# Family-Centered Early Intervention

# Family-Centered Early Intervention

## Supporting Infants and Toddlers in Natural Environments

by

**Sharon A. Raver, Ph.D.**

and

**Dana C. Childress, M.Ed.**

·P·A·U·L·H·
BROOKES
PUBLISHING CO.®

Baltimore • London • Sydney

**Paul H. Brookes Publishing Co.**
Post Office Box 10624
Baltimore, Maryland 21285-0624

www.brookespublishing.com

Typeset by Auburn Associates, Inc., Baltimore, Maryland.
Manufactured in the United States of America by
Sheridan Books, Inc., Chelsea, Michigan.

Cover image ©istockphoto/andipantz

The photographs that appear at the beginning of each chapter are ©istockphoto/monkeybusinessimages (Chapter 1), ©istockphoto/bo1982 (Chapter 2), ©istockphoto/Vita-lina (Chapter 3), ©istockphoto/akurtz (Chapter 4), ©istockphoto/lostinbids (Chapter 5), ©istockphoto/120b_rock (Chapter 7), ©istockphoto/andipantz (Chapter 8), and ©istockphoto/NolanWynne (Chapter 10). The photographs in Chapter 6 and Chapter 9 are used by permission of The Anchor Center for Blind Children, Denver, CO.

The individuals described in this book are composites or real people whose situations are masked and are based on the authors' experiences. In all instances, names and identifying details have been changed to protect confidentiality.

Per the Cincinnati Children's Hospital Medical Center: The contents of Figure 9.1, including text, graphics and other materials ("Contents") is a recitation of general scientific principles, intended for broad and general physician understanding and knowledge and is offered solely for educational and informational purposes as an academic service of CCHMC. The information should in no way be considered as an establishment of any type of standard of care, nor is it offering medical advice for a particular patient or as constituting medical consultation services, either formal or informal. While the Contents may be consulted for guidance, it is not intended for use as a substitute for independent professional medical judgment, advice, diagnosis, or treatment.

**Library of Congress Cataloging-in-Publication Data**

The Library of Congress has cataloged the print edition as follows:
Raver, Sharon A.
  Family-centered early intervention: supporting infants and toddlers in natural environments/Sharon A. Raver, Dana C Childress.
    pages    cm
  Includes bibliographical references and index.
  ISBN 978-1-59857-569-9 (paperback)—ISBN 978-1-59857-746-4 (epub3)
  1. Children with disabilities—Education (Early childhood)—United States.   2. Early childhood education—Parent participation—United States.   3. Early childhood special education—United States. 4. Family services—United States.   5. Children with disabilities—Family relationships—United States. 6. Children with disabilities—Services for—United States.   7. Infants—Services for—United States. 8. Toddlers—Services for—United States.   I. Childress, Dana C.   II. Title.
  LC4019.3.R39 2015
  371.9—dc23                                                2014031812

British Library Cataloguing in Publication data are available from the British Library.

2018   2017   2016   2015   2014

10    9    8    7    6    5    4    3    2    1

# Contents

# About the Authors

**Sharon A. Raver, Ph.D.,** a professor of special education at Old Dominion University, has worked in the area of early childhood special education (ECSE) for more than 35 years. She has worked with infants, toddlers, preschoolers, and school-age children with special needs and their families. Dr. Raver has administered programs, served as an international ECSE consultant, and published extensively. Her other books include *Early Childhood Special Education (0–8 Years): Strategies for Positive Outcomes* (Pearson, 2009), *Intervention Strategies for Infants and Toddlers with Special Needs: A Team Approach, Second Edition* (Pearson, 1999), and *Strategies for Teaching At-Risk and Handicapped Infants and Toddlers: A Transdisciplinary Approach* (Prentice Hall, 1991). She has been a Fulbright Scholar three times and received a number of awards for excellence in research and teaching. She currently lives in Norfolk, Virginia.

**Dana C. Childress, M.Ed.,** has worked in the field of early intervention for almost 20 years as an early childhood special educator, service coordinator, supervisor, professional development consultant, and writer. As an early intervention professional development consultant with the Partnership for People with Disabilities at Virginia Commonwealth University, she works as part of Virginia's early intervention professional development team. Ms. Childress develops resources, conducts web-based and in-person training, and manages the content for the Virginia Early Intervention Professional Development Center's web site (http://www.veipd.org/main). She also writes and manages the Early Intervention Strategies for Success blog (http://www.veipd.org/earlyintervention). Ms. Childress's interests include family-centered practices, autism spectrum disorder, supporting family implementation of intervention strategies, and finding ways to bridge the research-to-practice gap through interactive professional development for in-service early intervention practitioners. She regularly presents workshops in Virginia and has presented at state, national, and international conferences. She currently lives in Chesapeake, Virginia, with her family.

# Contributors

**Tanni L. Anthony, Ph.D.**
Director of Access, Learning, and Literacy
    Team
Exceptional Student Services Unit
Colorado Department of Education
1560 Broadway, Suite 1175
Denver, Colorado 80202

**Erika M. Baril, M.A., CCC-SLP**
Doctoral Fellow
University of Connecticut Health Center
The University of Connecticut
263 Farmington Avenue, MC6222
Farmington, Connecticut 06030

**Jonna L. Bobzien, Ph.D.**
Assistant Professor
Department of Communication Disorders
    and Special Education
Old Dominion University
111 Child Learning & Research Center
Norfolk, Virginia 23529

**Mary Beth Bruder, Ph.D.**
Professor and Director
A.J. Pappanikou Center for Excellence in
    Developmental Disabilities Education,
    Research, and Service
University of Connecticut Health Center
The University of Connecticut
263 Farmington Avenue, MC6222
Farmington, Connecticut 06030

**Anne George-Puskar, M.A.**
Doctoral Fellow
University of Connecticut Health Center
The University of Connecticut
263 Farmington Avenue, MC6222
Farmington, Connecticut 06030

**Corinne Foley Hill, M.Ed.**
Virginia Early Intervention Training
    Specialist
Partnership for People with Disabilities
Virginia Commonwealth University
34 Hermitage Estates Road
Waynesboro, Virginia 22980

**Toby M. Long, Ph.D., PT, FAPTA**
Associate Professor
Center for Child and Human Development
Georgetown University
3300 Whitehaven Street NW, Suite 3300
Washington, DC 20007

**Hedda Meadan, Ph.D., BCBA-D**
Assistant Professor
Department of Special Education
University of Illinois at Urbana–
    Champaign
1310 South Sixth Street
Champaign, Illinois 61820

**Lori E. Meyer, Ph.D.**
Assistant Professor
Department of Education
University of Vermont
633 Main Street
Burlington, Vermont 05405

**Corrin G. Richels, Ph.D.**
Assistant Professor
Department of Communication Disorders
    and Special Education
Old Dominion University
111 Child Learning & Research Center
Norfolk, Virginia 23529

**Mallene P. Wiggin, M.A., CCC-SLP**
Speech-Language Pathologist
Speech, Language & Hearing Sciences
University of Colorado Boulder
409 UCB
Boulder, Colorado 80309

**Christine Yoshinaga-Itano, Ph.D.**
Professor
Speech, Language & Hearing Sciences
University of Colorado Boulder
409 UCB
Boulder, Colorado 80309

# Foreword

*Family-Centered Early Intervention: Supporting Infants and Toddlers in Natural Environments* provides an important contribution to serving vulnerable young children—infants and toddlers with, or at risk for, delays and disabilities—and their families. It is written for service providers, teachers, administrators, and families, and it is especially useful for these stakeholders. It also serves as an excellent text for university faculty in personnel preparation—those who prepare students to be service providers.

This volume goes a long way to describe and explain, quite clearly, the early intervention system and the children and families served within it. It invites stakeholders into the world of early intervention in a way that is both accessible and meaningful. The book is organized into four sections, beginning with the system of early intervention; then detailing the services and participants; and ending with child development, including milestones and various threats to development. This organization introduces the reader to the beliefs and values embodied in the system of early intervention and the ways those beliefs and values are translated to practice (e.g., creation of the individualized family service plan, or IFSP). Theories and research that underlie development, as well as various methods of assessment and intervention, are emphasized in the chapters on typical and atypical child development.

More specifically, the first section introduces the overarching system of early intervention—the laws, policies, and practices in which early intervention services have been conceptualized and are being administered. It begins with a chapter on the foundations of early intervention, followed by a chapter on collaboration and teamwork with families and professionals. Raver and Childress provide a comprehensive and straightforward introduction to early intervention: where these services came from, what they are, why they are important, and who provides them. Each chapter begins with a case study of an infant or toddler served through early intervention. These cases are extended as new concepts are presented, which serves to deepen readers' understanding.

The second section focuses on supporting families in natural environments. The two chapters are especially useful for families and service providers because they describe the details of the IFSP (Chapter 3 by Hill & Childress) and how the goals of the IFSP are implemented in everyday routines, activities, and settings (Chapter 4 by Childress).

The three chapters in the third section, which are focused on the developing child, are explicitly organized around the three broad child outcomes specified by the Office of Special Education Programs (OSEP) of the U.S. Department of Education. The three child outcomes are children have positive social relationships (Chapter 5 by Richels & Raver), children acquire and use knowledge and skills (Chapter 6 by Bruder, Baril, & George-Puskar), and children take appropriate action to meet their needs (Chapter 7 by Long). Chapters 5–7 describe the developmental domains specified in federal law. They include typical development, the effects of experience on these domains, and relationships among the domains. Also included are assessment and intervention methods to use when development is threatened or delayed and clarification of the role of the service provider in natural environments. The chapters are supported by the theories and research that frame descriptions and explanations of child development.

The final section presents specific intervention strategies for facilitating development and learning in children with particular delays and disabilities, such as autism spectrum disorder (Chapter 8 by Childress, Meyer, & Meadan); sensory disabilities, such as visual impairments and hearing loss (Chapter 9 by Anthony, Wiggin, Yoshinaga-Itano, & Raver); and intellectual and motor disabilities, such as Down syndrome, cerebral palsy, and spina bifida (Chapter 10 by Bobzien, Childress, & Raver). These chapters provide very useful information on the impact of these disabilities on various developmental domains and what service providers, teachers, administrators, family members, and even researchers can do to promote development and learning.

As the field moves forward, stakeholders need to consider how the components of the early intervention system fit together and, in particular, how their beliefs and values intersect with theory and research. The larger culture's beliefs and values created the system of early intervention services, and the importance of promoting the development of children with delays and their families cannot be denied. Nevertheless, early intervention services must be evidence based and derived from evidence-based assessment activities that have been linked to intervention goals. These intervention activities, in turn, must be linked to the IFSP outcomes. Ensuring the connections among assessment, intervention, and outcomes is a tall order for administrators and practitioners. Researchers must be stakeholders in this process. An ongoing collaborative effort among research, policy, and practice would contribute to the productive linkage among components. This volume contributes substantially to the understandings that stakeholders need about the divergent perspectives and histories of each other, which affords increased opportunities for collaboration.

Theory and research heavily influence knowledge about child development. In describing the IFSP process in Chapter 3, Hill and Childress note that outcomes, among other things, should be "strengths-based," encouraging families and service providers to "start with skills the child already has and build toward the next developmental steps" (p. 65). This description of a strengths-based approach is very important in that it incorporates the child development perspective. Bruder, Baril, and George-Puskar (Chapter 6) invoke Piagetian theory to explain development, which conceptualizes children as active participants in their learning. This perspective, along with Vygotsky's zone of proximal development, is fundamental to understanding development. Early intervention assessments accordingly must capture the developmental steps in various developmental domains; in turn, the assessment activities must take into account where the child is along these continua of developmental steps to tap into the zone of active engagement. Intervention activities are enhanced when goals are finely tuned to the child's level of active engagement and interest.

Early intervention activities are largely based on behavioral theories—to manage the environment to promote development and learning in children who are developing more slowly than their peers. The linked components of assessment, intervention, and outcomes must be embedded into our knowledge of theory and research on the developing child and also in the context of the family. Raver and Childress contribute substantially to that effort in *Family-Centered Early Intervention*.

*Karin Lifter, Ph.D.*
*Northeastern University*
*Boston, Massachusetts*

# Preface

*Family-Centered Early Intervention: Supporting Infants and Toddlers in Natural Environments* covers knowledge and skill competencies service providers need to promote optimal development in children with and at risk for developmental delays and disabilities from birth through age 3. This introductory methods book uses the application of evidence-based strategies, family-centered approaches such as coaching and teaming, and services provided in an array of natural environments as thematic threads. Each chapter uses a case study to bring to life disability definitions and characteristics, informal and formal assessment practices, and practical strategies for supporting families as they foster the development and learning of their children. The book is unique in that it is organized around the three Office of Special Education Programs (OSEP) child outcomes or indicators that early intervention programs must address when assessing the impact of their program. This book is designed to meet the unique professional development needs of in-service and preservice early intervention providers across disciplinary and agency boundaries. It provides information and intervention strategies needed to ensure well-prepared, effective practitioners in the field of early intervention.

This book embeds techniques from early childhood special education, speech-language pathology, occupational and physical therapy, and vision and hearing education so that service providers can develop and implement integrated, comprehensive, and meaningful services for very young children and their families. Competencies identified by the Council for Exceptional Children (2014); Division for Early Childhood (2014); and Sandall, Hemmeter, Smith, and McLean (2005) are systematically incorporated throughout the book.

There are four major sections to this book. Section I examines the legal, philosophical, and instructional foundations of serving infants and toddlers with and at risk for special needs in early intervention programs. It discusses the historical perspective supporting early services, working in teams with professionals from diverse disciplines, supporting families, assessing young children, and utilizing evidence-based practices and strategies in a variety of settings. Section II discusses the rationale and development of the individualized family service plan and how to provide services within families' everyday routines. Section III describes practical techniques for maximizing communicative, cognitive, fine and gross motor, adaptive, and social-emotional development in young children using the three OSEP major child outcomes as a framework. Section IV emphasizes specific intervention strategies for promoting development and learning in children with specific needs, such as autism spectrum disorder, sensory disabilities, and cognitive and/or motor disabilities. It is our hope that service providers in early intervention, teachers in early childhood education, administrators, and families will find this book immediately useful.

## REFERENCES

Council for Exceptional Children. (2014). *Special education early childhood specialty competencies.* Retrieved from http://www.cec.sped.org/Standards/Special-Educator-Professional-Preparation/CEC-Initial-and-Advanced-Specialty-Sets

Division for Early Childhood. (2014). *DEC recommended practices in early intervention/early childhood special edu-* cation. Retrieved from http://www.dec-sped.org/recommendedpractices

Sandall, S.R., Hemmeter, M.L., Smith, B.J., & McLean, M. (2005). *DEC recommended practices: A comprehensive guide for practical application in early intervention/early childhood special education.* Longmont, CO: Sopris West.

# Acknowledgments

We extend appreciation to the families who allowed aspects of their stories to be shared in the case studies. A special thanks to our colleagues who contributed to the writing of this book: Tanni Anthony, Erika Baril, Jonna Bobzien, Mary Beth Bruder, Anne George-Puskar, Cori Hill, Toby Long, Hedda Meadan, Lori Meyer, Corrin Richels, Mallene Wiggin, and Christine Yoshinaga-Itano. We would like to thank our families, whose daily support aided the completion of this project, and our colleagues in the Department of Communication Disorders and Special Education at Old Dominion University and the Partnership for People with Disabilities at Virginia Commonwealth University for their encouragement. Furthermore, sincere appreciation is extended to the reviewers who guided the completion of this book.

A thank you goes to our copyeditor, Lori Barrett, for her work on the manuscript, and to our editor, Johanna Schmitter. However, our deepest appreciation goes to the infants and toddlers, and their families, who have enriched our lives. This book is the outcome of what they continue to teach us each day.

*To Greg, my husband, and Emmy, my daughter,*
*who provide me with continual support, love, and laughs*

—SAR


*To Michael and Caden, who balance me*
*with their love, laughter, and patience*

—DCC

# I

# Foundations of Early Intervention

# 1 | Early Education and Intervention for Children from Birth to Three

Sharon A. Raver and Dana C. Childress

This chapter discusses the foundations of early intervention, including the following:

- Definition and key principles of early intervention
- Current practices in infant and toddler intervention
- History of early intervention
- Provisions of the Individuals with Disabilities Education Improvement Act (IDEA) of 2004 (PL 108-446)
- Prevalence of children receiving early intervention
- Importance of early intervention and inclusive practices
- Best practice highlights

Welcome to the world of early childhood intervention, a field of study and practice that focuses on supporting the development of infants and toddlers, age birth to 36 months, who have developmental differences, delays, or disabilities. Support for these services is provided through partnership and collaboration with a child's caregivers and a team of professionals, all of whom are in the position to make a difference in the life of a child. As a professional in this field, you will play a significant role by working with caregivers to enhance their confidence, competence, and ability to meet the needs of their children. Whether you are training as an early childhood special educator, therapist, child care provider, or early childhood teacher, there is much you can do to help infants and toddlers grow, learn, and participate in their families' lives. In this book, you will learn about teamwork and collaboration, the individualized family service plan (IFSP) process, implementing interventions in the context of a family's everyday routines, techniques for enhancing development across key child outcomes, and strategies to support the development of very young children with a variety of specific developmental strengths and needs.

As you explore this field and acquire strategies that will help you support children and families, remember that, as a service provider, you have the special opportunity to make a profound difference in the life of each child and family you encounter. By sharing your knowledge of development and intervention strategies and supporting the efforts of families and caregivers, you can help each family build an intervention system and attitude of advocacy that will reach far beyond the first 3 years of a child's life. Now, let us meet Makeba and her family, who provide one example of what early childhood intervention looks like.

## Case Study: Makeba

Makeba is 30 months old and lives with her family in a small apartment near the city park. Makeba's father recently lost his job, and her mother works the evening shift at the local grocery store. Makeba spends her mornings at a local preschool program and her afternoons with her parents and older brother, who is 4 years old. Her mother, Imani, has noticed that Makeba is not talking like Makeba's brother did when he was the same age. Makeba is only saying five words but seems to understand most of what she hears. She is starting to have tantrums by screaming, crying, falling on the floor, and kicking her legs when her parents have difficulty understanding what she tries to say. Imani shared her concerns about Makeba's communication and behavior with the family's pediatrician, who suggested a referral to the local early childhood intervention program.

Soon after the referral was made, Makeba's family met with a service coordinator, who shared information about the early intervention program. The service coordinator gathered information about Makeba's development and discussed a convenient time for a developmental evaluation. Based on information gathered during the evaluation, Makeba was found to be eligible for early intervention services due to developmental delays in her expressive communication and social-emotional development. Child and family assessments were also conducted, during which Makeba's parents expressed their desire for Makeba to learn to talk so that she is less frustrated. They expressed an additional concern about being able to continue to pay for Makeba's preschool while her father searched for a new job. They asked if the service coordinator knew of community resources that could help them pay for preschool so that Makeba could continue to attend. An IFSP was developed, which focused on Makeba's family's priorities. The IFSP team, which included the family, decided that Makeba would receive intervention once per week, provided by an early childhood special educator at the family's home and at Makeba's preschool on alternating weeks. A speech therapy consultation once per month was also added to the IFSP, as well as service coordination. Makeba's family agreed to this plan and signed the IFSP. Services began the following week.

## WHAT IS EARLY INTERVENTION?

Makeba was referred to her local early childhood intervention program (sometimes also known as an infant-toddler program) by her pediatrician due to her mother's and the doctor's observations regarding Makeba's development. Children like Makeba are referred for intervention for many different reasons and have a range of abilities and needs. Each state in the United States operates early childhood intervention programs, as do many countries across the world, such as China, Australia, Sweden, Germany, and Canada (Guralnick, 2008). States and countries establish their own eligibility criteria and operational procedures for their programs. In the United States, there is a federal law that guides how early intervention is provided. This federal law is known as the *Individuals with Disabilities Education Improvement Act of 2004,* or *IDEA* (Trohanis, 2008).

## Early Intervention Under the Individuals with Disabilities Education Improvement Act

Under Part C of IDEA, early childhood intervention is referred to as "early intervention." For consistency with the federal regulations that describe this set of services, the same term will be used throughout this book. The term *early intervention* describes the process of offering family-oriented services for children from birth to age 3 who have disabilities, have identified special needs, or are at risk for developmental delays, as well as services for their parents or caregivers and other family members. Early intervention is a specialized area of early childhood special education (ECSE) that provides services for children with special needs who are between the ages of birth to 9 years. ECSE has a theory of practice and shared values rooted in evidence-based practices (Odom & Wolery, 2003). *Evidence-based practice* refers to decisions and activities that are grounded in published empirical research that documents the relationship between practices and outcomes for children, families, professionals, and systems (Buysse, Wesley, Snyder, & Winton, 2006; Klingner, Boardman, & McMaster, 2013). Evidence-based services in early intervention are *noncategorical* in nature, meaning that services are not organized by disability (e.g., children with motor impairments) but are individualized for a child's and family's strengths and needs. The individualized nature of early intervention services is a federal requirement and underlies effective practices with children and families.

The definition of early intervention services in the federal law includes nine important features. According to *Part C of IDEA*, the phrase *early intervention services* refers to developmental services that include each of the following characteristics.

***1. Services Are Provided Under Public Supervision***  Early intervention programs for infants and toddlers with developmental delays and disabilities are federally funded, meaning that funding is granted to states that choose to operate these programs within the parameters of Part C of IDEA. Providing early intervention services is discretionary, so states can choose whether or not to accept federal funding and offer these programs. All states currently provide early intervention programs using federal funding, and some states provide additional funding at the state and local levels. When states accept Part C funds, they also accept supervision and monitoring by the *Office of Special Education Programs (OSEP)*—the federal agency that is responsible for the implementation of IDEA. If a state is found to be noncompliant with OSEP or IDEA requirements, then that state's federal funding for early intervention services could be withdrawn.

***2. Services Are Selected in Collaboration with Parents***  The determination of which early intervention services most appropriately meet a child and family's needs is a team decision that includes the family, the service coordinator, and any other service provider who is assisting the family with developing the IFSP. The inclusion of this provision in the federal law emphasizes the essential role that the family–professional collaboration plays in early intervention.

***3. Services Are Provided at No Cost, Except Where Federal or State Law Provides for a System of Payments by Families***  In some states, all early intervention services are provided at no cost to families. In other states, services such as developmental screening, assessment, and service coordination are provided at no cost, while other services, such as special instruction, physical therapy, occupational therapy, and speech-language pathology (described in Chapter 2), have costs associated with them. A family's insurance or state funding sources, such as Medicaid, may be billed, but the family may also be responsible for paying insurance deductibles or copays. In states where services are billable, a *sliding-fee scale* must be available to families. The sliding-fee scale is used to calculate reduced costs based on factors such as a family's income and the number of people in the family. Even when services are billable, families cannot be denied services due to their inability to pay.

### 4. Services Must Meet the Developmental Needs of an Infant or Toddler with a Disability and the Needs of the Family to Assist the Child's Development as Identified by the Individualized Family Service Plan Team   Early

intervention is designed to address the development of infants or toddlers who are found to be eligible for services and their families. Part C of IDEA defines an "infant or toddler with a disability" using three categories of eligibility. An infant or toddler is eligible for early intervention if he or she

> Is experiencing developmental delays, as measured by appropriate diagnostic instruments and procedures in one or more of the areas of cognitive development, physical development, communication development, social or emotional development, and adaptive development; or has a diagnosed physical or mental condition that has a high probability of resulting in developmental delay. (IDEA 2004, § 303.21[a])

States may also choose to include children who are at risk for delay in their eligibility criteria; this option is the third category of eligibility.

Depending on the state, a child may be eligible for early intervention due to a certain percentage of delay (e.g., 25% delay) or level of deviation when compared to children with typical development (e.g., one standard deviation), a diagnosed condition (e.g., Down syndrome or cerebral palsy), or atypical or at-risk development (e.g., atypical sensorimotor development or a child who has been removed from his family due to abuse). *Developmental delay* is the term used to describe a child's eligibility when that child is demonstrating a significant delay in one or more domains of development. As defined in IDEA, a *diagnosed condition* refers to a physical or mental condition that has a high probability of resulting in a developmental delay. States determine the level of delay and which diagnosed conditions qualify a child for early intervention services. If they choose to serve children with atypical development or children who are at risk, states also define these parameters.

All early intervention programs that operate under IDEA must consider a child's functioning in each of the five areas, or *domains*, of development referenced in the federal definition: physical development, cognitive development, communication development, social-emotional development, and adaptive development. The area of physical development includes gross and fine motor development. *Gross motor development* deals with large muscle planning and coordination, such as squatting and walking. *Fine motor development* addresses small muscle planning and coordination, such as picking up small objects. *Cognitive development* involves thinking, solving problems, and communicating what one knows. *Communication development* includes both a child's *expressive communication* (the ability to produce language) and *receptive communication* (the ability to understand the communication of others). Interacting with others in meaningful ways and understanding and communicating emotions appropriately are aspects of *social-emotional development*. *Adaptive development*, also known as *self-help*, involves the ability to do things for oneself, such as dressing and eating. These five domains are examined during an *evaluation* of the child's development (Greenwood, Carta, & McConnell, 2011).

A child's eligibility for early intervention services is determined by an evaluation, which is conducted by a multidisciplinary team of at least two professionals. These professionals must be qualified in their disciplines to conduct the evaluation and may include an early childhood special educator, a physical therapist, an occupational therapist, a speech-language pathologist, and/or other appropriate professional depending on the child's needs. In addition, when appropriate, a functional child- and family-directed assessment is also conducted to determine strengths and needs in everyday life. This information becomes part of the *individualized family service plan (IFSP)* development process. Once the early intervention team confirms that the child is eligible, the IFSP is developed so that the child and family can receive services to help them work toward the *outcomes* (goals) that are outlined in the plan.

At the time of the initial evaluation and assessment, a child's development is also compared to same-age peers to determine how the child is functioning in three indicators of overall child development. These indicators have been determined by OSEP (2010) and are also referred to as *child outcomes*. This can be confusing because the OSEP child outcomes are not the same as the outcomes written in the IFSP. The child outcomes identified by OSEP refer to the functional outcomes that are expected to improve as a result of the child's participation in early intervention. The OSEP child outcomes are a global measure of a child's progress that the program reports to its funding agency, whereas the IFSP outcomes are an individualized measure that is specific to a child's strengths and needs and the family's particular priorities for that child's development.

The three OSEP child outcomes that are listed in Box 1.1 relate to a child's positive social-emotional skills, how the child gains and uses knowledge, and how the

---

**BOX 1.1.    The three child outcomes from the Office of Special Education Programs for comparing all children's broad developmental changes over time**

1. *Positive social-emotional skills (including social relationships):* How a child relates with adults and other children; how older children follow social rules. Includes the following:

   Attachment, separation, and autonomy
   Expressing emotions and feelings
   Learning rules and expectations
   Social interactions and play
   Language and communication

2. *Acquisition and use of knowledge and skills (including early language and communication):* How a child uses thinking and reasoning, memory, problem solving, and symbols and language; how a child understands the physical and social worlds. Includes the following:

   Early concepts such as symbols, pictures, numbers, classification, and spatial relationships
   Imitation
   Object permanence
   Expressive language and communication
   Early literacy

3. *Taking appropriate action to meet needs:* How a child takes care of basic needs, moves from place to place, and uses tools (e.g., fork, toothbrush, crayon); how older children contribute to their own health and safety. Includes the following:

   Using motor skills to complete tasks
   Self-help skills, such as dressing, feeding, and toileting
   Acting on the environment to get what one wants

From The Early Childhood Technical Assistance Center. (2009). *The child outcomes.* Retrieved from http://ectacenter.org/eco/assets/pdfs/Child_Outcomes_handout.pdf; adapted by permission.

child uses his or her abilities to get needs met. These outcomes are the same for all children and are used by OSEP as a broad measure of child progress across early intervention systems (Early Childhood Outcomes Center, 2005), offering a snapshot of the whole child and how the child is currently functioning in many settings and within real situations. They are considered to be *functional outcomes* because they refer to things that are meaningful to the child during his or her everyday living rather than isolated assessment skills, such as stacking three blocks when asked. These outcomes describe integrated behaviors or skills that allow the child to achieve important daily goals (Early Childhood Outcomes Center, 2005). Functionality means that the child is able to perform a series of integrated behaviors that include multiple domains. For example, it is clear from Box 1.1 that each of the OSEP outcomes involves language and communication.

States are required to report to OSEP the percentage of children who make improvements in each of these three outcomes as a result of their early intervention experience. The data are collected when children enter and exit the Part C system and are used by OSEP to determine the efficacy of early intervention across the United States. They are also measured when children enter and exit *early childhood special education* (ECSE; preschool) services, which are provided under Part B of IDEA.

The three OSEP outcomes are considered to be a more holistic way to view development, reflecting its interrelated nature in the blending of domains into three functional, overarching outcomes of typical development. Because of this, the OSEP child outcomes are also used as a framework for developing the IFSP and providing intervention to children and families. Much work is being done in the field to integrate this framework into actual intervention practices. This book is organized around the skills and strategies necessary to implement this framework. In particular, Chapters 5, 6, and 7 address multiple ways to support this new vision of promoting positive development in young children.

**5. Services Must Meet the Standards of the State in Which They Are Provided**   States that receive federal funding must follow the guidelines established at the federal level. Among these guidelines is the requirement that states set standards for how early intervention programs are implemented. These state-level policies and procedures describe how each state interprets federal guidance on the operation of programs. State-specific procedures may include state- and program-level infrastructure, eligibility criteria, service billing systems, monitoring and compliance procedures, and requirements and standards for service providers.

**6. Service Options Must Include Those Services that Are Identified in the Law**   A variety of services are available to eligible infants and toddlers and their families. Service type, length, frequency, location, and methods are determined by the IFSP team, with significant input from the family. Services are individualized based on the child's needs, family's priorities, and the outcomes written in the IFSP. The only service that all families in early intervention receive is *service coordination*. Possible services offered in early intervention are listed in Box 1.2.

---

**BOX 1.2.    Early intervention services available to families under Part C of the Individuals with Disabilities Education Improvement Act of 2004**

- Family training, counseling, and home visits
- Special instruction
- Speech-language pathology and audiology services, and sign language and cued language services
- Occupational therapy
- Physical therapy
- Psychological services
- Service coordination services
- Medical services, only for diagnostic or evaluation purposes
- Early identification, screening, and assessment services
- Health services
- Social work services
- Vision services
- Assistive technology devices and assistive technology services
- Transportation and related costs

*Source:* Individuals with Disabilities Education Improvement Act (2004).

---

***7. Services Must Be Provided by Qualified Personnel***    Each state determines the qualification standards of service providers who work within its early intervention system. These standards include minimum education, licensing, and competency requirements. Professional requirements vary greatly across states and may include requirements for state-level certification and ongoing professional development. Box 1.3 lists some of the professionals who may provide services and supports.

---

**BOX 1.3.    Qualified early intervention personnel who provide services to children and their families under Part C of the Individuals with Disabilities Education Improvement Act of 2004**

- Special educators
- Speech-language pathologists and audiologists
- Occupational therapists
- Physical therapists
- Psychologists
- Social workers
- Nurses
- Registered dietitians
- Family therapists
- Vision specialists, including ophthalmologists and optometrists
- Orientation and mobility specialists
- Pediatricians and other physicians

*Source:* Individuals with Disabilities Education Improvement Act (2004).

**8. To the Maximum Extent Appropriate, Services Must Be Provided in Natural Environments**   The *natural environment* refers to settings that are important to a specific child and family, as well as places and activities that the child and family would engage in if the child did not have a delay or disability. Early intervention services are provided in natural settings where children and families spend time, such as the home, child care center, local park, library, or the grocery store. These services are provided during *intervention visits* when the caregiver and service provider work together to enhance the child's development in the location where support is needed. This provision of the law has an inclusive component that describes how services are provided, emphasizing the importance of helping caregivers embed intervention into routines and activities that are familiar and natural for the child and family (Dunst, Hamby, Trivette, Raab, & Bruder, 2000). It also emphasizes the importance of encouraging the delivery of services in community placements where children and families without special needs participate. Specific ways to conduct intervention visits in natural environments are explored further in Chapter 4.

The majority of infants and toddlers with disabilities (80.6%) receive early intervention services in their homes, with their parents and families present (OSEP, 2010). Services are provided by early intervention professionals, therapists, and/or health care providers. Many service providers believe that this is the most effective model for delivering services because infants or toddlers are in a familiar, stress-free environment (Torrey, Leginus, & Cecere, 2011). Although this approach is the most common, there has been a shift toward a more community- and resource-based model. According to OSEP (2010), approximately 7.6% of infants and toddlers receive early intervention services in an established child care setting and approximately 5.6% receive center-based services. A *resource-based model* is built on the notion of providing intervention services in parks, libraries, child care centers, and/or community centers physically located in the family's community (Mott & Dunst, 2006). Families then have the opportunity to take their child to new environments to play and explore, and they may feel more comfortable taking their child into the community. In addition, parents may have the opportunity to see their child react and play differently in the presence of other children (Torrey et al., 2011). Similarly, some early intervention programs offer additional *center-based* or clinic-based services; families must bring their children to a center or clinic to take advantage of these services. Center-based services might include *intakes*, initial meetings with families, parent support groups and classes, and child playgroups.

**9. Services Are Provided in Conformity with the Family's Individualized Family Service Plan**   The IFSP is a written document that serves as a foundation for the early intervention process. The IFSP includes information about the child's development based on a team evaluation and assessment; the family's priorities, concerns, and resources related to the child's development; the outcomes to be expected from the child's and family's participation in intervention; the supports and services the child and/or family will receive; and the transition plan for when the child exits the system. The IFSP is discussed in detail in Chapter 3.

The federal guidelines outlined in Part C of IDEA were established by the U.S. Congress due to what is described in the law as an "urgent and substantial need" to support the development of infants and toddlers with disabilities, reduce long-term educational costs, maximize the independence of individuals with disabilities, enhance the capacity of families to meet the needs of their children, and enhance the capacity of states and local agencies to "identify, evaluate, and meet the needs of all children" (IDEA 2004, § 631). Congress recognized the importance of the first 3 years of life on a child's brain development. It also recognized the importance of supporting caregivers so they are able to meet their own needs, including those of their children. With the guidance in Part C and the financial assistance provided to implement it, a wide network of early intervention services and supports are now available to children and families who choose to participate.

## KEY PRINCIPLES OF EARLY INTERVENTION

According to the Workgroup on Principles and Practices in Natural Environments (2008a), the mission of early intervention is to build on and support the efforts of families and caregivers as they enhance the development of their children. The context for early intervention is the activities of everyday life, recognizing that all children learn best during interactions and experiences with the important people in their lives. As is seen with Makeba, infants and toddlers spend most of their time with their families, who naturally engage in activities that affect development. Early intervention is a supplement to these family activities and interactions, and it is most effective when provided within the family context.

The Workgroup (2008b) described seven key principles that guide the provision of early intervention. These principles focus on the importance of a flexible, family-centered, individualized, and evidence-based early intervention process that supports the capacity of families and caregivers to meet the needs of their children. Service providers are described as supports to *families and children,* rather than as the primary agents of change in the child's development. Each of these principles represents a foundational professional belief and standard that drives all interactions and assistance provided to very young children and their families (Pletcher & Younggren, 2013). Table 1.1 describes how these principles should be implemented with children and families.

### Key Principle 1: Infants and Toddlers Learn Best Through Everyday Experiences and Interactions with Familiar People in Familiar Contexts

All children, including infants and toddlers with developmental delays and disabilities, learn within the context of the interactions and activities that occur during their daily lives. Early intervention services can help families and caregivers learn additional strategies to use in their daily routines to support a child's development. This focus on learning in the context of natural daily routines with familiar people also reflects the importance of facilitating learning between visits, when the service provider is not with the family to provide support. Because most learning happens when the service provider is not with the family, intervention must focus on helping family members make the most out of these everyday experiences and interactions using the materials and activities that are natural to their family patterns and traditions. In practice, this principle is implemented when service providers respect the importance of unique family interactions, problem-solve with families, and help family members practice strategies during visits so that they are prepared for how to interact with the child between visits.

### Key Principle 2: All Families, with the Necessary Supports and Resources, Can Enhance Their Children's Learning and Development

This principle reflects the family-centered, strengths-based foundation of early intervention. Every family has strengths, and every family has the capacity to have a positive impact

**Table 1.1.**   Examples of how to implement the seven key principles of early intervention

| The principle DOES look like this | The principle DOES NOT look like this |
|---|---|
| **1. Infants and toddlers learn best through everyday experiences and interactions with familiar people in familiar contexts.** | |
| Using toys and materials found in the home or community setting | Using toys, materials, and other equipment the professional brings to the visit |
| Helping the family understand how its toys and materials can be used or adapted | Implying that the professional's toys, materials, or equipment are the "magic" necessary for the child's progress |
| Identifying activities the child and family like to do, which build on their strengths and interests | Designing activities for a child that focus on skill impairments or are not functional or enjoyable |
| Helping caregivers engage the child in enjoyable learning opportunities that allow for frequent practice and mastery of emerging skills in natural settings | Teaching specific skills in a specific order in a specific way through "massed trials and repetition" in a contrived setting |
| Focusing intervention on caregivers' ability to promote the child's participation in naturally occurring, developmentally appropriate activities with peers and family members | Conducting sessions or activities that isolate the child from his or her peers, family members, or naturally occurring activities |
| **2. All families, with the necessary supports and resources, can enhance their children's learning and development.** | |
| Assuming all families have strengths and competencies; appreciating the unique learning preferences of each adult; and matching teaching, coaching, and problem-solving styles accordingly | Basing expectations for families on characteristics, such as race, ethnicity, education, or income; categorizing families as those who are likely to work with early intervention and those who are not |
| Suspending judgment, building rapport, and gathering information from families about their needs and interests | Making assumptions about families' needs, interests, and ability to support their child because of life circumstances |
| Identifying with families how all significant people support the child's learning and development in care routines and activities meaningful and preferable to them | Expecting all families to have the same care routines, child-rearing practices, and play preferences |
| Matching outcomes and intervention strategies to the families' priorities, needs, and interests; building on routines and activities they want and need to do; collaboratively determining the supports, resources, and services they want to receive | Viewing families as apathetic or exiting them from services because they miss appointments or do not carry through on prescribed interventions, rather than refocusing interventions on family priorities |
| **3. The primary role of the service provider in early intervention is to work with and support family members and caregivers in a child's life.** | |
| Using professional behaviors that build trust and rapport and establish a working partnership with families | Being "nice" to families and becoming their friends |
| Valuing and understanding the provider's role as a collaborative coach working to support family members as they help their child; incorporating principles of adult learning styles | Focusing only on the child and assuming the family's role is to be a passive observer of what the provider is doing "to" the child |
| Providing information, materials, and emotional support to enhance families' natural role as the people who foster their child's learning and development | Training families to be "mini" therapists or interventionists |

*(continued)*

**Table 1.1.**    *(continued)*

| The principle DOES look like this | The principle DOES NOT look like this |
| --- | --- |
| Pointing out children's natural learning activities and discovering together the "incidental teaching" opportunities that families do naturally between the providers' visits | Giving families activity sheets or curriculum work pages to do between visits and checking to see if these were done |
| Involving families in discussions about what they want to do and enjoy doing; identifying the family's routines and activities that will support the desired outcomes; continually acknowledging the many things the family is doing to support the child | Showing strategies or activities to families that the provider has planned and then asking families to fit these into their routines |
| Allowing families to determine success based on how they feel about the learning opportunities and activities the child/family has chosen | Basing success on the child's ability to perform the professionally determined activities and parents' compliance with prescribed services and activities |

4. The early intervention process, from initial contacts through transition, must be dynamic and individualized to reflect the child's and family members' preferences, learning styles, and cultural beliefs.

| | |
| --- | --- |
| Evaluation/assessments address each family's initial priorities, and accommodate reasonable preferences for time, place, and the role the family will play | Providing the same "one-size-fits-all" evaluation and assessment process for each family/child regardless of the initial concerns |
| Collaboratively tailoring services to fit each family; providing services and supports in flexible ways that are responsive to each family's cultural, ethnic, racial, language, and socioeconomic characteristics and preferences | Expecting families to "fit" the services; giving families a list of available services to choose from and providing these services and supports in the same manner for every family |
| Treating each family member as a unique adult learner with valuable insights, interests, and skills | Treating the family as having one learning style that does not change |
| Acknowledging that the individualized family service plan (IFSP) can be changed as often as needed to reflect the changing needs, priorities, and lifestyle of the child and family | Expecting the IFSP document outcomes, strategies, and services not to change for a year |
| Recognizing one's own culturally and professionally driven child-rearing values, beliefs, and practices; seeking to understand, rather than judge, families with differing values and practices | Acting solely on one's personally held child-rearing beliefs and values and not fully acknowledging the importance of families' cultural perspectives |

5. IFSP outcomes must be functional and based on children's and families' needs and priorities.

| | |
| --- | --- |
| Writing IFSP outcomes based on the families' concerns, resources, and priorities | Writing IFSP outcomes based on test results only |
| Listening to families and believing what they say regarding their priorities and needs | Reinterpreting what families say in order to better match a service provider's ideas |
| Writing functional outcomes that result in functional support and intervention aimed at advancing children's engagement, independence, and social relationships | Writing IFSP outcomes focused on remediating developmental impairments |
| Writing integrated outcomes that focus on the child participating in community and family activities | Writing discipline-specific outcomes without full consideration of the whole child within the context of the family |

| The principle DOES look like this | The principle DOES NOT look like this |
|---|---|
| Having outcomes that build on a child's natural motivations to learn and do, match family priorities, strengthen naturally occurring routines, and enhance learning opportunities and enjoyment | Having outcomes that focus on impairments and problems to be fixed |
| Describing what the child or family will be able to do in the context of their typical routines and activities | Listing the services to be provided as an outcome (e.g., "Johnny will get physical therapy in order to walk") |
| Identifying how families will know a functional outcome is achieved by writing measurable criteria that anyone could use to review progress | Measuring a child's progress by "therapist checklist/ observation" or readministration of initial evaluation measures |

6. The family's priorities, needs, and interests are addressed most appropriately by a primary provider who represents and receives team and community support.

| | |
|---|---|
| Talking to the family about how children learn through play and practice in all their normally occurring activities | Giving the family the message that the more service providers that are involved, the more gains their child will make |
| Keeping abreast of changing circumstances, priorities, and needs and bringing in both formal and informal services and supports as necessary | Limiting the services and supports that a child and family receive |
| Having a primary provider, with necessary support from the team, maintain a focus on what is necessary to achieve functional outcomes | Having separate providers seeing the family at separate times and addressing narrowly defined, separate outcomes or issues |
| Coaching or supporting the family to carry out the strategies and activities developed with the team members with the appropriate expertise; directly engaging team members when needed | Providing services outside one's scope of expertise or beyond one's license or certification |
| Developing a team based on the child and family outcomes and priorities, which can include people important to the family and people from community supports and services, as well as early intervention providers from different disciplines | Defining the team from only the professional disciplines that match the child's impairments |
| Working as a team, sharing information from first contacts through the IFSP meeting when a primary service provider is assigned; all team members understanding each other's ongoing roles | Having a disjointed IFSP process, with different people in early contacts, different evaluators, and different service providers who do not meet and work together with the family as a team |
| Making time for team members to communicate formally and informally and recognizing that outcomes are a shared responsibility | Working in isolation from other team members with no regular scheduled time to discuss how things are going |

7. Interventions with young children and family members must be based on explicit principles, validated practices, the best available research, and relevant laws and regulations.

| | |
|---|---|
| Updating knowledge, skills, and strategies by keeping abreast of research | Thinking that the same skills and strategies one has always used will always be effective |

Adapted from Workgroup on Principles and Practices in Natural Environments, OSEP TA Community of Practice: Part C Settings. (2008, March). *Seven key principles: Looks like/doesn't look like.* Retrieved from http://www.ectacenter.org/~pdfs/topics/families/Principles_LooksLike_DoesntLookLike3_11_08.pdf; adapted by permission.

on their children's development. It is the job of the early intervention practitioner to recognize each family's strengths and build on them. Some families may want many supports or resources, whereas others may only want minimal supports. Families are part of the decision-making process and help identify how much support they think they need to help their children grow. When supports are implemented, service providers show respect for all families, use family-centered practices, and individualize the early intervention process to each family's priorities, needs, and resources.

### Key Principle 3: The Primary Role of the Service Provider in Early Intervention Is to Work with and Support Family Members and Caregivers in a Child's Life

This principle is especially important for early intervention service providers to understand. The role of the provider is not to focus on "working with the child" by playing with educational or therapeutic toys that teach developmental skills missed on the child's assessment, such as teaching the child to stack blocks. Instead, the role of the service provider is to collaborate with caregivers to identify and practice intervention strategies that support the child's development and ability to participate in and learn from everyday experiences. In the case of stacking blocks, this can be accomplished just as easily by the child helping the babysitter put canned goods away in the cabinet. The service provider should share his or her knowledge and expertise in instructional strategies that enhance development with the child's caregivers—those important people who are in the best position to make the biggest difference in the child's life. The implementation of this principle reflects a strong family–provider partnership that is built on the shared goal of increasing the family's competence and confidence with meeting the needs of the child.

### Key Principle 4: The Early Intervention Process, from Initial Contacts Through Transition, Must Be Dynamic and Individualized to Reflect the Child's and Family Members' Preferences, Learning Styles, and Cultural Beliefs

Although the steps of the early intervention process are similar across families, each family's experience in early intervention is unique. The process, much like the IFSP, should be flexible to adjust to the family members' changing priorities, resources, activities, and outcomes for their child. The process should also consider the family's cultural beliefs and values, which affect how the family members choose to participate and the decisions they make. This is not a "one-size-fits-all" approach. Rather, early intervention adjusts to fit families by considering their priorities and working together to implement meaningful and individualized supports that fit their lives. One key aspect of this principle centers on the idea that early intervention is only one part of family life and should not be its focus. Families should not have to rearrange their lives around intervention. When done well, early intervention blends into the family members' daily lives and becomes a part of how they interact with each other, rather than adding "therapy time" to their day.

### Key Principle 5: Individualized Family Service Plan Outcomes Must Be Functional and Based on Children's and Families' Needs and Priorities

The outcomes of the IFSP belong to families. Well-written outcomes reflect what is important to families and are functional, meaning that they describe activities the child needs to learn in order to accomplish activities that are necessary in the life of the child and his or her family. This is very different from writing outcomes based on skills the child missed on assessments. An IFSP's functional outcomes build on what naturally motivates and interests the child, fit into existing family routines, and help families learn to take advantage of natural learning opportunities as they happen to help their child develop because they see the importance of working on these outcomes for their child.

### Key Principle 6: The Family's Priorities, Needs, and Interests Are Addressed Most Appropriately by a Primary Provider Who Represents and Receives Team and Community Support

Early intervention is implemented by a team that includes the family, the service coordinator and service provider(s), and any other people who are important in the family's life, such as a child care provider, neighbor, or grandparent. Professional team members are included based on who has the appropriate expertise to support the child and family, rather than being assigned based on the child's impairments. The primary service provider's role is to collaborate closely with the family, keeping up with any changes and supporting the family in using intervention strategies between visits that are adapted for the child based on the team's input. The primary provider also communicates regularly with other team members to ensure that he or she is well prepared to coach the family on how to address the child's needs across developmental areas. When needed, other team members are brought in to meet with the family. The team's primary service provider may also change.

For example, Makeba had delays in communication and social-emotional areas of development. Rather than receiving weekly services from both the educator and the speech-language therapist, the educator acted as the primary provider with support from the speech therapist. When early intervention services are implemented using a primary provider, families are less likely to feel overwhelmed, the child is more likely to be viewed from a whole-child perspective, and services tend to be better coordinated.

### Key Principle 7: Interventions with Young Children and Family Members Must Be Based on Explicit Principles, Validated Practices, the Best Available Research, and Relevant Laws and Regulations

Providing high-quality services to all children and families must be a priority for all service providers. This principle stresses the importance of service providers making a commitment to keeping their discipline-specific knowledge current, as well as staying current in the field of early intervention. Being a lifelong learner helps providers to stay aware of changes in the laws and emerging evidence-based practices. Early interventionists must be committed to ongoing professional development so that they are ready to make good practice decisions when working with an array of very different children.

These key principles help service providers take the intention of federal regulations and link them to what they do each day in their actual practice. Using a common core of principles such as these helps all early intervention service providers, regardless of their discipline, to work as a team and provide services with a similar understanding of their program's mission. These principles are addressed repeatedly throughout this book and are woven through the professional competencies expected of all early interventionists.

## PROFESSIONAL COMPETENCIES

Similar to the key principles of early intervention, a standard set of competencies is required for all early intervention service providers. Regardless of their discipline, all early interventionists must demonstrate the following professional competencies, which were adapted from a position paper from the Council for Exceptional Children, Division for Early Childhood Task Force (1993), titled "Personnel Standards for Early Education and Early Intervention":

- View each family as unique and as being a part of a larger community
- Offer services and supports that enhance each child's and family's social networks and address the family's concerns, priorities, and needs
- Support and partner with families and caregivers to enhance the child's development
- Ensure that families are key decision makers
- Use communication that is respectful, unbiased, and focused on person-first language
- Recognize a continuum of services and supports based on a child's needs
- Understand the right of children to receive services with their peers in natural or inclusive environments
- Focus on inclusive practices that include the child with disabilities into the activities of his or her peers with and without disabilities, individualizing for the child's developmental status and age
- Facilitate a continuum of collaborative services and supports for children and their families
- Honor diverse backgrounds and develop cultural competence
- Maintain ethical conduct at all professional activities
- Engage in advocacy activities

Competency standards are intended to ensure that all service providers in the field have a similar foundation of knowledge and skills to best service children and families. These competencies may be developed through both education and experience and require ongoing professional development in order to stay current with best practices. Because the field of early intervention is relatively young and what is known about quality practices is constantly evolving, a commitment to remaining current in knowledge and skills is a necessity for all early interventionists.

## CURRENT PRACTICES IN INFANT AND TODDLER INTERVENTION

Early intervention has evolved since it first appeared as a new field in the 1970s. Family-centered practices, intervention in natural learning environments, routine-based intervention, participation-based intervention, and coaching and consultation are now considered to be evidence-based practices that offer the best possible outcomes for young children and their families. Each approach is discussed in the following sections.

### Family-Centered Practices

Early intervention employs an ecological approach to supporting children and families by attempting to strengthen the following (Bronfenbrenner, 1986):

1. The child–family relationship, such as relationships with parents, siblings, and significant individuals outside the family
2. The family's resources, such as improving access to services, information, skills, and knowledge for supporting a child's development

3.   The family's social supports, including those who assist a family in meeting the needs of the child and family

This approach highlights the importance of the child's family on influencing the child's development.

Because learning and development for all infants and toddlers occurs within the context of the family, early intervention is described as being family centered. *Family-centered practice* refers to a way of organizing and delivering assistance and support to families based on distinct, interconnected beliefs and attitudes that are expressed through the behavior of service providers (Pletcher & McBride, 2004). This practice has been described as using families' strengths, encouraging collaborative partnerships with families, supporting informed family decision making, and developing families' independence and competence (Keilty, 2008; Tomasello, Manning, & Dulmus, 2010). Box 1.4 shows the assumptions rooted in family-centered practices. This approach is discussed further in subsequent chapters.

### Interventions in Natural Learning Environments

According to Dunst, Trivette, Humphries, Raab, and Roper (2001), *natural learning environment interventions* are intervention methods and practices that focus on teaching and providing support in settings that are common, natural, and familiar to a child and family. These interventions can be conceptualized by thinking about the degree to which they are *contextualized* (provided in the context of natural or contrived activities), adult or child focused, and implemented by the interventionist or the family during or between visits. These three distinctions will be discussed further in Chapter 4. Natural learning environment interventions focus on helping families learn to use the many natural learning opportunities that occur in their daily lives.

The routines and activities that are part of a family's life offer many *natural learning opportunities,* in which the child can practice a skill or learn a new one during a regular routine. Guiding caregivers so they recognize and seize natural learning opportunities whenever they occur is a primary goal of early intervention. When families are able to successfully use the natural learning opportunities that occur during their daily lives, they become more competent in supporting their child's development between intervention visits (McWilliam, 2010).

---

**BOX 1.4.     Assumptions grounding family-centered practices and services**

- All people are basically good.
- All people have strengths.
- All people need support and encouragement.
- All people have different but equally important skills, abilities, and knowledge.
- All families have hopes, dreams, and wishes for their children.
- Families are resourceful, but all families do not have equal access to resources.
- Families should be assisted in ways that help them maintain their dignity and hope.
- Families should be equal partners in the relationship with service providers.
- Service providers work for families.

From Pletcher, L.C., & McBride, S. (2004). *Family-centered services: Guiding principles and practices for delivery of family-centered services.* Retrieved from https://www.educateiowa.gov/sites/files/ed/documents/Family%20 Centered%20Services.pdf

Prior to this current focus on interventions in natural learning environments, early intervention was child focused, with the service provider working with the child while the caregiver passively observed (Campbell & Sawyer, 2007). Intervention centered on what could be accomplished during the brief intervention visit, and the caregiver was given "homework" to do with the child between visits. This approach focused on what could be accomplished with the child during visits and provided limited support to caregivers for the time between visits. Early intervention has evolved to a more triadic approach, in which the service provider helps the caregiver practice strategies during visits with the child in the context of a target routine. The natural learning environment is broadened beyond the intervention visit. The visit is used as a practice session so that the caregiver learns strategies he or she can use every day with the child when those learning opportunities occur. The focus of intervention visits now supports the child's development through the parent–child interaction, as opposed to through the service provider working primarily with the child (Woods, Wilcox, Friedman, & Murch, 2011).

For example, Mullins (2002), the mother of a toddler with Down syndrome, stated that having her child walk along the bleachers while at his brother's baseball games allowed him to have fun practicing walking while reinforcing a narrow center of gravity, which improved his gait. This activity, embedded into a regular family routine of baseball practice and games, allowed the child to practice a new skill in a way that was enjoyable for him and his parents. The baseball field was one of this family's natural environments at that point in their lives. Mullins stated that early intervention in natural environments allowed "learning to be embedded into our daily activities … so intervention became a *part* of our lives" (p. 23). In this example, the service provider might have joined the Mullins family at the baseball field for the intervention visit. The service provider could help the mother think about and try out ways to help her child practice walking, rather than constraining intervention to therapeutic exercises for the child during the intervention visit in the family's home. This example is contextualized because the intervention is provided in the context of the family's routine of visiting the baseball field. The intervention, which is adult and child focused, can be implemented by the family because the mother knows how to support the child's walking between visits.

## Routine-Based Intervention

*Routine-based intervention* uses a family's routines and activities as the context for intervention (McWilliam, 2010). Everyday caregiving routines such as mealtimes, dressing, diapering, and other family activities such as camping, child care, and "mommy and me" groups are common settings for caregivers to embed parent-selected outcomes and objectives. Many families find that embedding the teaching of needed skills into their routines feels comfortable and generally saves them time. When routine-based intervention is not used, many natural learning opportunities are overlooked, and intervention can feel as if it is "owned" by the service provider.

The mother of a toddler with motor delays stated the following about her child's physical therapy:

> The therapists did not often include me in the actual "hands-on" therapy so I was not comfortable trying at home what they did in the therapy session. I did not know what to do, or when or how, or why to do it. (Mullins, 2002, p. 23)

When therapists and service providers support parents as they learn the "how" and "why" of learning activities, the child benefits from the extra time learning and practicing skills between intervention visits because the parent is confident in how to use those strategies.

Routine-based intervention encourages all family members or friends who wish to be involved to participate in assisting the child's development. Intervention that is contextualized in child and family routines makes sense because the consistent adults in a child's life—not the early interventionist—have the greatest influence on learning and development.

## Participation-Based Intervention

In *participation-based intervention,* the emphasis is placed on a child's participation in natural family and community activities and daily routines, rather than only teaching skills missed on assessments (Campbell, 2004; Campbell & Sawyer, 2007). In other words, the focus is on increasing a child's involvement and *participation* with his or her family, and other people important to the child, by increasing the child's functional skills and learning opportunities. The service provider's interactions with parents and caregivers should be relaxed, structured, supportive, and professional. The service provider must have the intent of enhancing parents' or caregivers' confidence in their role of fostering their child's development. Functional outcomes improve participation in meaningful activities for both the child and parent because they build on natural motivations to learn and participate. The family comes to understand that collaboratively determined strategies and outcomes are worth using because they lead to practical improvements in the child's development and, consequently, in the family's life.

## Coaching and Consultation

*Coaching* and *collaborative consultation* involve the use of specific strategies and interactions to support and guide the learning of adults who can be of assistance to a child with special needs (Rush & Shelden, 2011; Woods et al., 2011). Both of these strategies are types of *indirect services* because the service provider is training another adult who will be implementing the interventions with the child when the service provider is not present. Although the service provider may work with the child to model or demonstrate how to play with a toy or engage the child, the objective is to support the other adult in feeling confident in performing these interventions when the provider is not in that setting. Using coaching and collaboration with parents or caregivers involves helping them reflect on what they currently are doing with their child, engaging in shared problem solving and planning to develop intervention strategies that can be used during those interactions, developing a joint plan for how the family or caregivers will implement intervention in their daily routines, and following up at each intervention visit to answer questions and provide support (Rush & Shelden, 2011). Helping families understand how their toys, activities, and interactions can be used or adapted to promote positive developmental changes in their child is a key focus of coaching and collaboration. Examples of this are evident in Makeba's case.

## Case Study: Makeba

Makeba and her family have been partnering with the early childhood special educator and speech therapist for 3 months now. During each intervention visit, the educator talks with family members about what is going well and discusses any challenges they have faced regarding Makeba's communication and social-emotional development. Together, they identify a familiar routine to target that visit, and the educator observes the parent–child interactions during the activity. The educator then coaches the parents (often both are present) in ways to interact with Makeba to encourage her to learn to use more words. The educator also has helped the parents learn strategies to manage Makeba's tantrums. They report that ignoring her tantrums works well most of the time. When the speech therapist joins them for visits, he consults by problem solving with them on strategies and activities that will boost Makeba's variety of sounds, use of purposeful communication, and overall vocabulary. The services focus on how to support this family by building intervention around what they are already doing with Makeba and her interests, as well as by suggesting strategies that the family members can embed in their routines to help Makeba learn.

The service providers check in with the family at each visit to see if the parents have been able to successfully use the intervention strategies between visits; then, they brainstorm and plan together for the next intervention visit. The service coordinator also visits the family about once each month; she has worked closely with the family to find a community group that provides stipends to families for preschool costs. The service coordinator has helped Makeba's father take advantage of a local job center, where he is taking a class to gain computer skills, which he hopes will help him find a job in sales.

The early intervention services Makeba and her family received reflected the Workgroup (2008a, 2008b) practices, which emphasize the importance of parent–child interactions during daily routines. Recognizing the centrality of parent–child interactions and building interventions around supporting and adapting what families already do are the characteristics of early intervention that have most changed in recent years.

## HISTORY OF EARLY INTERVENTION

Early intervention is a relatively young specialty area of special education. Although the history of special education dates back to the 1800s, the early intervention provision of IDEA only became part of the law in the United States in 1986. Services for infants and toddlers with disabilities were available in some states before they became a federal priority, although most special education services focused on the education of older children who attended public schools. Progress with implementing early intervention internationally has varied from country to country.

Before 1986 in the United States, families who were interested and could afford it sought private therapy through local hospital programs or private agencies. Families who were unable to access private services worked with their children at home using more informal family and community supports. It was not until after provisions were added to IDEA to mandate educational support for preschoolers with special needs that similar services were considered for children younger than 3 years old.

The federal law known today as IDEA was originally called the Education for All Handicapped Children Act (EHA) of 1975 (PL 94-142). When originally passed, EHA represented a landmark in special education law because it afforded all school-age children the right to a free appropriate public education, regardless of disability. EHA was also important because it was the first time that federal funding was provided for the education of school-age children with special needs. The law included a voluntary option for states to serve preschoolers with disabilities under the Preschool Incentive Grant program, but this option did not include serving children younger than 3 years of age (Raver, 1999, 2009).

It was not until the 1986 reauthorization of EHA that special education services for infants and toddlers were addressed in the law. Under Part H of EHA, discretionary funds became available for states to operate early intervention programs. The addition of Part H (similar to what we now know as Part C of IDEA) came about through the efforts of organizations and families who lobbied on behalf of infants and toddlers (Erickson & Kurz-Riemer, 1999). Once the reauthorization took effect, all states began the process of developing federally funded early intervention programs or helping local and state programs make the transition to match the requirements in the federal law. In 1990, EHA was amended again and renamed the *Individuals with Disabilities Education Act (IDEA) of 1990* (PL 101-476). Part C of this law outlined early intervention services for infants and toddlers and their families.

Part C of IDEA (2004) includes provisions for offering early intervention services. These provisions have been implemented by states and include the following criteria: 1) eligibility, 2) time lines, 3) evaluation and assessment, 4) the IFSP, 5) early intervention services, 6) natural environments, 7) transitions, and 8) procedural safeguards. These criteria are discussed in the following sections.

## Eligibility

As mentioned previously, IDEA provides guidance regarding eligibility criteria for early intervention, but states define the specific criteria for services in their state. Some states include children who are at risk for developmental issues, whereas others do not.

## Time Lines

IDEA designates time lines for the completion of some parts of the early intervention process, such as the completion of the IFSP and requirements for IFSP reviews (which will be discussed in Chapter 3). IDEA also describes the need for timely initiation of early intervention services, resolution of disputes with families and/or agencies, and the development of the transition plan. Some functions, such as transition planning, do not have a specified time line, but states are responsible for choosing time lines to ensure that these actions are timely.

## Evaluation and Assessment

Under the law, families have the right to a "timely, comprehensive, multidisciplinary evaluation" (IDEA 2004, 34 CFR Part 303.113) of their child's development and a determination of the child's eligibility for early intervention services. IDEA describes an assessment of the family's resources, priorities, and concerns related to their child's development and their family's functioning. It is stipulated that evaluation and assessment must be conducted by qualified personnel and must include the use of *informed clinical opinion* (the perceptions and observations of professionals trained in a specific discipline), as well as the administration of evaluation instruments that determine the child's functioning in each domain of development. Procedures for completing the evaluation and assessment are further outlined in the federal regulations.

## Individualized Family Service Plan

IDEA requires that an IFSP be developed by a multidisciplinary team for each eligible child. The multidisciplinary team must include the child's parent(s), the service coordinator, and professionals representing at least two different disciplines of service, such as a physical therapist and an educator. Among other things, the IFSP documents the early intervention services that will be provided to the child and family. Specific requirements related to the plan and its development are addressed in Chapter 3.

## Early Intervention Services

The federal regulations designate the kind of information that must be addressed in the provision of early intervention services. Services must be *outcome driven*—that is, driven by the outcomes the family desires to see as a result of the child's participation in the program. IDEA requires that service frequency (i.e., the number of sessions, such as once per month), intensity (i.e., individual or group services), method (i.e., how a service will be provided, such as using coaching), length (i.e., length of time, such as 60 minutes per visit), duration (i.e., how long the services will be provided, such as 3 months or 1 year), and location (i.e., the place[s] where the service will be provided, such as the home or child care center) must be specified.

## Natural Environments

IDEA defines *natural environments* as settings such as the family's home or other community places where the child's same-age peers who do not have disabilities spend time. Services must be provided in natural environments to the maximum extent possible and must be justified in the rare circumstances where they are provided in nonnatural settings.

## Transitions

Each child's IFSP must include a plan that outlines the steps to be taken to ensure a smooth transition from the early intervention system. IDEA describes the specific steps that must be included, such as developing activities that will help the child prepare for the next setting. Specific information about this process is discussed in Chapter 3.

## Procedural Safeguards

According to IDEA, families who choose to participate in early intervention have certain rights and procedural safeguards available to them. Some of these procedural safeguards address confidentiality, parental consent, prior notice of proposed activities, access to the child's records, and the right to dispute resolution.

The careful implementation and monitoring of each of these key provisions is vital to creating a successful early intervention experience. These provisions are discussed in more detail in later chapters.

Part C of IDEA currently remains a discretionary program, meaning that states can choose to accept or decline federal funds and thereby agree or decline to operate this kind of program. When a state agrees to offer a Part C early intervention program, the state is also agreeing to comply with federal regulations, including these major provisions, and to federal oversight and monitoring by OSEP. Although the provision of early intervention services continues to be a priority at the federal and state levels, challenges continue as programs face inadequate funding and struggle to serve the growing number of children and families who are in need of these services.

## PREVALENCE OF CHILDREN RECEIVING EARLY INTERVENTION

According to the Data Accountability Center (2011), 453,406 infants and toddlers ages birth to 36 months received early intervention services under Part C of IDEA in 2011. This number represented approximately 2.79% of the entire population of infants and toddlers living in the United States. Attempts to estimate the number of children who are in need of early intervention services are known to underestimate the actual number of children who are potentially eligible but who do not receive services (Rosenberg, Robinson, Shaw, & Ellison, 2013). One study examined prevalence data from a nationally representative sample of children, ages 9–24 months, who were enrolled in early intervention programs; the authors found that 17% of children under the age of 5 years who were potentially eligible for early intervention or special education services did not receive them (Rosenberg, Zhang, & Robinson, 2008). Ongoing and comprehensive *Child Find activities* are an important part of early intervention. These programs try to identify and recruit these potentially eligible children and families who are in need of these services.

To investigate who actually participates in early intervention, the National Early Intervention Longitudinal Study (NEILS; Hebbeler et al., 2007) was conducted as a 10-year project under the U.S. Department of Education and OSEP. According to the NEILS report, children entered early intervention at an average age of 17 months. Most children were male, and most were enrolled due to a communication delay or a disability. Other common reasons for enrollment included motor delays, prenatal and perinatal factors (one third of children were premature), and global developmental delays (i.e., delays in all areas of development). Children who were found to be eligible due to a developmental delay tended to enter programs after the age of 24 months due to concerns about communication. Children who were found to be eligible due to a diagnosed condition, such as Down syndrome or visual impairment, typically entered intervention earlier, before their first birthdays.

Demographically, an overrepresentation of children from low-income families was noted, and there was a higher proportion of Caucasian children receiving intervention. Children from ethnic minorities were also represented, with children of African American and Hispanic origin representing the two other populations most often receiving early intervention. A large number of children receiving early intervention have also been found to receive foster care, have low birth weight, and be more likely to be rated as having only fair health (Scarborough, Spiker, Mallik, Bailey, & Simeonsson, 2004).

The most common services received, in order of frequency, were service coordination, speech therapy, special instruction, occupational therapy, and physical therapy. These services were provided in families' or child care providers' homes, with most families receiving one to two services at a time for 2 hours or less each week. The average length of stay in early intervention was approximately 17 months. Most children received services until they reached their third birthday, at which point they were no longer age-eligible for early intervention. The trajectory of a child's participation in early intervention differed depending on the child's reason for eligibility. Children with speech or communication problems remained in the program for the shortest amount of time, and those with at-risk or diagnosed conditions tended to receive intervention the longest.

Children with diagnosed conditions may have received early intervention longer because many disabilities can be identified at birth. A diagnosis of Down syndrome is one example. Children with *Down syndrome* manifest the most common biological condition associated with intellectual disability and can demonstrate a range of intellectual abilities (American Association on Intellectual and Developmental Disabilities, 2010). During the first or second year of life, children with *cerebral palsy,* which results from a brain lesion or abnormal brain growth, are often identified. This condition, a disorder affecting voluntary movement and posture, is commonly served in early intervention programs.

Less than 1% of infants who receive services typically have low vision or blindness (discussed in Chapter 9); hearing impairment or deafness (discussed in Chapter 9); or multiple and complex disabilities, such as fragile X syndrome (discussed in Chapter 10). *Fragile X syndrome* is a chromosomal abnormality associated with mild to severe intellectual disabilities; it affects males more often and more severely than females. The behavioral characteristics of this condition can be similar to those seen in children with autism spectrum disorder (ASD; Meyer & Batshaw, 2005). The incidence of children with ASD has significantly increased in recent years to 1 in 88 births (Centers for Disease Control and Prevention, 2012). As a consequence, serving infants and toddlers with this condition is becoming increasingly more common in early intervention programs. ASD is further discussed in Chapter 8.

## IMPORTANCE OF EARLY INTERVENTION

It is now well established that early experiences can have significant long-term effects on the developmental outcomes of children, regardless of the level of delay or disability (Ramey & Ramey, 2004). A child's brain is highly responsive to early experiences because these experiences directly affect the neural connections and functions within the brain. In fact, early experiences can actually change the way a child's genes are expressed or alter the types and amount of neural connections in the brain, with both negative and positive trajectories possible (Medina, 2011; National Scientific Council on the Developing Child, 2010). This *neural plasticity* is why early intervention is so important, especially for children who live in impoverished circumstances and those with limited early childhood experiences. Although early intervention cannot eliminate most disabilities, it can have a positive effect on the development of many young children and lessen the effects of the disability or delay on the child's interactions and participation in everyday life.

A child's foundation for all learning for the rest of the child's life is established during the first 5 years of life (Ramey & Ramey, 2004); as the child ages, this foundation is elaborated and refined. Early childhood specialists agree that infancy is the right time to begin providing support to children with special needs or those who are at risk for developmental difficulties. Services should generally begin as early as possible. A child's age at the start of services has been found to be a significant variable in predicting a child's later intellectual or cognitive progress (Lee & Kahn, 1998).

This early start unfortunately does not always occur. Many children are referred to early intervention later in the first 3 years of life—or not at all—for a variety of factors, including the family's or physician's preference to "wait and see" if the child's development catches up, ineffective or no developmental screening efforts, a family's choice to obtain similar services outside of the Part C system (e.g., outpatient therapy services), cultural factors, or late diagnoses. To address these issues, IDEA stipulated that early intervention programs conduct ongoing Child Find efforts to raise public awareness among potential referral sources and families regarding the positive benefits of individualized support during the first 3 years. Child Find efforts also concentrate on locating children who are in need of services. These efforts are important because of the complexity and array of challenges that can be associated with having a developmental disability early in life.

A child with cognitive delays may also have motor or language delays, sensory difficulties, or health conditions such as seizure disorders. Because of the complexity of these problems, it can be difficult to determine precisely how much children have benefited from early intervention. However, there is strong evidence that the declines in child functioning that occur in the absence of early intervention can be substantially reduced by providing services to a child and the child's family during the early years (Guralnick, 1997, 1998,

2005a, 2005b; Pungello, Campbell, & Barnett, 2006). Furthermore, early intervention programs have been shown to mitigate the stresses and challenges associated with family and child risks or a child's disability or delay. Today, it is accepted that the benefits of early intervention justify its costs (Barnett, 2000; Trohanis, 2008). Makeba's family's story is a good example of this.

 **Case Study: Makeba**

Makeba and her family continued to receive early intervention services until her third birthday. Just before her birthday, Makeba's father found work at a local car dealership and the family's concern about paying for preschool was resolved. To prepare for the transition out of early intervention, the family's service coordinator assisted them with developing a transition plan for the services they wanted Makeba to receive after she was no longer age-eligible for the program. Because she continued to show a developmental delay, her family was interested in a referral to the local ECSE preschool program at her neighborhood school. Following her discharge from early intervention, Makeba began attending the school system's preschool morning class four days a week, where she also received speech therapy. In the afternoons, the ECSE preschool teacher offered continued support to the teacher in the community child care preschool Makeba had been attending. As her vocabulary increased, Makeba had fewer tantrums, which made life at home and school easier. Makeba's family was pleased with the support they received in early intervention and commented that Makeba was making progress every day.

## INCLUSIVE PRACTICES IN EARLY INTERVENTION

In early intervention, *inclusion* refers to helping families, child care providers, preschool teachers, and other adults in a child's natural environments to support the child's participation in activities that are typical for a particular setting. At their core, inclusive practices for early intervention focus on the idea that all children are valued and have the right to participate in activities that are typical for infants and toddlers without special needs. Inclusive practices involve guiding adult providers to use strategies and accommodations that increase a child's participation in the setting. For example, it could be collaboratively decided that taping down the paper for a child with cerebral palsy (see Jennifer's case study in Chapter 10), could help the child better manage painting at the art table. Embedding sign language or a communication switch into the welcome routine may support a child with limited communication abilities in asking for what he or she wants to do during the day. These are examples of easily implemented changes, or *adaptations*, in a setting that will allow a child to more effectively participate.

 **Case Study: Makeba**

While Makeba was still enrolled in early intervention, the family's service providers visited with her child care center's preschool teacher to help her support Makeba's communication and social-emotional development. They collaborated with the teacher about once every 2 weeks to find out how Makeba was managing. The child care provider indicated that group activities were especially challenging for Makeba. Together, they decided that providing

Makeba with an *activity mini-schedule,* a Velcro list of the four different activities that occurred during opening circle, might help Makeba, as well as the other children, feel less anxiety and have more understanding of what was about to occur. This strategy has been found to be effective in improving the attention of children with ASD, behavior challenges, or hearing loss (Raver, Hester, Michalek, Cho, & Anthony, 2013). As one activity was completed, the label for it was removed; then, the teacher pointed to the next activity to help guide Makeba's attention to the appropriate materials. The collaborative process involved a lot of give and take, with the child care provider developing several strategies that proved to be helpful. After Makeba made the transition out of early intervention, the speech therapist from the ECSE preschool program continued this collaboration. The purpose of these consultations was to support Makeba's inclusion in classroom activities so she could fully participate in ways that enhanced all of her development.

A principal tenet of inclusion in early childhood education and early intervention is using *developmentally appropriate practice* (DAP; Garguilo & Kilgo, 2000). This means creating environments that match every child's developmental level and are also appropriate for a child chronologically. In this way, each child's individual abilities and interests are supported (Bredekamp & Copple, 1997). The principle of DAP supports developing individualized activities for children, including those with and without disabilities. When Makeba attended her inclusive child care preschool class, her family, the program staff, and the early interventionist met frequently to discuss the type of instructional supports and accommodations necessary for Makeba to be included successfully in that program. Through observation, the service provider noted what seemed to work for Makeba and areas that presented challenges for Makeba and her child care teacher. Through indirect services, such as monitoring and consultation, Makeba's service providers provided informal coaching to the child care staff. It was important during this process that the service providers helped the early childhood staff understand how the consultation process worked.

Some early interventionists have unfortunately expressed concern about poorly coordinated interventions in inclusive settings and a lack of understanding regarding what early childhood staff can expect from the consultation process (Horn & Sandall, 2000; Wesley, Buysse, & Skinner, 2001). This book discusses ways to individualize inclusion so that both the child and the professional in the inclusive setting feel supported. Just like services provided to young children and their families, each inclusive situation requires a slightly different kind and style of support for the adults involved to learn ways to facilitate a particular child's learning. By using contextualized, collaborative interventions that are embedded into the setting's routines, professionals are supported in enhancing children's development. Successful inclusion of infants and toddlers with special needs requires good communication, clear expectations for the consultative process, and regular monitoring by the adults in the inclusive setting.

## BEST PRACTICE HIGHLIGHTS

Specific best practices used in the field of early intervention will be highlighted in each chapter of this book to help you remember and apply key information. As you begin your exploration of the field of early intervention, keep these best practices in mind:

- Effective early intervention programs focus on the importance of providing flexible, family-centered, and individualized supports that intentionally develop the capacity and competence of families and caregivers to meet the needs of their young children with special needs.

- Early intervention programs provide a variety of supports to children and families—not merely to children—because caregivers are the primary agents of change in a child's development.

- Programs follow seven key principles in providing early intervention (Workgroup on Principles and Practices in Natural Environments, 2008b):

  1. Infants and toddlers learn best through everyday experiences and interactions with familiar people in familiar contexts.

  2. All families, with the necessary supports and resources, can enhance their children's learning and development.

  3. The primary role of a service provider is to work with and support family members and caregivers in a child's life.

  4. The early intervention process, from initial contacts through transition, must be dynamic and individualized to reflect the child's and family members' preferences, learning styles, and cultural beliefs.

  5. IFSP outcomes must be functional and based on children's and families' needs and priorities.

  6. The family's priorities, needs, and interests are addressed most appropriately by a primary provider who represents and receives team and community support.

  7. Interventions with young children and family members must be based on explicit principles, validated practices, the best available research, and relevant laws and regulations.

- An understanding of federal regulations and state procedures helps service providers in presenting interventions that are respectful of families' rights and preferences and are aligned with a state's early intervention system expectations.

- According to Part C of IDEA, effective early intervention programs do the following:

  1. Support the development of infants and toddlers with disabilities and delays

  2. Reduce long-term educational costs

  3. Maximize children's independence

  4. Enhance the capacity of families to meet the needs of their children

- Service providers must meet established professional competencies; commit to following explicit early intervention principles; and use validated, evidence-based practices so that interventions are effective, appropriate, meaningful, and supportive of each child's participation in his or her family's natural environments.

- The primary objective of early intervention is to offer an array of services and supports that helps families and caregivers know how to support the child's development in his or her daily living routines so that the child learns between intervention visits, when most learning naturally occurs.

## CONCLUSION

As Makeba's story demonstrates, early intervention involves a number of professionals using a family-centered approach to support children and their families in order to provide coordinated services. The first 3 years of a child's life are critical for later development. As

Part C of IDEA explains, services and interventions must be tailored to the unique needs of each child and family and should begin as soon as possible. The best outcomes occur when caregivers and early intervention professionals work together because the majority of change occurs while children are interacting with their families. Early intervention service providers use coaching and consultation to guide parents or caregivers, as well as other adults who are important to the family, in developing participation-based interventions within the routines of families' natural environments. As much as possible, inclusive activities that involve children without disabilities are encouraged. Encouraging families to use natural learning environment interventions is a good way to support the learning of children. Service providers need to remember the fundamental purpose of early intervention: to help families and caregivers know how to support a child's development using individualized intervention strategies between visits, when most learning naturally occurs.

## DISCUSSION QUESTIONS AND APPLIED ACTIVITIES

1.  Using at least three of the Workgroup's (2008b) seven key principles, write a one-paragraph definition of early intervention. Use common language so the definition could be shared with a parent or caregiver who is considering having his or her child assessed to determine if the child is eligible for services.

2.  Write the nine provisions of Part C of IDEA (2004) and describe each as if you were sharing them with a parent or caregiver.

3.  Visit an early intervention program in your community. Ask the director the following questions:

    •  What is the process by which a child, and the child's family, are determined to be eligible for services?

    •  How are services paid for?

    •  What is the most common type of service setting your program offers (e.g., intervention visits in the home, inclusion setting consultations, community location)?

    •  What are the three greatest challenges your staff face in providing early intervention services? Describe how you and your team have responded to these challenges.

## REFERENCES

American Association on Intellectual and Developmental Disabilities, Ad Hoc Committee on Terminology and Classification. (2010). *Intellectual disability: Definition, classification, and systems of supports* (11th ed.). Washington, DC: Author.

Barnett, W.S. (2000). Economics of early childhood intervention. In S.J. Meisels (Ed.), *Handbook of early childhood intervention* (2nd ed., pp. 589–610). New York, NY: Cambridge University Press.

Bredekamp, S., & Copple, C. (Eds.) (1997). *Developmentally appropriate practice in early childhood programs* (Rev. ed.). Washington, DC: National Association for the Education of Young Children.

Bronfenbrenner, U. (1986). Ecology of the family as a context for human development: Research perspectives. *Developmental Psychology, 22*(6), 723–742.

Buysse, V., Wesley, P.W., Snyder, P., & Winton, P. (2006). Evidence-based practice: What does it really mean for the early childhood field? *Young Exceptional Children, 9*(4), 2–11. doi:10.1177/109625060600900401

Campbell, P.H. (2004). Participation-based services: Promoting children's participation in natural settings.

*Young Exceptional Children, 8*(1), 20–29. doi:10.1177/109625060400800103

Campbell, P.H., & Sawyer, L.B. (2007). Supporting learning opportunities in natural settings through participation-based services. *Journal of Early Intervention, 29,* 287–305. doi:10.1177/105381510702900402

Centers for Disease Control and Prevention. (2012). *Autism spectrum disorders (ASDs): Data and statistics.* Retrieved from http://www.cdc.gov/ncbddd/autism/data .html

Council for Exceptional Children, Division for Early Childhood Task Force. (1993). *Personnel standards for early education and early intervention* [Position statement]. Missoula, MT: Author.

Data Accountability Center. (2011). *Part C data and notes: IDEA 618 data tables.* Retrieved from https://www.idea data.org/tools-and-products

Dunst, C.J., Hamby, D., Trivette, C.M., Raab, M., & Bruder, M. (2000). Everyday family and community life and children's naturally occurring learning opportunities. *Journal of Early Intervention, 23,* 151–164. doi: 10.1177/105381510002300301

Dunst, C.J., Trivette, C.M., Humphries, T., Raab, M., & Roper, N. (2001). Contrasting approaches to natural learning environment interventions. *Infants & Young Children, 14*, 48–63. doi:10.1097/00001163-2001140 20-00007

Early Childhood Outcomes Center. (2005). *Family and child outcomes for early intervention and early childhood special education.* Retrieved from http://www.ectacenter.org/~pdfs/eco/Family_Outcomes_Issues_01-17-05.pdf

Early Childhood Technical Assistance Center. (2009). *The child outcomes.* Retrieved from http://ectacenter.org/eco/assets/pdfs/Child_Outcomes_handout.pdf

Education for All Handicapped Children Act of 1975, PL 94-142, 20 U.S.C. §§ 1400 *et seq.*

Erickson, M.F., & Kurz-Riemer, K. (1999). *Infants, toddlers, and families: A framework for support and intervention.* New York, NY: Guilford Press.

Garguilo, R., & Kilgo, J. (2000). *Young children with special needs.* Albany, NY: Delmar.

Greenwood, C., Carta, J.J., & McConnell, S. (2011). Advances in measurement for universal screening and individual progress monitoring of young children. *Journal of Early Intervention, 33*(4), 254–267. doi: 10.1177/1053815111428467

Guralnick, M.J. (Ed.). (1997). *The effectiveness of early intervention.* Baltimore, MD: Paul H. Brookes Publishing Co.

Guralnick, M.J. (1998). Effectiveness of early intervention for vulnerable children: A developmental perspective. *American Journal on Mental Retardation, 102*, 319–345. doi:10.1352/0895-8017

Guralnick, M.J. (2005a). Early intervention for children with intellectual disabilities: Current knowledge and future prospects. *Journal of Applied Research in Intellectual Disabilities, 18*, 313–324. doi:10.1111/j.1468-3148 .2005.00270.x

Guralnick, M.J. (2005b). Second-generation research in the field of early intervention. In M.J. Guralnick (Ed.), *The effectiveness of early intervention* (pp. 3–20). Baltimore, MD: Paul H. Brookes Publishing Co.

Guralnick, M.J. (2008). International perspectives on early intervention: A search for common ground. *Journal of Early Intervention, 30*, 90–101.

Hebbeler, K., Spiker, D., Bailey, D., Scarborough, A., Mallik, S., Simeonsson, R., … Nelson, L. (2007). *Early intervention for infants and toddlers with disabilities and their families: Participants, services, and outcomes. Final report of the National Early Intervention Longitudinal Study [NEILS].* Retrieved from http://www.sri.com/sites/default/files/publications/neils_finalreport_200 702.pdf

Horn, E., & Sandall, S. (2000). The visiting teacher: A model of inclusive ECSE service delivery. In S. Sandall & M. Ostrosky (Eds.), *Natural environments and inclusion* (pp. 49–58). Longmont, CO: Sopris West.

Individuals with Disabilities Education Act of 1990, PL 101-476, 20 U.S.C. §§ 1400 *et seq.*

Individuals with Disabilities Education Improvement Act (IDEA) of 2004, PL 108-446, 20 U.S.C. §§ 1400 *et seq.*

Keilty, B. (2008). Early intervention home-visiting principles in practice: A reflective approach. *Young Exceptional Children, 11*(2), 29–40. doi:10.1177/1096250607311 933

Klingner, J.K., Boardman, A.G., & McMaster, K.L. (2013). What does it take to scale up and sustain evidence-based practices? *Exceptional Children, 79*, 195–212.

Lee, S., & Kahn, J. (1998). Relationships of child progress with selected child, family and program variables in early intervention. *Infant-Toddler Intervention, 8*(1), 85–101.

McWilliam, R.A. (2010). *Routines-based early intervention: Supporting young children and their families.* Baltimore, MD: Paul H. Brookes Publishing Co.

Medina, J. (2011). *Brain rules for baby: How to raise a smart, happy child from zero to five.* Seattle, WA: Pear Press.

Meyer, G., & Batshaw, M. (2005). Fragile X syndrome. In M. Batshaw (Ed.), *Children with disabilities* (5th ed., pp. 321–332), Baltimore, MD: Paul H. Brookes Publishing Co.

Mott, D.W., & Dunst, C.J. (2006). Influences of resource-based intervention practices on parent and child outcomes. *CASEinPoint, 2*(6), 1–8.

Mullins, L. (2002). Natural environments: A letter from a mother to friends, families and professionals. *Young Exceptional Children, 5*(3), 21–24. doi:10.1177/109625 060200500303

National Scientific Council on the Developing Child. (2010). *Early experiences can alter gene expression and affect long-term development.* Retrieved from http://developingchild.harvard.edu/index.php/download_file/-/view/666/

Odom, S.L., & Wolery, M. (2003). A unified theory of practice in early intervention/early childhood special education: Evidence-based practices. *Journal of Special Education, 37*(3), 164–173. doi:10.1177/002246690303 70030601

Office of Special Education Programs. (2010). *29th annual report to Congress on the implementation of the Individuals with Disabilities Education Act, 2007* (Vol. 1). Washington, DC: Author.

Pletcher, L.C., & McBride, S. (2004). *Family-centered services: Guiding principles and practices for delivery of family-centered services.* Retrieved from http://www.learningace.com/doc/535648/f0944db94571fda4e 09769382cd40479/famlcntrdsrvc

Pletcher, L.C., & Younggren, N.O. (2013). *The early intervention workbook: Essential practices for quality services.* Baltimore, MD: Paul H. Brookes Publishing Co.

Pungello, E.P., Campbell, F.A., & Barnett, W.S. (2006). *Poverty and early childhood educational intervention.* Retrieved from http://www.law.unc.edu/documents/poverty/publications/pungelloandcampbellpolicybrief .pdf

Ramey, C.T., & Ramey, S.L. (2004). Early learning and school readiness: Can early intervention make a difference? *Merrill-Palmer Quarterly, 50*, 471–491. doi:10 .1353/mpq.2004.0034

Raver, S.A. (1999). *Intervention strategies for infants and toddlers with special needs: A team approach.* Upper Saddle River, NJ: Prentice-Hall.

Raver, S.A. (2009). *Early childhood special education— 0–8 years: Strategies for positive outcomes.* Upper Saddle River, NJ: Pearson.

Raver, S.A., Hester, P., Michalek, A., Cho, D., & Anthony, N. (2013). Impact of an activity mini-schedule on the attention of preschoolers with cochlear implants during a group activity. *Education and Treatment of Children, 36*(2), 15–32. doi:10.1353/etc.2013.0014

Rosenberg, S.A., Robinson, C.C., Shaw, E.F., & Ellison M.C. (2013). Part C early intervention for infants and toddlers: Percentage eligible versus served. *Pediatrics, 131*(1), 38–46. doi:10.1542/peds.2012-1662

Rosenberg, S.A., Zhang, D., & Robinson, C.C. (2008). Prevalence of developmental delays and participation in early intervention services for young children. *Pediatrics, 121*(6), e1503–e1509. doi:10.1542/peds.2007-1680

Rush, D.D., & Shelden, M.L. (2011). *The early childhood coaching handbook.* Baltimore, MD: Paul H. Brookes Publishing Co.

Scarborough, A.A., Spiker, D., Mallik, S., Bailey, D.B., & Simeonsson, R.J. (2004). A national look at children and families entering early intervention. *Exceptional Children, 70,* 469–483.

Tomasello, N.M., Manning, A.R., & Dulmus, C.N. (2010). Family-centered early intervention for infants and toddlers with disabilities. *Journal of Family Social Work, 13,* 163–172. doi:10.1080/10522150903503010

Torrey, M.K., Leginus, M.A., & Cecere, S. (2011). Resource-based intervention: Success with community-centered practices. *Physical & Occupational Therapy in Pediatrics, 31*(2), 115–119. doi:10.3109/01942638 .2001.563663

Trohanis, P.L. (2008). Progress in providing services to young children with special needs and their families: An overview to and update on the implementation of the Individuals with Disabilities Education Act (IDEA). *Journal of Early Intervention, 30*(2), 140–151. doi:10.1177/1053815107312050

Wesley, P., Buysse, V., & Skinner, D. (2001). Early interventionists' perspectives on professional comfort as consultants. *Journal of Early Intervention, 24,* 112–128. doi:10.1177/105381510102400206

Woods, J.J., Wilcox, M.J., Friedman, M., & Murch, T. (2011). Collaborative consultation in natural environments: Strategies to enhance family-centered supports and services. *Language, Speech, and Hearing Services in Schools, 42,* 379–392. doi:10.1044/0161-1461(2011/10-0016)

Workgroup on Principles and Practices in Natural Environments, OSEP TA Community of Practice: Part C Settings. (2008a, March). *Agreed upon mission and key principles for providing early intervention services in natural environments.* Retrieved from http://ectacenter .org/~pdfs/topics/families/Finalmissionandprinciples 3_11_08.pdf

Workgroup on Principles and Practices in Natural Environments, OSEP TA Community of Practice: Part C Settings. (2008b, March). *Seven key principles: Looks like/doesn't look like.* Retrieved from http://www.ecta center.org/~pdfs/topics/families/Principles_Looks Like_DoesntLookLike3_11_08.pdf

# 2 | Collaboration and Teamwork with Families and Professionals

Sharon A. Raver and Dana C. Childress

This chapter discusses issues related to the creation of collaborative relationships with families, team members, and other professionals, including the following:

- The importance of family–professional collaboration
- The family-centered approach and family systems theory
- The early intervention team
- Team models in early intervention
- Strategies for effective collaboration and communication
- Best practice highlights

## Case Study: Mason

Mason is a 5-month-old child who was born 8 weeks early because his mother was in a car accident. Because of complications associated with the accident and his premature birth, Mason has a brain injury and has been diagnosed with cerebral palsy and visual impairment. He is the fourth child in his family. Mason was referred to a local early intervention program by his pediatrician shortly after being discharged from the hospital at 3 months old. Following the evaluation and assessment of his development, Mason was found to be eligible for early intervention services, and an individualized family service plan (IFSP) was developed. Mason's parents and child care provider were present during the initial IFSP meeting, where outcomes were written and service recommendations were discussed.

The team had to sort through several differing recommendations before reaching consensus. Some team members recommended that Mason receive services from a primary service provider, who could help the family with integrating strategies from all disciplines into Mason's daily life. Another team member strongly felt that Mason should receive multiple services, such as special instruction, physical therapy, and speech therapy weekly due to his significant disabilities. To reach a consensus, the service coordinator facilitated an open discussion that allowed all team members, including Mason's parents, to express their positions. Finally, the team determined that Mason would receive services from a physical therapist, who would be his primary service provider, as well as special instruction services from an educator as a consulting service, to help his family and child care provider encourage his development in a variety of settings throughout the day. The parents stated that they felt comfortable with this approach, knowing that further consultations with the speech-language pathologist may be added to the IFSP at a later date as Mason began to communicate more purposefully. In fact, when Mason was 2.5 years old, his primary provider changed to the educator as his intervention outcomes began to focus on more learning and communication issues in preparation for transition to preschool. Mason received early intervention services until his third birthday.

Because Part C of the Individuals with Disabilities Education Improvement Act (IDEA) of 2004 (PL 108-446) requires family members to be involved in all aspects of their child's services—to the extent that they choose—caregivers are clearly essential players in the implementation of early intervention. Mason's parents were involved in the early intervention process from the beginning and actively contributed their insights and opinions about Mason's strengths and needs during the evaluation and assessment, as well as throughout the development of his IFSP. They participated in the discussion about services as equal team members with the professionals at the IFSP meeting. Mason's parents' participation was critical to ensuring that the services on the IFSP met their family's needs and the needs of their son.

There has been a paradigm shift in early intervention from viewing the child with special needs as the key recipient of services to viewing the *child's parents, caregivers, and family* as the principal recipients of services and supports. The process of family–professional collaboration enhances parents' natural abilities to influence their child's development and learning. Parents have been found to be good advocates for their children when they are provided with information, encouragement, and optimism (Trivette & Dunst, 2004). Through meaningful family–professional relationships, parents receive experiences that will hopefully lead to positive outcomes for themselves, their child, and their family.

## IMPORTANCE OF FAMILY–PROFESSIONAL COLLABORATION

A child's family spends the most time with a child and is the real constant in a child's life. Involving parents and other family members in the intervention process is more powerful than focusing exclusively on the child. If Mason's team had determined services from the perspective of what *he alone* would receive during intervention visits, then prescribing multiple services might have made sense. Instead, they considered what supports his *family* would need to support Mason's development and together, with his parents, determined that fewer direct services were more appropriate. This is because team members would be consulting across their disciplines and providing integrated intervention alongside his family; consequently, Mason would ultimately receive more intervention during and between visits. When families are involved, trained, and supported, children are given the opportunity to receive interventions when professionals are not present because their parents or caregivers feel prepared to provide the intervention. Encouraging family members to choose their level of involvement in intervention, program planning, decision making, and service delivery benefits both the child and the family (Sandall, Hemmeter, Smith, & McLean, 2005), and it also permits service providers to be more effective.

Interventionists must prepare parents or caregivers to understand how and why interventions can be used in their daily lives because parents are the ones who will be interacting with the child long after professionals leave. Formal early intervention accounts for less than 20% of an infant's or toddler's awake time (Bruder, 2001). For this reason, service providers need to develop outstanding communication skills to interact successfully with the range of adult personalities and styles they will encounter in families in order to reach the child (Turnbull et al., 2007). Basic effective interpersonal skills, such as building trust by following through on plans, actively showing attention during conversations, and pausing (Cheatham & Ostrosky, 2009), are courtesies viewed as critical to successful collaboration from a parent's point of view. Because positive parent–professional collaboration is essential for meaningful services and outcomes, attempts are now being made to develop training and assessment instruments that evaluate the use of parent–professional collaboration in the field with families (Basu, Salisbury, & Thorkildsen, 2010).

The reality is that the field of early intervention is a relationship-based discipline. Without a sound relationship with the child, the child's family and extended family, and other important people in the family's life, it is impossible to make meaningful changes in a child's development. To achieve this, service providers must develop respectful, nonjudgmental reactions to families' values, beliefs, and lifestyles (Zhang & Bennett, 2001). This will lead to strong, lasting relationships with families that are undeniably strengthened by the amount of time that families and interventionists share. The parent–professional relationship should not be confused with a friendship. Although collaborations with families are cordial and supportive, there is a necessary professional boundary established, which is not present in friendships.

Time is a fundamental resource for any family (Brotherson & Goldstein, 1992). When time is not available, it can cause major stresses in a family's life. In the process of parent–professional collaboration, it is critical that service providers understand the importance of using their time with families efficiently and recognize time as a resource that is limited for many families. Time is always a key factor in the involvement level of a family with the early intervention team.

Parents and caregivers are viewed as fully participating team members on the early intervention team. They are given the opportunity to be the primary decision makers regarding planning services, identifying the locations for the delivery of services (e.g., the child care provider's home), identifying outcomes, and determining whether collaborative recommendations have benefited the child and family. Parents also provide necessary information for evaluations and assessments. Although all decisions are team decisions, the family members have the final word on the services the child receives, and their commitment to the process is critical to the success of their child's intervention. Since the family is the primary change agent in the child's life and directly influences the child's development, family members are invited to participate in all aspects of the child's intervention. In addition, families should be encouraged to do so in a way that best suits them. Some families, such as Mason's family, elect to be directly involved in every aspect of their child's services, while others may choose to participate in a less active way. Each choice is followed because it represents the preference of that family. When families are encouraged to be active members of the team, parents tend to participate more, their children tend to have positive long-term developmental outcomes, and parents report an increase in their sense of *empowerment*—the belief that they can make a difference in another person's life (Trivette & Dunst, 2004). Supportive parent–professional collaboration is one of the key principles of family-centered intervention (Wolery & Hemmeter, 2011).

## THE PROCESS OF THE FAMILY-CENTERED APPROACH

The family-centered approach to early intervention is a way of thinking that leads to a set of practices in which families or parents are considered as the most important decision makers in a child's life (Sandall et al., 2005). It involves a process that acknowledges that early intervention programs and professionals must respect the unique values and priorities of families, encourage families' strengths, and support parents' sense of competence in order to foster a child's progress (Dunst, 2001; Keilty, 2010). During every interaction, professionals should express their belief in the capability of parents to support their own children. Trivette and Dunst (2004) found that a staff's strong beliefs about parents' abilities to support their child's learning were linked to more positive parental judgments about their parenting competence. In other words, when professionals provide family-specific coaching and support, family members are better equipped to support their child's development.

The family-centered approach is based on the belief that most parents of children with special needs possess the emotional investment necessary to encourage and motivate their child's development, particularly when given appropriate and individualized supports from professionals (Trivette & Dunst, 2004). Families who are not able to focus on the child's needs may have issues that are more pressing, such as when a family is facing homelessness or when a parent has substance abuse or mental health challenges. Other families may not feel that intervention is necessary, so they may be reluctant to participate, such as when a family is mandated to receive early intervention by the court system or when the family does not recognize the child's special needs. In any of these cases, the family-centered approach is individualized to meet families where they are, meaning that time is taken to build rapport with family members and ensure that supports revolve around their priorities and strengths. This approach acknowledges that children and their families possess strengths that are just as important as their needs.

These beliefs lead to offering families *positive helpgiving,* which is a style of offering assistance to children or families with the intent that the help will have positive consequences for those receiving it (Sandall et al., 2005). One way of achieving this is using family priorities for establishing outcomes and using multiple techniques to engage family members in discussions about how to develop their child's needed skills during the process of daily living. This kind of capacity-building, positive helpgiving (Dunst, Trivette, & Hamby, 2007) builds on the strengths the child and family displayed during the initial assessment and uses new strengths as they emerge. This approach is exemplified by Mason's case. Because Mason's older sisters were clearly very attached to him, the strategies for implementing some of his outcomes on the IFSP involved his sisters interacting with Mason while their mother prepared dinner, which was a particularly busy time of day for the family. Research has shown that meeting family-selected outcomes during family routines can improve parents' reported perceptions of their family's quality of life (Epley, Summers, & Turnbull, 2011). Once again, professionals are reminded that they are not working with the child but rather with the entire family, which can lead to positive changes for both.

When implementing this approach, professionals should ask parents what amount and type of involvement and services are best suited for their child and family, then attempt to provide services that match these priorities. This information is generally gathered through the process of collaborative consultation. Service providers should also use *coaching*—a collection of strategies such as listening, prompting, joint problem-solving, and planning—to promote changes in a child's outcomes by strengthening parent–child interactions and expanding parents' abilities to foster their children's learning throughout the day (McCollum, Gooler, Appl, & Yates, 2001; Rush & Shelden, 2011). Coaching is described in detail in Chapter 4.

Two common strategies are used in a family-centered approach. First, supports are provided to families in their selected natural environments. Within these settings, service providers and caregivers brainstorm ways to embed goals for the child into natural learning opportunities within families' daily routines (Raver, 2005, 2009). When working with infants and toddlers, professionals do not remove a family from its regular environment; rather, they work in conjunction with a family to make established routines more responsive to the child's current needs. For example, when Mason was approximately 2 years old, a priority for his family was for him to sit in the shopping cart at the grocery store for the entire trip. This was a very functional priority that directly related to Mason's motor skills and his ability to participate and learn during a regular family routine. Rather than only provide his family with exercises they could use at home to strengthen Mason's muscles, the educator and the physical therapist accompanied Mason's family on a trip to the grocery store to problem-solve with his mother about strategies to help Mason sit with appropriate support in the cart. Taking intervention out into the specific natural setting where it is needed makes intervention more meaningful for the family and is aligned with family-centered practices.

A second common strategy is attempting to support parents in their efforts to manage their own and their family's stress. Families of children with disabilities appear to be susceptible to increased stress. They report feeling isolated and may have smaller support networks than families of children without disabilities (Raver, Michalek, & Gillespie, 2011). All parents have to cope with family stress. However, parents of children with special needs tend to have additional daily stressors that may impede their child's development or negatively affect how the family functions (Hooste & Maes, 2003). Again, consider Mason's family. During the first year of intervention visits, Mason's mother frequently talked about the strain of making the many doctors' appointments required for him, as well as the difficulty of finding a child care provider who was comfortable managing Mason's needs. Mason's mother stated later that just being able to discuss these concerns with the interventionist seemed to ease the stress of these realities.

Even the best-intentioned early intervention programs may inadvertently introduce stress into a family's life. Therefore, service providers must take special care in the way they manage services to ensure that unintended stress is not introduced. To monitor this with Mason's family, the service coordinator regularly checked in with family members about how they were feeling about their services and if changes were needed. Services were coordinated so that providers consulted one another and avoided conflicting recommendations, which could be frustrating for the family. When requested, providers also conducted co-treatments, visiting the home at the same time when the family's schedule was busy, to reduce the number of visits to the home. The service coordinator coached the family in requesting that doctors' appointments in the same hospital be scheduled either on the same day or across several weeks to reduce the amount of appointments in any one week. The service coordinator and Mason's mother also discussed child care options among family members and friends who might be able to assist with child care, ultimately identifying a friend at the family's church who was comfortable caring for Mason.

## FAMILY SYSTEMS THEORY

Family systems theory is the foundation for the most integral guiding philosophy of early intervention. A family is an interconnected system, with the activities of each member affecting all other members as well as the family unit as a whole (Turnbull, Turnbull, Erwin,

Soodak, & Shogren, 2010). In other words, what benefits or stresses the child is also likely to benefit or stress the family as a whole because of the connections among family members. For example, when Mason was having significant sleep disturbances, his parents were sleep deprived, which affected their interactions with one another and with Mason and his sisters. Once Mason's sleep was regulated, all members of the family eventually experienced relief; they were able to feel more like "themselves" and manage the needs of the family better.

Family systems theory describes three major characteristics that influence how a family manages family life: 1) family characteristics, 2) family interaction, and 3) family functioning. Family characteristics are attributes that a family shares as a unit, such as a family's size, cultural background, socioeconomic status, and the characteristics of individual members. Each of these may influence a family's adaptation to receiving early intervention services and the family's response to a child having special needs. This is illustrated by one of Mason's mother's comments during the first months of services: "With all of Mason's health problems and my own recovery from his birth, I have been thinking about leaving my job. It will be tight. I think we can make it but it won't be easy—and Mason isn't an easy baby, either." Obviously, the severity of a child's disability, temperament, and behavior can influence a family's adjustment and functioning.

Family interaction involves the relationships between individual members of a family (Turnbull et al., 2007). When there are changes within a family, as with the birth of a child with a disability or the identification of a developmental delay, dramatic changes may occur in the roles of individuals within a family. Mason's father's remarks show how relationships within families can change, resulting in either positive or negative consequences for individual members that also may have an influence on the family as a unit: "At first I was obsessed about Mason's future. Would he be able to support himself or ever live alone? But my mother loved him from the beginning. He was just her little grandson—her first grandson.... She didn't see any differences. Honestly, that has helped me."

Family functions involve the needs that families are responsible for, such as economic support, daily care, recreation, socialization, and affection (Turnbull et al., 2010). Mason's mother made this observation about the family's daily lives: "With three other kids, sometimes it is hard to find the time that Mason needs.... I worry that the other kids are getting the short end of the stick." It was suggested that the other children help with Mason's learning activities while the family members went through their usual routines; in this way, the older children, as well as Mason and his mother, could benefit. Every family is unique and manages challenges differently. Parents, siblings, and extended family members frequently respond to delays in a child's development or the identification of a disability in different ways as well.

## Parents' Reactions to Delayed Development or a Disability

Parents often do not perceive a disability in the same way as professionals. Mothers have described feelings of denial and wishful thinking, followed by searching for information, seeking social support, and *reframing* (i.e., restating a situation in a more hopeful way) to cope with their children's initial diagnoses (Bingham, Correa, & Huber, 2012). Within the same family, mothers and fathers usually experience different emotions. The sequence of reactions and the time needed for adjustment are different for each parent—and each family. Service providers must remind themselves of this fact often. However, the diagnosis of a disability or delayed development may not alter established routines of caregiving. For instance, research has found that there is no difference in the level of involvement between fathers of very young children with disabilities and fathers of children without disabilities

(Dyer, McBride, Santos, & Jeans, 2009). Although there was no evidence that fathers of children with developmental delays were less involved with their children, the results did not show that responding to a diagnosis of a disability resulted in fathers becoming more involved. Despite the fact that mothers of children with special needs are likely to have increased child care responsibilities, there is also no evidence that fathers tend to increase their engagement with their children to relieve maternal burdens (Dyer et al., 2009). This information should be useful to service providers who often find that mothers report feeling overwhelmed and lacking in daily family support. Developing a personalized approach to each child and each family is the best way to support families with varying resources and needs (Bailey et al., 2006).

## Siblings' Reactions to Delayed Development or a Disability

Parents' attitudes about a disability or developmental delay are critical in shaping siblings' adjustment. When parents take a positive view, siblings tend to follow their lead. However, in some families, siblings' needs may be neglected due to disproportionate parental time being devoted to the child with special needs, which may encourage siblings' negative feelings. For this reason, service providers must help support parents in creating a balanced family life. A balanced family is one in which the needs of all family members are appropriately and equally addressed across time. To support families in maintaining this balance, service providers should be flexible when scheduling visits to accommodate changing family needs, try to include siblings and other family members during visits, and help families develop strategies that encourage interaction between siblings and inclusion of the child with disabilities in activities that the whole family enjoys.

Encouraging open communication regarding both positive and negative feelings can also aide sibling adjustment. Siblings need accurate information about a disability to allay fears that may stem from misunderstandings. It is beneficial for professionals to promote strong sibling relationships in families. During the family's visits with the service provider, Mason's older siblings were invited to join intervention activities and ask questions. By participating during the visit, Mason's siblings learned simple activities that they could do with him, such as holding a rattle in his hand and helping him shake it. The oldest siblings enjoyed having special intervention "jobs," such as playing with Mason with his lighted toys each day or helping him learn what simple words meant, such as asking him, "Want to be picked up?" then touching his sides before getting him out of his crib after naptime. They enjoyed having important roles to play in Mason's intervention and felt proud when they "taught" him something. Activities such as these help siblings develop strong bonds. Children with disabilities or developmental delays tend to develop better social skills, and families seem to report less stress.

Most families eventually make successful adjustments to their situations and report positive effects, such as increased family cohesion and a renewed appreciation for life (Raver et al., 2011). Over time, most parents and extended family members rebuild their hopes and learn to adapt to the new circumstances of their lives (Gallagher, Fialka, Rhodes, & Arceneaux, 2003). The reactions and behaviors of caregivers, siblings, and extended family members are important to service providers because they work with the entire family, not merely the child.

Early intervention views child, parent, and family functioning as complex processes (Bruder, 2010). Early learning and development are influenced by interactions between environments experienced by a child, as well as the characteristics of the child and the adults around that child. Family systems theory is a way of conceptualizing how the characteristics of families, and those important to them, affect their response to critical events. Understanding this theory permits service providers on the early intervention team to more effectively support very young children and their families during a vulnerable time in families' lives (Davis & Gavidia-Payne, 2009).

## EARLY INTERVENTION TEAM

From its inception, early intervention has involved many disciplines and fields of study, such as psychology, health, early childhood education, special education, physical therapy, occupational therapy, and speech-language pathology—all working together to support a child and the child's family (Bruder, 2010). The actual combination of professionals who make up the early intervention team depends on the child's IFSP. Regardless of team composition, the primary task of this team is to support the family's competence and confidence with promoting a child's development toward the outcomes desired by the family in the child's everyday life.

By definition, a *team* is a small group of people with complementary skills, common purposes, goals, and approaches for which they hold themselves jointly accountable (Katzenbach & Smith, 1993). These characteristics of a team are key to successful early intervention and to ensuring collaborative and nonduplicative services and supports. Two main types of teams provide supports to families during the early intervention process: evaluation and assessment teams and IFSP teams.

### Evaluation and Assessment Team

The evaluation and assessment team is typically composed of a small group of two or three professionals and family members who meet to gather information about a child's development. This information is collected by formal developmental assessments, observation, parents' reports, and review of the child's medical and developmental history. The evaluation and assessment team uses this information to determine a child's eligibility for IDEA Part C services, identify the child's functional strengths and needs, collaboratively identify with the family ideas for interventions, and gather information needed to develop the IFSP for children found to be eligible for services. The evaluation and assessment team may or may not be the same group of professionals who will also help the family develop the IFSP. The composition of both teams is usually determined by a family's stated priorities, a child's strengths and needs, and state and local policies and procedures.

Parents are important members of the evaluation and assessment team because they are the only team members who can report on the child's behaviors and abilities in everyday activities. Professional team members can facilitate active parental involvement on the team by preparing families for what questions they will be asked and what activities the child will be expected to do, as well as helping families prepare information they would like to share. Parents or caregivers generally become more active contributors in the assessment and planning process when they feel comfortable and prepared (Byington & Whitby, 2011).

### Individualized Family Service Plan Team

The task of the IFSP team focuses on the development of the IFSP, which involves collaborating with parents to determine appropriate outcomes for the child's development based on assessment information and the family's stated priorities. The IFSP team determines which supports (e.g., assisting the parents in finding reliable child care) and services (e.g., vision services for a child with a visual impairment) are necessary to help the child and family achieve their goals. A team representative, known as the *primary service provider,* works directly with the child and family or caregivers during visits to develop individualized intervention strategies to address IFSP outcomes. Support is provided to help families understand their important role in enhancing the child's development and to feel confident implementing learning activities during their daily lives. The primary service provider also collaborates with all team members to provide individualized support to the family. IFSP team members conduct ongoing assessments and link the family to needed resources such as housing assistance, evaluation for equipment (e.g., gait trainer, wheelchair), or counseling, when appropriate. As the child approaches his or her third birthday, the IFSP team begins a formal transition process and develops a plan for easing the shift from early intervention to preschool special education, which is provided under Part B of IDEA (2004, § 619), or another community service option.

The roles of IFSP team members often change over the course of the child's participation in early intervention. Who participates on the IFSP team and what role each professional plays is individualized to the child and family outcomes, priorities, and resources and the team's decision-making process.

## Professional Team Members' Roles

The most important member of the early intervention team is the parent or caregiver. Another very important member is the professional who is identified as a family's primary service provider. Service providers from any discipline can be designated as the primary service provider, depending on who is most appropriate to help the family and child. This designation may change over the time that services are offered as a child's and family's needs change. The process for determining services and service providers is discussed further in Chapter 3.

Although the same team members worked with Mason and his family throughout their early intervention experience, the primary service provider changed when Mason was approaching his third birthday to meet his changing needs. It is the primary service provider's responsibility to support the child and family by integrating information from consulting team members and helping the family address the child's development in all areas of need. The roles of educators, therapists, service coordinators, medical personnel, and other specialists are described in the following sections.

***Educator***    The educator usually has training in early childhood education, early childhood special education, or child development. This provider helps the team gain a global, whole-child perspective of a child's development. The educator participates in screenings, evaluations, and assessments; assists in developing IFSPs; and provides special instruction if he or she is selected as the primary service provider. *Special instruction* is the phrase used in Part C of IDEA to describe educational services provided to infants and toddlers and their families. Educators may also facilitate playgroups or other group activities with children, siblings, and families. If group activities are arranged, they are often funded with money from outside of Part C funding. This service is discussed further in Chapters 3 and 4.

***Therapists***    Speech-language pathologists and physical or occupational therapists also serve on early intervention teams. The roles are discussed further in Chapter 10.

*Speech-Language Pathologist*    The speech-language pathologist has training in developing and improving communication and speech. Speech-language pathologists typically get little direct experience with infants and toddlers with special needs during their graduate training, although the field is embracing family-centered practices in natural environments (Woods, Wilcox, Friedman, & Murch, 2011). These specialists address communication development; participate in screenings, evaluations, and assessments; participate in IFSP development; and provide specific speech and/or language interventions in natural settings. Some speech-language pathologists also treat oral-motor and feeding issues.

*Physical Therapist*  Physical therapists have been trained to facilitate, improve, and maintain motor development and functioning. They are involved in screenings, evaluations, assessments, and IFSP development; they also provide motor interventions in natural settings. Because infants and toddlers with developmental disabilities and/or delays often have difficulty generalizing and maintaining new skills, these children learn motor skills best through high-frequency, naturally occurring activities in their natural environments (Shelden & Rush, 2001). Providing motor-related services in natural settings decreases the problems related to poor generalization because the child has an opportunity to use and practice skills in the very environments in which he or she needs to use those skills.

*Occupational Therapist*  Occupational therapists are trained to maximize fine motor development, play, feeding, and other adaptive skills. Like physical therapists and speech-language therapists, they may have minimal experience working with infants and toddlers in their training programs. Occupational therapists may also address sensory processing issues. They tend to participate in screenings, evaluations and assessments, and IFSP development and offer interventions in natural settings. As mentioned in Chapter 1, the emphasis in early intervention is to provide all supports to children with special needs and their families in their natural environments, rather than asking parents to take their children to clinics or an early intervention program office to receive therapy. Occupational therapists tend to use more family-centered approaches when they work in families' natural environments in early intervention than when they provide school-based services with older students, although strong differences occur among therapists and practice settings (Fingerhut et al., 2013).

When services are provided in natural settings, parents are immediately more involved in intervention visits; they learn by practicing intervention strategies with their child and by watching professionals use techniques that can later be used in the family's daily lives. Training parents to provide the intervention is a viable, time-saving, and evidence-based alternative to clinic-based services for all therapists (e.g., speech-language pathologists, physical therapists, occupational therapists). The time saved through the use of coaching the parent in skills and therapies the child needs makes it possible for more children to be served at a lower cost per child (Hanft & Pilkington, 2000). In addition, children seem to learn more because intervention or therapy is ongoing and not separate from life experiences. As Shelden and Rush (2001) stated, "Intervention is not tied to a specific person at a specific place at a specific time" (p. 4). The child actually receives more intervention when the parents and caregivers are able to use intervention strategies throughout the day—more than the child could receive if intervention focused on what could be accomplished by one person during one visit to the home each week.

**Service Coordinator**  The service coordinator usually has training in a variety of child- and/or family-related disciplines. This person acts as a case manager who oversees the implementation of the IFSP; collaborates with families' other team members and community partners; and links families to resources such as health, social services, or respite care services. In some programs, team members may have blended roles, serving as both a service coordinator and an educator or therapist, or they may have a "dedicated role" and only provide service coordination. The primary duties of a service coordinator are participation in screenings, evaluations, and assessments (but not necessarily conducting testing); facilitating IFSP development; ensuring that the IFSP is implemented as agreed; and serving as the primary point of contact for families.

**Medical Personnel**    Any medical professional who works with the child and family can participate on the early intervention team. This may be a pediatrician, primary care physician, or specialist, such as a geneticist, developmental pediatrician, neurologist, physiatrist, audiologist, or nutritionist. These professionals usually serve on the team in a consulting role to ensure that interventions support a child's development and learning without interfering with a child's health needs.

**Other Professional Members**    Depending on a child's delays or disabilities, other professionals may need to be included on the team. These team members commonly include a vision specialist, a hearing specialist, an infant mental health/behavioral specialist, or the family's child care providers.

## Other Family-Selected Members

In addition to these professionals, parents or caregivers can designate other individuals whom they consider important to their family to serve on the team, such as extended family members and family friends.

To some extent, the role that each team member plays on the early intervention team depends on the model of service delivery used in the specific program. The interactions among team members of different disciplines and between the family and professional team members contribute to the success of the team and are linked to the teaming model. Understanding how team members interact and which practices are recommended for early intervention teams is important as teams come together to support families.

## TEAM MODELS IN EARLY INTERVENTION

The needs of infants and their families often extend beyond the expertise of a single discipline. Teaming permits professionals from different disciplines to work collaboratively to implement services that will support a very young child in reaching his or her potential. To improve the efficiency of the different individuals who provide early intervention services, services should be delivered through an integrated team approach (Bruder, 2010). Most early intervention programs use some variation of three team models—multidisciplinary, interdisciplinary, and transdisciplinary—to deliver services.

*Multidisciplinary teams* include professionals from different disciplines who typically work with limited opportunities for collaboration across disciplines. Team members may obtain consultations from different disciplines, but assessments are conducted individually by each team member. For example, the speech-language pathologist and the physical therapist may independently conduct the communication and motor-related assessments. Parents may meet with individual team members alone. This professional is responsible for implementing his or her "portion" of the IFSP. For example, the speech-language pathologist only addresses IFSP outcomes related to communication. Discipline-specific members of these teams recognize the importance of the contributions of other disciplines but may have only informal, infrequent communication with other team members. This approach lacks the benefits of team synthesis and, in some cases, may result in duplicative services for families.

*Interdisciplinary teams* involve professionals from different disciplines conducting their assessments separately but sharing this information with one another. Members may be willing to share development of the IFSP, but they tend to provide services that relate directly to "their part" of the IFSP. Periodic case-specific team meetings usually occur in an effort to manage problems by participating in group decision making.

*Transdisciplinary teams* make every effort to work together as an integrated team rather than as isolated discipline-specific professionals. This approach not only involves sharing the assessment process, outcome selection (in collaboration with the family), intervention strategies, and implementing services, but it also requires members to function as a cohesive unit by sharing knowledge and skills among the members (Raver, 2009). There is a strong sense of shared responsibility for all team activities and functions. The regular and systematic sharing of knowledge and skills across disciplines among diverse members of a team is called *role sharing.*

Transdisciplinary teaming uses role sharing to provide a child and family with the benefits of the whole team's expertise through collaboration between the primary service provider and other team members, who provide indirect support to the family through the primary service provider. Team members actively support each other in developing a good "working knowledge" of the other members' disciplines. Therefore, if they are selected to be the primary service provider and offer direct services to a child and family, all team members feel comfortable representing their colleagues (King et al., 2009). For example, consider Mason's transdisciplinary team. When the physical therapist was the primary service provider, she addressed all IFSP outcomes—not just those related to motor development—with the support of the educator, who acted in a consultative role. Later, the speech-language pathologist joined the physical therapist once a month during visits with the family to help integrate learning and communication strategies into home routines. As the primary service provider, the physical therapist represented the educator and speech-language pathologist by coaching the family to continue to use selected strategies throughout the month. Under the transdisciplinary model, no part of the IFSP is recognized as "belonging" to a particular discipline or provider; rather, the IFSP and all outcomes "belong" to the family.

The transdisciplinary team approach provides several benefits to families (Raver, 2009):

1. The approach involves fewer people working directly with the child and family.
2. It improves continuity and integration of information to the family, which can enhance embedding interventions into the family's routines and activities.
3. It increases consistency in services and information offered in the family's selected natural environments, saving the family time and increasing the variety of natural learning opportunities available to the child.

With infants and toddlers, transdisciplinary team members tend to conduct assessments together, often in the form of arena assessments (discussed in Chapter 3), share assessment results, and write integrated outcomes. The goal of transdisciplinary teaming is to provide services to children and families that might not be possible if strict discipline divisions were employed (Sandall et al., 2005). For example, a speech-language pathologist could teach all members of the team to use general techniques that foster early language development during an office team meeting before the designated primary care provider visits the family. One strategy commonly taught is the use of *parallel talk,* in which the objects and actions in a child's play environment are narrated (e.g.,

"You are looking at a book," "That is a ball"; Raver et al., 2012). This parent-implemented intervention is the same strategy that the speech-language pathologist would have demonstrated and trained the parent to use if he or she had been the primary service provider (Kaiser & Roberts, 2011). This kind of knowledge and skill sharing does not mean that professionals give up their specific discipline-based skills, but that they use their discipline-specific training in a way that ultimately saves the family time and helps the family understand the interrelated nature of development. Regular contact and communication are important for any of the team models, but transdisciplinary teams cannot perform effectively without both.

Information and skill sharing is a characteristic commonly associated with transdisciplinary teaming, but it can also occur in interdisciplinary and multidisciplinary teams, although it rarely occurs as systematically. Often, a program will change the team model it uses to suit a particular program's purpose. Some programs use interdisciplinary teaming for evaluations and assessments, whereas they use transdisciplinary teaming for implementing services.

Frequent team meetings and consultations must be scheduled for team members to discuss assessments, outcome development, planning and strategy selection, evaluation of the IFSP, and family-specific issues, irrespective of the team model followed. The location, frequency, and method of team meetings and consultations depend on a variety of factors, such as program policies, team members' preferences (including the family), and the purpose of the activity. Team meetings might be scheduled to occur in the office, with or without the family present, or in the family's home or other natural environment. Consultations can occur by phone or e-mail, during shared visits, or in office meetings. When team members cannot be in a family's home, teaming strategies (e.g., videotaping a problematic or targeted routine) can help team members understand the context of a situation so that their feedback is more useful during team meetings. Even though teaming can be conducted in several ways, effective teams tend to be described as possessing a clear, common purpose and displaying sound communication.

## DEVELOPING EFFECTIVE TEAMS

Effective teaming requires a good deal of communication, collaboration, and planning. To function successfully, teams also need leadership and direction. The early intervention team is led by the service coordinator, who keeps the team's activities focused on supporting the family and addressing the outcomes written in the child's IFSP. All team members, including the family, must be able to engage in open and honest communication about what supports are needed and how they should be provided, as well as challenges as they arise. Professional team members need to understand their roles, respect the opinions and roles of others, and collaborate across disciplines by sharing information and ideas and engaging in thoughtful discussions about how to best support the child's development within the context of the family. Frequent communication and regular meetings to share ideas and review the IFSP are important to keep the team cohesive and focused.

It is the job of service providers to ensure that families are supported, not overburdened. Therefore, effective teams offer supports in a competency-enhancing manner, which features these characteristics (Bricker, Pretti-Frontczak, Johnson, & Straka, 2002):

1. Mobilizing resources in ways that do not disrupt family life
2. Using supportive communication styles
3. Not overwhelming a family with information or services

When team members fail to integrate these competency-enhancing characteristics into their interactions with families, problems can occur, which must be addressed in a timely and responsive manner. It is not uncommon for families to express concerns related to services being disruptive, providers not communicating enough with them, or feelings of being overburdened. When these problems occur, it is time for the IFSP team to pull together to identify a solution that results in services that better meet the needs of that child and family.

Problems with teaming have been reported in all disciplines, not just in education. Developing an effective team takes time; it is unrealistic to expect a team to work well together immediately or to expect a team to operate smoothly indefinitely. Being aware of other common team problems and how to manage them will help team members overcome challenges and collaborate effectively to resolve them.

## Common Team Problems

The following are some common problems teams experience.

***Differing Expectations About the Purpose of the Team and Team Members' Roles***    Understanding the purpose of the early intervention team is vital to the success of teaming. Problems will arise when staff and administrators do not share the same expectations about the team's purpose, duties, roles, and goals. Teams must come to a consensus on the team's family-centered mission if they are to operate effectively for the benefit of the child and family.

An effective team does not result from simply placing professionals from different disciplines in the same room. Team members with different discipline backgrounds have likely been trained in different missions, which may result in differing goals and solutions to problems. One common cause of conflicts in teams is having team members who have different expectations for the team or for the roles of team members. Team members may have been trained to focus on the child as the client rather than the family; thus, they may intend to provide child-centered rather than family-centered services. Some members may not have been trained in role sharing, which can make them uncomfortable or unfamiliar with addressing outcomes that they do not recognize as within their area of expertise. For example, a physical therapist might express discomfort with addressing outcomes that are not directly related to motor development. However, with the support of other team members, the physical therapist can come to understand how to support other areas of development, such as by talking or playing with a child while helping the child learn to plan motor movements that prepare for walking. Shared communication and support are essential to any team in which role sharing is an expectation.

***Team Communication and Disagreements***    Poor communication is another common cause of problems in teams. Good communication is essential for every aspect of early intervention, including working in teams. The best teams are described as being relaxed with open, direct communication (Beninghof & Singer, 1992). Using conduct guidelines may improve communication during early intervention team meetings and may prevent a meeting from becoming contentious. Byington and Whitby (2011) suggested the following basic guidelines for communicating during team meetings:

- Allow one person to speak at a time.
- Focus all comments on the needs of the child and family.
- Listen and respect the opinions of others.

- Encourage everyone to participate equally.
- Find solutions to issues.
- Be willing to respectfully compromise for the good of the child, family, and program.

Helping all team members honor these basic guidelines is typically one of the duties of the service coordinator. In the role of team leader, the service coordinator monitors team communication and collaboration for both successes and challenges related to the implementation of the IFSP.

All IFSP decisions include all team members, with the family members having the final say because they are in the best position to gauge their own needs. Teaming can be challenging when team members disagree on IFSP decisions, such as the type or frequency of services. Disagreements like these tend to be based on differing philosophies of intervention service delivery or different expectations for team member roles, particularly when role sharing is not a comfortable interaction style for all team members. A common understanding of the purpose and goal of early intervention, as covered in the key principles outlined in Chapter 1, and direct facilitation by the service coordinator can help early intervention teams navigate disagreements and come to a consensus.

Role sharing demands that team members have consistent and positive communication with one another. Maintaining a communication log, record, or notebook to track communications between team members can also be a useful tool (Byington & Whitby, 2011). Regular communication by phone, e-mail, online communication, or video conferencing is also necessary to ensure that strategies learned through role sharing continue to be used as intended.

**Confidentiality**    Confidentiality must be strictly followed when communicating about families. Personal information about a child and his or her family must not be shared with anyone unless the family has given written consent for the release or exchange of that information. It is never permissible for a service provider to discuss information about one family with another family or a service provider who is not part of the team. The Health Insurance Portability and Accountability Act (HIPAA) of 1996 (PL 104-191) and the Family Educational Rights and Privacy Act (FERPA) of 1974 (PL 93-380) are laws that provide guidance related to confidentiality and must be followed in early intervention. Table 2.1 summarizes the nature of these legal requirements (U.S. Department of Health and Human Services & U.S. Department of Education, 2008).

**Table 2.1.**    Privacy laws that affect early intervention

| | |
|---|---|
| Health Insurance Portability and Accountability Act (HIPAA) of 1996 (PL 104-191) | Protects the privacy of personally identifiable information in health records |
| | May apply to early intervention programs that operate under health care providers and agencies, such as hospitals and other applicable community health agencies |
| Family Educational Rights and Privacy Act (FERPA) of 1974 (PL 93-380) | Protects the privacy of personally identifiable information in educational records |
| | May apply to early intervention programs that operate under agencies that receive funding under the U.S. Department of Education, such as public schools, school districts, and universities |

*Source:* U.S. Department of Health and Human Services and U.S. Department of Education (2008).

Challenges can arise among team members when there are limitations to what information can be shared. For example, a family may choose not to permit the sharing of information to certain team members, such as a child care provider or case manager from another community program involved with the family. When issues related to confidentiality affect team collaborations, the service coordinator can help the family understand why consent to share information is being requested and how sharing information can benefit the family or help the team operate within the limitations of communication.

## Managing Team Conflicts

When conflicts are experienced, team members need to address the dispute directly and with professional courtesy. Team members must state a conflict as explicitly as possible, generate several ways for resolving it, and be open to the service coordinator's suggested solutions (Ostrosky & Cheatham, 2005). When disagreements occur, professionals need to remain calm, soften their voice, and permit the colleague with the concern to express his or her point of view. The key ingredient to resolving conflict with colleagues—and with parents or caregivers—is listening empathetically and making sincere efforts to come to a mutually acceptable resolution.

All team members want the same thing: what is best for the child and family. Listening empathetically involves trying to emotionally place one's self in the situation of another person and actively taking that person's viewpoint. When service providers acknowledge the legitimacy of someone else's point of view, negotiation will generally follow. Involving families as team members may lessen professional conflicts and discipline loyalties because the team is unified by families' priorities.

The objective of teaming is to access multiple perspectives to develop the best intervention plans for children. This involves input from a wide variety of professionals who are learning from one another (LaRocco & Bruns, 2013; Murray & Mandell, 2006).

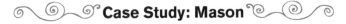 **Case Study: Mason**

Mason's team was able to collaborate to solve a persistent problem his family had in the car. When the family rode in the van, Mason always cried, making the trip difficult for everyone. Had this problem been viewed from an isolated, discipline-specific perspective, the family might have been given conflicting suggestions. For instance, the special educator might have suggested they play music to calm Mason during the ride, and the physical therapist might have recommended that they keep the ride quiet with less stimulation. Instead, team members, including Mason's family, discussed the problem together and decided that the physical therapist would join the family for a car ride. During the ride, the therapist determined that Mason was becoming distressed by the light flashing in his eyes from the window. Mason was also having difficulty managing his head control in his car seat. Joining the ride revealed that the noise level in the car was not the issue at all. Based on these observations, the therapist and educator worked together with Mason's mother to develop solutions. They decided that covering the window with a shade and adding two small towel rolls on either side of Mason's shoulders would make the rides easier for him. These strategies reduced the light in his eyes and helped him support his head in a more comfortable position. These simple yet effective solutions were facilitated because Mason's team was able to share ideas across disciplines and engage in problem solving to meet Mason's family's specific needs.

Innovative approaches and solutions often result from a team composed of diverse professionals discussing and working toward solutions based on the expertise of each team member. Effective early intervention teams learn to reach consensus by respecting diverse perspectives, assuming shared responsibilities related to a child and family's successes and challenges, and respecting the interaction between the family system and early intervention supports and services.

## STRATEGIES FOR SUPPORTING TEAM COLLABORATION AND COMMUNICATION

Overcoming problems associated with team collaboration is the responsibility of all team members, especially those in a professional role. There are two mechanisms built into the early intervention team process that support team collaboration: the activities of the service coordinator and the IFSP meeting.

The role of the service coordinator has been viewed as "a linchpin to quality service delivery" (Harbin et al., 2004, p. 95). By actively monitoring service delivery and team collaboration, the service coordinator keeps abreast of family satisfaction, child progress, team cohesion, and successes or challenges with the implementation of the IFSP. The service coordinator maintains regular communication with and among all team members and documents these interactions in the child's intervention record. By communicating regularly with all team members, the service coordinator can link needs and resources in the most efficient manner. The activities of the service coordinator are critical for helping the family to navigate a positive intervention experience; without an actively involved service coordinator, services for families can seem disjointed or redundant or fail to follow the service plan as intended.

When the early intervention team faces a challenge or needs to communicate as a group, the service coordinator (or any other team member) can arrange an IFSP meeting. The IFSP team meets, in a face-to-face meeting or by other electronic means, to respond to changes in the child's development or family situation or to process any challenges or problems. The regularity of these team meetings depends on the needs of the team. The minimum standards for certain types of IFSP meetings are established in Part C of IDEA and are discussed in Chapter 3. IFSP meetings can occur at any time and for any reason, and they can be requested by any team member. They are a useful means of communication and collaboration for teams.

Between IFSP meetings, team members are encouraged to communicate regularly by sharing notes, discussing strategies, and collaborating to solve difficulties that arise based on the child's development, disability, or family situation. Regular communication among professional team members can be challenging with busy schedules and the isolation that comes with providing services outside of a single office location. Service providers are often out in the field, traveling from intervention visit to visit, and can go an entire workday or more without seeing another colleague. Staying in touch about a child's progress across services takes effort and can be managed by reading contact notes in the child's record and/or communicating by phone or e-mail with other team members between visits. Service providers who build in scheduled regular communication with team members find that it is often easier to do their job.

Early intervention team activities revolve around regular communication with families, as well as professional colleagues. Communicating well with families is critical to their role as active participants in the early intervention process and to their feelings of satisfaction. Good communication and collaboration among professional team members strengthens a team and builds positive relationships. Table 2.2 lists 14 strategies that service providers can use when communicating and collaborating effectively as part of an early intervention team. These strategies may be used with both colleagues and families.

**Table 2.2.**  Communication strategies for effective collaboration

| Strategy | Description |
| --- | --- |
| Explain collaboration and communication expectations to new team members. | Assist new team members with understanding what is expected of them as part of their participation on the early intervention team. When each person understands what is expected, the team is more likely to function well. |
| Ask team members about their preferred mode of communication. | Find out if families and colleagues prefer to be contacted by phone, e-mail, or text (if allowed by the early intervention programs) and honor that preference. |
| Check-in regularly with team members, especially the family. | Ask how they feel about intervention, whether or not they are having success with intervention strategies, and about any new needs. Families have reported that regular communication with service providers is key for collaboration. |
| Maintain a nonjudgmental, supportive attitude and manner. | Focus on child and family strengths and have a positive attitude about the family and other team members both in and outside of the family's presence. |
| Be honest and open. | Address needs or concerns expressed by the family or other team members in an unbiased manner. When needed, help families consider their options so that they can make informed decisions that are best for them. Avoid imposing professionals' viewpoints on the family. |
| Show that you are interested. | Use good eye contact and positive body language that shows that you are attending and interested, such as facing the speaker, leaning in toward him or her, and verbally acknowledging what is being said. Let the speaker know that his or her input is valued. |
| Schedule team meetings at places and times that are convenient for team members. | Schedule meetings when most, if not all, team members can participate. If a team member is absent, include information from that member to ensure that he or she has a voice. |
| Use language that all team members can understand. | Use language with families and other team members that is free of technical jargon. Define new terms when used in speech or in the body of the individualized family service plan or other reports. |
| Invite the family and other team members to share. | Invite families to share their priorities, concerns, and knowledge of their child during all team meetings. Help families feel that they have an active role and their opinion is respected. Ask for input from all members and be sure to consider all points of view when there is a decision to be made. |
| Use open-ended questions to gather information. | Use open-ended questions to gather information regarding a parent's or colleague's perspective on an issue or concern. |
| Follow through. | When a professional follows through, team members see that he or she is reliable. It is easier to collaborate with a trusted colleague. |

| Strategy | Description |
| --- | --- |
| Communicate with team members with and without other team members present. | Join visits with other team members for collaboration. Find time to speak with team members in private. This is especially important when communicating with families to find out their satisfaction with intervention service providers, intervention strategies, and child progress. |
| Use interpreters when language barriers exist. | Ensure that families of differing cultural and linguistic backgrounds can understand and participate in team collaborations by providing information in the family's preferred language or mode of communication. |
| Use the child's record as a central repository of information. | Document all communication and activities with or on behalf of the child and family. Team members can then review the record to maintain supports and services. |

One important communication strategy used with families and other professionals is the use of open-ended questions. *Open-ended questions* ask for information that cannot be answered in a few words or with a yes-or-no response. Because open-ended questions elicit complete responses, they are useful when more information is desired. Questions such as, "Tell me about why you feel that way," or "What makes Mason smile?" prompt a caregiver or colleague to give more elaborate and detailed responses. By gaining someone's impression first, open-ended questions allow service providers to be reflective and avoid jumping in and offering "solutions" before sufficient information is known. These kinds of questions also promote collaboration (shared problem solving) because they facilitate brainstorming, which is more likely to result in collaboratively designed interventions. How these effective communication strategies are implemented depends on who is on the team, individual preferences, state and local policies and requirements, and the leadership and teaming skills of professional team members.

## BEST PRACTICE HIGHLIGHTS

The following best practices should guide service providers as they participate on early intervention teams:

- Using a family-centered approach to early intervention recognizes that each family is a unique, interconnected system, with the activities of each member affecting all others as well as the family unit as a whole.

- When early interventionists use family-centered practices, they understand that the child's parents and caregivers are the most important decision makers in the child's life and are the most important members on the early intervention team.

- Because early intervention is a relationship-based discipline, actively developing strong family–professional and professional-to-professional relationships and collaborations increases the chances of families participating in experiences that lead to positive outcomes for themselves and their child.

- Family members experience different reactions and ways of coping with a child's developmental delay or disability. While they are participating in early intervention, families are also negotiating a vulnerable time in their lives, so early interventionists must display empathy and patience.

- Early intervention teams with a clearly delineated purpose—supporting each family's competence in promoting their child's development within everyday routines—tend to be more collaborative and, consequently, more successful teams.

- Innovative approaches and solutions often result from an early intervention team comprised of diverse professionals working collaboratively toward solutions based on the expertise of each team member.

- Effective teams use good communication with professional team members and families as they hold the team jointly accountable for helping families reach their identified outcomes for early intervention.

- The transdisciplinary team model, when used to conduct assessments and deliver competency-enhancing early intervention services, mobilizes resources in ways that do not disrupt family life, uses supportive and effective communication styles, and avoids overwhelming families with information or services.

- Successful early intervention teams communicate regularly with the service coordinator and other team members to ensure regular collaboration, have established ways for handling disagreements, and have a sense of shared responsibility for team success.

- The IFSP is used as the primary guide for all team decisions.

## CONCLUSION

Mason's case study shows that early intervention can offer families a source of information, guidance, and emotional support during a time in which many families express that they feel overwhelmed, powerless, and unsure how to best support their child with special needs. The team members that worked with Mason worked collaboratively among themselves and with his family to develop a system of intervention supports that would immediately help the family members as they negotiated a very challenging time in their family's life. After much respectful dialogue, the team found a level of services that suited the family's lifestyle without overburdening them. After services began, Mason's primary service provider maintained regular interaction with the family and worked directly with the child care provider, Mason's three sisters, and occasionally, Mason's grandparents. The primary service provider also consulted regularly with the educator, and later with the speech-language pathologist, to ensure that he was well prepared to address all areas of Mason's development and Mason's IFSP outcomes.

Maintaining this collaborative communication made it easier for services to be adjusted when important events occurred in the family's life, including when Mason's mother eventually left her job and when a health crisis occurred with Mason that changed the family's most pressing needs for approximately 6 months. Because this transdisciplinary team had been systematic about how to work together, during the transition process near Mason's third birthday, his father described the family's experiences with early intervention in this way: "[Early intervention services] were a lifesaver for Mason and all of us. The encouragement and support were what I needed."

Early intervention provides a process that demands highly committed, professional, collaborative service providers who come together as a team to help families develop their own abilities in parenting their child. The quality of any early intervention program is determined by the quality of the disciplinary expertise, mutual respect, and communication skills of the team members. Effective teamwork permits interventionists to expand their individual knowledge as they offer support to parents who are learning ways to improve their child's development and learning.

## DISCUSSION QUESTIONS AND APPLIED ACTIVITIES

1.  Identify five characteristics of family-centered practices and discuss in detail how they would be implemented during a 45-minute home intervention visit with a teenage single mother whose 6-month-old child, Toby, has global developmental delays. This mother lives with her parents in her family home. Both Toby's mother and grandmother are usually present for visits.

2.  Name and discuss the 14 effective communication strategies that service providers use when collaborating with families and professional team members.

3.  Role play a team meeting in which team members decide how they will conduct their IFSP meetings, which later will include a parent or caregiver. As a team, identify at least four guidelines for the team's meetings so they are positive, cordial, collaborative environments for team members as well as families. Come to a resolution that has consensus.

## REFERENCES

Bailey, D., Bruder, M.B., Hebbeler, K., Carta, J., Defosset, M., Greenwood, C., …Barton, L. (2006). Recommended outcomes for families of young children with disabilities. *Journal of Early Intervention, 28*(4), 227–251. doi:10.1177/105381510602800401

Basu, S., Salisbury, C., & Thorkildsen, T. (2010). Measuring collaborative consultation practices in natural environments. *Journal of Early Intervention, 32*(2), 127–150. doi:10.1177/1053815110362991

Beninghof, A., & Singer, A. (1992). Transdisciplinary teaming: An inservice training activity. *Teaching Exceptional Children, 58*(3), 58–60.

Bingham, A.J., Correa, V.I., & Huber, J.J. (2012). Mothers' voices: Coping with their children's initial disability diagnosis. *Infant Mental Health Journal, 33*(4), 372–385. doi:10.1002/imhj.21341

Bricker, D., Pretti-Frontczak, K., Johnson, J., & Straka, E. (2002). *Assessment, Evaluation, and Programming System for infants and children (AEPS®): Administration guide* (2nd ed.). Baltimore, MD: Paul H. Brookes Publishing Co.

Brotherson, M., & Goldstein, B. (1992). Time as a resource and constraint for parents of young children with disabilities: Implications for early intervention services. *Topics in Early Childhood Special Education, 12,* 508–527. doi:10.1177/027112149201200408

Bruder, M.B. (2001). Infants and toddlers: Outcomes and ecology. In M.J. Guralnick (Ed.), *Early childhood inclusion: Focus on change* (pp. 203–228). Baltimore, MD: Paul H. Brookes Publishing Co.

Bruder, M.B. (2010). Early childhood intervention: A promise to children and families for their future. *Exceptional Children, 76*(3), 339–355.

Byington, T., & Whitby, P. (2011). Empowering families during the early intervention planning process. *Young Exceptional Children, 14*(4), 44–56. doi:10.1177/1096250611428878

Cheatham, G.A. & Ostrosky, M. (2009). Listening for details of talk: Early childhood parent-teacher conference communication facilitators. *Young Exceptional Children, 13*(1), 36–49. doi:10.1177/1096250609357282

Davis, K., & Gavidia-Payne, S. (2009). The impact of child, family and professional support characteristics on the quality of life in families of young children with disabilities. *Journal of Intellectual & Developmental Disability, 34*(2), 153–162. doi:10.1080/13668250902874608

Dunst, C.J. (2001). Participation of young children with disabilities in community learning activities. In M. Guralnick (Ed.), *Early childhood inclusion: Focus on change* (pp. 307–333). Baltimore, MD: Paul H. Brookes Publishing Co.

Dunst, C., Trivette, C., & Hamby, D. (2007). *Research synthesis and meta-analysis of studies of family-centered practices.* Asheville, NC: Winterberry Press.

Dyer, W.J., McBride, B., Santos, R., & Jeans, L. (2009). A longitudinal examination of father involvement with children with developmental delays: Does timing of diagnosis matter? *Journal of Early Intervention, 31*(3), 265–281. doi:10.1077/0192513X09340386

Epley, P.H., Summers, J.A., & Turnbull, A. (2011). Family outcomes of early intervention: Families' perceptions of need, services, and outcomes. *Journal of Early Intervention, 33*(3), 201–219. doi:10.1177/1053815111425929

Family Educational Rights and Privacy Act (FERPA) of 1974, PL 93-380, 20 U.S.C. §§ 1232g *et seq.*

Fingerhut, P.E., Piro, J., Sutton, A., Campbell, R., Lewis, C., Lawji, D., & Martinez, N. (2013). Family-centered principles implemented in home-based, clinic-based, and school-based pediatric settings. *American Journal of Occupational Therapy, 67*(2), 228–235. doi:10.5014/ajot.2013.006957

Gallagher, P., Fialka, J., Rhodes, C., & Arceneaux, C. (2003). Working with families: Rethinking denial. *Young Exceptional Children, 5*(2), 11–17. doi:10.1177/109625060200500202

Hanft, B., & Pilkington, K. (2000). Therapy in natural environments: The means or end goal of early intervention? *Infants & Young Children, 12,* 1–13.

Harbin, G.L., Bruder, M.B., Adams, C., Mazzarella, C., Whitbread, K., Gabbard, G., & Staff, I. (2004). Early intervention service coordination policies: National policy infrastructure. *Topics in Early Childhood Special Education, 24*(2), 89–97. doi:10.1177/02711214040240020401

Health Insurance Portability and Accountability Act (HIPAA) of 1996, PL 104-191, 42 U.S.C. §§ 201 *et seq.*

Hooste, A., & Maes, B. (2003). Family factors in the early development of children with Down syndrome. *Journal of Early Intervention, 25*(4), 296–309. doi:10.1177/105381510302500405

Individuals with Disabilities Education Improvement Act (IDEA) of 2004, PL 108-446, 20 U.S.C. §§ 1400 *et seq.*

Kaiser, A., & Roberts, M. (2011). Advances in early communication and language intervention. *Journal of Early Intervention, 33*(4), 298–309. doi:1177/1053815111429968

Katzenbach, J., & Smith, D. (1993). *Wisdom of teams*. New York, NY: Harper Business.

Keilty, B. (2010). *The early intervention guidebook for families and professionals: Partnering for success*. New York, NY: Teachers College Press.

King, G., Strachan, D., Tucker, M., Duwyn, B., Desserud, S., & Shillington, M. (2009). The application of a transdisciplinary model for early intervention services. *Infants & Young Children, 22*(3), 211–223. doi:10.1097/IYC.0b013e3181abe1c3

LaRocco, D.J., & Bruns, D.A. (2013). It's not the "what," it's the "how": Four key behaviors for authentic leadership in early intervention. *Young Exceptional Children, 16*(2), 33–44. doi:10.1177/1096250612473120

McCollum, J., Gooler, F., Appl, D., & Yates, T. (2001). PIWI: Enhancing parent–child interactions as a foundation for early intervention. *Infants & Young Children, 14*, 34–45.

Murray, M., & Mandell, C. (2006). On-the-job practices of early childhood special education providers trained in family-centered practices. *Journal of Early Intervention, 28*(2), 125–138. doi:10.1177/105381510602800204

Ostrosky, M., & Cheatham, G. (2005). Teaching the use of a problem-solving process to early childhood educators. *Young Exceptional Children, 9*(1), 12–19. doi:10.1177/109625060500900102

Raver, S.A. (2005). Using family-based practices for young children with special needs in preschool programs. *Childhood Education, 82*(1), 9–13. doi:10.1080/00094056.2005.10521333

Raver. S.A. (2009). *Early childhood special education—0 to 8 years: Strategies for positive outcomes*. Upper Saddle River, NJ: Pearson.

Raver, S., Bobzien, J., Richels, C., Hester, P., Michalek, A., & Anthony, N. (2012). Effect of parallel talk on the language and interactional skills of preschoolers with cochlear implants and hearing aids. *Literacy Information and Computer Education Journal, 3*(1), 530–538.

Raver, S.A., Michalek, A., & Gillespie, A. (2011). Major stressors and life goals of caregivers of individuals with disabilities. *Journal of Social Work in Disability & Rehabilitation, 10*(2), 115–128. doi:0.1080/1536710X.2011.571536

Rush, D.D., & Shelden, M.L. (2011). *The early childhood coaching handbook*. Baltimore, MD: Paul H. Brookes Publishing Co.

Sandall, S., Hemmeter, M., Smith, B., & McLean, M. (2005). *DEC recommended practices: A comprehensive guide to practical application in early intervention/early childhood special education*. Longmont, CO: Sopris West.

Shelden, M., & Rush, D.D. (2001). The ten myths about providing early intervention services in natural environments. *Infants & Young Children, 14*(10), 1–13.

Trivette, C., & Dunst, C. (2004). Evaluating family-focused practices: Parenting Experiences Scale. *Young Exceptional Children, 7*(3), 12–19. doi:10.1177/109625060400700302

Turnbull, A., Summers, J., Turnbull, R., Brotherson, M., Winton, P., Roberts, R.,…Stroup-Rentier, V. (2007). Family supports and services in early intervention: A bold vision. *Journal of Early Intervention, 29*, 187–206. doi:10.1177/105381510702900301

Turnbull, A., Turnbull, H.R., Erwin, E.J., Soodak, L.C., & Shogren, K.A. (2010). *Families, professionals, and exceptionality: Positive outcomes through partnership and trust* (6th ed.). Upper Saddle River, NJ: Pearson.

U.S. Department of Health and Human Services & U.S. Department of Education. (2008, November). *Joint guidance on the application of the Family Educational Rights and Privacy Act (FERPA) and the Health Insurance Portability and Accountability Act of 1996 (HIPAA) to student health records*. Retrieved from http://www.hhs.gov/ocr/privacy/hipaa/understanding/coveredentities/hipaaferpajointguide.pdf

Wolery, M., & Hemmeter, M.L. (2011). Classroom instruction: Background, assumptions, and challenges. *Journal of Early Intervention, 33*(4), 371–380. doi:v1177/1053815111429119

Woods, J.J., Wilcox, M., Friedman, M., & Murch, T. (2011). Collaborative consultation in natural environments: Strategies to enhance family-centered supports and services. *Language, Speech & Hearing Services In Schools, 42*(3), 379–392. doi:10.1044/0161-1461(2011/10-0016)

Zhang, C., & Bennett, T. (2001). Multicultural views of disability: Implications for early intervention professionals. *Infant-Toddler Intervention, 11*(2), 143–154.

# II

# Supporting Families
# in Natural Environments

# 3 | The Individualized Family Service Plan Process

Corinne Foley Hill and Dana C. Childress

This chapter discusses the development of the individualized family service plan (IFSP), including the following:

- Referral, intake, evaluation, and assessment
- Federal requirements
- Development of the IFSP, including the roles of team members
- IFSP outcome development
- Determination of supports and services
- Inclusive practices
- Best practice highlights

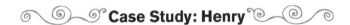

## Case Study: Henry

The Garrisons, a military family, currently live with Mrs. Garrison's parents while her husband, Derek, is stationed overseas. The family recently learned that Sgt. Garrison's tour had been extended by 9 months. The family stays in contact through videoconferences, periodic telephone calls, e-mail, and social media.

Julie Garrison is a kindergarten teacher whose father was also a career Army officer, so the military lifestyle is familiar to her. She reports that she feels lucky that her parents are so involved in helping raise her two children, 4-year-old Lucy and 26-month-old Henry, while her husband is out of the country. Julie and her mother, Jean, were both worried about Henry, who does not use many words but often makes a high-pitch squealing sound. He is a picky eater who likes chicken nuggets and macaroni and cheese, but he gags if other foods are offered. Henry prefers to play by himself and likes to watch television while lying on the sofa with his head hanging upside down.

At Henry's 24-month checkup, his pediatrician suggested that Henry receive an evaluation at the developmental clinic of a nearby children's hospital. Henry was evaluated by a developmental pediatrician, a speech-language pathologist, and an occupational therapist from the clinic. Following this multidisciplinary evaluation, Henry received a diagnosis of autism spectrum disorder. Although this diagnosis was hard to hear, Julie had suspected it and was eager to get started in early intervention, so Henry was referred to the local program.

The early intervention service coordinator, Talisha, met with Julie for an intake visit, during which Julie learned more details about the program. Talisha explained that she would obtain copies of Henry's medical records from his pediatrician and copies of the reports from all of the evaluators from the developmental clinic. They also agreed that it would be helpful to have Brad, the early intervention occupational therapist, become a part of their team. Henry's autism diagnosis made him eligible for early intervention, so Talisha and Brad scheduled a time to visit Henry and Julie at home when Lucy and his grandparents would be available.

During this assessment visit, Talisha and Brad talked with Julie and her parents. They also had the opportunity to watch Henry play with the dinosaurs that he carried everywhere, even when watching his favorite television shows. Talisha and Brad also observed snack time, and Julie talked about how hard it was at lunch and dinner because Henry refused to try new foods and often cried. Jean reported that Henry really does not pay any attention to Lucy and will not play with her. Jean and Tom, Henry's grandfather, have tried taking both of the children to the local children's museum, but Henry seems to get overwhelmed easily.

The early intervention team discussed the next step in the early intervention process, which was to schedule the initial IFSP meeting. Working together, the early intervention team—including Julie, Jean, and Tom as important team members—found a date and time when they could videoconference Derek so that he could join the meeting. Everyone agreed that they were most concerned about Henry's limited language and the difficulties with eating. They also hoped he would learn to play better with other children.

## WHAT IS THE INDIVIDUALIZED FAMILY SERVICE PLAN DEVELOPMENT PROCESS?

The development of the IFSP can be thought of as a collaborative process involving all members of the child's early intervention team. The process of developing and monitoring the IFSP involves a great deal of information gathering and synthesis related to the child's development, with an ongoing focus on how a child's abilities and needs affect his or her participation in natural daily routines and activities. This information gathering begins immediately when a child is referred for possible early intervention services and continues during the intake, evaluation, and assessment—all of which occur before the actual IFSP is written. The IFSP process is family centered and individualized, reflecting what is important to each family. In other words, the plan is considered to be the family's document, belonging to them rather than to the professional team members or the program. The process must be flexible, changing as the child grows and as family priorities change, while also being the mechanism for tracking whether early intervention services are addressing the child's and family's needs. How the IFSP is developed—including how the team works together, how well the document is individualized, and how it reflects the outcomes desired by the family—forms the backbone of the broader early intervention process for each family.

## REFERRAL, INTAKE, EVALUATION, AND ASSESSMENT

Before the initial IFSP is developed, several important activities occur. These activities provide information about the child and family that are essential to developing an individualized plan of supports and services. These activities include referral, intake, evaluation, and assessment.

## Referral

An infant or toddler can be referred to the early intervention system by anyone who has concerns about the child's development. In many instances, the referral comes from the child's health care provider. Family members and caregivers are also frequent referral sources, as described in Henry's case with his mother's referral. Other referral sources include hospital staff, who may refer children from the neonatal intensive care unit (NICU); the health department, who may refer children from programs such as the Special Supplemental Nutrition Program for Women, Infants, and Children (WIC) nutritional clinic; and the social services department, who may refer children whose families are involved in child protective services or other programs.

Every early intervention program establishes a system to ensure that referrals are promptly received and managed in a timely manner. This system often includes a designated person who accepts referrals. Regardless of the system that is in place, the date of referral to the early intervention system begins the 45-day time line that will be discussed later in this chapter.

## Intake

Once a child is referred for possible early intervention services, an *intake visit* is scheduled. This first meeting is a time to begin to establish trust and rapport with the family, which will be the foundation for all early intervention supports. The first meeting also sets the stage for the rest of the early intervention process. It should be conducted in a way that orients family members to what is to come and prepares them for being an active part of their child's services (Applequist, Umphrey, Moan, & Raabe, 2008).

During the intake, family members receive information about the program, their rights, and procedural safeguards. They provide information about their child and family. This mutual sharing is important and offers the family the opportunity to experience the reciprocal interaction that is most effective for successful intervention (Woods & Lindeman, 2008). Developmental screenings may also be conducted to assist the family and service provider in determining whether or not further evaluation of the child's development is needed. Paperwork is completed during the intake to begin the child's enrollment in the program.

Early intervention service providers begin to gather information about the child and the family during the intake to help form a picture of what makes the family unique, including family priorities, favorite activities, important people in their lives, and their concerns. Learning how to gather this crucial information in a sensitive, respectful, and compassionate manner requires practice. Interventionists must have the ability to make the family feel comfortable while asking detailed questions that may be personal in nature. They must also understand that families are often just beginning to learn about their child's developmental delay or disability; thus, they may feel vulnerable and unsure how the early intervention system works (Woods & Lindeman, 2008). A combination of good listening skills and sensitive interviewing techniques is essential during this first meeting.

Some early intervention systems have an established family interview that includes information about the child's birth and health history, family demographics, and family concerns. Although these more formalized family questionnaires will provide general information, the service provider must learn how to go beyond these basic questions to gather information that will later become an important part of IFSP outcome development (McWilliam et al., 2011). Using open-ended questions about the child's likes and dislikes, typical family routines, and parts of the day that are challenging for the family gives family members the opportunity to share detailed information about their preferences and how their family functions. Table 3.1 presents specific examples of open-ended questions that are family sensitive and provide the building blocks that lead to an individualized plan (Childress, Hill, & Buck, 2011).

## Evaluation and Assessment

The next steps in the early intervention process include evaluation and assessment. An *evaluation* is defined in the Individuals with Disabilities Education Improvement Act (IDEA) of 2004 (PL 108-446, §303.321) as "the procedures used by qualified personnel to determine a child's initial and continuing eligibility. An initial evaluation refers to the evaluation to determine his or her initial eligibility." These procedures may include the use of developmental checklists, standardized tests, review of the child's record, observation, parental report, and informed clinical opinion. This multidisciplinary evaluation must be conducted by at least two qualified service providers from different disciplines. Henry's multidisciplinary evaluation was conducted at the developmental clinic; the providers included a physician, occupational therapist, and speech-language pathologist.

If a child is referred to early intervention and has previously been diagnosed with a condition that has a high probability of resulting in a developmental delay, such as vision and/or hearing loss, the child is considered to be eligible for services (IDEA 2004). If the child does not have a diagnosis, however, the multidisciplinary evaluation is used to determine the child's eligibility for services. Because Henry had received a diagnosis of autism based on the multidisciplinary evaluation from the developmental clinic, the early intervention team knew that he was eligible.

*Assessment* is defined in IDEA 2004 as

> The on-going procedures used by qualified personnel to identify the child's unique strengths and needs and the Early Intervention service appropriate to meet those needs throughout the period of the child's eligibility. Initial assessment refers to the assessment of the child and family prior to the IFSP meeting. (§ 303.321[a][2][ii])

**Table 3.1.**  Open-ended questions for gathering information

| Gathering information about priorities, concerns, and daily routines | Gathering specific information about an individualized family service plan outcome |
|---|---|
| What would you like for your child to be able to do? | If your child could ____, what would that look like to you? |
| What parts of your day go well or do not go well? | How could you help your child learn to do this? |
| Are there parts of the day that frustrate your child? Or you? | When during the day could your child practice this activity? |
| Where do you like to go? Where would you like to be able to go as a family? | Who could help your child learn this activity? |
| What does your child like to do? What makes your child laugh? | What does your child need to do before, during, or after this activity to be successful? What do you need to do? |
| What do you and your child like to do together? | How will you know when your child has met this goal? |

*Source:* Childress, Hill, and Buck (2011).

To truly understand how children function, their likes and dislikes, and what priorities the family may have for them, it is important to go beyond the more formalized evaluation process. Through the use of *authentic assessment,* early interventionists use observations, their experiences and expertise, and conversations with the family to obtain information about how the child interacts and participates in family routines and everyday activities (Sandall, Hemmeter, Smith, & McLean, 2005). Authentic assessment draws the attention away from missed items on a test or evaluation tool while focusing on how the child is able to actively participate with his or her family and community (Bagnato, 2005; Bagnato, McLean, Macy, & Neisworth, 2011; Keilty, LaRocco, & Casell, 2009). Family members can also provide details about their hopes and dreams for their child. This information is crucial to the development of the IFSP outcomes because it informs the rest of the IFSP team about what is important to the family as well as the contexts in which intervention might occur (Keilty, 2010).

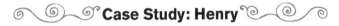 **Case Study: Henry**

Using authentic assessment, Brad and Talisha learned important information about Henry and his family. For example, by watching the Garrisons' lunchtime routine, they observed that Henry gagged when Julie tried to offer him green beans. Henry also refused to put his dinosaurs down during the meal, which made it difficult for him to use his hands to eat. Julie reported that Henry is able to feed himself, but he refuses to release his dinosaurs. The interventionists witnessed how agitated Henry became during lunch. His high-pitched squealing and crying were upsetting to the whole family. This observation helped Talisha and Brad better understand Julie's priority regarding mealtimes and provided detailed information that they would use when crafting outcomes with the family.

## FEDERAL REQUIREMENTS FOR THE INDIVIDUALIZED FAMILY SERVICE PLAN

The IFSP is the document described in Part C of IDEA that guides the early intervention process. The IFSP serves as documentation of how the child qualifies for early intervention services, the outcomes or goals that will be addressed, and the supports and services that will be provided. The plan also provides a record of the child's progress. Most important, however, the IFSP must be a fluid document that changes as a family's priorities change and a child's progress occurs. When a truly individualized IFSP is developed, it represents a commitment to the family from the early intervention team. McGonigel, Kaufman, and Johnson described it this way:

> The IFSP is a promise to children and families—a promise that strengths will be recognized and built on, that their beliefs and values will be respected, that their choices will be honored, and that their hopes and aspirations will be encouraged and enabled. (1991, p. 2)

### Components of the Individualized Family Service Plan

According to Part C regulations, the IFSP is "a written plan for providing Early Intervention services to an infant or toddler with a disability...and the infant's or toddler's family" (IDEA 2004, § 303.20). This definition reflects the family-focused nature of the IFSP in that the services described in the plan address both the child's and family's strengths and needs. The regulations further state that the IFSP must be based on information gathered from the evaluation and assessment and be developed by a multidisciplinary team, including the parents.

Although the federal definition is broad, the law provides specific details about the requirements that must be included in every IFSP, such as the following eight components (IDEA 2004):

1. "A statement of the infant's or toddler's present levels of physical development, cognitive development, communication development, social or emotional development, and adaptive development, based on objective criteria" (§ 303.344[a])

   When a child is evaluated for eligibility for early intervention, all five of the developmental domains must be evaluated to determine the child's current level of development. The statement in the IFSP that describes the child's abilities and needs across all areas of development is based on input from all team members and is most useful when it includes functional information about how the child's present levels relate to his or her everyday life. Chapter 1 offers descriptions of these domains.

2. "A statement of the family's resources, priorities, and concerns relating to enhancing the development of the family's infant or toddler with a disability" (§ 303.344[b])

   Information is gathered throughout the IFSP development process to understand the family members' concerns and priorities for their child. This includes information about their everyday routines and activities, important people in the lives of the child and family, and resources that can be used to support early intervention activities. The family assessment is voluntary, and families may choose how much or how little they wish to share in the development of the IFSP. For Henry's family, Talisha and Brad learned that Jean and Tom really hoped to find a way to use their local children's museum as a fun and educational outing for their grandchildren. Since Julie was at work during the day, the museum offered Lucy and Henry an opportunity to play with other children, too. Henry's grandparents were eager for ideas that could make this experience more enjoyable for him.

3. "A statement of the measurable results or outcomes expected to be achieved for the infant or toddler and the family, including pre-literacy and language skills, as developmentally appropriate for the child, and the criteria, procedures, and timelines used to determine the degree to which progress toward achieving the results or outcomes is being made and whether modifications or revisions of the results or outcomes or services are necessary" (§ 303.344[c])

   IFSP outcomes provide information about the developmental goals that it is hoped the child will achieve, such as self-feeding. These outcomes are based on what the family would like to see the child achieve and what was learned about the child's development through the evaluation and assessment. In addition, IFSP outcomes can also include goals for the family that will have a lasting impact on the child's developmental progress, such as finding additional resources related to their child's disability. It is important to note that IFSP outcomes are separate from the child and family outcomes identified by the Office of Special Education Programs (OSEP), reviewed in Chapter 1.

4. "A statement of specific early intervention services based on peer-reviewed research, to the extent practical, necessary to meet the unique needs of the infant or toddler and the family, including the frequency, length, and method of delivering services" (§ 303.344[d])

After outcomes are written, the early intervention team determines the appropriate services that will support the child and family in addressing these goals. The team discusses frequency (how often the service will occur; e.g., twice per month), the length of each session (e.g., 30 minutes), and the method or mode by which the service will be delivered (e.g., coaching). In the Garrisons' case, Henry received occupational therapy twice per week for 30 minutes each session. Brad, the occupational therapist, used coaching to provide information to Henry's mother and grandparents about how to engage Henry in ways that helped him develop the skills and abilities identified in his IFSP outcomes. Chapter 1 lists some of the possible early intervention services.

5.  "A statement of the natural environments in which early intervention services will appropriately be provided, including a justification of the extent, if any, to which the services will not be provided in a natural environment" (§ 303.344[e])

    Because early intervention services must be provided in natural environments, the IFSP must include a statement indicating specifically where the service will occur, such as in the family's home, at the shopping mall's play area, or at the child care center. Where services will occur is another team decision based on the priorities and resources of the family and the IFSP outcomes in the plan. Henry's IFSP listed his home and the children's museum as the natural environments where his services would occur. In the rare circumstance that it is not possible to provide early intervention services in the natural environment, the IFSP must include a justification about why this is not possible for the child and family. The justification must also include a plan to work toward implementing services within the natural environment.

6.  "The projected dates for initiation of services and the anticipated length, duration, and frequency of the services" (§ 303.344[f])

    For every service that the child will receive, documentation must be provided that includes the projected date (month, date, and year) of the initiation of services. The IFSP also must document how long it is anticipated that the child will receive the service.

7.  "The identification of the service coordinator from the profession most immediately relevant to the infant's or toddler's or family's needs (or who is otherwise qualified to carry out all applicable responsibilities under this part) who will be responsible for the implementation of the plan and coordination with other agencies and persons, including transition services" (§ 303.344[g])

    The service coordinator serves as the central point of contact for the family, providing a link to needed supports and resources. The service coordinator's name is prominently identified on the IFSP form for easy access for the family. As the service coordinator for Henry's family, Talisha assisted the Garrisons by providing information about autism spectrum disorder and coordinating their early intervention services.

8.  "The steps to be taken to support the transition of the toddler with a disability to preschool or other appropriate services" (§ 303.344[h])

    Transition planning begins with the initial IFSP to help the family begin the process of preparing for the next steps after early intervention. The IFSP contains documentation and procedures that will be used to support the toddler as he or she moves to early childhood special education or other services outside of the Part C system.

Although these eight required components must be in every child's IFSP, each state or territory has the option to develop its own IFSP form. Many states use a standardized IFSP form, which allows for consistency across the state. Completing the form correctly and ensuring that these requirements are addressed are the responsibility of the service coordinator, with the assistance of other team members. All team members must remember to balance the emphasis on correctly completing the form with the importance of conducting a collaborative IFSP development process. It is the collaborative process of developing the plan, rather than the act of completing the form, that is most important to a meaningful and supportive experience for children and families.

## DEVELOPMENT OF THE INDIVIDUALIZED FAMILY SERVICE PLAN

This collaborative process uses the experience and expertise of all team members—including the family—to develop an IFSP that will serve as the launching point for effective and significant early intervention services. Collaboration occurs most easily when all team members understand their roles in the process.

### Roles of Team Members in Individualized Family Service Plan Development

Team members involved in IFSP development often include people from a variety of backgrounds, depending on who is most appropriate to develop an individualized plan for the child and family. At a minimum, all IFSP teams include the service coordinator and the parent. Other team members may include people who are important to the family, such as neighbors, friends, or extended family, and other service providers, such as therapists, educators, child care providers, physicians, or social workers. The roles of team members, including the family, service provider, service coordinator, and others important to the family, are discussed in the following sections.

**Family**     Because of the family-centered nature of the IFSP, the process of developing an IFSP must empower family members to be active participants in their child's intervention. Parents know the child best and are the experts on their family's routines and activities, so they are the primary source of information regarding how the child interacts, communicates, moves, plays, and solves problems in his or her daily life. Rather than having the professional team members develop the IFSP based on their goals for the child, the family members' expertise about the child and their daily life is combined with the professionals' knowledge of development and intervention to develop outcomes and service recommendations that meet child and family needs. This collaborative effort provides the balance needed to develop a meaningful plan.

**Service Provider**     Depending on how the IFSP team works, the service provider may have conducted part of the evaluation and assessment or may be meeting the family for the first time to help develop the IFSP. During IFSP development, the provider listens carefully to the information shared by the family and the service coordinator about the child's development. The provider may ask questions to gather additional information about the family's priorities and desired outcomes for the child, then assist with writing outcomes to be included in the plan. The provider, with other team members, then actively discusses what service(s) would be most appropriate to help the family work toward the IFSP outcomes. Again, depending on individual program policies and on the final services written on the plan, the provider who helps the family develop the IFSP may or may not continue to support the family by being its ongoing service provider.

An important aspect of the service provider's role in IFSP development is maintaining a balance between sharing professional expertise and listening to the family. Providers have a responsibility to share their knowledge with families, but they must do so in a way that is respectful of the family's role in the process. Understanding that IFSP development is driven by family priorities, rather than child impairments, can ensure that the process is collaborative.

**Service Coordinator**     The service coordinator is typically the leader of the IFSP team. He or she coordinates the IFSP development process by gathering information from the family, physician, and other sources before the actual IFSP meeting occurs and then scheduling the meeting when team members can participate. The service coordinator is the facilitator of the meeting and the writer of the plan. An important duty of the service coordinator is to closely monitor the family's comfort with the process, ensuring that questions are answered and that the family clearly understands what is happening. The service coordinator also mediates the discussion during IFSP outcome development so that outcomes tie back to family priorities, address the child's functional development, and lead to appropriate service recommendations. This is accomplished by intentionally asking family members for input throughout the process and helping them participate in whatever way they are comfortable, whether verbally, in writing, or through an interpreter. The service coordinator is the person on the team who connects the parts of the IFSP development process together (Jung & Grisham-Brown, 2006). Once the IFSP is written, the service coordinator completes documentation of the process and provides a copy of the plan to all team members, including the child's physician.

**Other Team Members**     The role of the child's primary care physician or pediatrician is mainly to provide information about developmental and medical history, including information about diagnoses or medical precautions that are necessary during intervention. Physicians may contribute to recommendations for services, but they do so as part of the team. The actual decision about which service(s) a child and family will receive is a team decision that includes input from all members. The same is true for other medical specialists, such as neurologists, or other types of consultants, such as vision specialists or behavior consultants. These team members often have important information to contribute.

Another important team member who may be asked to participate in IFSP development is the child care provider. The decision to include this provider is based on the family's preference. Child care providers can provide useful information about the child's functional strengths and needs in the child care environment. For many children, child care providers will be important partners during intervention, so including them in the development of the plan is helpful.

Other team members could include a neighbor who is a significant resource to the family, a grandmother in another state who helps the family make important decisions, or a social worker from another agency with whom the family is working. The people the family members identify as important to them in the IFSP development process will vary. Service providers must be flexible to work with whomever the family identifies, knowing that the more people who are supporting the family in working toward their goals for the child, the greater the chances are of positive developmental outcomes for the child.

Once the IFSP team members have been identified, the service coordinator makes arrangements so that all members can participate in the process. Some team members might participate by attending the IFSP meeting, whereas other members might provide input by phone, in writing, or by other means. The service coordinator is responsible for facilitating the IFSP development process to combine the expertise of all team members, including the family. No one team member is more important than another; all team members have equal input, with the parents being the ultimate decision makers about what outcomes they want to address for their child and what services they agree to receive. Through discussion about what has been learned about the child from the intake, evaluation, and assessment, as well as what the family shares about its everyday life, the team works together to reach consensus that results in a meaningful IFSP.

## Initial Individualized Family Service Plan

The initial IFSP represents family members' first experience with developing a plan to address their child's development with the assistance of early intervention supports and services. This can be a time during which families receive a great deal of information and have important decisions to make. Professional team members should be careful to respect family preferences while providing information and appropriate support for family decision making about what outcomes and services family members feel are most appropriate for their child. The service coordinator plays a key role in this process by supporting family participation and decision making; receiving input from all team members; and facilitating the process so that the IFSP meets federal, state, and local program requirements.

The initial IFSP meeting to develop the plan must be held within 45 calendar days of the date the child was referred to the early intervention program (IDEA 2004). The purpose of this time line is to protect children and families from having to wait for extended periods of time to begin the early intervention process. If a mitigating circumstance occurs that affects the time line, such as when a child is ill, the service coordinator must document the circumstances in the child's record. When scheduling the meeting, the family's service coordinator must ensure that the IFSP meeting is held at a time and place that is convenient to the family. The family must also be extended the right to invite anyone to the IFSP meeting who will be able to share information or provide family support. According to Part C of IDEA 2004, all information presented during the IFSP meeting must be in the family's native language or other mode of communication unless it is clearly not feasible to do so.

### Using Information from Intake, Evaluation, and Assessment
Information that was gathered from the evaluation and assessment process informs the initial IFSP development process. What the team learned about the child's skills and abilities and how he or she uses them in daily life is what will be considered when identifying the outcomes and services to be written on the IFSP. When discussing the evaluation and assessment results with the family, professionals should relate what was learned about the child's development to his or her functioning in everyday life. This helps families understand the link between skills that were tested and the skills the child needs to participate more fully in daily activities (Campbell, 2011).

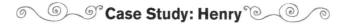 **Case Study: Henry**

During Henry's evaluation, he did not imitate the task of stirring with a spoon in a cup, which is a skill that most toddlers can imitate by around 10 months of age (Glover, Preminger, & Sanford, 1995). This test skill is not particularly important in Henry's daily life; however, by observing Henry's difficulty with this task, the occupational therapist learned that Henry is not yet able to imitate some simple motor tasks and does not yet understand how to combine objects to play, such as putting a shape in a shape sorter or a ring on a ring stand. This is important because it relates to what Henry's mother described as his tendency to throw his toys rather than play with them. Brad speculated that Henry may be throwing his toys because he is unable to figure out how to play with them and is not yet able to imitate others who try to show him how to play. The skill on the developmental test, in and of itself, was not very important, but what it showed about Henry's development helped his team determine why he might be struggling with functional play. This information was then used to determine outcomes for Henry's IFSP.

Information gathered from the intake and assessment about family members' priorities for the child's development and their concerns also informs the development of the IFSP. The team should review this information and continue to ask questions that help family members identify what they would like to address with their child. The open-ended questions listed in Table 3.1 are also useful when making the transition from the evaluation and assessment to developing the IFSP because they focus the discussion. Asking a parent or caregiver the direct question, "What are your goals for your child?" can be intimidating, especially if the family is feeling vulnerable and unsure of the process. Some families will be able to answer this question clearly, whereas others will need assistance identifying what outcomes they want on the plan. Revisiting what they shared during the intake about their child and summarizing what was learned during the evaluation and assessment process can be helpful for focusing the discussion. Rather than asking a broad question about what the family wants as a goal, the service coordinator or service provider can help the parent identify what is most important to begin addressing by asking a question such as, "Based on what we've learned so far and what you know about your child, where would you like to begin?" Instead of professional team members jumping in and beginning to list developmental goals for the child, the parent should be given the first opportunity to identify what is important to the family. The professionals then can help the parent specify what the activity might look like while the child is learning and once the child has mastered it. This discussion combines the knowledge of all team members and, with careful facilitation, results in functional IFSP outcomes and services that meet the child's developmental needs.

**Individualized Family Service Plan Outcome Development**    IFSP outcomes are statements that describe what the child is expected to achieve by participating in early intervention. Outcomes address the child's developmental strengths and needs in the context of his or her everyday routines and activities. They are written to include 1) specific information regarding what the child will do, 2) the circumstances in which the skill or behavior will be learned, and 3) the criteria for achievement.

Developing meaningful, functional, and individualized IFSP outcomes is often the most challenging part of writing an IFSP. Service providers must learn to synthesize the information that has been gathered throughout the IFSP process. The interventionist simultaneously uses his or her educational training and experiences to consider the developmental skills and abilities the child needs to learn, as well as what instructional strategies might be useful to help the child learn. In addition, the provider must ensure that the IFSP outcomes meet the requirements of *payors,* which are the funding streams, such as the family's insurance or Medicaid, that are used to pay for early intervention services. (In most states, early intervention is not a free resource to families.) Writing meaningful outcomes takes skill and practice. When interventionists understand the key characteristics of IFSP outcomes, the process becomes more manageable.

The following are six essential characteristics of well-written IFSP outcomes:

1. *Strengths-based:* IFSP outcomes should be based on the strengths of the child and family. This encourages the family as well as service providers to start with skills the child already has and build toward the next developmental steps.

2. *Focused on family members' hopes and dreams for their child:* When the team understands and acknowledges the family's vision for the child's future, IFSP outcomes can be written to include developmental skills and behaviors that work toward these long-term goals. Service providers can support the family in understanding the smaller developmental steps that are necessary to reach larger developmental milestones. For example, family members might dream that their child with spastic cerebral palsy will walk someday. Team members are unlikely to know for sure if or when the child will walk, but they can still respect the family's dream and explain that, before walking, certain developmental abilities must be mastered. That is, the child must be able to support his or her head and maintain trunk control (or control of the middle of his or her body) prior to walking. If the family agrees, these steps can be included as outcomes on the IFSP and addressed during intervention visits to help the child develop skills related to the family's dream.

3. *Individualized:* Well-written IFSP outcomes must be individualized to reflect the strengths, needs, interests, and the environment in which the child and family live. By including a child's favorite activity, a special toy, or an important person in the child's life, the outcome becomes significant and more meaningful to family members because they can relate it to their everyday life.

4. *Contextualized:* When IFSP outcomes are contextualized, they are addressed within the context of a family's activities and routines. Contextualized IFSP outcomes also help family members understand how the outcomes can be incorporated throughout their daily activities. For example, if parents who want their daughter to eventually walk spend much of their weekends attending sporting events for their older child, they can learn ways to help their daughter practice head control while watching her sibling's games. Incorporating this specific routine into the IFSP outcome for walking will help family members better understand how to include their younger child in these activities while supporting frequent practice of this new skill. Describing this outcome in the context of the weekend routine also reminds the service provider of when and where the family is likely to practice and monitor the child's development, which is important to know when developing intervention strategies with the family.

5. *Functional:* Functional IFSP outcomes reflect real-life activities that are important to the child's everyday interactions with others and his or her environment. IFSP outcomes should not be tied to missed evaluation items or isolated developmental skills, such as nesting a smaller cup into a larger cup, which frequently have less functional use in the reality of everyday tasks. A child who understands that a certain shape fits into a specific opening develops better eye–hand coordination, which supports eating and dressing. When an infant learns that a smaller bowl fits inside a bigger bowl, he or she is developing spatial skills that will be used throughout life, such as when putting bowls into a kitchen cabinet. Understanding the purpose of the developmental skill that each test item is targeting assists the early intervention team in writing more practical and functional outcomes.

6. *Measurable:* To determine a child's progress, IFSP outcomes should be written using practical and everyday measurability criteria that make sense to both caregivers and service providers (Jung & Grisham-Brown, 2006; Pletcher & Younggren, 2013). Families typically do not think of their child's progress in terms of a particular skill or activity occurring "80% of the time" or "during three out of four trials." Criteria like these tend to reflect how a service provider would measure progress in a more clinical setting, rather than how a family would measure a child's progress in the natural environment. Using family-friendly measurements, such as "takes two bites of Stage 3 baby food without gagging" or "walks up two steps to get into the family's house," make it much easier for a parent to report and determine progress (Partnership for People with Disabilities, 2012).

Writing a strengths-based, individualized, functional, and measurable IFSP outcome that includes the family's routines or activities and also supports the family's dreams for the child may seem like a daunting task. Having a basic structure for writing outcomes helps the IFSP team ensure that each outcome includes the key components discussed above. At a minimum, outcomes should include the following:

- *Who:* Each outcome should start with the child's name.
- *What:* This is typically a verb that indicates the skill or task that is being addressed in the outcome.
- *Where:* This part of the outcome focuses on the everyday routine or family activity in which the outcome will be practiced.
- *How:* Identifying how the outcome is to be achieved helps ensure that it is measurable. This part of the outcome might include how often the child is supposed to do the skill or over how long a period of time the skill should be observed to determine that it has been mastered.

Using this simple format, Henry's IFSP team developed the following outcome based on his family's priority to address feeding: *Henry will taste two new foods at dinner each week during one month.* This IFSP outcome includes each outcome component: who (*Henry*), what (*will taste two new foods*), where (*at dinner*), and how (*each week during one month*). This outcome is functional and individualized to one of Henry's needs, will be addressed in a daily routine, and is measurable because the team will know that Henry has met it when he is able to try new foods consistently each evening at dinner across the span of a month. Once he is able to manage new foods this frequently, the team will be able to consider the goal as being met. Box 3.1 shows other outcomes the team, with the family, identified during Henry's initial IFSP development.

---

**BOX 3.1.    Examples of initial individualized family service plan outcomes for Henry**

- Henry will taste two new foods at dinner each week during 1 month.
- Henry will take three turns with Lucy while playing with his dinosaurs in the sandbox each afternoon for 1 week.
- Henry will use 10 words or signs (e.g., *up, down, go, uh-oh, mine*) while playing with the blocks at the children's museum once each week over 2 months.

Writing quality outcomes requires more than just following this simple format, however. For outcomes to "belong" to the family and be useful to all members of the team, they must also be *discipline free,* assuring that the outcome does not imply that a certain type of team member with specific training is the only person who can support the child on this outcome (Lucas, Gillaspy, Peters, & Hurth, 2012). For example, if someone identifies an outcome as a "speech goal," implying that only the speech-language pathologist will address it, the outcome is not discipline free. Outcomes should also be free of technical jargon and written in common language understandable by all team members (Jung, 2007; Jung & Grisham-Brown, 2006). An outcome might describe a child learning to roll bilaterally, for example. Rather than use the technical term *bilaterally,* the outcome could be better worded to say that the child will roll to both sides of his or her body.

Another good rule of thumb when writing quality outcomes is to avoid passive words, such as *participate* or *tolerate,* which may have different meanings to different people (Lucas et al., 2012). IFSP team members can apply the *third-word rule,* which emphasizes using an active verb as the third word in the outcome (Shelden & Rush, 2009). The verb should be specific and have the same meaning regardless of who reads the outcome. For example, the outcome *Dimitri will participate in play activities with his mother* could mean many things because the outcome does not define how Dimitri will participate in play or what he will be doing. The revised outcome, *Dimitri will bang toys together using both hands during playtime with his mother each day for 2 weeks,* is much more specific. It clearly describes what Dimitri will accomplish so that all team members will understand what Dimitri is learning to do.

Developing the outcomes with these considerations in mind requires the service coordinator and service provider to pay close attention to the information provided by the family. The discussion must be facilitated to bring out the information needed to ensure that the outcomes are written well, and team members must collaborate to ensure that outcomes are reflective of the family's priorities and the child's developmental needs. This takes skillful team collaboration and practice.

The number of outcomes actually written on the IFSP is variable and depends on the family's priorities and preferences for the child. It is not necessary to write an outcome for every developmental domain in which the child is exhibiting delays (McWilliam, 2010). Instead, when outcomes focus on functional activities, rather than isolated skills, a single outcome can address multiple areas of development. For example, a toddler who is showing delays in gross motor, communication, and cognition might have an outcome that combines activities addressing several skills, such as *Arnold will crawl 8 feet across the living room to get to his father when he calls Arnold's name at least 5 evenings in 1 week.* This outcome includes an important gross motor skill (crawling) that Arnold is learning as well as receptive communication and the cognitive skills of localizing the speaker and understanding and responding to his name. Having fewer, more functional outcomes on the IFSP allows family members to focus their attention and efforts on how to use the strategies they practiced to support their child each day, rather than feeling overwhelmed by having so many different things to work on. Service providers can also more easily track the child's progress on more focused outcomes. Because of the fluid nature of the IFSP, outcomes can be modified, added, or deleted as needed to reflect changing family priorities or changes in the child's development that occur after services have begun.

**Determining Supports and Services**        Once the IFSP outcomes are written, it is time to determine which supports and services are most appropriate to assist the child and family in meeting those outcomes. Services are always determined after IFSP outcomes are developed. This ensures that the early intervention team has determined what needs to be addressed before it can be assumed that any particular service is required (Partnership for People with Disabilities, 2012). Following this process also allows the team to consider which service provider might provide the best support to the family. Perhaps one service provider has specialized training in working with children with autism spectrum disorder. Another provider might work well with family members with intellectual disabilities. When the strengths and skills of early intervention providers are appropriately matched with outcomes based on family priorities, it eliminates outdated or inflexible thinking that a child with a certain delay or disability must have a certain type of service or provider. For example, it is no longer thought that a child with motor delays must have physical therapy or a child with language delays must be seen by a speech-language pathologist. Rather, providers are matched with families based on the knowledge and skills needed to support the family, rather than solely on the child's delay or diagnosis.

Through thoughtful discussion, the early intervention team can reach consensus regarding the needed service(s) and the appropriate service provider(s). The conversation includes determining how often the service will be provided (frequency), how long each session will last (intensity), and the location of the services. Important considerations for determining frequency and intensity include how often intervention strategies will need to be changed and how often the family needs support to be able to implement interventions in their everyday life (Jung, 2003).

Although most early intervention services continue to be provided in the home, the discussion about location should include all of the places where families go as part of their routines (Keilty, 2008). The grocery store, the Laundromat, religious services, and community events such as swimming lessons, ballet classes, or art activities at the local craft store can provide rich opportunities to address IFSP outcomes. The interventionist and the family should also discuss inclusive practices and strategies to determine what supports are needed to promote the child's active participation in these settings. In the Garrisons' case, the team determined that Brad would be the family's primary service provider, and he would receive support through consultation with the team speech-language pathologist. Henry would receive occupational therapy with Brad two times a week for 30 minutes per session for the first 3 months, then services would be reduced to once a week until it was time for Henry's 6-month IFSP review. Henry's services would take place at both home and the children's museum.

After service(s), provider(s), frequency, intensity, and location are determined, it is important that the child's services begin in a timely manner. Each state has the opportunity to define what is deemed as timely. Although wide variations across states are reported, from within 10 days after parental consent is received to up to 45 days, the majority of states use a time line of within 30 days from the date that parental consent for services was obtained (National Early Childhood Technical Assistance Center, 2011).

**Transitions**    In early intervention, transitions may occur numerous times, such as when an infant leaves the NICU to come home, when there is a change in service providers, and when the child is being discharged from early intervention services. *Transition services* are the supports and activities that are established to help the family prepare for a smooth and seamless transition when their child leaves the early intervention system (Office of Special Education Programs, 2011). All of the activities related to a transition should be outlined on the IFSP and are individualized to the child and family's interests, priorities, and concerns.

Transition planning begins at the initial IFSP and continues during each IFSP review. Families are initially informed of the age requirements for early intervention and that children must be discharged by age 3, unless the family lives in a state that has taken advantage of the option under IDEA 2004 to extend early intervention services to the state's entry age for kindergarten. During each IFSP review, the transition is discussed to ensure that families are aware of their options following early intervention. These options may include transition to early childhood special education through Part B of IDEA, community settings such as Early Head Start or Head Start, or private child care or preschool.

Children make the transition out of early intervention either because they have met all of their outcomes and no longer qualify for services or they reach the age limitation that mandates discharge from services. As children are nearing the age of transition, two important meetings are held:

1. *A meeting to develop the transition plan:* This meeting is held for all children regardless of their transition destination. The service coordinator and the parent(s) are required attendees, although others who can support the transition process may also be invited. During this meeting, plans and strategies are developed, such as visiting the new destination or writing additional outcomes to support the child in group activities to prepare the child for the next setting.

2. *A transition planning conference:* For children who are potentially eligible for early childhood special education, the second meeting—called the *transition planning conference*—is held with parental approval. This meeting must include an early intervention representative, the parent(s), and a representative from the local school division or other community program.

Both of these meetings must be held at least 90 days but no more than 9 months before a child makes the transition from the early intervention system (IDEA 2004).

A transition can be a stressful time for families as they leave the supports they have become accustomed to and enter a new service system. Parents who are used to having service providers join them in their natural environments may find it unsettling to send their toddler to an unfamiliar classroom environment. Parents may also find the different focus between family-centered early intervention and a more child-centered early childhood special education program to be a significant change. On the other hand, some parents find relief in sending their child to school and look forward to the social opportunities that the classroom environment provides. For families who choose a transition to a preschool environment for their toddler, this change marks a significant milestone. The support offered by the service coordinator and other team members during this time is invaluable to a successful transition process.

## INDIVIDUALIZED FAMILY SERVICE PLAN IMPLEMENTATION AND REVIEW

Once the initial IFSP is completed, the services designated on the plan begin. Services are provided in the family's home or other natural environment, and the ongoing collaboration between the family and the service provider is initiated. The service coordinator is instrumental in ensuring that services are implemented in accordance with the IFSP. He or she closely monitors services by checking in regularly with the family and service provider, monitoring the child's progress toward IFSP outcomes, and convening IFSP meetings to make changes to the plan as needed. Teamwork and collaboration are essential during IFSP implementation.

At any time during the implementation of the IFSP, any team member may request a meeting to discuss the plan. Common reasons for requesting an IFSP meeting include the need to review outcomes that the child may have met, the need to discuss a possible change in service frequency, or the need to change services or service providers. When such a need arises, the service coordinator works with the family and other team members to schedule an IFSP meeting where the team can consider the issue and come to consensus on changes to the plan.

IFSP reviews are required any time there are changes to the outcomes or to the services being provided, including changes to the frequency, intensity, method, or natural environment. Infancy and toddlerhood are periods of rapid growth and development. Because these changes occur so quickly, it is important that the IFSP remains current and accurately reflects the child's status and progress toward outcomes. To ensure regular monitoring and review of the plan, IDEA 2004 requires the IFSP to be reviewed at least every 6 months and annually, as described in the following sections.

## Six-Month Review

The IFSP must be reviewed at a minimum of every 6 months, although it may be revised more frequently. At the 6-month review, the participants must include, at minimum, the parent(s) and the service coordinator, although all early interventionists providing services are encouraged to attend and are given the opportunity to participate in writing or by other means.

During the 6-month IFSP review, the early intervention team, including the family, considers the child's progress on all outcomes. The team should consider the questions shown in Box 3.2 as they review each outcome. These questions help the team consider whether an outcome is still relevant, whether the child has met the outcome, or whether the outcome needs modifications. The team also reviews all supports and services to determine if any changes are needed. For example, a father may indicate that he is feeling more confident about the strategies that he and the physical therapist have discussed and practiced with his child. An IFSP review meeting is scheduled and, after some discussion, the father may indicate that he would be comfortable reducing the number of visits from one time per week or might like to reduce the amount of session time from 60 minutes to 30 minutes. The changes that the team agrees on would then be documented in the IFSP.

---

**BOX 3.2.    Questions to ask when reviewing individualized family service plan (IFSP) outcomes**

- What progress has your child made on this outcome?
- Is this outcome still meaningful and relevant for your child?
- Does this outcome need to be modified to reflect developmental progress or a change in family priorities?
- If your child has not made progress, should this outcome be revised into smaller, more achievable steps?
- Does your family have a new priority or concern related to your child's development? Does a new outcome need to be added to the plan to address this priority or concern?
- If your child has met the outcome, are there any other outcomes that need to be added to the IFSP?
- If your child has met all IFSP outcomes, how do you feel about your child's development now? What outcomes and services are now needed?
- Do you believe there are now changes to services that are needed based on this review?

## Annual Review

Most infants and toddlers achieve numerous developmental milestones rapidly during the first 3 years. Even children with more significant developmental delays or disabilities exhibit changes in their development that affect their IFSP outcomes and services. To accommodate and adjust for changes that occur over the course of a year, each child's IFSP must be reviewed and rewritten annually (IDEA 2004).

Prior to writing the annual IFSP, the child's continued eligibility for services must be confirmed. A full multidisciplinary evaluation is not required; however, enough information must be gathered to be able to complete the eight required components of the IFSP, including the child's present levels of development in all domains. Early interventionists who are currently providing services to the child and family can frequently provide this information using an evaluation tool and their informed clinical opinion. Once the child is determined to still be eligible for services, a new IFSP is written.

The annual IFSP review meeting must include, at minimum, the family and the service coordinator, as well as anyone involved in new or ongoing assessment. Service providers who are currently supporting the family also provide valuable input to the process. During the annual review, the IFSP team considers the child's progress during the past year; reviews the family's current concerns, priorities, and daily routines (which likely have changed); and discusses outcomes based on the previous IFSP. The new IFSP reflects the child's current developmental status, new outcomes, any outcomes that are being continued from the previous plan, and new or continuing services. The transition plan is also updated at this time. The annual IFSP review offers the family and other team members a time to come together to plan for the child's continuing supports and services to ensure that the family's intervention experience continues to meet their needs.

## INCLUSIVE PRACTICES

Throughout the IFSP development process, the importance of everyday routines and family activities is emphasized. By using natural learning opportunities that occur in the child's life and building IFSP outcomes around them, children and families have multiple opportunities to practice and master skills during regularly occurring activities. The early intervention team considers how to incorporate those natural environments and activities into the IFSP to promote inclusive practices throughout the implementation of the plan.

Two professional organizations—the National Association for the Education of Young Children (NAEYC), which focuses on high-quality early childhood education, and the Division for Early Childhood of the Council for Exceptional Children (DEC), which promotes the use of evidence-based practices for children with disabilities and other special needs—published the following joint position statement in order to define inclusion in early childhood:

> Early childhood inclusion embodies the values, policies, and practices that support the right of every infant and young child and his or her family, regardless of ability, to participate in a broad range of activities and contexts as full members of families, communities, and society. The desired results of inclusive experiences for children with and without disabilities and their families include a sense of belonging and membership, positive social relationships and friendships, and development and learning to reach their full potential. (DEC & NAEYC, 2009, p. 2)

By understanding this joint position statement, interventionists can work together with families to build and enhance the three key elements of inclusive practices: 1) access, 2) participation, and 3) support (Buysse, 2011):

- *Access:* For children and families to have access to a variety of community resources, simple to advanced modifications may need to be made. An automatic door-opening button allows easy access for those who use a walker but it also assists anyone whose hands are full. A more complex modification, such as a waterproof wheelchair with specialized wheels that moves easily through the sand, allows a child access to the fun of the beach and the ocean with his or her family.

- *Participation:* Promoting opportunities that enable children and families to gain access to community resources provides chances to interact and engage with others in the community. For example, during activities at the children's museum, Brad assisted Henry's mother and grandparents in helping Henry and Lucy join other children in a fun construction area where the children were building with foam blocks. By problem-solving together how to help Henry stay in the area and take turns building with the other children, Henry's family was able to see Henry become more involved in his community and learn to socialize in that environment.

- *Support:* Interventionists must recognize the need for collaboration to build a supportive infrastructure to encourage inclusive practices. Creativity and flexibility will benefit service providers as they interact with community members who may have less experience with children with developmental delays or disabilities. Before a fingerpainting activity at the children's museum, Brad and Julie met briefly with the museum educator to discuss ways to support Henry's inclusion in that activity. They brainstormed strategies and determined that Henry could paint using a paintbrush instead of using his fingers, which was likely to make him uncomfortable due to his sensitivity to textures on his hands. While sitting on his mother's lap, Henry was then able to participate in the art activity without leaving or becoming upset. Taping his paper down ensured his work did not slide away from him and he could place more attention on the task. By supporting the educator before the activity, they were able to collaboratively come up with a modification for the activity. These simple supports allowed Henry to have access to a learning and social opportunity that he previously had avoided.

When an IFSP team considers outcomes and services to meet a child's and family's needs, strategies that promote access and opportunities for children to participate and interact in community settings take high priority. These strategies are woven into the IFSP and implemented during the provision of services. Inclusive practices and strategies also align well with the concept of supporting families in their natural environments during activities and routines that are of interest to them. Viewing the IFSP from the lens of inclusive practices reminds service providers that early intervention supports can—and must—extend far beyond the living room.

## BEST PRACTICE HIGHLIGHTS

The following best practices should guide service providers as they collaborate with families to develop meaningful IFSPs:

- The IFSP is a fluid document that belongs to the family and should reflect the priorities family members have for their child's development, focusing on the everyday activities and routines of their life.

- Information gathered during the referral, intake, evaluation, and assessment is essential to developing a family-centered, individualized plan for intervention.

- The development of the IFSP is a team process based on multiple sources, including what was learned about the child during the evaluation and the assessment, information from the family, and the expertise of all team members.
- Understanding that IFSP development is driven by family priorities, rather than child impairments, will ensure that the process is collaborative.
- IFSP outcomes must be strengths-based, focused on the family's hopes and dreams for the child, individualized, contextualized, functional, and measurable.
- A well-written IFSP outcome includes the following components: *who* (the child's name), *what* (a verb indicating the skill or task being addressed), *where* (the everyday routine or family activity in which the outcome will be practiced), and *how* (how achievement of the outcome will be measured).
- IFSP services are determined after outcomes are developed and are based on team discussion about how often strategies may change and how much support family members need to implement strategies with their child.
- According to Part C of IDEA, the initial IFSP meeting must be held within 45 calendar days from the date of the child's referral. Once developed, services must begin in a timely manner, and the IFSP must be reviewed at least every 6 months and annually.
- Inclusive practices that promote the child's access and participation and provide support to caregivers should be considered during IFSP development and continue throughout the implementation of services in the child's natural environments.

## CONCLUSION

The process of developing and reviewing the IFSP is one that begins from the child's initial referral and continues until the child makes the transition from early intervention. Each IFSP should be individualized because it reflects what is unique about the child and family receiving supports and services. Developing the IFSP is a process, rather than a single event, because the document is constantly changing as the child grows and the family's priorities and routines change. By using family-centered, collaborative practices that combine the expertise of all team members, the IFSP process reflects these important changes and prepares family members for active participation in their child's early intervention services.

## DISCUSSION QUESTIONS AND APPLIED ACTIVITIES

1. List and describe the eight required components of the IFSP as described in Part C of IDEA 2004.
2. Describe why it is important that IFSP outcomes are based on the family's priorities rather than on items missed on the child's evaluation and assessment.
3. Observe an initial IFSP development meeting at your local early intervention program. After the meeting, review the IFSP and critique the outcomes to determine whether they meet the criteria described in this chapter. Answer the following questions:
   - Are the outcomes strengths-based?
   - Do the outcomes relate to the family's priorities and dreams for the child?
   - Are the outcomes functional and contextualized?
   - Are the outcomes individualized and clearly measurable?
   - Do the outcomes include the components of who, what, where, and how?

If you answer *no* to any of these questions, pick one outcome and revise it according to the characteristics learned in this chapter. If all of the outcomes meet the criteria, then practice your outcome development skills by writing one new outcome for the child.

## REFERENCES

Applequist, K.L., Umphrey, L., Moan, E., & Raabe, B. (2008). Using effective communication techniques when presenting initial information to families. In C.A. Peterson, L. Fox, & P.M. Blasco (Eds.), *Early intervention for infants and toddlers and their families: Practices and outcomes* (pp. 19–31). Missoula, MT: Division for Early Childhood of the Council for Exceptional Children.

Bagnato, S.J. (2005). The authentic alternative for assessment in early intervention: An emerging evidence-based practice. *Journal of Early Intervention, 28*(1), 17–28. doi:10.1177/105381510502800102

Bagnato, S.J., McLean, M., Macy, M., & Neisworth, J.T. (2011). Identifying instructional targets for early childhood via authentic assessment: Alignment of professional standards and practice-based evidence. *Journal of Early Intervention, 33*(4), 243–253. doi:10.1177/1053815111427565

Buysse, V. (2011). Access, participation, and supports: The defining features of high-quality inclusion. *Zero to Three, 31*(4), 24–31.

Campbell, P.H. (2011). Using the assessment of family activities and routines to develop embedded programming. In C.A. Peterson, L. Fox, & P.M. Blasco (Eds.), *Early intervention for infants and toddlers and their families: Practices and outcomes* (pp. 64–78). Missoula, MT: Division for Early Childhood of the Council for Exceptional Children.

Childress, D.C., Hill, C.F., & Buck, D.M. (2011, November). *A family-centered approach to developing quality outcomes.* Paper presented at a workshop for the Infant and Toddler Connection of Virginia, Richmond, VA.

Division for Early Childhood & National Association for the Education of Young Children. (2009). *Early childhood inclusion: A joint position statement of the Division for Early Childhood (DEC) and the National Association for the Education of Young Children (NAEYC).* Chapel Hill: The University of North Carolina, FPG Child Development Institute.

Glover, M.E., Preminger, J.L., & Sanford, A.R. (1995). *The Early Learning Accomplishment Profile for developmentally young children* (Rev. ed.). Chapel Hill, NC: Chapel Hill Training-Outreach Project.

Individuals with Disabilities Education Improvement Act (IDEA) of 2004, PL 108-446, 20 U.S.C. §§ 1400 *et seq.*

Jung, L.A. (2003). More better: Maximizing natural learning opportunities. *Young Exceptional Children, 6,* 21–26. doi:10.1177/109625060300600303

Jung, L.A. (2007). Writing individualized family service plan strategies that fit into the routine. *Young Exceptional Children, 10,* 2–9. doi:10.1177/10962506070100301

Jung, L.A., & Grisham-Brown, J. (2006). Moving from assessment information to IFSPs: Guidelines for a family-centered process. *Young Exceptional Children, 9,* 2–11. doi:10.1177/109625060600900201

Keilty, B. (2008). Early intervention home-visiting principles in practice: A reflective approach. *Young Exceptional Children, 11,* 29–40. doi:10.1177/1096250607311933

Keilty, B. (2010). *The early intervention guidebook for families and professionals: Partnering for success.* New York, NY: Teachers College Press.

Keilty, B., LaRocco, D.J., & Casell, F.B. (2009). Early interventionists' reports of authentic assessment methods through focus group research. *Topics in Early Childhood Special Education, 28*(4), 244–256. doi:10.1177/0271121408327477

Lucas, A., Gillaspy, K., Peters, M.L., & Hurth, J. (2012). *Enhancing recognition of high-quality, functional IFSP outcomes and IEP goals: A training activity for infant and toddler service providers and ECSE teachers.* Retrieved from http://ectacenter.org/~pdfs/pubs/rating-ifsp-iep-training.pdf

McGonigel, M.J., Kaufman, R.K., & Johnson, B.H. (Eds.). (1991). *Guidelines and recommended practices for the individualized family service plan* (2nd ed.). Retrieved from http://files.eric.ed.gov/fulltext/ED336907.pdf

McWilliam, R.A. (2010). *Routines-based early intervention: Supporting young children and their families.* Baltimore, MD: Paul H. Brookes Publishing Co.

McWilliam, R.A., Casey, A.M., Ashley, D., Fielder, J., Rowley, P., DeJong, K., …Votava, K. (2011). Assessment of family-identified needs through the routines-based interview. In C.A. Peterson, L. Fox, & P.M. Blasco (Eds.), *Early intervention for infants and toddlers and their families: Practices and outcomes* (pp. 43–63). Missoula, MT: Division for Early Childhood of the Council for Exceptional Children.

National Early Childhood Technical Assistance Center. (2011). *Part C SPP/APR 2011 indicator analysis—(FFY 2009).* Retrieved from http://www.nectac.org/~pdfs/partc/part-c_sppapr_11.pdf

Office of Special Education Programs. (2011, November). *Part C of the Individuals with Disabilities Education Act: Final regulations: Nonregulatory guidance.* Retrieved from http://osep-part-c.tadnet.org/uploads/file_assets/attachments/12/original_Final_Regulations-_Part-C-DOC-ALL.pdf

Partnership for People with Disabilities. (2012). *Kaleidoscope: New perspectives in service coordination, level I.* Richmond: Virginia Commonwealth University.

Pletcher, L.C., & Younggren, N.O. (2013). *The early intervention workbook: Essential practices for quality services.* Baltimore, MD: Paul H. Brookes Publishing Co.

Sandall, S., Hemmeter, M.L., Smith, B.J., & McLean, M.E. (2005). *DEC recommended practices: A comprehensive guide for practical application in early intervention/early childhood special education.* Missoula, MT: Division for Early Childhood.

Shelden, M.L., & Rush, D.D. (2009, March). Tips and techniques for developing participation-based IFSP outcome statements. *BriefCASE, 2*(1).

Woods, J.J., & Lindeman, D.P. (2008). Gathering and giving information with families. *Infants & Young Children, 21*(4), 272–284. doi:10.1097/01.IYC.0000336540.60250.f2

# 4 | Implementing Intervention in Everyday Routines, Activities, and Settings

Dana C. Childress

This chapter discusses the implementation of early intervention within the context of families' natural routines, activities, and settings, including the following:

- Key concepts from the Individuals with Disabilities Education Improvement Act (IDEA) of 2004 (PL 108-446)
- A natural environments framework
- Child and family routines and activities
- Implementing early intervention with children and families
- Conducting intervention visits
- Inclusive practices
- Best practice highlights

## Case Study: Ryan

Ryan is 30 months old and has been receiving early intervention services for 2 months. He was found to be eligible for services due to global developmental delays. On a weekly basis, Ryan's mother and an educator, Alicia, meet to talk about his development and progress on the outcomes written in his individualized family service plan (IFSP), including what is going well and what is challenging about the daily routine. During these visits, Ryan's mother and Alicia interact with Ryan in ways that allow them to discover which intervention strategies might be effective to support his development. They problem-solve together, practice strategies, and plan for how Ryan's family will use these strategies between visits during their daily routines. Alicia acts as Ryan's primary service provider, with regular support from the occupational therapist and a speech-language pathologist on the team.

The outcomes on Ryan's IFSP focus on learning to engage and communicate with others, playing with toys and with his brother, and reducing the number of tantrums he has at home and when they go out in the community. Ryan's parents told the team that they were not able to go out to dinner or to take Ryan to a playgroup because of his difficulties.

He struggles with engagement and tantrums whenever anyone tries to play with him or when his needs are not met quickly enough.

For the first few intervention visits, Alicia used the time to observe Ryan and talk with his mother about what Ryan liked and disliked, his favorite activities, which daily activities went well for Ryan, and which activities were challenging. Alicia tried to get to know Ryan and his family and began to explore which priorities his mother wanted to address first. They decided to start with teaching Ryan to engage and take turns in play using one of his favorite activities, which was being pushed on the swing in the backyard. After Alicia observed them playing on the swing, she and Ryan's mother problem-solved how to teach Ryan to engage during swinging so that he could communicate that he wanted to swing more when the swing stopped (rather than cry, which was his typical reaction). They developed a strategy in which Ryan's mother stopped the swing, looked at Ryan expectantly, asked him, "Swing?" and waited briefly for his response. Alicia taught Ryan's mother to swing Ryan when he showed any sign of communication, including looking at her, making a sound, or moving his body, and to do so before he began to fuss. Alicia eventually said that they would try to teach him to say the word *swing*, but initially they just wanted him to take a turn to show that he was communicating. After several attempts, Ryan vocalized, "ing!" and his mother celebrated with an extra big push on the swing, which made Ryan laugh.

After this activity, Ryan's mother and Alicia reflected on how the strategy of prompting Ryan and waiting for his response could be used during the week in similar routines. Ryan's mother decided to try to get her husband to use this strategy when he wrestles with Ryan in the evening. Together, they wrote down their plan for how to use the strategy before the next visit and posted it on the refrigerator. The next visit was scheduled, and Alicia left the home. Ryan's mother reviewed the plan throughout the week and found that before she saw Alicia again, she was able to use the strategies that she learned to teach Ryan to look at her to get his snack in the afternoon each day. This was a significant improvement for the family because, before learning the strategies, Ryan would have a tantrum if his mother did not give him his snack immediately.

Intervention visits continued in a similar manner over the next month, addressing Ryan's development in the context of family routines. On each visit, a new routine or activity was explored that related to Ryan's IFSP outcomes. Ryan learned to use two new words to communicate and was beginning to roll a ball back and forth with his brother. His parents were not yet able to take him out in the community with any success, so Ryan's mother and Alicia decided to schedule an intervention visit to occur at the grocery store. In this way, they could problem-solve together to find ways to make the experience more successful for Ryan and the whole family.

Once the IFSP is developed, the actual implementation phase of the early intervention process begins. During the implementation of supports and services, the family–provider partnership grows, and individualized intervention strategies are developed. These strategies are used by the family during everyday routines to help the child learn functional skills and abilities, such as learning to interact with others, walk independently, play, or communicate using signs or words. The child's learning is situated within the context of the familiar activities, using the family's toys and materials, and using the child's interactions with others. The early intervention service provider supports the parent in learning how to seize the natural learning opportunities that occur in the familiar environment by using the intervention visit as a time for problem solving and practicing strategies that the parent can use to support the child's learning and participation during and between visits. The focus of intervention becomes both the child's and the parent's learning, with the service provider acting as a facilitator and coach and the parent acting as the primary agent of change for the child's development. Intervention that is provided within the context of family routines and activities builds on what families are already doing, supports them as the most important teachers in their child's life, and recognizes that most of the child's learning will occur when the service provider is not present.

For many families like Ryan's, the implementation of the IFSP is the longest phase of their early intervention experience. It is a time during which they will work collaboratively with service providers to help their children meet their goals. How this time is spent and where services occur are important and affect the impact that these services have on the child's development and the family's quality of life (Dunst, Bruder, Trivette, & Hamby, 2006). It is well established in the field of early intervention that the most effective services support families' efforts with their children in the context of daily life, rather than the early intervention service provider working directly with the child during infrequent visits. This broader view of early intervention, which moves away from a clinical model to a more family-centered approach, seeks to build family members' capacity to meet the needs of their child in the context of the natural activities and settings that they find familiar. This is where learning occurs for all children, including those with developmental delays and disabilities.

## KEY CONCEPTS FROM THE INDIVIDUALS WITH DISABILITIES EDUCATION IMPROVEMENT ACT

As was discussed in Chapter 1, early intervention has evolved in how services are provided to families since its induction to federal law in 1986. Two important concepts from IDEA 2004 are closely linked with how to provide meaningful early intervention supports and services, as discussed in the next sections.

### Enhancing the Capacity of Families

When IDEA was reauthorized, U.S. Congress recognized five "urgent and substantial needs," for providing services for young children and their families with the inception and funding of Part C early intervention. The fourth need described by U.S. Congress refers to enhancing the capacity of families to meet the needs of their children (IDEA 2004, § 631). This is a key concept in early intervention because it recognizes that families have the abilities to positively influence their children's development.

When the early intervention team builds the family's capacity, efforts focus on exploring what is important to the family, what family members are already doing to support their child's development, what resources they have, what they need to know, and how they can find and obtain resources to achieve their desired outcomes for their child. This is done through collaboration between the service provider, service coordinator, and family with the idea that the family is fully participating in the process and learning needed skills and information. Research in the field has indicated that this is what parents want from early intervention as well (Allen, 2007; Campbell, Sawyer, & Muhlenhaupt, 2009; Woods & Lindeman, 2008).

In a series of focus groups with parents of children receiving early intervention services, Campbell et al. (2009) found that parents wanted support that included information on child development and strategies they could use with their children during family activities. Parents also wanted relationships with their service providers in which providers listened to them, provided information and resources, and helped them problem-solve how to support their child's development in natural environments. Parents wanted support that prepared them to know what to do with their children to promote development, rather than relying on the service provider to work with the child. This is an important distinction because it differs from the traditional view of child intervention. Parents want to learn from early intervention service providers and apply what they learn during their natural parenting activities.

In order for early intervention to build the family's capacity, the goal of intervention must be clear from the beginning. The service provider's goal in the home (or wherever the visit may occur) is to help the parent learn strategies that he or she can use with the child to address IFSP outcomes during activities and routines that occur in daily life, which mostly happen *between* visits. The provider and parent must understand that the child's development will be most positively affected by working within the context of parent–child interactions (or interactions with other caregivers such as grandparents, child care providers, or other family members) to help the child learn the functional skills and abilities needed to participate in familiar activities (rather than the provider spending the session playing with the child). For example, a parent who might have thought she needed to leave the interventionist and her child alone during the visit to avoid interrupting "their" work will understand her important role in intervention and stay to participate in the visit. This equips the mother so that she knows how to support her child's development between visits when the provider is not present. Another example might be the parent who typically would have called her service coordinator to ask for help when she ran out of diapers for her child instead of learning to ask her neighbor or a friend for help first. This way, she learns to use familiar resources that she will have access to long after her child leaves the early intervention system.

## Natural Environments

Natural environments are another important concept that originates from the law. In IDEA 2004, the term *natural environment* appears to focus on settings where early intervention takes place, including the family's home and community settings that are typical for the child's peers without disabilities. Amendments to IDEA in the 1990s strengthened the natural environments provisions by including the wording in the definition of *early intervention services* and requiring justification for when services cannot be provided in natural environments. Similar to the emphasis on enhancing family capacity, this stronger language recognized that using a family's natural environments makes the most sense because that is where most learning happens. This provision is especially important because it also guards against early intervention services being provided in nonnatural settings, such as classrooms where the parent is not in attendance or therapy clinics that are removed from the child's normal life (Bruder, 2010).

Prior to the inclusion of the natural environments provisions in the law, services for infants and toddlers with special needs were likely to be available through outpatient clinics or other programs, if at all. Families took their children to therapy sessions or educational playgroups, and services were not available in families' homes or other community settings. As the legislation began to evolve and early intervention services became available in natural settings, the field initially saw the relocation of clinic-style interventions to family homes (Jung, 2003). Service providers brought therapy or educational materials to the home (commonly known as the "bringing the toy bag" or the "toy bag approach") and worked directly with the child while the parent observed (McBride & Peterson, 1997), using what is now known as a more traditional style of intervention. At that time, the professional was still viewed as the primary agent of change in the child's development. The activities that were accomplished during the visit were considered to be the most important activities that would affect developmental changes. The IFSP was often written with a focus on what the service provider could accomplish with the child during the intervention visit, with outcomes focused on teaching the child skills that were missed on evaluations. Early intervention programs thought they were meeting the requirements of the natural environments provisions simply by moving services into the home.

Over time, *natural environments* has come to be understood as a concept rather than primarily a setting (Woods & Kashinath, 2007). The concept of natural environments refers to the idea that infants and toddlers with delays and disabilities are best supported in their natural settings through collaboration with caregivers who can use strategies to support the child's development during natural learning opportunities occurring in daily routines throughout the week (Bruder, 2010; Dunst, Bruder, Trivette, Raab, & McLean, 2001; McWilliam, 2010; Raab & Dunst, 2004) because supports and services have enhanced the caregiver's capacity to meet the child's needs. The parent or caregiver is the agent of change, and intervention occurs wherever family members find themselves (e.g., the home, the park, grocery store, the child care provider's home). Children learn the skills they need to participate in family and community life through interactions with familiar people, using familiar materials, and in familiar contexts. Expanding beyond the law's focus on setting and revolving around the idea that the goal of intervention is to enhance the family's capacity to meet the child's needs, the concept of the natural environment provides an underlying foundation for how to implement early intervention services.

## NATURAL ENVIRONMENTS FRAMEWORK

Best practices in early intervention generally include both concepts of enhancing family capacity and supporting families in natural environments. To illustrate the characteristics of these best practices, Dunst, Trivette, Humphries, Raab, and Roper (2001) used a framework that described natural learning environment practices in terms of intervention setting, type of activity, and how intervention is provided. Using their framework, each of these characteristics can be explained as a continuum that illustrates the desired characteristics of effective early intervention.

### Intervention Setting: Contextualized or Decontextualized Learning

According to Dunst, Trivette, et al. (2001), when a child's learning is contextualized, it occurs in the context that is most meaningful to the child. This includes the experiences and settings where the behavior being learned naturally occurs. When learning is contextualized, it is more meaningful to the child and offers more opportunities for the child to practice and adapt the behavior and to generalize it to other situations (Woods & Kashinath, 2007). In contrast, learning in decontextualized settings refers to learning outside of the experiences and places where the behavior would naturally occur. When this happens, behaviors are taught in isolation outside of the functional context, and the child's ability to use the skills learned in other contexts is likely to be diminished. For example, Ryan's parents wanted him to respond when they called his name. Teaching Ryan to respond to his name would be decontextualized if it were only practiced during intervention visits, perhaps by calling Ryan's name several times without any purpose for him to respond. However, practicing this behavior during his favorite parts of the day, such as when his father arrives home from work or when playing Hide and Seek with his brother, would make this learning activity contextualized. As is apparent from the examples, contextualized learning is preferred in early intervention.

## Type of Activity: Child-Initiated or Adult-Directed Learning

The type of activity used to support learning is closely related to the context of the learning setting. When activities are child initiated, they are based on the child's interests and motivations because the child chose the activity during which intervention occurs. Information about the child's interests is gathered during the IFSP development process and is constantly updated during intervention visits by observing the child and gathering information from the family. In contrast, adult-directed activities are those that are chosen by the adult in order for the child to achieve an objective identified by the adult as important. Information relating to the objectives adults think are important is also gathered during IFSP development and ongoing assessment of the child's development. Intervention in natural environments often includes both types of activities, with adults being keenly aware of what behaviors children need to learn but using child-initiated activities as the context for learning those behaviors. Research with families has established that interventions that are both adult and child focused (i.e., they are blended to include both the child's and adult caregiver's learning and priorities) are most effective (Dunst, Trivette, et al., 2001; Woods, Wilcox, Friedman, & Murch, 2011).

Ryan regularly took his blanket to his mother and put it on her head. When he initiated this activity, his mother knew he wanted to play the Peekaboo game, which Ryan enjoyed. After talking with the educator about how to help Ryan learn his name in the context of this familiar game, Ryan's mother decided to add the phrase "Where's Ryan?" before uncovering his face to help him learn his name. She also added, "Where's Mama?" when uncovering her face to help Ryan learn her name, too. This activity is both child initiated and adult directed. It also was enjoyed by both Ryan and his mother, so it was more likely to be repeated throughout the day. Ryan got more practice learning his name than he would have if he only practiced the game during the hour each week when Alicia visited with the family.

## Practitioner: Practitioner-Absent or Practitioner-Implemented Learning

This dimension of the framework examines who is the primary supporter of the child's development and when most learning for the child occurs. Learning opportunities can and do occur when the service provider is present during intervention visits, but these visits represent a very small portion of a child's life (Bruder, 2010). The majority of learning occurs between visits, when the practitioner is not available to provide support (McWilliam, 2000), so it is reasonable that these learning opportunities should be considered and planned for as well. Therefore, learning opportunities that are implemented by the service provider without consideration for what happens between visits limit the amount of intervention the child receives (Dunst, Trivette, et al., 2001)—and ultimately limit the effectiveness of early intervention.

Practitioner-absent learning opportunities include the many rich opportunities that occur in family life that support child development. Practitioner-implemented learning opportunities are those that are provided by the practitioner with the child in the natural environment. These are not necessarily aligned with natural environment practices. A blended approach to how practitioners and families interact is preferable, with practitioners actively working with families to identify learning opportunities for the child. The parent and service provider share information and collaborate, with the goal of ensuring that the family is prepared to support the child's development whenever opportunities for learning occur.

Across these three dimensions, the most effective early intervention services are those that are contextualized, include both child-initiated and adult-directed learning, and focus on building the capacity of the family to support the child's development when professionals are not present. How these broad ideas look in practice will be different for each family. To truly individualize intervention within each family's natural environment, early interventionists must learn about child and family routines and activities, including what goes well and what is challenging, because daily life is where children learn and practice skills, interact with others, and explore their world—and that is where intervention should occur.

## CHILD AND FAMILY ROUTINES AND ACTIVITIES

On a practical level, early intervention that is aligned with the natural environments framework and the seven key principles (discussed in Chapter 1) is most effectively built around child and family routines and activities. *Routines-based intervention* refers to intervention in which a service provider collaborates with the family to practice and develop intervention strategies that can be used during specific routines that are individualized to the family's priorities and way of life. In this model, service providers must understand that they do not create or implement the routines with the family; instead, routines are defined by the family and happen naturally as part of the family's daily life, which could occur during the intervention visit but are more likely to occur between visits (McWilliam, 2010, 2012). Routines-based intervention takes the concept of natural environments and further individualizes it to the child and family level.

Researchers have found that parents of young children with disabilities can be naturally skilled with engaging their children during daily routines (Buchanan, 2009; Dunst, Hamby, Trivette, Raab, & Bruder, 2000) and are readily able to accommodate their family's activities to include their children (Diamond & Kontos, 2004; Guralnick, Neville, Hammond, & Connor, 2008; Keilty & Galvin, 2006). Parent responsiveness, or the quality of parent–child interactions, has also been found to be a key factor influencing the development of children with and without disabilities (Mahoney, 2009). Working within the context of the family routines and parent–child interactions, service providers help parents learn to identify and build on what they are already doing that supports development to help them reach their goals for their child. Intervention becomes about more than just what the child can learn by playing with toys; it strengthens the parent–child interaction so that, no matter what routine or activity is occurring, the parent can support the child's development.

Learning during familiar routines and activities benefits the child and family in many ways. Routines provide context and natural motivation for the child and family because activities are interesting to them and materials are used that they have in their environment, allowing them to have what they need to support the child's learning at any time (Woods et al., 2011). Learning within routines is also predictable for the child and parent and offers repeated opportunities for the child to practice the skill being taught (Spagnola & Fiese, 2007). Perhaps most important, routines-based intervention helps families to bridge the gap between intervention visit activities and daily life, which increases the likelihood that the skills and abilities the child learns will be maintained and generalized.

## Daily Routines and Activities Are Unique

The daily routines and activities of each child and family will be unique. This is important to remember when interacting with families because it can be easy to assume that common routines, such as mealtime or bath time, operate generally the same across families. For example, bath time in one family might occur before dinner and offer a fun time for the parent and child to play and enjoy each other. In this family, embedding intervention strategies to support the child's communication during bath time might be useful. For another family, bath time occurs before bed with three tired children in the tub. It is a necessary daily activity but not one that allows the parent to focus on the child with the delay or to think beyond completing the task at hand, which is bathing and getting the children to bed. For this family, the bath time routine is not likely to be a place where the parent can use strategies unless something about the routine is not going well and the parent wants to address that. In order to implement early intervention within the context of the natural environment, practitioners must start with learning about how families operate within their routines (Woods & Lindeman, 2008).

As discussed in Chapter 3, service providers can use a variety of questions to start conversations with families about a child's development and functioning in daily life. This conversation is continuous and occurs throughout the implementation of early intervention services, with service providers checking in with families at each visit about how routines are going, identifying any concerns or changes, and discussing progress. Because not all routines are equal in terms of opportunities to address IFSP outcomes (Woods & Kashinath, 2007), providers must listen for information about two types of routines: those that go well and those that present challenges for the child and family. Both routines offer opportunities for intervention.

**_Routines that Go Well_**    Although early interventionists tend to focus more on routines that are challenging, routines that are going well offer a rich context for intervention. Service providers can ask families if they are interested in using these routines to help their children learn the skills and activities that will promote their child's development. Routines that go well, such as wrestling with the child's father, playing in the sandbox at the park, or taking turns during playtime after breakfast, are more likely to be repeated throughout the week, offering the child repeated opportunities to learn and practice new developmental abilities during the times in which the skills are needed. Ryan's family routine of swinging in the backyard provides an example of a routine that went well and offered a natural opportunity for Ryan to learn and practice social-communication skills. As a consequence, his parents liked the idea of using this activity to promote those skills.

**_Routines that Are Challenging_**    Professionals tend to focus more on routines that are challenging by attempting to help families find ways to make them more successful. Routines that present challenges to families are important because they often involve issues related to the child's delays or disabilities. For example, Ryan's difficulties with regulating his behavior during trips to the grocery store are likely related to his difficulties with social-communication. For another family, trips to the grocery store might be challenging because the parent struggles to find a safe way for her child with cerebral palsy to sit in the shopping cart. Both are similar routines but are challenging to the families for different reasons. To learn more about why these routines are challenging, additional information must be gathered from the parent about the particulars of the routine.

## Gathering Information About Routines and Activities

As discussed in Chapter 3, information about routines, activities, priorities, and concerns is gathered during the initial IFSP development process, which occurs prior to the first intervention visit. Because this information was used to develop the IFSP outcomes, the service provider has some information with which to begin supporting the family from the very first contact. In reality, however, the IFSP is not likely to provide enough detail to design meaningful intervention strategies (McWilliam, 2010). To begin to do that, the service provider must gather more detailed information, which can be accomplished through a variety of means, including informal conversations; interviews, questionnaires, and checklists; and direct observation of the selected routine or activity (Spagnola & Fiese, 2007; Woods & Lindeman, 2008). Each is discussed here.

*Informal Conversation*    A conversation allows the provider and parent to get to know each other, establish rapport, and learn about how they can work together. Conversations during intervention visits are important means of gathering information about family routines and activities, what the child enjoys and dislikes, and what is important to the family. These conversations are important because often they uncover underlying concerns and priorities that the family did not share during the more formal IFSP development process. Early interventionists can explore specifically how the child is functioning in the daily routines and where the caregivers would like to focus their effort. When a routine is identified by the family, the interventionist should use open-ended questions to determine if the routine is one during which strategies can be embedded to support the child's development. Before assuming that a routine is an option for intervention, the interventionist should be sure to ask the parent and let him or her make this decision.

*Interviews, Questionnaires, and Checklists*    An interview, questionnaire, or checklist can be used to ensure that specific information is captured about family priorities and routines. These are typically more formal than a conversation but can be effective ways of obtaining information. Depending on the format of the tool, it can be left with the parent to be completed before the next visit, allowing him or her time to think about how to respond, or be used during the intake visit or another meeting with the family.

The Routines-Based Interview (RBI; McWilliam, 2010) is an example of a semistructured interview process that some programs conduct prior to IFSP development and the implementation of services. Information about the family's concerns, the activities and routines of a typical day, and their satisfaction with their daily routines is discussed. With each routine, very specific questions are asked regarding what everyone does during the routine (including the child) and about factors such as engagement, the child's independence, and social relationships (McWilliam, 2010). Child- and family-level needs are noted and, based on this information, IFSP outcomes are chosen and prioritized by the family to be included on the IFSP. The service provider then collaborates with the family to address the IFSP outcomes based on the rich information gathered during this assessment process.

*Direct Observation*    Direct observation of a child and family routine is another purposeful avenue for gathering information about the mechanics of a routine. When it is possible, this is usually the best method for learning how a routine works. The observation can be planned or spontaneous and is often initiated when a parent mentions a problematic or enjoyable routine during the information-gathering process. If the routine does not occur during the visit, then the provider and the parent can schedule the next visit to occur when the routine can be observed.

If the opportunity to observe presents itself during the visit, the provider should ask for the parent's permission to observe and clearly establish the purpose of the observation. For example, one of Ryan's IFSP outcomes addressed his ability to use words and approximations to request his favorite activities. During an intervention visit, Alicia observed Ryan going to the gate at the kitchen doorway and pulling on it to get to the family's new puppy. His mother said that this happens frequently throughout the day because they were house-training the puppy, who must stay in the kitchen. Alicia asked Ryan's mother what she typically does when Ryan wants the gate open. She said she opens the gate and lets Ryan in for a few minutes to play with the dog. The educator then asked if she could observe the routine to understand more about how Ryan communicated. While Ryan pulled on the gate, his mother walked over to him and said, "Okay, Ryan, step back," and then opened the latch. Ryan eagerly rushed into the kitchen and sat by the puppy. After a few minutes, Ryan's mother picked him up, which set off a tantrum, and brought him back out of the kitchen. Within moments, Ryan was back at the gate.

Because Alicia observed this frequently occurring routine, she was better equipped to more effectively problem-solve with Ryan's mother about how to turn this event into a learning opportunity for her son. Box 4.1 outlines the steps for purposeful observation of a family routine or activity.

## Exploring a Targeted Routine

Information gathering is an ongoing process that occurs at each intervention visit and informs the direction that the visit takes. Early intervention service providers must know how to gather general information about family routines as well as how to explore a specific, targeted routine in the intervention setting with the parent. Gathering information about a targeted routine typically includes at least conversation and direct observation, then quickly proceeds to considering intervention strategies based on what the parent or caregiver has already tried, as well as what needs to happen to help the child learn the targeted skills and behaviors described in the IFSP outcomes. How the service provider collaborates with the parent for this process is critically important because it is actually the parent, rather than the provider, who will be intervening with the child most often. This requires professionals to have a clear understanding of how to implement early intervention that supports both the child's and adult's learning so that intervention can occur across many routines beyond the intervention visit.

---

**BOX 4.1.    Steps for purposeful observation of a child and family routine**

- Ask for the parent's permission to observe the routine.
- Choose a vantage point that allows you to see all aspects of the routine.
- Avoid interfering with the routine and remember your role as an observer.
- Note the behaviors of each participant (parent, child, siblings).
- Note what occurs before, during, and after the routine.
- After the routine, ask if this was typically how the routine works.
- Ask for the parent's observations and reflections.
- Identify (with the parent) one aspect of the routine that he or she would like to change, improve, or use for enhancing the child's development.

After observing Ryan's routine with the puppy, Alicia asked Ryan's mother if this might be a routine where they could try to use a learning strategy to help him communicate more clearly. Ryan's mother said that she would like for Ryan to be able to ask her to open the gate to get in the kitchen. She had previously tried to teach him this phrase, but he became upset when she tried. When Ryan went to the gate again, this time Alicia coached Ryan's mother on how to prompt him to say "open" by kneeling down to Ryan's eye level, using a single-word prompt of "Open?" and waiting several seconds for Ryan to respond. After trying these strategies several times during the visit, Ryan eventually made an "oh" sound as his attempt to say "open." This frequently occurring routine became a learning opportunity for Ryan and his mother that they could implement during the week.

## IMPLEMENTING EARLY INTERVENTION WITH CHILDREN AND FAMILIES

Successful implementation of early intervention requires that service providers understand the various roles played by team members and are knowledgeable about methods for supporting child and adult learning during and between visits. Providers must also be able to adapt intervention approaches to support child development and progress toward IFSP outcomes. This knowledge of intervention roles, methods, and approaches provides a foundation on which the provider can build individualized strategies and activities that match the family's priorities and address the child's needs.

### Role of Team Members

Similar to the IFSP development process, each member of the team has an important role to play in the implementation of supports and services. The interactions that occur during intervention visits have been described as *triadic* in nature, meaning that there is a triad including the parent, child, and service provider, who interact together to support the child's development (Salisbury & Cushing, 2013; Woods et al., 2011). When the intervention triad works together, each learns from the other during visits, and the child's development is enhanced (see Figure 4.1).

***Service Provider*** The service provider sets the tone for the intervention visit based on the goals and activities of the visit and whether or not they focus on the provider's priorities or those of the family (Brorson, 2005). The provider is a facilitator of learning for both the child and the adult, as well as an explorer who intentionally tries to learn about the family's daily life.

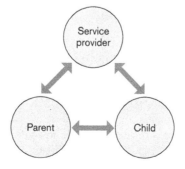

**Figure 4.1.** The early intervention triad.

Providing early intervention is a reciprocal process. When the provider interacts with the parent and the child, the provider is learning information that is needed to individualize intervention strategies to support the child's development, information about how they interact, and information about how to help the parent use strategies during daily routines. The provider is also sharing information, discussing strategies, modeling techniques, and coaching the parent or caregiver with the child. The interventionist's role is ultimately to take what he or she knows about child development, teaching, and learning, then individualize that knowledge to each child's strengths and needs, the family's priorities, and their daily lives. He or she then uses a variety of instructional strategies to help both the parent and the child learn (Sandall, Hemmeter, Smith, & McLean, 2005).

**Family Members**    Family members are encouraged to take active roles in their child's intervention. The extent of their participation will depend on their comfort level with the process and with the interventionist, as well as their general understanding of what their roles should be. It is important to remember that families do not enter the early intervention system understanding their roles (Brorson, 2005). These roles should be explained to the families so that they understand the importance of their participation and can make decisions about how they will receive support and use what they learn with their children. Clearly explaining the family's role in successful intervention also sets the tone for the relationship, so it should occur early in the intervention process. When family members understand the powerful influence they have on their child's development and are extended the invitation to participate rather than observe, then they will be more likely to take on active roles.

**Child**    The role of the child in early intervention is also one of an active participant. Intervention visits should be enjoyable for children and families. Children should be engaged and interacting with their parents during visits, with the service provider acting as a facilitator of activities that support learning for both. In fact, children should not realize that they are "working" at all because the activities that challenge the child are masked as motivating, fun, and playful interactions with people and interesting objects in their environment. The child's main role during the intervention visit is to be an engaged learner.

Within these roles, a key concept is *who* is facilitating learning for *whom*. The service provider facilitates learning for both the child and the parent, keeping in mind that facilitating the parent's learning builds his or her capacity to support the child's development. The parent facilitates the child's learning during and between visits based on what he or she learns from the service provider and how that information is integrated into what the family already does or learns to do with the child.

## Facilitating Child and Adult Learning

Because early intervention is most effective when it is both child and adult focused, interventionists must have knowledge and skills in how to support both types of learners. With infants and toddlers, development unfolds in a predictable pattern. It may unfold at a slower pace for children with developmental delays or in a different pattern for children with disabilities. Understanding infant and toddler development and instructional strategies that support development are important for all early interventionists, across all disciplines. Similarly, there are consistencies with how adults learn that are important to understand. Having knowledge of what adults need in order to learn new information, gain and use skills, and apply what they learn with their children enriches the intervention experience, making the difference between children receiving intervention once per week versus receiving intervention repeatedly in daily activities.

***Infant and Toddler Learning***   Infants and toddlers learn and develop within the context of the activities and interactions they encounter every day (Shonkoff & Phillips, 2000). They learn the skills they need through interactions with their environment, including the people, materials, and experiences in their daily lives. This is true for all children, including those with developmental delays and disabilities. Children who qualify for early intervention services may require additional support to fully participate in these activities or to learn from them, but they still learn in ways that are similar to their peers with typical development.

Infants and toddlers learn best through *interest-based activities,* which are grounded in what the child finds interesting and motivating. They learn through playful experiences and opportunities to explore the effect they have on the world around them. They enjoy repeating actions and sounds as they are learning new skills, and they often try to apply them to new activities to expand their understanding of the world.

*Multisensory learning*—learning using more than one sense (e.g., learning about cookies by feeling the squishy batter, hearing words that describe the baking process, helping to stir the ingredients, smelling the cookies baking, and tasting the warm cookies)—helps very young children to expand their knowledge and use multiple parts of the brain to absorb new information. *Repetition* is also important with infants and toddlers, who need to practice new skills over and over, typically with different people, materials, and environments, before they master them. For example, an 8-month-old child who is learning to hold and bang toys will repeatedly bang them on her high chair tray, drop them over the edge, and eventually bang them together. These repeated, playful actions teach the child how he or she relates to the environment, how to grasp and release objects, and, if the child's parents play along, how to engage others in a favorite game.

Although they have many things in common with children with typical development, infants and toddlers with delays and disabilities show developmental differences in terms of skills and abilities that they have not yet mastered. It can be easy to focus on the skills that a child has not yet mastered, according to the evaluation, and can be tempting to teach those skills, which is known as "teaching to the test." Many of the skills on developmental assessments are not particularly important to a child's development; rather, they are a way for the child to demonstrate mastery of other abilities. For example, Ryan was not able to stack three 1-inch cubes during the developmental team evaluation. His inability does not mean that he should have a stacking goal on his IFSP so that he can learn this skill. His IFSP team needs to instead consider the underlying abilities that Ryan needs to learn that can interfere with this activity, such as the fact that he is not yet engaging with another person for a social exchange longer than a few seconds, has not yet learned to imitate others or take turns (both of which would interfere with Ryan attending to, learning, or imitating the stacking task), and has difficulties with using his fingertips to hold small objects. Service providers must understand the underlying abilities that a child needs to learn in order to master a skill or participate in a family routine. Intentionally addressing these underlying abilities is more functional for the child and is more likely to result in positive effects on development than is solely teaching skills missed on a test.

As with all very young children, play and caregiving routines offer frequent opportunities for learning. Infants and toddlers learn best when they have a variety of stimulating materials, engage with responsive adults who read and respond to their cues, and are in environments that allow them to move about and hear rich vocabulary (Medina, 2010). When children have disabilities that limit their abilities to explore, hold toys, attend to others, or move their bodies in purposeful ways, the service provider and the parent must work together to adapt the environment so that the child is able to more fully participate and learn. Important developmental milestones, learning strategies, and adaptations and modifications for children with delays and disabilities will be discussed in subsequent chapters.

***Adult Learning***    Reflecting on how adults learn is integral to successful early intervention, but it is a topic about which many service providers do not receive adequate training or fully consider in their work with families. It is often erroneously assumed that parents will watch what the service provider does with the child, discuss strategies, and know what to do with their child, when in fact it is well established in the literature that adults learn through a much more active process (Trivette, Dunst, Hamby, & O'Herin, 2009). With knowledge of adult learning principles, service providers can facilitate parents' learning in ways that expand capacity and increase the parents' confidence and competence with enhancing the child's development (Raab, Dunst, & Trivette, 2010). Supporting adult learning is also aligned with the strong research consensus in the field that parents can be skilled implementers of intervention strategies with their children (Kashinath, Woods, & Goldstein, 2006; Matson, Mahan, & LoVullo, 2009; Reese, Sparks, & Leyva, 2010; Woods & Kashinath, 2007).

The following five key adult learning principles are important for early interventionists to understand when partnering with parents and other caregivers (Raab et al., 2010; Trivette et al., 2009):

1. *Adults learn best when what is being learned is immediately relevant and useful to them.* This links directly with why it is important to base the IFSP outcomes on family priorities. When the outcomes and intervention strategies address the parent's most important priorities for their child, then the parent is likely to be more invested in intervention. On the other hand, when intervention is not useful to families, or when they do not understand the relevance, service providers might find that child progress is slowed or intervention visits are missed. When these things occur, it is a good time to check in with the parent and the service coordinator to make sure that intervention is still meeting the family's most pressing needs.

2. *Adults learn best when new knowledge is built on prior knowledge.* Service providers should use open-ended questions and direct observations to find out what parents know and what they have tried to do with their children in the past. Providers can take the additional step of helping the parent reflect on what he or she knows in order to develop meaningful intervention strategies based on prior knowledge. Finding out what the parent already knows and has tried is an especially useful step in supporting the family because it helps the provider avoid giving general and unhelpful strategies and thereby wasting time. Building on what parents already know also emphasizes their roles as the main agents of change.

3. *Adults learn best through active participation and practice.* When setting the tone of the intervention visit, service providers should prepare families for active participation by assuming more of a coaching role that places the provider in the background, rather than as the primary person interacting with the child. Providers should encourage adult learners to engage the child during the visit and structure the visit so that it is viewed as an interactive learning session for the parent or caregiver, too.

4. *Adults learn and remember most successfully when what they are learning is practiced in context and in real time.* This is very different from the service provider planning activities and asking the parent to come sit on the floor to play for each visit. To use this learning principle, the service provider supports learning in the contexts where the parent and child naturally play and interact. This could be during playtime or having a snack in the kitchen, during which the provider intentionally helps the parent address IFSP outcomes within those activities. This helps the parent learn intervention strategies actively in real time, so the parent knows what to do and how to do it later in the week when the service provider is not present.

5. *Adult learners want feedback on their learning and their performance.* This positive, encouraging feedback should occur during a shared interaction during the visit or following the implementation of an intervention strategy. Providing feedback should involve the parent's reflections on how the activity went as well as the service provider sharing feedback on the activity. It is this reciprocal process of providing reflective feedback that builds and expands the parent's understanding of how to better help the child.

By addressing how both children and adults learn during visits, service providers share their knowledge and skills more directly with parents and other adult caregivers, rather than primarily using their skills to teach the child. Interventionists still interact directly with the child when needed, but they do so for the purpose of modeling activities for the adult learner so that he or she can learn to do them too. For example, Ryan's educator, Alicia, used a combination of child and adult learning techniques during their intervention trip to the grocery store. When entering the store, Ryan quickly became upset when his mother tried to place him in the cart, which was his typical response. Alicia and his mother discussed the situation and determined that Ryan might do better with a distraction before getting in the cart to make the activity more pleasant. Ryan's mother offered him a snack and gave him a playful verbal warning ("Up you go!") to prepare him for being put in the cart. While he ate his snack, Alicia and Ryan's mother discussed ways to entertain Ryan by describing the sights around the store, labeling the items being placed in the cart, and letting Ryan hold items that were appropriate. Ryan was able to sit in the cart for 10 minutes before fussing to get down, which was an important step toward his family's goal of being able to include him in family outings. It also represented a step toward opening up a new learning setting for Ryan where he could learn and practice new abilities, such as labeling foods and pictures, following directions, and interacting with others.

Early intervention, as in this example with Ryan's family, supports learning for the whole family. It can be thought of as addressing the child's development through the actions of the adult caregivers, who, with appropriate support, are in the best position to make the biggest difference in the development of the child.

## Specific Intervention Approaches

How early interventionists provide services depends on many factors, including the provider's professional and educational background and experience, his or her beliefs and values related to working with children and families, program-specific requirements, and the strengths and needs of the provider, the specific child, and the family (Bruder, 2010; Campbell & Sawyer, 2009; Raab & Dunst, 2004). Intervention is also affected by the specific intervention approach used by the professional. Three specific approaches for providing early intervention are described in the following sections.

***Routines-Based Early Intervention***    The routines-based early intervention (RBEI) approach emphasizes the importance of gathering detailed information from the family that is used to individualize the IFSP and services and then providing supportive intervention using a primary service provider (McWilliam, 2010). In this approach, detailed information is collected prior to writing the IFSP about family members' support networks, daily lives, and concerns and goals for their child and themselves. This information is gathered using two procedures: the ecomap and the Routines-Based Interview (RBI).

During the intake visit, the service coordinator works with the family to complete an *ecomap,* which is an informal representation of how the family connects to their resources. To complete the ecomap, the service coordinator asks the parent questions about who lives in the home, extended family, friends, neighbors, and others who are supports to family members, such as work colleagues or child care providers. The names of these people are placed on the ecomap and are connected by lines to indicate the levels of support provided (see McWilliam, 2010, for further details about how to draw an ecomap). The ecomap is then used by the team to try to understand the family's support system, as well as the family's strengths and needs, and to prepare for intervention. For example, Ryan's ecomap showed that his family's closest supports included his grandparents, who lived nearby, and a neighbor. As Ryan's social, communication, and play skills developed, his mother began having Ryan spend time at the neighbor's home to play with her daughter, who was close to Ryan's age. These playtimes helped to prepare Ryan for later trips to a local playgroup and eventually preschool. The process of developing and updating the ecomap helped Ryan's team use his family's resources to work toward the family's IFSP outcomes.

In the next part of the RBEI process, further information is gathered from family members about their concerns, daily routines, satisfaction with their daily routines, and their worries by using McWilliam's RBI, which was previously discussed in this chapter. The RBI helps the IFSP team to better understand the child's and family's needs, prioritize, and choose outcomes that will become part of the IFSP.

The RBEI approach also describes the implementation of a primary service provider (PSP) model of service delivery. The PSP is determined based on which professional team member has the knowledge and expertise to support the child and family based on the outcomes written in the IFSP. The PSP then visits with the family regularly to address all IFSP outcomes. The PSP and family also receive support from other consulting professional team members through *joint visits,* in which the consulting team member joins the regular intervention visit with the PSP and the family, or through team meetings without the family present. The consulting team member interacts with the family less regularly than the PSP, relying on the PSP to help the family implement strategies that are suggested by the consultant.

Using a PSP model has many benefits, including reducing the number of people and visits the family has to contend with. Early intervention should not require families to change their lives to revolve around scheduled visits. When a skilled PSP is used, there are generally fewer visits, and intervention is better coordinated. The family has one main point of contact for intervention, and this individual helps the family to integrate strategies that may have been suggested by professionals from different disciplines. The PSP works with the family to understand how to enhance the child's development across domains, contexts, and routines in a coordinated way that is difficult to achieve when multiple service providers are visiting the family separately.

Finally, the RBEI approach describes intervention visits that are support based using the four principles found in Box 4.2. These principles underscore what has been discussed

---

**BOX 4.2.    McWilliam's four principles of support-based home visits**

- The family and other constant caregivers influence the child, and we can influence the family and other caregivers.
- Children learn throughout the day—not in lessons, sessions, work times, exercise times, or goal times that concentrate the learning into just one time a day.
- All the intervention for a child occurs between visits.
- The child needs maximal intervention, not maximal services.

From McWilliam, R.A. (2010). *Routines-based early intervention: Supporting young children and their families.* Baltimore, MD: Paul H. Brookes Publishing Co.; adapted by permission.

---

so far. According to McWilliam (2010), visits that support families must also address families' emotional, material, and informational needs. Service providers must again be flexible to meet these varied needs, understanding that some families will have more needs during intervention visits than others. For instance, some families, such as Ryan's, may request more information about their child's disability; other families will ask for very little or even avoid the topic. Another parent might have significant emotional needs that distract from intervention efforts with the child, whereas other parents need little emotional support. It is possible to visit one family that has an abundance of toys and resources, then go to the next visit with a family that is unsure where its next meal will come from. Being able to manage the diversity of needs that occurs across families and across intervention visits is an essential skill for early interventionists. Gathering information from families, acting in the role of primary or consulting service provider, and providing supportive intervention visits are typical activities for providers from any discipline working in early intervention.

***Family Guided Routines Based Intervention***    The Family Guided Routines Based Intervention (FGRBI) model can also be employed by any early intervention provider, although it was initially developed for use by speech-language pathologists (Woods, 2012). It was developed to incorporate natural environment practices and includes four phases: program planning, intervention, community teaming and collaboration, and progress monitoring and transition. Prior to these phases, a welcome phase is suggested, which is similar to the intake activities described in Chapter 3.

The first phase, *program planning,* includes gathering information and developing intervention outcomes and strategies. An interview and parent–child observation is conducted. Following the child's developmental assessment, results are discussed. One or two outcomes are developed, with target routines identified as the context for addressing the outcomes. These routines must meet three criteria: 1) they must occur frequently throughout the day, 2) they are identified by the caregiver and are motivating to the child, and 3) they offer multiple opportunities for embedding learning experiences (Woods, 2012). Strategies are then identified that work across these routines to address the child's outcomes.

The second phase, *intervention,* describes how intervention visits are conducted with families in three parts:

1. *Setting the stage:* This occurs at the beginning of a visit as the interventionist gets updates about the child and family, typically relating to IFSP outcomes.

2. *Planned activities:* The service provider joins the parent and child during a planned routine that was mutually targeted based on the strategy being taught. A specific teaching strategy is taught to the parent. Then, the provider observes the parent interacting with the child and shares feedback about the use of the strategy. Examples of specific strategies used in this model include teaching the parent to use time delay (or waiting for the child to respond appropriately after a prompt), balanced turn-taking, or arranging the environment to challenge the child's development (The Florida State University, 2013). The parent and provider problem-solve together to identify other routines where the parent could use the strategy, as well as discuss a method for the family to collect data to monitor the strategy's use and the child's progress.

3. *Plans for the next visit:* The parent and service provider collaborate to identify which routines they will target on the next visit. They also discuss routines to address between visits, with emphasis on generalization and maintenance of the strategy use by the parent.

In the FGRBI model, these three steps for the intervention phase are repeated each time a new instructional strategy is taught to the parent. The focus of this model is on teaching families specific strategies that address their outcomes for their child. These steps are followed as a structure for intervention visits and as a way to monitor progress for learning in the home.

The final two phases of the FGRBI model are the *community teaming and collaboration phase* and the *progress monitoring and transition phase*. Community teaming and collaboration represents a broad effort to collaborate with any team members who are important to the child and family, including other family members, physicians, or child care providers. The progress monitoring and transition phase refers to monitoring the child's ongoing progress and preparation for transition out of the program.

The FGRBI model is a more specific intervention protocol, especially regarding what occurs during intervention visits, than the RBEI approach. The emphasis on teaching specific strategies and the format for how to teach them also differentiates this model. The next approach to early intervention, coaching, is not actually a model of intervention but rather a style of interacting with the parent during the visit, which supports the parent's learning and positively affects the child's development.

### Coaching    *Coaching is defined as*

> An adult learning strategy in which the coach promotes the learner's (coachee's) ability to reflect on his or her actions as a means to determine the effectiveness of an action or practice and develop a plan for refinement and use of the action in immediate and future situations. (Rush & Shelden, 2011, p 8)

A critical component of this interaction style is reflection, which is essential for supporting adult learning.

The intention of coaching is to help service providers move away from a role where they provide the parent with answers, give them "homework," or are the main providers of the intervention, and toward a more purposeful and collaborative role that builds the parent's capacity to work with the child. Coaching is considered to be a way of interacting with parents and others by using a series of five evidence-based practices: observation, action, reflection, feedback, and joint planning (Rush & Shelden, 2011). These practices are discussed in the following sections.

*Observation*    The preceding approaches to intervention included observation of the parent and child during their natural routines. Coaching includes parent–child observation as well, but it also includes, when needed, the parent observing the coach as the coach models a strategy with the child in the context of the routine. When the coach models for the parent, it is a purposeful learning activity to help the parent learn. The parent is instructed in specifically what to watch for during the modeling episode to support his or her reflection and understanding of the strategy.

*Action*    Actions represent how parents practice what they are learning during and between intervention visits with their children. This can occur during any activity that offers parents the opportunity to try out new skills, refine learned skills, or reflect on their use of what they are learning. If the coach is present, he or she can help the parent plan, problem-solve, and reflect on the action to make improvements and changes as needed based on the parent–child interaction and the desired outcomes of the action.

*Reflection*    Reflection refers to the process of helping parents analyze what they know or are doing so that they can recognize what they need to know or do to achieve their goals for their children and themselves. The coach should facilitate the reflection process by asking open-ended questions that enhance the parent's awareness of his or her thoughts and actions, such as "Why do you think that worked for Ryan?" The reflection process can occur during a routine with the coach present or can be used to discuss an action that occurred between visits. The idea of reflection is to help parents learn to think critically about their interactions, play, and caregiving tasks with their children and use that analysis to monitor and adjust their interactions to better support the child's development. The practice of reflection is what differentiates coaching from other approaches to early intervention.

*Feedback*    Feedback is important to supporting parents as adult learners because it helps them to understand if they are using intervention strategies correctly. It also helps parents see the positive effects of their interactions with their children. When needed, feedback also takes the form of sharing additional information to help the parent know what he or she needs to learn or to refine a skill. Parents should be encouraged to provide feedback to the coach as well about the routine and strategy use. Their feedback about the process is integral to ensuring that it is meaningful and doable in their lives.

*Joint Planning*    The joint planning step in the coaching process also differentiates it from other approaches, as it capitalizes on the adult learner's needs. *Joint planning* is a collaborative effort that involves the coach and the parent working together to identify priorities to address between visits based on what was discussed and learned during the visit. Rather than the coach (or service provider) prescribing a list of activities or exercises, the parent identifies what he or she wants to focus on or accomplish with the child before the next visit. Joint planning puts the parent in a more active role in determining what is appropriate and manageable for his or her family to address when the service provider is absent. At the beginning of the next visit, the coach reviews the joint plan with the parent to find out what successes and challenges the family has experienced since the last visit. This discussion—and in fact, the entire coaching process—supports the idea of a *shared* responsibility for the child's progress. From the joint plan discussion, the activities of the current visit flow as challenges experienced during the week are addressed and new routines are identified for embedding strategies.

According to Rush and Shelden (2011), these coaching practices do not necessarily have to occur in this order. The coach engages the family with the appropriate practice depending on the activity during which the coaching conversation occurs. Interacting with families using these practices can happen within any routine when a learning opportunity presents itself. Early intervention service providers often find that coaching some families is easier than others, depending on the family's prior knowledge of child development or expectations about intervention. Coaching can be used with all families, however, as an evidence-based practice that promotes child and adult learning.

These three approaches to providing early intervention overlap in their alignment with the natural environments framework in that they all focus on family-centered practices, emphasize contextualized learning for the child and family within familiar routines, and designate the role of the early interventionist as a learning facilitator and collaborative partner to the parent rather than a child-centered service provider. Each approach or interaction style can be employed by interventionists from any discipline as a means of sharing expertise and information with families. Perhaps most important, these approaches also include a focus on helping the family know what to do with the child between visits. Because the intervention visit represents such a short amount of time in the child's and family's life, service providers must know how to make the best use of this time so that families are well prepared to independently support their child's learning when the visit is over.

## CONDUCTING INTERVENTION VISITS

While most early intervention visits occur on a weekly schedule, for about an hour-long visit with the family, the actual decisions about how often to visit, how long a visit should last, and what to address with the family are determined during IFSP development. Intervention frequency and length are designated on the IFSP, remaining consistent until a family's priorities or needs change. What is addressed during visits and how they are conducted are more flexible, adjusting with each visit depending on the outcomes and the most pressing concerns of the child and family. It is important for service providers to be flexible and responsive to feedback from families because intervention varies across families and visits. This flexibility may also contribute to families being more successful with using the strategies as well (Kashinath et al., 2006).

Early intervention service providers must be knowledgeable about how to conduct visits that follow the family's and child's lead while also addressing the developmental outcomes written into the IFSP (Ridgley & O'Kelley, 2008). This is a delicate balance to maintain—to be responsive to the family while sharing expertise and guidance within the context of their activities. Many service providers enter the field without training in how to do this, having only had preservice training in clinical or classroom settings where they focused specifically on teaching the child (Stremel & Campbell, 2007). Providers who are more familiar with a traditional, clinical approach to intervention will find the tone of their visits feels very different from more routines-based, child- and adult-focused, collaborative intervention visits. Collaborative intervention visits are described next to prepare service providers to recognize intervention that is provided using the recommended practices described in this book.

## Collaborative Intervention Visits

Intervention visits that are responsive to both child and adult learners and are contextualized within family routines look different each time the service provider and family interact. The scheduled time and location of visits ideally change depending on the needs of the child, family, and the routine or outcome being addressed. Rather than occurring in a single static location (e.g., the living room floor), visits should occur in a variety of natural environments, such as the backyard, the playroom, the grocery store, or a local restaurant—wherever the family needs supports. The toys and materials that are present in the environment are the tools used to support learning. Although play activities are still often used as the means for teaching the child new skills and facilitating parent–child engagement and learning (Campbell & Coletti, 2013), caregiving routines are also an important context for learning opportunities and should be explored (Woods & Kashinath, 2007).

The parent is frequently and actively engaged in collaborative intervention sessions. Intervention visit time is spent as a practice session for the parent so that he or she can try out strategies with the child with the support of the service provider. The activities of the visit may be planned or may follow the child's lead. Intervention strategies are adapted to the activities and routines that occur during the visit. Direct instruction of the child is used as a technique to find out how to help the child learn, as a means of modeling strategy use, and, when needed, to facilitate the parent's learning; it is not used as the primary activity during the visit.

Because so much of what occurs during collaborative intervention visits happens through the partnership between the interventionist and the parent, their interactions must be based on a strong rapport, mutual respect and trust, and a shared understanding of each other's roles. This relationship is also important when planning for the strategies that will be tried between visits. The interventionist must be able to share his or her knowledge and expertise in such a way that allows the parent to understand how to apply it to the family's activities that occur when the intervention is not present. The interventionist and parent also plan for what to do on the next visit, meaning what routine or skill to target or what developmental issue to explore next.

## Steps for Conducting Collaborative Intervention Visits

Early intervention service providers who conduct collaborative intervention visits, such as Alicia, understand that it is their role to facilitate learning during the visit that translates into learning for the parent or caregiver and regular practice throughout the week for the child. The following seven specific steps were used by Alicia during each of her collaborative intervention visits with Ryan's family, including their visit to the grocery store.

***Step 1: Greeting and Checking In***   Upon arrival at the store, Alicia greeted Ryan and his mother. She inquired about the family's week and any new information regarding Ryan's development. The previous week's intervention plan was revisited and successes and challenges with implementing the designated strategies were discussed before they entered the store. This information was used to help Alicia and Ryan's mother determine what to do during the current visit. They decided to identify ways to help Ryan tolerate riding in the grocery cart. Once this target routine was identified, it was used as the context for the present visit's activities.

***Step 2: Discussion and Observation***   Before trying to put Ryan in the cart, the grocery store routine was discussed, with Alicia using open-ended questions to help Ryan's mother describe the routine, including what went well and what was challenging about it. Ryan's mother described their struggle with getting Ryan to sit in the cart. She would typically find a cart while still in the parking lot, pick Ryan up, and wrestle with him to place him in the seat as he squirmed and began to fuss. Once he was finally placed in the seat, he would cry and try to climb out while she pushed him into the store. Alicia then observed Ryan and his mother interacting as they normally would while Ryan's mother tried to put him in the seat. At this stage, Alicia was not yet "intervening" but was simply observing while keeping the family's goals for Ryan and the routine in mind.

When observing the family's routine is not possible, such as when the routine occurs outside of the interventionist's working hours, this discussion must be extremely detailed to include what occurs before, during, and after the routine, as well as what each participant does. This discussion, although rarely as effective as actually joining the routine, can be very useful when helping family members reflect on what they can do to improve a routine and support the child's development. Another option for remotely observing a routine is to ask the parent to digitally record the routine, if possible, so that the provider can watch the recording on the next visit and they can problem-solve together at that time.

***Step 3: Problem Solving***   After observation and discussion of the routine, Alicia opened up a problem-solving discussion using coaching techniques to encourage Ryan's mother to think through how to make changes to the routine to help Ryan learn to sit in the seat without crying or struggling. This involved identifying strategies to try with Ryan to facilitate learning of needed functional skills and abilities, such as learning to regulate his behavior and communicate using simple words.

This problem-solving discussion involved exploring Ryan's mother's prior knowledge and what she had already tried during the routine, what she needed to know in order to improve the routine, what would be most useful to her, and how she wanted to move forward to the next step, which involved practicing a strategy with Ryan. Problem solving also involved exploring the mother's need for information about the skills Ryan needed to learn. Ryan's mother shared her frustration that this routine was so troublesome. She had tried distracting Ryan with a special toy, singing to him, and letting him walk beside her (which was problematic because he tended to sit down or pull away). She recognized that Ryan did not like to ride in the cart but needed him to do it so that she could complete her shopping while her older children were at school.

Knowledge is shared by both the parent and the service provider during this step, which is important especially if it is found that the parent does not yet have the knowledge or understanding needed to help the child and would benefit from specific support, such as suggestions for what skills the child needs to learn or instructional techniques modeled with the child. It is important to avoid overloading the child or the parent during this step; otherwise, one or both of them may become frustrated. Strategies are discussed collaboratively, resulting in typically one to two new strategies that the parent is comfortable with learning during the visit.

During this discussion, Ryan's mother revealed that sometimes he behaved well when they went to a local department store and rode in a cart located in the store. Alicia asked Ryan's mother what was different about these experiences, and his mother realized that Ryan did better when placed in the cart inside the store. She wondered if Ryan was becoming upset because of the bumpy ride into the store, which might be uncomfortable for his sensory system. Together, Alicia and Ryan's mother discussed several strategies to try to change this routine and walked back out to the car to try them.

**Step 4: Practicing the Strategy**    During this step, Ryan's mother learned to use the strategies she and Alicia discussed. To get from the car to the grocery store entrance, Alicia suggested she hold Ryan's hand and walk with him. Once they reached the carts inside the store, Ryan's mother counted down "3...2...1...lift off!" and swung Ryan up into the air. After playing this game three times, Ryan "landed" in the cart seat. His mother quickly buckled him in and moved the cart forward while using her voice playfully to say, "Ready, set, go!" which was a phrase used when Ryan played on the swings in the backyard. This familiar phrase engaged Ryan and calmed him as the cart began to move. Once the cart was moving smoothly, Ryan's mother talked about the sights inside the store and let Ryan carry a banana, his favorite fruit. He tolerated riding in the cart for 5 minutes before wanting to get down.

Practicing takes different forms depending on the parent's learning needs, the child's abilities, and the tools and circumstances in the environment. Some parents benefit from seeing the interventionist model the strategy first. Other parents, such as Ryan's mother, may prefer to try to use the strategy with the child while the interventionist provides coaching and support. Other active learning techniques could include viewing a video of another parent using the strategy or recording the parent using the strategy and then watching the clip together to reflect on it.

While practicing the strategy, Ryan's mother and Alicia worked closely together to determine the most effective way for Ryan's mother to use the strategies to help him be successful. While the mother practiced the strategies with Ryan, observation and discussion continued as ways to facilitate the learning process. Over time, Alicia's support, which included modeling how to help Ryan communicate "down" to get out of the cart, will be faded out as Ryan's mother becomes more comfortable with using the strategies with him.

**Step 5: Reflection**    After the practice activity, Alicia and Ryan's mother reflected on the successes and challenges of using the strategies. Ryan's mother provided feedback about how it felt to use the strategies with her son and whether or not the new routine would be manageable within the family's daily lives. This is important information to gather. Simply because a parent is skillful with learning a strategy does not necessarily mean that it is a realistic or useful strategy for that family. Ryan's mother felt that she would be able to use these strategies when they visited the grocery store in the future, especially after she and Alicia discussed how to begin the routine again after giving Ryan a break from riding in the cart, with the goal of extending how long he tolerates the ride.

Alicia also provided feedback on her observations of the mother's use of the strategy and Ryan's reactions during the practice. She observed that Ryan tolerated the cart ride well once he was put in the cart while inside the store. She complimented his mother on her use of the strategies, noting that Ryan looked at his mother twice and approximated "Go!" when she pushed the cart forward. Helping Ryan learn to sit in the cart was becoming another learning opportunity during which Ryan could engage with his mother and practice his new expressive communication skills. If the practice session had not been successful, Alicia and Ryan's mother would have reflected on how to use the strategies differently with Ryan, then would have tried again to implement them. Practice and reflection go hand in hand in the adult learning process that occurs during the intervention visit.

***Step 6: Planning for Between Visits***   Anytime during the visit, and especially at the end, the service provider and parent should discuss what the parent is interested in doing with the child based on what was learned during the visit. Together, Alicia and Ryan's mother planned for how to implement the strategies practiced during the visit in similar routines, such as getting Ryan to sit in his highchair, that would occur after the intervention visit ended. This planning was specific and included the steps Ryan's mother will take when using these strategies, as well as an alternate plan in case she finds it challenging to use these strategies later in the week.

Some parents benefit from having this plan written down and posted in an obvious place, such as on the refrigerator, to act as a visual reminder of how to use the strategy (Childress, 2004; Dunst, Bruder, et al., 2001; Ridgley & O'Kelley, 2008). Another option for recording the plan might be digitally recording the parent using the strategy (e.g., using the parent's camera). The recording of the strategy or written plan can also be shared with other caregivers. Table 4.1 shows the intervention plan that Alicia and Ryan's mother developed at the conclusion of this visit.

***Step 7: Wrap-Up and Scheduling***   This final step involved Alicia making sure that the next visit was scheduled and that the family was comfortable with the between-visits plan. When possible, the next visit should be scheduled according to the target routine that the parent had chosen to be addressed the next time. Flexibility with scheduling is often challenging in early intervention, but it can be very beneficial when helping families and children learn across different people, places, and activities.

During any intervention visit, these steps can occur multiple times as learning opportunities present themselves. With the general exception of the first and final steps, the facilitation process used by the skillful service provider moves in and out of the other steps, helping the parent learn how to think about how any activity can present an opportunity for enhancing development, supporting the child's participation, or simply engaging the child in a playful and loving interaction. The toys and materials become less important as the parent learns how the family's interactions and activities are the keys to the child's learning.

## SPECIAL CIRCUMSTANCES THAT OCCUR DURING EARLY INTERVENTION VISITS

Even with a clear understanding of the goal of early intervention, a strong foundation in how the services should be provided, and an understanding of the steps for conducting intervention visits, many issues can arise that affect the success of intervention. How these issues are dealt with depends on the individual strengths of the service provider, but having some knowledge of these circumstances and being aware of strategies to deal with them can be helpful.

### Families Who Are Not Actively Involved During Visits

Family members choose how they wish to participate during visits. Some parents will be active from the first visit, whereas others will need time to warm up and learn how to participate. When a parent is not actively involved during visits, the service provider should first consider whether or not the parent understands his or her role in the process and what the provider can do to support the parent's participation. Considering whether or not the visits are focusing on the family's priorities and whether the strategies are helpful to the

**Table 4.1.** Intervention plan for Ryan's family

| Intervention strategy | Who will use it? | When? | Why? |
|---|---|---|---|
| Hold Ryan's hand and walk into the grocery store before getting a cart. | Ryan's parents | On each visit to the grocery store or other store with a cart | Ryan is sensitive to movement and seems to get upset by the bumpy ride across the parking lot. If you avoid this bumpy ride, you might avoid what triggers his distress at the grocery store. |
| Once in the store, play the Lift Off game several times before placing Ryan in the seat of the cart. | | When helping Ryan sit in his highchair (use similar strategies) | Learning to ride in the cart allows Ryan to join you in a new environment where he can learn to understand and say new words. Being face-to-face with you encourages his engagement and attention. |
| Once buckled in, play the Ready, Set, Go! game using an expressive voice and face to make sitting in the cart a fun activity. On "Go!" push the cart forward. | | | Using phrases such as "3…2…1…lift off!" and "Ready, set, go!" help Ryan anticipate what is coming next, making it easier for him to manage his behavior. |
| If Ryan is engaged with you, say, "Ready, set…" and wait a few seconds while looking at him with an expectant look on your face. This will communicate that it is his turn to make a sound or gesture. Once he vocalizes, waves his hand, or says, "Go," repeat, "Go!" and move the cart forward. | | | Pushing the cart when Ryan says, "Go," and allowing Ryan breaks when he communicates that he wants out of the seat help him understand that his sounds, gestures, and words have meaning and can be used to get his needs met. |
| Talk to Ryan about the sights around the store. | | | |
| Visit the fruits and vegetables first. Let Ryan hold a fruit or vegetable to keep his hands busy or offer Ryan a special snack to eat while sitting in the cart. | | | |
| Let Ryan handle safe objects, such as small vegetable cans. Ask him to help you choose between foods. Keep him engaged during the ride. | | | |
| If he wants to get down, push the cart forward another foot and ask him, "You want down?" Lift him out of the cart for a short break. | | | |
| Repeat the routine to get him back in the cart if possible. | | | |
| Keep your visits to the grocery store short at first, just as long as Ryan can tolerate. Over time, you will work on extending how long he can ride in the cart. | | | |

family are also important. Another reason parents might be unable to actively focus on the activities of the visit could be related to their concern with greater needs, such as impending homelessness, a job loss, or the complexity of the child's health care needs. Regularly checking in with families and with the service coordinator are very useful strategies when questions arise about how to help families get the most out of their visits.

## Lack of Materials in the Home

Providing services in settings that lack toys and other developmentally appropriate materials can be challenging for interventionists. It is important to keep in mind that the majority of what children learn is not from their toys; it is from the interactions that occur in their environment. Similar interactions can and often do occur with other materials. Regardless of the quality or amount of materials available, the service provider should work closely with the parent to find ways to use what the family has and what they like to do to support the development of skills the child needs to participate in daily activities. New activities and interactions that fit into the family's day may also be suggested. For example, rather than emphasizing that Ryan needs to learn to stack 1-inch cubes because he did not pass that item on the assessment, he could practice helping his brother put canned goods away in the pantry, which would let him practice how to grasp and release objects as the cube activity would. This activity also allows Ryan to take turns and pay attention long enough so that the cans line up and stay stacked. If a child and family would benefit from a particular toy or piece of equipment to help the child learn, loaning the family the item could also be an option.

## Families Who Do Not Use Strategies Between Visits

When families are not using strategies between visits, they could be struggling with making the leap from what happens during the visit when they have the provider's immediate support to being on their own. In this case, having a coaching conversation with the family can be very helpful to uncover the source of the problem and then to brainstorm solutions. The family might need a better developed plan, or perhaps there is another priority that is more important for the family. More practice or problem solving might be needed during the visit to better prepare the parent or caregiver. Another possibility might be that the child is spending time with another caregiver who needs to be included in intervention planning. Perhaps the family is overwhelmed with early intervention strategies and needs to work on one at a time, rather than receiving multiple strategies at once. Gauging a family's comfort level and success requires regular check-ins at each visit.

## Siblings

Siblings are some of the most important people in an infant's or toddler's life. Siblings often know how to motivate each other and what activities the child prefers. They enjoy being a part of the intervention process. Including them in intervention visit activities is essential and often highly desired by the sibling and parent. The service provider and parent can develop strategies based on an activity that the siblings enjoy doing together or build activities that develop positive relationships between siblings.

However, siblings can also be distracting during visits, such as when they seek the attention of the parent or service provider. Managing the inclusion of siblings during visits depends on the preferences of the parent and the ages of the siblings. Older siblings can be involved by being given a specific job to do, such as holding the toy while the toddler tries to activate it or calling the child's name to encourage crawling. Visits can be scheduled when younger siblings are napping or in child care, if this is preferred by the family. Asking families how they would like a sibling to be involved during visits is always a good idea.

## Parents with Special Needs

Supporting parents with special needs offers its own set of unique challenges for the service provider. Family-centered practices continue to guide service provision, but how the parent is supported may need to be further individualized. Parents with special needs might require additional time to learn how to use strategies with their children and might benefit from strategies being broken down into smaller steps. If the parent struggles to maintain attention to the child and provider during the visit, taking frequent breaks, adjusting the length of visits, or scheduling visits when there are fewer distractions could be helpful. Additional supports might also be needed to help parents remember scheduled visits, such as recording the date of the next visit on a calendar in the home or in the parent's mobile phone. When other people are involved in assisting the parent, such as relatives or case managers, the early intervention team may find communicating with them to be valuable as well, with parental permission.

## Cultural and Linguistic Issues

Working with families from different cultural and linguistic backgrounds often requires that service providers collaborate across agencies. Intervention providers and service coordinators might collaborate with refugee resettlement programs, social service agencies, and community churches that provide resources to families who are new to the country. Communication is typically the most pressing issue, requiring that the service provider work closely with an interpreter to ensure that the family understands and is able to participate in the activities of the visit. Documentation that the family receives, such as the IFSP, must be translated into the family's native language as well, either in writing or orally. Service providers should also make efforts to learn about family members' culture and how their priorities for their child are affected by their beliefs and values. This is true for every family, but it can be challenging for providers when collaborating with families from backgrounds that are different from their own. Print and online resources are available to help early intervention providers learn about different cultures. When in doubt, having a conversation with family members about their cultural beliefs can be an important and respectful step.

## Safety

The safety of service providers is a high priority for any early intervention program. Many programs offer safety trainings and other protocol to keep their staff safe. For example, shared calendars or other electronic systems that track the schedules of providers are common so that a provider's whereabouts are known at all times. When making a visit in an area of the community where safety is a concern, program protocol might require the service provider to check in with the office throughout the day, make visits in the morning when fewer people are milling around, bring a colleague, and/or make visits in pairs. Two important safety tips for all early intervention service providers include always keeping a mobile phone with them during visits and being aware of their surroundings. When service providers feel that their safety is in question, the most important thing to remember is to excuse themselves from the situation and call their supervisor.

The provider's supervisor and colleagues are some of the best resources for assistance when managing special circumstances such as these. Asking questions, learning strategies for managing different situations, and growing as a professional are actually very similar to how the knowledge and skills of families grow while in early intervention. Through collaboration, maintaining a strong interest in learning, and the willingness to share expertise, the service provider is better prepared for conducting successful intervention visits.

## INCLUSIVE PRACTICES

In addition to supporting the child's development within the context of everyday family activities, the early intervention team also helps the family ensure that the child is included in activities and settings beyond the family and home environment. These activities and settings might include child care settings, playgroups, or family outings such as trips into the community for shopping, dining out, visiting a museum, or whatever activity the family likes to do or would like to do.

Inclusive practices underlie the provision of early intervention services that enhance family capacity in natural environments. When families need support and children need to learn functional skills in settings other than the home environment, the same practices are used as those already described in this and previous chapters. Whenever possible, the service provider should join the family in the alternate setting and help family members find ways to promote the child's learning and participation in the desired activity. For example, if Ryan's IFSP included an outcome related to being able to join his family for an entire meal without having a tantrum, then this outcome might be addressed at the kitchen table as well as in the family's favorite restaurant, both of which could be locations for visits and require different intervention strategies.

### Community-Based Playgroups

Attending a playgroup, storytime in a local library, or a swim class can offer infants and toddlers rich opportunities to interact with peers and develop social-communication skills. Families of very young children with disabilities can find it challenging to participate in these community groups because of their child's behavioral or developmental differences or the parent's discomfort. Talking with the group leader prior to attending, observing the group, and sharing ideas on how to adapt activities can be ways that the interventionist may help the parent prepare for participating in a community outing. The early interventionist can also accompany the family to provide support during the group activities, then fade out the support as the parent and child feel comfortable and the child is fully included.

### Child Care Settings

Promoting inclusive practices in child care settings represents a special situation for the early intervention service provider. In this setting, the interventionist works closely with the child care provider or teacher to consider how to take advantage of and adapt natural learning opportunities as they occur to address the child's development (Winton, Buysse, Turnbull, Rous, & Hollingsworth, 2010). Building an equal partnership with the child care provider is important because he or she will be using strategies with the child while the child is attending child care. This situation requires that the provider not only help the child care provider develop strategies to use with the child to teach needed skills and abilities, but that the strategies must be manageable for the child care provider to use while caring for other children. In addition, the child care provider also needs to think beyond teaching specific skills and consider how to ensure that the child is able to fully participate in the activities offered to all children in the classroom. This might involve considering appropriate positioning of the child and ordering equipment, learning how to adapt classroom activities, supporting peer interaction, and clarifying expectations regarding the child's participation. Any strategies used at child care should also be shared with the parent so that the family can use them at home with the child as well. This can be accomplished through phone calls or e-mails with the parent, digitally recording the visit at child care and sending it to the parent, exchanging a notebook describing the visit, or scheduling an occasional visit with the parent present (whenever possible for the parent's schedule). It is vital to maintain regular contact with the parent when the service provider has primary contact with the child care provider.

The natural environments provision of IDEA addresses helping children engage in activities that their peers without disabilities would be doing, but this does not mean that programs must create playgroups or that attending a group should be a requirement for all children enrolled in a program. Rather, this provision means that children and families should have the support they need to be able to engage in the activities they desire, within their families and their communities. How these natural learning opportunities occur will depend on the resources of a specific program and community. The purpose is the same, however—for all children and families to be valued and included in the community.

## BEST PRACTICE HIGHLIGHTS

The following best practices should guide service providers as they collaborate with families to implement early intervention supports and services in everyday routines, activities, and settings:

- Implementing early intervention supports and services in natural environments builds the family's capacity to meet the child's needs and promotes the child's development during daily activities and routines.

- All children learn in the context of their everyday activities. Early interventionists help families recognize what they are already doing and build on that to help children learn the skills and abilities they need in order to achieve their IFSP outcomes and more fully participate in family and community life.

- Early intervention service providers are facilitators of child and adult learning. They use a variety of instructional strategies to help both learners gain knowledge and skills. Providers take what they know about child development, teaching, and learning, then individualize that knowledge to each child's strengths and needs, the family's priorities, and their routines and activities.

- Recommended practices for implementing effective early intervention include providing support that is contextualized, is child and adult focused, and emphasizes the interactions and learning opportunities that occur between visits when the interventionist is not available to provide parents or caregivers with support.

- Gathering information from families is an ongoing process. Each interaction between parents and service providers should be used to learn about child and family routines and activities, including what goes well and when challenges occur.

- Routines-based, collaborative intervention visits include the following steps: greeting and checking in, discussion and observation, problem solving, practicing the strategy, reflection, planning for between visits, and wrap-up and scheduling.

- Interventionists must be flexible to adjust to families' changing needs and the special circumstances that arise when providing early intervention. They should understand that no two families are the same, just as no two intervention visits are the same.

## CONCLUSION

Implementing early intervention in natural routines, activities, and settings opens up many more learning opportunities for the child than can possibly happen during a visit with a service provider that occurs once or twice per week (Dunst et al., 2000). When interventionists adopt the perspective that they can help families affect the child's learning across the broader scope of the activities of the family's daily life, as well as engage parents in ways that increase their ability to support their child's development, infants and toddlers ultimately receive more intervention because it is provided both during and between visits. For Ryan and his family, this meant taking advantage of intervention visit time to explore activities that Ryan enjoyed or routines that were challenging; problem-solving and reflecting together with Alicia; and developing strategies that, once embedded into their routines, were effective at helping Ryan learn the skills and abilities he needed to further his development and reach his IFSP outcomes.

## DISCUSSION QUESTIONS AND APPLIED ACTIVITIES

1. Explain the natural environments framework in your own words and provide two examples of intervention activities that illustrate each component of the framework.
2. Describe why having knowledge of adult learning principles is important when providing early intervention.
3. Observe an intervention visit with your local early intervention program. Summarize your observation of the visit by discussing the following:
   - The activities and settings of the visit
   - How the parent and provider interacted
   - What questions the service provider used to gather information
   - How the provider supported parent–child interactions
   - What developmental skills and abilities the child was learning
   - Whether or not the visit included the steps of a collaborative intervention visit

   Did the visit fit the concept of natural environments described in this chapter? Why or why not? Be sure to include suggestions for how the visit could be improved.

## REFERENCES

Allen, S.F. (2007). Parents' perceptions of intervention practices in home visiting programs. *Infants & Young Children, 20*(3), 266–281. doi:10.1097/01.IYC.0000277757.95099.47

Brorson, K. (2005). The culture of a home visit in early intervention. *Journal of Early Childhood Research, 3*(1), 51–76. doi:10.1177/1476718X05051346

Bruder, M.B. (2010). Early childhood intervention: A promise to children and families for their future. *Exceptional Children, 76*(3), 339–355.

Buchanan, M. (2009). The home play of toddlers with disabilities: Contexts and maternal perspectives.

*International Journal of Disability, Development, and Education, 56*(3), 263–283. doi:10.1080/10349120903102296

Campbell, P.H., & Coletti, C.E. (2013). Early intervention provider use of child caregiver-teaching strategies. *Infants & Young Children, 26*(3), 235–248. doi:10.1097/IYC.0b013e318299918f

Campbell, P.H., & Sawyer, L.B. (2009). Changing early intervention providers' home visiting skills through participation in professional development. *Topics in Early Childhood Special Education, 28*(4), 219–234. doi:10.1177/0271121408328481

Campbell, P.H., Sawyer, L.B., & Muhlenhaupt, M. (2009). The meaning of natural environments for parents and professionals. *Infants & Young Children, 22*(4), 264–278. doi:10.1177/0271121408328481

Childress, D.C. (2004). Special instruction and natural environments: Best practices in early intervention. *Infants & Young Children, 17*(2), 162–170.

Diamond, K.E., & Kontos, S. (2004). Families' resources and accommodations: Toddlers with Down syndrome, cerebral palsy, and developmental delay. *Journal of Early Intervention, 26*(4), 253–265. doi:0.1177/105381 510402600402

Dunst, C.J., Bruder, M.B., Trivette, C.M., & Hamby, D.W. (2006). Everyday activity settings, natural learning environments, and early intervention practices. *Journal of Policy and Practice in Intellectual Disabilities, 3*(1), 3–10. doi:10.1111/j.1741-1130.2006.00047.x

Dunst, C.J., Bruder, M.B., Trivette, C.M., Raab, M., & McLean, M. (2001). Natural learning opportunities for infants, toddlers, and preschoolers. *Young Exceptional Children, 4*(3), 18–25. doi:10.1177/109625060100400 303

Dunst, C.J., Hamby, D., Trivette, C.M., Raab, M., & Bruder, M.B. (2000). Everyday family and community life and children's naturally occurring learning opportunities. *Journal of Early Intervention, 23*(3), 151–164. doi:10.1177/105381510002300030501

Dunst, C.J., Trivette, C.M., Humphries, T., Raab, M., & Roper, N. (2001). Contrasting approaches to natural learning environment interventions. *Infants and Young Children, 14*(2), 48–63.

Florida State University, The. (2013). *Parent Strategy Handouts.* Retrieved from http://fgrbi.fsu.edu/model.html

Guralnick, M.J., Neville, B., Hammond, M.A., & Connor, R.T. (2008). Mothers' social communicative adjustments to young children with mild developmental delays. *American Journal of Mental Retardation, 113*(1), 1–18.

Individuals with Disabilities Education Improvement Act (IDEA) of 2004, PL 108-446, 20 U.S.C. §§ 1400 *et seq.*

Jung, L. (2003). More is better: Maximizing natural learning opportunities. *Young Exceptional Children, 6*(3), 21–26. doi:10.1177/109625060300600303

Kashinath, S., Woods, J., & Goldstein, H. (2006). Enhancing generalized teaching strategy use in daily routines by parents with children with autism. *Journal of Speech, Language, and Hearing Research, 49,* 466–485. doi:10.1044/1092-4388(2006/036)

Keilty, B., & Galvin, K.M. (2006). Physical and social adaptations of families to promote learning in everyday experiences. *Topics in Early Childhood Special Education, 26*(4), 219–233. doi:10.1177/027112140602600 40301

Mahoney, G. (2009). Relationship focused intervention (RFI): Enhancing the role of parents in children's developmental intervention. *International Journal of Early Childhood Special Education, 1*(1), 79–94.

Matson, J.L., Mahan, S., & LoVullo, S.V. (2009). Parent training: A review of methods for children with developmental disabilities. *Research in Developmental Disabilities, 30,* 961–968. doi:10.1016/j.ridd.2009.01.009

McBride, S.L., & Peterson, C. (1997). Home-based early intervention with families of children with disabilities: Who is doing what? *Topics in Early Childhood Special Education, 17*(2), 209–233. doi:10.1177/0271121497017 00206

McWilliam, R.A. (2000). It's only natural...to have early intervention in the environments where it's needed. In S. Sandall & M. Ostrosky (Eds.), *Young Exceptional Children Monograph Series No. 2: Natural Environments and Inclusion* (pp. 17–26). Denver, CO: Division for Early Childhood of the Council for Exceptional Children.

McWilliam, R.A. (2010). *Routines-based early intervention: Supporting young children and their families.* Baltimore, MD: Paul H. Brookes Publishing Co.

McWilliam, R.A. (2012). Implementing and preparing for home visits. *Topics in Early Childhood Special Education, 31*(4), 224–231.

Medina, J. (2010). *Brain rules for baby: How to raise a smart and happy child from zero to five.* Seattle, WA: Pear Press.

Raab, M., & Dunst, C.J. (2004). Early intervention practitioner approaches to natural environment interventions. *Journal of Early Intervention, 27*(1), 15–26. doi:10.1177/105381510402700102

Raab, M., Dunst, C.J., & Trivette, C.M. (2010). Adult learning process for promoting caregiver adoption of everyday child language learning practices: Revised and updated. *Practically Speaking, 2*(1). Retrieved from http://www.cecll.org/download/Practically_Speaking _v2n1.pdf

Reese, E., Sparks, A., & Leyva, D. (2010). A review of parent interventions for preschool children's language and emergent literacy. *Journal of Early Childhood Literacy, 10*(1), 97–117. doi:10.1177/1468798409356 987

Ridgley, R., & O'Kelley, K. (2008). Providing individually responsive home visits. *Young Exceptional Children, 11,* 17–26. doi:10.1177/1096250608315936

Rush, D.D., & Shelden, M.L. (2011). *The early childhood coaching handbook.* Baltimore, MD: Paul H. Brookes Publishing Co.

Salisbury, C.L., & Cushing, L.S. (2013). Comparison of triadic and provider-led intervention practices in early intervention home visits. *Infants & Young Children, 26*(1), 28–41. doi:10.1097/IYC.0b013e3182736fc0

Sandall, S., Hemmeter, M.L., Smith, B.J., & McLean, M.E. (2005). *DEC recommended practices: A comprehensive guide for practical application in early intervention/early childhood special education.* Missoula, MT: Division for Early Childhood.

Shonkoff, J.P., & Phillips, D.A. (2000). *From neurons to neighborhoods: The science of early childhood development.* Washington, DC: National Academies Press.

Spagnola, M., & Fiese, B.H. (2007). Family routines and rituals: A context for development in the lives of young children. *Infants & Young Children, 20*(4), 284–299. doi:10.1097/01.IYC.0000290352.32170.5a

Stremel, K., & Campbell, P.H. (2007). Implementation of early intervention within natural environments. *Early Childhood Services, 1*(2), 83–105.

Trivette, C.M., Dunst, C.J., Hamby, D.W., & O'Herin, C.E. (2009). *Characteristics and consequences of adult learning methods and strategies.* Retrieved from http://tnt.asu.edu/files/AdultLearning_rev7-04-09.pdf

Winton, P.J., Buysse, V., Turnbull, A., Rous, B., & Hollingsworth, H. (2010). *CONNECT Module 1: Embedded interventions.* Chapel Hill: The University of North Carolina, FPG Child Development Institute.

Woods, J. (2012). *Final report: Family guided routines based intervention (FGRBI) model.* Retrieved from http://fgrbi .fsu.edu/final.html

Woods, J.J., & Kashinath, S. (2007). Expanding opportunities for social communication into daily routines. *Early Childhood Services, 1*(2), 137–154.

Woods, J.J., & Lindeman, D.P. (2008). Gathering and giving information with families. *Infants & Young Children, 21*(4), 272–284. doi:10.1097/01.IYC.0000336540.60250.f2

Woods, J.J., Wilcox, M.J., Friedman, M., & Murch, T. (2011). Collaborative consultation in natural environments: Strategies to enhance family-centered supports and services. *Language, Speech, and Hearing Services in Schools, 42*, 379–392. doi:10.1044/0161-1461(2011/10-0016)

# III

Enhancing Infant and Toddler
Development and Participation

# 5 | Developing Positive Social-Emotional and Communication Skills

Corrin G. Richels and Sharon A. Raver

This chapter discusses the foundations of social-communicative skills, including the following:

- Typical communication and social development
- Effects of early experience on communication, language and social-emotional development
- Practices for encouraging the first Office of Special Education Programs (OSEP) child outcome
- Principles and practices of early language intervention
- Best practice highlights

## Case Study: Joel

Joel is an 11-month-old boy who was born full term following a prolonged, complicated labor. Since his birth, Joel showed signs of low muscle tone, which affected his ability to breast feed and resulted in a dramatic weight loss in his first weeks of his life. Joel is the second child born to a two-parent family. He was referred to his local early intervention program by his pediatrician at 4 months old due to his failure to meet early motor milestones. An individualized family service plan (IFSP) was developed with outcomes that reflected Joel's family's desire to integrate his speech-language, social-emotional, motor, and cognitive needs. Services began immediately and were provided by an early childhood special educator, who initially acted as the primary service provider and met with the family once every 2 weeks. The educator supported the family in encouraging Joel's abilities to feed himself, socially engage others, use early gestures and words, and explore his environment. As Joel's feeding needs progressed, an occupational therapist became the primary service provider. The team focused on improving Joel's pinching and grasping skills that were important for his independent feeding. They also continued to monitor his development in other areas. Joel's 8-year-old sister, Melissa, was present for all intervention visits and was a great support to Joel, according to her parents.

The first OSEP (2010) child outcome, "Positive social-emotional skills (including social relationships)," addresses how a child's attachment to the significant others in the child's world provides the foundation for learning. This outcome includes how a child expresses emotions and feelings, how the child responds to social rules and situations, and how these relationships and other knowledge help a child to make sense of his or her physical and social worlds. In other words, children learn through communication and positive social interactions about how to engage, respond, and interact meaningfully with others. The Early Childhood Outcomes Center (ECO) elaborated on this outcome:

> Making new friends and learning to get along with others is an important accomplishment of the early childhood years. Children develop a sense of who they are by having rich and rewarding experiences interacting with adults and peers. They also learn that different rules and norms apply to different everyday settings and that they need to adjust their behavior accordingly. This outcome involves relating to adults, relating to other children, and (for older children) following rules related to groups or interacting with others. The outcome includes concepts and behaviors such as attachment/separation/autonomy, expressing emotions and feelings, learning rules and expectations in social situations, and social interactions and social play. (2009, p. 1)

Like all three OSEP child outcomes, this outcome statement does not address one or two developmental domains. Rather, it integrates multiple domains as it attempts to look at a child's functional competence in a variety of settings, with a variety of materials and a variety of people. As stated, this outcome addresses many traditional domains: fine and gross motor skills, as well as cognitive, communication, and social-emotional development. Following a strict domain-focused intervention approach will not allow service providers to gather information that reflects a child's progress on this child outcome because it is concerned with more subtle, integrated functioning. Assuming a "big picture" approach is the best way to address the broad, nonlinear philosophy exemplified in the OSEP child outcomes. This outcome is attempting to capture how a very young child integrates these multiple domains to show how the child interacts with his or her social world (positive social relationships) and how the child manages his or her expression of feelings and emotions. This first OSEP child outcome attempts to answer the following questions:

- How does the child relate to family members, close family friends, caregivers, and strangers?
- How does the child relate to other children at child care or in the neighborhood?
- How does the child show his or her feelings? How does the child calm down when upset?
- How does the child show that he or she understands social rules, such as sharing and taking turns? (National Parent Technical Assistance Center, 2013)

Social development and communicative development are explicitly linked in the birth-to-3 period of development. This chapter provides background knowledge regarding the typical acquisition of skills and knowledge in social-communicative development. Social-communicative development involves social skills, such as interaction and the expression of emotions, as well as the child's ability to comprehend and produce communication (Rossetti, 1996). This developmental coverage will provide a foundation for best practices and recommended interventions. There is also a discussion of how to integrate the teaching of these skills in a number of ways within families' daily routines.

Appropriate communication, social, and emotional development is crucial for being able to function in any community. Even before birth, infants with normal hearing mechanisms receive information about their social world by hearing their mother's voice and the sounds of her environment. Infants' womb experiences prepare them for entering the world with the capacity to interact. Infants' first cries, grunts, yawns, and head turns begin their attempts to communicate with their caregivers and begin the process of getting their needs met. How their needs are met helps to shape infants' emotional health, and it either strengthens or deters their desire to be part of the social world. Children born with disabilities may miss some of these first opportunities to take part in the social-communicative exchanges that define the human experience.

Early intervention service providers, whether they are early childhood special educators or professionals from other disciplines, are essential in teaching caregivers strategies to ensure that every child has as much access as possible to opportunities to successfully interact with his or her environment. Infants and toddlers with disabilities or delays have the potential to achieve an impressive number of foundational skills before their third birthday in the areas of social-emotional and communication development. To identify what a child needs to learn, professionals use typical communication and social development as a measurement in combination with family priorities for these areas of development.

## TYPICAL COMMUNICATION AND SOCIAL DEVELOPMENT

As noted, communication and social development are often referred to as social-communicative development in children younger than 3 years because they are interdependent domains of development. *Communication* occurs when a person receives information from or conveys feelings, emotions, ideas, thoughts, or desires with someone else. Communication can involve the use of words, sounds, signs, gestures, or alternative or assistive devices. Human beings are social creatures; as a consequence, social and emotional skills develop out of a need to communicate with others. Communication skills develop when people interact socially and express their thoughts and emotions. This direct interplay makes it essential that service providers target communication, social, and emotional skills as a unit rather than as a series of independent skills.

One theory supporting the interaction of these domains is called the transactional theory of skill development. The *transactional theory* asserts that the child both shapes and is shaped by his or her environment, and the interplay between the two is pivotal to learning (Lazarus & Folkman, 1987). From birth to 3 years, infants and toddlers learn to integrate their sensory sensations and use their motor skills to engage the social and inanimate worlds around them. This transactional relationship is easiest to see as children progress from their first sounds to eventual conversations. This period of development is called the prelinguistic period.

### Prelinguistic Communication Development

*Prelinguistic development* is the period that generally spans from birth until the first year, when infants begin to meaningfully combine sounds into words. Infants come into the world equipped to make sounds. The progression of these noises and sounds, also called *vocalizations*, to true words is divided into five stages that become progressively more complex as development occurs. The stages of prelinguistic sound development have been described by Stark (1986) as the following:

- *Stage 1:* reflexive crying and vegetative sounds
- *Stage 2:* cooing and laughter
- *Stage 3:* vocal play

- *Stage 4*: canonical babbling
- *Stage 5*: jargon

These stages are described in Table 5.1. It is important to remember that all children show a good deal of variability in when specific skills develop, so the developmental age references provided reflect the months that most children move from one stage to the next.

As early interventionists, it is necessary to understand the reason a particular child has been referred for early intervention services or is currently being served. This is frequently because the child has already shown that he or she is not able to acquire social-communicative skills in the way children without delays have been able. However, through coaching and collaboration, parents and other caregivers can be guided to provide the repetition, positioning, or stimulation necessary to foster those essential skills. Each prelinguistic stage is discussed in the following sections.

**Stage 1: Reflexive Crying and Vegetative Sounds**    This stage of prelinguistic development generally spans from birth through the first 8 weeks, or approximately the first 2 months of life. During this time, infants manifest very little gross and fine motor control. As a consequence, sound production is a virtually random act resulting from air passing through the vocal folds of the voice box. This stage is defined by the nonintentional production of noises. Early crying is a reflexive behavior that is believed to stem from an automatic response to internal stimuli or the physical states of the child. Vegetative sounds are generally associated with nonfeeding and feeding activities. Nonfeeding sounds are generally grunts and sighs produced during various activities, such as stretching, yawning, or moving. Feeding sounds are burps, snorts, lip smacking, and tongue clicks associated with eating.

**Stage 2: Cooing and Laughter**    This stage of development generally spans from 8 weeks (2 months) to 16 weeks, or approximately 4 months of life. Infants begin to develop gross motor control and are beginning to roll over and independently hold up their heads. Sound production consequently becomes more controlled as well. This stage is defined by the emergence of laughing at approximately 8 weeks of age and a reduction in crying around 12 weeks. Infants also begin the production of consonant-like and vowel-like combinations. The consonant-like sounds include /k/, /g/, /m/, and /n/ sounds typically made when the infant is in a content state. These consonant-like sounds are usually paired with vowels like /u/, so infants frequently vocalize a "coo" sound—hence the name of the stage.

**Table 5.1.**    Prelinguistic stages of communication development

| Skill | Age of acquisition | Examples |
| --- | --- | --- |
| *Stage 1:* Reflexive crying and vegetative sounds | Birth to 2 months | Cries, coughs, grunts, burps, sighs |
| *Stage 2:* Cooing and laughter | 2–4 months | Consonant-like and vowel-like combinations that are made when infants are in a content state |
| *Stage 3:* Vocal play | 4–6 months | Vowel-like variations, pitch and volume play |
| *Stage 4:* Canonical babbling | 6 months to first words | Reduplicated babbling (/baba/) and variegated babbling (/adabaga/) |
| *Stage 5:* Jargon | 10 months and older | Sound combinations and intonation that are adultlike without being actual words |

*Source:* Stark (1986).

In the case study, Joel's communication development was approximately in this stage. Despite being 11 months old, he was unable to sit independently or consistently grasp and hold objects. Nonetheless, he smiled frequently and had a strong giggle. His connection to others was strong, so social interactions were used as motivators to build skills in the gross and fine motor domains, which were difficult for him.

**Stage 3: Vocal Play**    This stage of prelinguistic development overlaps with Stage 2, but it generally spans from 4 to 6 months old. During this period, infants gain more control over their bodies and are able to roll in both directions and sit with support while managing their own head control. They also begin to be able to support their own weight on their legs when held in standing position and transfer an object from one hand to the other when playing in a *supine position* (lying on his or her back) or in supported sitting.

This new supported sitting posture and beginning locomotion also coincide with more variety in infants' vocal behavior. Being in a sitting position changes the pull of gravity on oral structures, such as the tongue and jaw, which allows for the development of vocal production skills that cannot be achieved when an infant is lying flat on his or her back. For this reason, a child such as Joel, who is older but physically delayed, would need to be placed in the sitting position often by caregivers to facilitate vocal and motor development.

The major feature of this stage is the variation in tongue height and position that infants achieve, leading to sounds that are vowel-like with squeals, squeaks, and raspberries (i.e., blowing of air through both lips). Furthermore, infants in this stage also play with their volume control, resulting in squeals that can start out as a quiet growl and quickly achieve a high pitch at a volume that draws attention from others around them.

**Stage 4: Canonical Babbling**    This stage generally spans from approximately 6 months old and can continue to about the time that first words appear, generally occurring between 10 and 12 months of age. Again, major strides in motor development emerge. Infants are sitting up independently, can easily roll from stomach to back and back to stomach, and are typically crawling. Some infants may also be taking their first steps toward walking. Another major milestone involves the introduction of foods other than milk. With the advent of solid food consumption around 6 months of age, infants have the opportunity to get more face-to-face interaction time with parents as the parent sits in front of the child and offers food on a spoon.

In this stage, infants begin to deliberately make noises and combinations of noises. At first, these vocalizations are repetitions of the same consonant-vowel, vowel-consonant combinations, such as /bababa/, /dadada/, /mamamama/. This behavior is called *reduplicated babbling* because the sound combinations are repeated. As time passes, infants learn to vary the consonants and vowels in the same string, such as /mabada/ and /wodibabu/. This behavior is called *variegated babbling* because the infant is varying the sounds in the production string. Reduplicated and variegated babbling together are termed *canonical babbling*—hence the name of this stage.

**Stage 5: Jargon**    This stage of prelinguistic development generally spans from 10 months old through the production of true words. At this time, growth in motor development continues. Infants are beginning to make the transition from being infants to becoming toddlers. Crawling gives way to standing, standing to cruising, and cruising to walking. As toddlerhood emerges, so does more sophisticated vocal play, variegated babbling, pitch, and volume control. Toddlers are capable of varying their sounds, pitch, and volume in ways that make it sound as if they are having a conversation that adults may not yet be able to understand. Toddlers often pair these conversational streams with eye contact, gestures, pausing, and turn-taking behavior. These behaviors are the foundation for meaningful and effective communication and social-emotional development. The development of these skills is the function of the prelinguistic communication period.

## Prelinguistic Social Development

*Social development*—the establishment of relationships through interaction with the environment—is an extremely complex process. As with communication, social development is a central part of the human experience. *Attachment* is one of the earliest foundations for developing positive social skills; it involves the bond between an infant and his or her parents and other adult caregivers in his or her environment (Deiner, 1997). Like prelinguistic communication development, attachment is thought to evolve in stages that are tied to infants' brain, motor, and communication development (Ainsworth, 1969). Also like communication development, social skill development is transactional. In other words, social and emotional skills are dependent on what the infant brings to the process and how the infant's environment responds to his or her behaviors. As a consequence, intervention that helps to build and refine skills in the child's caregivers can be highly effective, resulting in improved developmental outcomes for the child and the family. The most important thing to remember about attachment and social skill development is that they depend on all five senses delivering quality information to the infant's brain. First, the role of hearing in the development of social skills is discussed.

**_Hearing_**    As mentioned, infants receive information through their ears even before they are born. However, infants who are born deaf or hard of hearing are unable to take advantage of these earliest sounds used for language learning (Kisilevsky et al., 2003), as discussed further in Chapter 9. Infants as young as a few days old will turn their heads when they hear their mother's voice (DeCasper & Fifer, 1980).

The desire for an infant to turn toward the sound of the mother's voice is a cornerstone of attachment. Even before they are born, infants appear to understand that their safety, nourishment, and comfort are associated with the sound of their mother's voice. Those early sensations are strengthened as mothers attempt to comfort their infants by feeding, changing, swaddling, talking to, and holding them. It is important to remember that infants who are adopted or do not live with their biological parents are still able to form strong attachments to new adult caregivers. They adapt quickly to associating positive feelings with the voices of their primary caregivers because the sensations of safety, nourishment, and contentment are learned through having these needs consistently met by the same person or people.

For example, infants learn that when they make laughing sounds, the people around them do the same, and that is a positive feeling (Messinger & Fogel, 2007). Before laughing develops, infants learn that making the noise of crying can bring an adult who provides comfort, and it also serves to block out any other noises that may be unpleasant in the environment. Another crucial use of hearing is how it is used to discern the sound qualities of speech to determine the intent of the person talking. For instance, higher pitch, slower speech rate, and moderate loudness characterize how mothers talk to their infants—often termed *motherese* (Fernald & Kuhl, 1987).

Being able to turn their heads toward a sound and having a preference for voices makes isolating the sounds of infants' native language easier as it spurs sound development. Hearing provides infants with many clues as to what is being said beyond discerning the words and the individual sounds. Infants use their vision, in conjunction with their hearing, to interpret cues from their environment to gather information about the intentions of the people and objects they encounter in the world.

**Vision**    By the end of the first month of life, infants are able to see between 8 and 12 inches away. They use this limited field of vision to find faces, especially when they are held in the parent's arms. Research has shown that infants display a preference for faces above any other stimuli in the first days of life (American Academy of Pediatrics, 1998). The preference for faces is a skill called *sensitivity,* which means that infants are sensitive to the fact that someone is looking at them. By 3 months old, infants are not only sensitive to someone else's eyes looking at them, but they are also able to use their own eyes, or their gaze, to look at someone in order to get that person's attention. Around 6 months old, they have expanded their sensitivity to not only include faces but objects. Table 5.2 shows key prelinguistic stages of social development from birth to approximately 9 months old, as they relate to visual development (Striano, Kopp, Grossmann, & Reid, 2006).

The ability to attend to an object, as well as a face, has profound implications for communication development because first words are generally acquired by the skills used in initiating and responding to joint attention. *Joint attention* involves sharing a common experience with another person, which may or may not involve objects. *Initiating joint attention* is the attempt to get a communication partner to look at an object of interest. Adults and infants do this: 1) by holding out an object, 2) picking up an object and looking from the object to the communication partner and back, 3) pointing to an object, 4) vocalizing and/or verbalizing, or 5) crying. This skill develops around 6 months old.

**Table 5.2**    Key prelinguistic stages of social development from birth to approximately 9 months old

| Skill | Age of acquisition | Examples |
|---|---|---|
| Sensitivity to someone looking at him or her | Birth | Infants attend to faces more than any other stimuli |
| Sensitivity and initiation of being looked at by or looking at another person | 3 months | Infants attend to others' eye gaze and deliberately look at others' faces to draw their attention |
| Sensitivity to someone else looking at an object | 3 months | Infants are able to follow not only faces but someone else looking at an object |
| Sensitivity to someone else looking at an object and initiation of attention to an object by looking from the object to the person | 6 months | Infants are able to direct their own looking to an object another person has as well as using their own looking to direct another person's eyes |
| Sensitivity and initiation similar to what was found at 6 months but now can tell if the object will be given to him or her | 9 months | Infants are better able to gauge from the adult's gaze and facial features if he or she is willing or able to give the infant a desired object |

*Source:* Striano, Kopp, Grossmann, and Reid (2006).

When an infant has joint attention, he or she can tell that the other person's gaze shifted from looking at him or her to looking at an object; in response, the infant then also looks at the object. This ability to shift focus to an object that someone else is looking at is called *responding to joint attention*. Adults and infants try to recruit a response from each other by pointing, vocalizing, verbalizing, or drawing the object into the other person's line of sight. Establishing meaningful joint attention is an important skill to help parents learn as a means of engaging a child and encouraging social-communication intent and response.

Being able to initiate and respond to bids for joint attention is a cornerstone of language development because object labeling typically occurs during these interchanges (Baldwin & Moses, 2001). By 9 months of age, most infants can predict whether initiating joint attention to an object they want is actually going to get them what they want. Eye contact, gaze direction, touch, and movement are critical skills in developing early social abilities.

**Touch and Movement**    In utero, infants are surrounded by the temperature-regulated amniotic fluid and are swaddled by their diminishing surroundings as they grow. They are gently rocked by their mother's walking, sitting, and general movement. Birth disrupts this temperature regulation and leads to pronounced changes to the sense of touch as the arms and legs that were tightly pressed to the body are allowed to fall open and flail around. These changes can have a significant impact on children who are not able to receive the regulation provided by the parent in the form of being handled and held in the months following delivery.

In neonatal intensive care units, infants who are born prematurely or have urgent medical needs encounter a world of tubes, lights, unusual sounds, and potentially invasive procedures. Recent insight into the need for all infants to have skin-to-skin contact has fostered research into what is termed *kangaroo care* (KC; Feldman, Weller, Eidelman, & Sirota, 2002; Ferber & Makhoul, 2004). During KC, an infant who is wearing only a diaper is placed on the bare chest of his or her mother or father. Feldman et al. (2002) found that when mothers of premature infants were able to participate in KC, the family benefited in many ways. The infants who had KC had better perceptual-cognitive and motor development. In addition, the mothers were less likely to experience depression. Overall, the families that participated in KC had better interactions and positive social outcomes. Even in full-term infants, some positive outcomes after KC have been found, including infants who sleep longer and generally show less physical signs of stress (Ferber & Makhoul, 2004). This research demonstrates how powerful and necessary touch is to positive development in infants and their families.

Touch is central to everyday routines and interactions. How adults touch infants is highly communicative. Activities such as diaper changing, rocking, tickling, or rubbing lotion on an infant can provide opportunities to strengthen social bonds and attachment through touch. Service providers must remember that each infant is different in how he or she likes to be touched. Some infants love to be swaddled, whereas others find it uncomfortable. Joel's mother reported that her oldest daughter liked to have one arm hanging out of her swaddle, whereas Joel seemed to prefer being completely wrapped. Some infants like to be patted, some gently jiggled, some rocked, and some prefer to be left to themselves occasionally. Infants will usually communicate, in some way, to caregivers what types of touch they prefer through their behavior.

Infants may communicate that they are overwhelmed or stressed by throwing an arm out and spreading their fingers, arching their backs, closing their eyes or looking away, yawning, or sneezing. Infants also engage in these behavioral responses spontaneously, or they may indicate other needs, such as the need to stretch or rest or that the child is developing a cold. When the infant displays these behaviors consistently in response to particular stimuli, he or she may be communicating feelings of stress and the need for the stimuli to be removed or reduced. All of these behaviors are ways that infants attempt to communicate before they can use words. Reading these signs is not always easy for new parents or when the infant has limited motor or visual control. At times, it may be necessary for service providers to help parents and family members understand the kind of touch their infant seems to take comfort from and explain how the child communicates distress. It is critical that caregivers understand that all of an infant's gestures, eye contact, vocalizations, and crying are essential foundations for later competence in the social-communicative domain, and that these are clear ways that their child is attempting to communicate. It is equally important that parents are responsive to these cues to meet the infant's needs.

***Smell and Taste***    Smell and taste are closely interrelated. Blass (1990) suggested that the sense of smell serves a crucial role in newborns as they learn about familiar people. Because of newborns' limited vision, the sense of smell provides them with another way to identify caregivers while their vision develops. In the first month of life, infants can recognize the smell of their mother's breast milk. They also prefer sweet smells to smells that are bitter or acidic. Infants tend to prefer sweet tastes over bitter tastes. A sense of salty taste develops sometime around 5 months old. This is the time that infants start tasting foods other than milk.

Feeding plays a major role in social and communication development. Basic communication skills and attachment are established and strengthened during the face-to-face interactions that occur while infants are being fed by bottle, breast, or spoon. This association of food with contentment is a physiological reaction that is strengthened while infants are held, fed, and have an enjoyable meal. As discussed in Chapter 10, children with disabilities who are fed with alternative methods, such as tube feeding, may miss out on the social aspects and bonding time associated with typical feedings if parents are not provided with support on how to interact with their children during these alternative feeding times. It is important for families to hold and interact with their infants whenever possible, whether they are being fed through tube feedings or orally.

## Prelinguistic Emotional Development

*Emotional development* is the translation of physiological states to labels that serve to define how people regard themselves, connect to others, and respond to social situations. One of the cornerstones of social and emotional development is the concept of contingency (Gergely & Watson, 1999). *Contingency* is the idea that infants understand that what they are doing has an impact on someone else and causes a reaction. The infant must be aware that actions have reactions. This concept is also sometimes called *means–end theory*—a critical concept in cognitive development discussed in Chapter 6. Means–end theory is the notion that an infant deliberately acts on a person or object in order to begin or end a specific event. The concepts of contingency and means–end connect emotion to social behavior. Infants learn that their distress, usually expressed by crying, is responded to by a caregiver, who then begins a chain of behaviors to alleviate the infant's distress (Gergely & Watson, 1999). The same principle occurs when infants and toddlers learn how to activate a toy in the way it was intended. The child experiments with ways to play with the object and then discovers how to make it function each time it is played with. Caregiver responsiveness is believed to influence an infant's development of emotional self-awareness and control.

Crying serves many purposes for infants and toddlers. It is the ultimate tie between communication, social exchange, and emotional outlet. For a newborn, crying is the physiological response to his or her entrance into the world. Over time, crying is used to signal more specific physical states, such as being hungry, tired, needing a diaper change, or needing a change of activity or position. Parents and caregivers provide the social reinforcement or behavioral responses that strengthen the association of the infant's behavior to particular physiological states. Even in the first month of life, infants are able to communicate their physiological states by using facial expressions, as well as crying. Infants convey interest, distress, and disgust through facial expressions and crying (Kuebli, 1994). The first months of life also bring about the development of the intentional smile.

Smiling has the ability to both convey joy and bring joy to the person smiling (Messinger & Fogel, 2007). There are different theories regarding how and why smiling develops, but the universally agreed-on idea is that smiling conveys emotion, is communicative, and has a social purpose. Messinger and Fogel (2007) discussed research that has documented the development of social smiling, even in infants with visual impairment. This work illustrates that smiling is an important developmental skill; it is not just a reflexive imitation that comes from seeing someone else smiling. These researchers noted that the smiles of infants who are visually impaired do not have the intensity and duration as smiles exhibited by infants without visual impairments. They make this distinction to emphasize that being able to see someone else smile back reinforces the intensity and duration of smiles. Smiling is one of the earliest evolving signs of positive emotion. Although Joel's gross and fine motor milestone skills were delayed, his onset of smiling was age appropriate, which likely was an additional aid in forming the strong parent–child and sibling–sibling relationships commented on by the service providers who worked with the family.

Over the next several months after the first smiles occur, infants begin to show more complex emotions. Around 7 months old, infants begin to show surprise, sadness, fear, and anger. Table 5.3 shows early emotional development until about 18 months old. At the end of this time, toddlers begin to use others' reactions to situations to judge what their own reactions should be. This skill is referred to as *social referencing*, which is a child's use of the facial expressions and reactions of others to judge what his or her own reaction should be in a particular situation (Gross & Ballif, 1991). Research has shown that children first interpret facial expressions in terms of the broad categories of pleasant and unpleasant, with all other emotions with similar positive or negative feelings being overgeneralized into these two broad distinctions (Widen & Russell, 2003, 2008). By the time infants have reached 12 months old, they begin to show an understanding of specific emotion words. As language skills develop, children begin to label the emotions of others as well as their own emotions. The typical progression of the development of labels for emotions is *happy, sad,* and *angry* (Visser, Alant, & Harty, 2008). The use of emotion words marks another transition point for infants at the prelinguistic level.

**Table 5.3.**  Early stages of emotional development (birth to approximately 18 months old)

| Skill | Age of acquisition | Examples |
|---|---|---|
| Displays emotions | Birth to 7 months | Interest, distress, and disgust at birth |
| | | Around 1 month: enjoyment |
| | | Between 1 and 2 months: intentional smiling |
| | | Responds to emotions in others |
| Social referencing | 7 months old | Infants show surprise, sadness, fear, and anger |
| | | Infants use social referencing to guide their own responses |
| Comprehension and labeling of emotion words | 12–18 months old | Labeling of emotions begins with understanding first and then verbal use |
| | | First emotion words appear |

*Source:* Kuebli (1994).

## Communication, Social, and Emotional Development from 12 to 36 Months of Age

Throughout this stage of development, distinguishing social development from speech-language and emotional development is challenging. Developing effective communication skills depends on the interplay of children's social and emotional need to be active participants in their environments. It is also dependent on the environment effectively responding to a child's social-emotional and communication needs. Between 12 and 18 months of age, researchers have shown that word learning becomes a socially driven process (Baldwin & Moses, 2001). As humans, the complex behavior of language is used to accomplish communication.

Language skills are generally separated into two broad areas: receptive language and expressive language. *Receptive language* is the ability to make sense of and understand what is being said. Receptive language skills precede expressive skills during typical development. According to Fenson et al. (1994), 8-month-old children are able to understand approximately six commonly used phrases, such as *stop* and *come here*. Between 11 and 13 months old, most children comprehend at least 50 words. By 16 months old, children are reported to understand approximately 169 words and 23 of 28 commonly used phrases. The number of words and phrases that toddlers understand varies depending on an individual child's development and exposure to language. Even more variation should be expected for children with disabilities and/or delays. When infants can understand approximately 50 words, generally by 12–13 months of age, understanding begins to translate into expression.

*Expressive language* is the ability to communicate emotions, ideas, thoughts, or desires in a variety of ways. Expressive language can be nonverbal or verbal. Nonverbal or visual modes of expression include facial expressions, gestures, tone of voice, signing, and proximity to the person with whom the child is communicating. Fenson et al. (1994) reported that the highest distribution of 8-month-old infants were producing up to 20 different communicative gestures. However, at these early ages, there is a great deal of variability between children. Some infants were not producing gestures at all or only a median of three different gestures. At 14 months of age, the differences between what individual children could produce was the greatest, with the lower 10% of these typically developing toddlers producing 23 different gestures and the upper 90% producing 52 (Fenson et al., 1994).

Some of these gestures include showing an object, blowing kisses, pointing, shaking the head *no*, nodding *yes*, waving good-bye, and extending the arms to be picked up. Around 12 months of age, gestures are paired with the verbal productions of words (i.e., speech). *Speech* occurs when oral structures are used to shape sounds into words. In the following sections, expressive speech-language development will be discussed in three broad stages: the production of single words, putting words together, and grammatical development.

**Production of Single Words**    The first word occurs when a child consistently uses the same strings of sounds when presented with a particular person, place, or thing. These words are often not clearly articulated, adult-style productions. For example, Joel's parents reported that when the dog walked into the room, Joel said, "Dah." They shared that he said it consistently while looking straight at or pointing to the family's dog. Joel's first word was developmentally appropriate because the /d/, /b/, and /m/ consonants tend to be among the earliest developing sounds. Vowel sounds emerge and are mastered between 12 and 18 months old. Consequently, *mama, dada,* and *baba* tend to be some of the first meaningful words children use.

Rescorla, Alley, and Christine (2001) indicated that first words reported on the MacArthur Communicative Development Inventory generally fall into the following categories:

1.  Sound effects and animal sounds (e.g., *uh oh, woof, moo*)
2.  Games and routines (e.g., *bye-bye, no, night-night*)
3.  Animals (e.g., *dog, kitty, bird*)
4.  Food and drink (e.g., *banana, juice, cookie*)
5.  People (e.g., *daddy, mommy, baby*)
6.  Toys (e.g., *ball, book, balloon*)

In general, nouns are understood and used before other types of words. Verbs, nouns (e.g., people, games, routines), adjectives, sound effects, and other words (e.g., *a, the, will*) are understood and used by 30-month-old children. Between 16 and 30 months, children develop from producing fewer than 100 words to producing approximately 450 words.

**Putting Words Together**    The transition from using single words to producing two-word combinations typically occurs between 14 and 18 months of age. Children also tend to begin using two-word combinations after they are able to successfully produce at least 50 individual words; this seems to be the necessary condition for putting words together because the child needs to have a minimum number of different words before he or she is able to combine them. These first two-word combinations are produced for the purpose of meeting the child's needs. Later, these combinations serve as a tool for learning about the child's environment, enabling the child to make comments on what he or she sees or experiences. During this stage, children may use the same two-word combination to indicate a variety of ideas. Many times, the purpose is to request something. For example, an infant may hold a ball out to his father and say, "Daddy ball?" as a request for daddy to play ball with him. "Daddy ball" can also indicate possession, as in "This is Daddy's ball."

Core words that toddlers frequently use are *no, more, mine, go,* and *all gone* (Fensen et al., 1994). *No* is one of the earliest used words for a variety of reasons. First, the /n/ and the /o/ sounds are very early developing sounds and are easy for infants to produce. In addition, infants and toddlers are frequently told "no" as they explore their environments.

As toddlers' vocabularies increase, they begin to move from two-word utterances to three- and four-word utterances. There is a tradeoff effect between the length of the utterance and the intelligibility of the utterance in young children. As children push the limits of their oral-motor capacities by putting together more words, their speech is typically harder to understand. Their ability to make all of the individual sounds in the words they are producing is complicated by their limited oral-motor coordination, decreasing the clarity of the individual sounds. With time and practice, utterances become more intelligible because the children have strengthened their oral-motor planning for the individual sounds. Once children reach the level of putting three to four words together into short phrases, they are beginning to learn the rules of grammar as well.

***Grammar Development***    Children begin to use the past tense around their second birthdays. They also tend to overgeneralize the use of the regular past tense marker *-ed*, using it incorrectly with verbs, such as "I goed school." Irregular verbs, such as *was,* are generally learned out of imitation of what others in the environment are using. Irregular plurals are problematic for young children and can result in words such as *childrens, deers,* and *mans.* However, these overgeneralizations reflect the fact that the toddler knows to add /s/ to the end of the word when speaking about more than one of something. At this point in development, the toddler's social and emotional world expands to being able to talk about things that are not anchored in the present or about things that are not currently in the environment. This expanded ability to communicate also results in an expanded ability to express emotions and relate to others.

Many children who are referred to early intervention are not yet meeting the developmental milestones described in this chapter. When a child is exhibiting delays in social-communicative development, early intervention services can assist the child's parents and other caregivers in exploring the natural environment and finding ways to facilitate this development within the context of everyday interactions and experiences.

## EFFECTS OF EARLY EXPERIENCE ON COMMUNICATION, LANGUAGE, AND SOCIAL-EMOTIONAL DEVELOPMENT

Earlier in the chapter, the transactional theory of development was discussed. Recall that this theory states that learning is a bidirectional activity that involves the skills of the child and the responses of the environment. With this in mind, activities in any natural environment can be adjusted or modified in many ways to better support a child's communication and social-emotional development.

### Early Language and Preliteracy Experiences

Infants come into the world wired to interact with their families and caregivers. Infants crave the sounds of voices speaking to them. Parents of children with disabilities may find it frustrating or challenging to talk or play with a child who does not respond, who responds inconsistently, or who responds in a slower or different way from other children in the family. It is important for parents to understand that all infants depend on human interactions to facilitate communication, social, and emotional development. Infants are learning from the interactions even if it is not immediately apparent, as it might be with infants who are developing typically. Talking to infants during daily family routines teaches them the purpose of communication, demonstrates the sounds and prosody (i.e., rhythm) of language, and provides opportunities for learning words. Simply put, repeated experiences with hearing and using communication are at the root of early language learning.

Infants need the repetitive nature of routines, as well as the words that go with those routines, to foster the development of a variety of skills. For example, before feeding, Joel's mother consistently used the following routine: She said, "Time to eat," while putting on Joel's bib, then put Joel in the highchair with his bolster supports. Next, she placed the food in a bowl on the tray, scooped up a spoonful of food, held it in front of Joel's mouth, and said, "Open up." By keeping this sequence consistent every time Joel ate, Joel learned that *time to eat* meant that food was coming and that *open up* meant to open his mouth. This kind of reciprocal interaction strengthened the attachment between Joel and his mother, and it built a foundation for receptive and expressive language development during a daily routine. The routine also was social in nature and provided an emotional sense of security and predictability for them both.

Another early experience that provides focused language facilitation and social-emotional growth is shared book reading. Research has consistently shown that children have better literacy outcomes later in life when they are read to earlier and more consistently (Raikes et al., 2006). To engage infants and toddlers in book reading, the adult must make the reading interesting and engaging by using an expressive voice, encouraging the child to point to pictures and interact with the book, and using high-interest materials and subjects (Lonigan, 1994). The process of sitting together and looking at a book can also foster stronger emotional bonds between the child and parent through the shared experience (Scarborough & Dobrich, 1994). The novel vocabulary and sounds produced when reading create an effective context for promoting both expressive and receptive communication development. The social nature of book reading builds joint attention skills that have also been shown to foster speech and language development.

A simple book-reading modification that Joel's family used was "reading" a small photo album with pictures of people, objects, or events/activities that the family identified as important to them. The photo book included images of immediate and extended family members; Joel's favorite toys; Joel and his family doing daily routines, such as bath time and playing in the backyard; the family pet; and other images the family believed captured their everyday lives, values, and preferred activities, such as their family's evening walk. Joel's sister enjoyed making the photo book and reading it with Joel after school. Their parents encouraged this interaction because it was rewarding for Melissa, and Joel seemed to enjoy this time with his sister.

## Attachment and Reciprocal Interactions

The first OSEP child outcome involves facilitating attachment, separation, and autonomy, which are aspects of typical social-emotional development. Successful separation without anxiety and a healthy sense of autonomy can only be achieved if the child already has secure attachment. Infants learn to feel safe and secure by experiencing responsive caregiving, during which caregivers appropriately react to the child's bids for attention and communication and consistently meet the child's needs. Bowlby (1982) explained that the attachment figure can be "a secure base from which to explore" (p. 675). Having this secure base allows an infant or toddler to physically move away from the parent or caregiver to explore the world because the emotional connection remains. Without this secure base, a child may feel insecure and cling to the parent, feel detached and too easily move away, or fail to respond to the parent because of the lack of connection. This metaphor of the secure base illustrates how important it is that families learn to read their children's cues and respond to them with love and compassion so that a healthy attachment occurs.

Attachment includes the desire to seek out an individual in times of stress and distress in order to feel loved and cared for. Infants with secure attachments have been found to have a lower risk of later peer and behavior problems (Erickson, Sroufe, & Egeland, 1985). Infants and toddlers who experience secure attachments and know that they are loved despite challenging behaviors or other developmental differences gradually come to develop positive self-esteem and the ability to relate to others in a healthy way. Children with weak attachments have no one to anchor their self-esteem in times of stress and may struggle with building relationships with others.

How caregivers respond to crying is a cornerstone of attachment. Infants who have unresponsive or hostile caregivers may develop disorganized neurological systems and have difficulty with regulating their communicative and social-emotional behavior in later life (Mikulincer, Shaver, & Pereg, 2003). Infants with developmental delays or disabilities are at a higher risk for displaying excessive fussiness or may be slow to respond to traditional methods of comforting. These behaviors can present unexpected challenges and, at times, cause disruptions in the attachment process. For this reason, service providers are pivotal in explaining concepts and coaching caregivers who are struggling with attachment by discussing its importance and modeling responsive behaviors when appropriate. In this way, caregivers come to see the critical importance of providing predictable, appropriately stimulating, and loving interactions during a child's daily caregiving routines.

## Impact of Adverse Environmental Conditions

When children are born into environments where their caregivers are having difficulty meeting basic needs (e.g., securing sufficient food, shelter, or clothing), have an addiction and/or mental illness, or have intellectual disabilities, these adverse conditions can have profound effects on development. An overwhelmed parent may have difficulty responding to the round-the-clock needs of an infant and toddler. Similarly, a parent who is focused on meeting the basic safety or security needs of the family may not be able to sufficiently attend to a child's developmental needs. Insufficiency in areas such as nutrition in early childhood can result in compromised neurological development.

Service providers who support families experiencing these conditions can offer assistance in many ways. The service coordinator, for example, can link families with other agencies to secure support for a family's needs. The service coordinator might refer the parent to a local food pantry for assistance with groceries or to a community counseling program if the parent experiences depression and requests support. When a family's needs are met, the child with developmental delays or disabilities also benefits from the stable environment. Because it has been well established that low socioeconomic status (SES) is one of the greatest risk factors for all developmental disabilities (Morisset, Barnard, Greenberg, Booth, & Spieker, 1990), service coordinators and providers must be aware of the unique needs of children and families experiencing these challenges as well as the community resources that are available to help.

In areas of cognition and language, researchers have reported significant differences between economically disadvantaged children and their more advantaged counterparts (Feldman et al., 2003; Hoff & Tian, 2005; National Institute of Child Health and Human Development, 2000; Pan, Rowe, Singer, & Snow, 2005; Petrill, Pike, Price, & Plomin, 2004; Rescorla & Achenbach, 2002). For example, language development appears to develop at a faster rate for children with high SES. The difference between children of high SES and low SES is most apparent at 2 years of age (Hoff & Tian, 2005) in terms of the number of words the children use and understand. Such delays in skills are thought to be related to specific properties of the language experience provided within the home environment, with children who hear less rich vocabulary and shorter sentences spoken to them showing slower rates of vocabulary growth (Hoff, 2003). This work illustrates the importance of collaborating with families to help them modify their interactions with their children and promote early language-focused experiences, such as shared book reading and engaging children in conversation. These interactive activities have a positive impact on communication and social-emotional development.

The impact of children's environments on their development of speech, language, and cognition has typically been studied by looking at the quantity and quality of input given by the mothers of the children rather than the fathers (e.g., Dollaghan et al., 1999; Hoff, 2003; Huttenlocher, Vasilyeva, Waterfall, & Vevea, 2007). Although this traditional view of parenting acknowledges mothers as the primary caregivers of young children, fathers make a unique contribution to their child's vocabulary and language development (Pancsofar & Vernon-Feagans, 2006, 2010). Research has shown that fathers offer a unique source of stimulation to their infants and young children and, in some respects, the father's speech serves different developmental needs (McLaughlin, White, McDevitt, & Raskin, 1983; Rutherford & Przednowek, 2012). Tamis-LeMonda, Shannon, Cabrera, and Lamb (2004) stated that the father's engagement directly affects children's linguistic, literacy, and cognitive abilities; in addition, a father's demographic characteristics, such as years of education and income, might indirectly influence a child's outcomes on these variables. Because of their important contributions, fathers should be included in all aspects of the early intervention process, including intervention visits, as frequently as possible.

Regardless of whether it is the mother or father engaging the child, the amount and quality of talking that is directed to children helps build vocabulary and language processing skills (Weisleder & Fernald, 2013). Regularly talking to children also develops positive social skills and is important for helping children learn to follow social rules. Early intervention service providers should work closely with both parents, whenever possible, to help them learn ways to interact and communicate with their child to build these important skills.

## Challenging Behaviors in Toddlers

Researchers have become interested in effective, comprehensive models for promoting healthy social-emotional development and preventing persistent challenging behavior in early care and education programs (Boulware, Schwartz, & McBride, 1999). Children with language impairments are at increased risk for behavior problems (Kaiser & Roberts, 2011). As a consequence, early language interventions create a foundation for increased positive behavior.

Noncompliant behavior serves a specific purpose and is predicted by the events that take place before (i.e., antecedents) and is maintained by events that take place after the behavior (i.e., consequences; Neilsen, Olive, Donovan, & McEvoy, 1998). It is now a recommended practice to examine refusals and tantrums from a function-based perspective rather than by their topographies, or what they look like (Dunlap & Fox, 2011). The term *function-based* means looking at what motivated the child to display these behaviors. Noncompliant behavior may be attempting to achieve attention, avoidance, or both for the child. Often, children engage in these behaviors because they have been the most effective way to escape from or avoid an undesired activity. In a way, infants and toddlers are using these behaviors to communicate. Instead of reacting, it is better if caregivers focus on teaching the child a more appropriate way to obtain attention or cope with an unpleasant activity.

When adults look at what function the behavior is attempting to serve, it becomes easier to identify replacement communication behaviors, which can be taught to allow the child to accomplish the same outcome in a more socially acceptable manner. One way to do this is to consistently respond to a positive behavior (usually one that caregivers have taught the child to use) and not react to the challenging behavior (Branson & Demchak, 2011). For example, if a child's tantrum is being used to communicate that he or she would like to reject a toy or wants a break, the caregiver would systematically teach a communication replacement for these behaviors. This replacement could be saying "all done," gesturing or signing NO or FINISHED, or touching a symbol for BREAK or NO. The goal would then become to train the child to use the appropriate communication behavior rather than the negative behavior. At first, the communicative replacement is taught after the negative behavior. As the caregiver improves in identifying the signs that a tantrum is about to occur, the child can be prompted to use the designated communication replacement to achieve the same outcome. The caregiver might say, "Use your words. Say 'all done,'" while using the sign if this is the agreed-on behavior (Neilsen et al., 1998).

## PRACTICES FOR ACHIEVING THE FIRST OFFICE OF SPECIAL EDUCATION PROGRAMS CHILD OUTCOME

To support infants and toddlers as they improve their skills and knowledge encompassed in the first OSEP child outcome, service providers conduct assessments, identify strategies that can be easily embedded into families' routines, and stay in regular contact with families so that interventions and services can be adjusted as needed. Each of these components of intervention are discussed in the following sections.

### Assessment

Communication, social, and emotional skills are typically assessed with infants and toddlers by using checklists that combine direct observation of behaviors, direct elicitation of behaviors, and information provided through interviews with caregivers. Many tools are available for the assessment of communication, social, and emotional skills in the birth-to-3 population. When assessment is undertaken, a good rule of thumb is that the child should be assessed in more than one familiar environment. That is, assessment should occur in places where the child's different activities occur, such as the living room, kitchen, bathroom, playground, or child care setting. Observing the child in these different settings allows the professional to gather a more complete picture of the child's communication and social strengths and needs, more so than only assessing development in a single isolated situation. This is important because infants and toddlers may communicate and interact in different ways depending on the situations in which they find themselves. For example, they may be friendly and engaging at home but quiet at the child care center.

The primary focus of any developmental and/or communication assessment instrument is to determine how and if the child is getting his or her needs met. An assessment should attempt to identify the following:

- What mode of communication (e.g., sign language, augmentative and alternative communication methods, speech) will the child be able to use to communicate successfully?

- Is the child able to understand the communication of others?
- Is the behavior that the service provider is observing or the parent is reporting a result of not having an effective mode of communication?
- Does the child have an appropriate mode for expressing emotions?
- Is the child able to successfully interact with others, including family members, for play, communication, and learning?

Answering these questions requires the provider to observe the child directly and try to elicit behaviors from the child during the assessment.

On occasion, a child's behavior is so fussy that completing an assessment is simply impractical. In these cases, a team approach is beneficial because other team members may have observed some of the skills on the assessment instruments in other situations. Playing with the child until the child is more comfortable or beginning with skills that do not appear to frustrate or overwhelm the child can frequently allow service providers to gain enough information to determine if a child is in need of services or has made developmental gains as a result of services. In addition, parents are an invaluable resource for filling in the gaps in unsuccessful or incomplete assessments.

## Intervention

The outcomes of intervention for communication, social, and emotional skills should be focused on establishing successful relationships and purposeful, spontaneous communication interactions that allow the child to get his or her wants and needs satisfied. The teaching of these skills should always be incorporated into daily routines and should include words, phrases, or skills that are a priority for the family. Service providers have the critical role of coaching parents in how to support their children's communication and social development. Research has shown that what parents say to their children and how they interact with them directly affects children's language development (Kaiser & Roberts, 2011). Offering coaching to parents on how to facilitate language and social development in their children can take many forms.

Naturalistic interventions are among the most effective for supporting the development of infants and toddlers. In social-communicative development, naturalistic interventions are achieved by following a child's lead. *Following a child's lead* occurs when an adult, such as a service provider, parent, or other caregiver, observes what the child is doing and then joins the child in that activity. It does not mean directing the child to do what the adult would like the child to do. Naturalistic interventions seek to take advantage of the child's interest in an object or activity to create new opportunities to work on skills that the child needs to learn or practice. There are many strategies for these interventions, as discussed in the following sections.

### *Strategies for Encouraging Communication, Social, and Emotional Development*     For young children, play and interactions during caregiver routines are the primary modes of social exchange (Honig, 2001). During play and caregiving, adults have the opportunity to teach and model vocabulary, grammar, and desired social interactions. There are many naturalistic social-communicative techniques used to scaffold verbal skills during these routines, including recast therapy (Camarata & Nelson, 2006; Camarata, Yoder, & Camarata, 2006), enhanced milieu teaching (Kaiser, Hancock, & Nietfeld, 2000; Qi, Kaiser, & Milan, 2006; Robertson & Weismer, 1999; Warren, Yoder, Gazdag, Kim, & Jones, 1993; Yoder & Warren, 2002), parallel and self-talk (Honig, 1989, 2001),

and appropriate use of questioning. Educators and speech-language therapists report that these types of child-directed interactions facilitate language skills in preschool-age children who are developing typically as well as those who are not (McDuffie, Yoder, & Stone, 2006; Tomasello & Farrar, 1986). Words are learned because the production of these strings of sounds is socially reinforced by the adults in the environment. Professionals and parents do this by imitating, modeling, labeling, commenting, and expanding on what the child has said. There are many strategies for doing this in natural environments, including the following.

*Recast Therapy*    Recast therapy occurs when an adult's response uses the child's topic, content, and point of reference. Recasting adds or modifies one or more of the language elements the child used. Recasting is often used with the language stimulation techniques of imitation, modeling, and expansion.

*Imitating* is the simplest form of reinforcement and is done by making the same noises (e.g., blowing raspberries), gestures (e.g., clapping hands), vocalizations (e.g., "wheeee"), or verbalizations (e.g., "go, go, go") as the child. Imitating is most appropriate for younger children who are just learning the importance of words and word meanings and are still playing with the sounds of their native language. It offers immediate reinforcement of a child's own productions. Imitation helps with both sound and word development because it creates the most timely link between the child's efforts and the adult's model. In recast therapy, the child's utterance is usually followed by modeling of the target word or structure.

*Modeling* is another technique that is commonly used when another person in the environment, who could be an adult or another child, gives a few slightly different utterances that have the same critical language feature that the child is trying to learn. Using modeling, the service provider shows the parent or other family members as many examples of the communication and/or social-emotional target as possible so that the child hears and sees the target skills in many different contexts in a concentrated space of time. To model the target word or behavior, often the adult must expand the child's original utterance. For example, when Joel was shown the picture of his father and said, "Daaaaa," his sister had been shown how to say "daddy" after Joel's attempt to provide him with the model; she then tickled his tummy after each turn to make the interaction enjoyable for Joel.

*Expanding* a child's language occurs when the adult adds to what the child says in any of the following ways:

- Grammatically (e.g., The child says, "Mommy bye-bye," and the mother says, "Mommy went bye-bye")
- With more words (e.g., The child says, "Mommy bye-bye," and the mother says, "Mommy bye-bye now")
- With grammar, more words, and more information (e.g., The child says, "Mommy go bye-bye," and the mother says, "Mommy went bye-bye. I came back")

Expansions and providing models should not exceed a child's zone of proximal development. The *zone of proximal development* refers to providing input at the level that is just slightly above what the child is currently able to do (Chaiklin, 2003). The idea is to challenge the child's social-communicative system to move forward in development without overwhelming the system into shutdown. The target behavior and the subsequent input from the early interventionists and/or parent should be at a level that is just above the child's current functioning. For example, if the child is at the single-word level of production, providing models and expansions that are 6–10 words is not facilitative. Providing models and expansions that are at the two- or three-word level are appropriate. Keeping the models and expansions closer to the child's level allows the child to more easily process and identify the salient message from the adult's output or comment. It also is easier for the child to imitate the adult's communication and add vocabulary.

The following is an example of an interaction from an intervention visit in which recast therapy was being used. The mother had been coached on how to use these strategies by the family's primary service provider.

- *Target:* The child is working on subject + verb (e.g., "Daddy go").
- *Context:* The mother and child are telling the father good-bye in the morning as he leaves for work.

> Child:    "Daddy."
>
> Mother:   "Yes, Daddy *go.* Daddy go bye-bye."

**Enhanced Milieu Teaching**   Enhanced *milieu teaching* incorporates the same basic elements of recast therapy but includes a prompt for production following the model. Enhanced milieu teaching is a naturalistic intervention that uses structured and semistructured play while following a child's lead. The advantage of using enhanced milieu teaching over recast therapy is that it provides a greater degree of adult support, or scaffolding, for expected utterances. Using the previous example for recast therapy, the following example incorporates enhanced milieu teaching.

> Child:    "Daddy."
>
> Mother:   "Yes, Daddy go."
>
> Child:    "Daddy."
>
> Mother:   "Nice try. Daddy go."
>
> Child:    "Daddy go." (while waving good-bye)
>
> Mother:   "That's right! You said, 'Daddy go.'"

**Parallel Talk and Self-Talk**   Parallel *talk* is an intervention strategy in which an interactional partner comments on a child's play by stating what the child is doing, thinking, or feeling, rather than requiring the child to answer direct questions or produce particular responses (Honig, 2001). With *self-talk,* the adult describes what he or she is doing, thinking, or feeling. With both, no particular communication targets may be specified. These strategies are adult directed in that they do not require the child to make a response or repeat a particular verbal model to stay in the interaction. These strategies tend to be easy for parents to learn and can be easily incorporated into daily caregiving and play routines. Parallel talk and self-talk primarily use the techniques of labeling and commenting and have been found to be effective in increasing communication skills in an array of children with diverse communication needs (Raver, Bobzien, Richels, Hester, Michalek, & Anthony, 2012).

Labeling is more sophisticated than imitating and can be used to establish joint attention. *Labeling* involves providing: 1) the name for objects (e.g., "ball"), 2) actions (e.g., "run"), or 3) feelings (e.g., "happy"). With this strategy, adults initiate and respond to joint attention by narrating the child's world with words that match the objects, actions, and feelings that are holding a child's attention. For example, when Joel looked at or pointed to an object, his mother looked in the direction Joel was indicating and provided the label. Reciprocally, when Joel's mother held out Joel's blanket, she frequently said, "blankie," as she put the blanket around Joel's shoulders. Then, to further elaborate, she said, "Wearing blanket. All warm."

As children become more proficient with single words, imitation and labels grow into comments. *Commenting* is making statements about the child's environment such as, "I like the flower on your dress"; commenting about what the child is doing, such as "You're going fast"; or commenting about what the child may be displaying or feeling, such as "You are mad." Commenting is an important aspect of creating links between emotions and emotion labels. When an adult comments on a child's behavior and provides a label for what the child is doing or feeling, the child begins to be able to make the connections between how he or she feels and the words that go with that feeling.

Parallel talk and self-talk work particularly well with infants and toddlers, primarily because these strategies do not demand a reply from a child to stay in the interaction. Parallel talk essentially provides a continuous narrative about the child's day. Self-talk provides a narrative of what the adult is doing. Just the process of using parallel talk can serve to create joint attention between adults and children, which is an established natural mechanism of teaching speech and language skills. Consider again the previous example:

- Parallel talk (Example 1)
    Child:    "Daddy." (waves good-bye)

    Mother:   "Daddy go. You're waving bye-bye."

- Parallel talk (Example 2)
    Child:    "Daddy go."

    Mother:   "Daddy's going bye-bye. He's waving to us."

- Self-talk
    Child:    "Daddy go bye-bye."

    Mother:   "Yes, bye-bye, Daddy. I'm waving bye-bye too." (waves)

The key elements involved in any successful social-communicative intervention stem from creating the expectation that the child must communicate in some way to get what he or she wants. One way to inspire communication is to withhold a motivating object or activity until the child provides an appropriate level of communication. For example, blowing bubbles is extremely motivating for children of all ages. The interventionist might show the parent or caregiver how to hold the bubbles and the bubble wand, blow a few bubbles, and then wait. This is called expectant waiting, or using wait time. *Wait time* provides the child an opportunity to produce the target behavior. While waiting, the adult makes eye contact and assumes an expectant facial expression and body posture. The child should be encouraged to use whatever mode of communication he or she has to request bubbles. This could be reaching for the wand while vocalizing, signing, pressing a switch, or saying "bubbles." If the child makes an attempt to communicate in any of these ways, the adult would provide the verbal model "more bubbles," just prior to blowing more.

When providing a model of a target, the adult must use high-intensity facial and vocal expressions to stress what the target is. The child should be prompted for a response two to three times. If no response occurs, then the adult should attempt to physically prompt a motor response (e.g., guiding the child to activate the switch, guiding the child's hands to sign BUBBLES, pointing to the wand), as the adult says, "Show me what you want." After the child has attempted to respond, either independently or after being physically prompted, the child should be provided with the desired object or activity. In this example, it would be another round of bubble blowing. Keep in mind that these play episodes should be relaxed and playful for both the child and the caregiver. It is also important to keep in mind the zone of proximal development, ensuring that the service provider or the parent does not bombard the child with too many different targets or prompts at once.

When the child's intent is not clear, the interventionist must help the parents and caregivers learn to recognize and reinforce any attempt at social engagement or communication in infants and toddlers. It can be difficult to read an eye gaze and other body language when the child's ability to communicate is compromised by developmental delays or disability. Because children with delays and/or disabilities may present subtle social-emotional and communicative behaviors, service providers can be helpful in alerting caregivers to these nontraditional behaviors so that the child's communicative behaviors are responded to appropriately more frequently.

Joel was delayed in the production of vocalizations (sounds) when he was first enrolled in the early intervention program. The speech-language pathologist was helpful to the team by pointing out how Joel used his body language to attempt to communicate and interact with others. Joel tended to display a subtle shift in his right hand position and a slight twitching of muscles around the eyes and mouth, which communicated that he was alert and wanted to play. Once his family learned to read these social-communicative bids, or attempts, Joel received more attention and was rewarded by their smiles, holding, and playing. All communication attempts should be rewarded with praise that is appropriate for the child's age. For most infants, including Joel, clapping, cheering, smiling, and tickling were more appropriate than using long sentences. High-fives, "Good job," or "You did it!" along with smiling, clapping, and cheering are usually appreciated by toddlers. However, some children have a low threshold for noise and startle easily. Service providers consequently need to be careful to tailor praise recommendations to each child's preferences.

*Using Questions Effectively*     When adults address questions to children, there are three basic types of questions that can be used: yes-no, forced-choice, and open-ended questions. The type of question used should be based on the complexity and nature of the response the adult is trying to elicit. Yes-no questions are questions that can only be answered with a yes or no response (e.g., "Do you want more?" "Do you want up?"). *Yes-no questions* are appropriate when trying to keep the communicative demand low. Because there are only two possible answers, yes-no questions lend themselves well to use with gesture, augmentative and alternative communication, and simple sound or word modes of communication. However, this type of question should not be used if *no* is not an acceptable option.

*Forced-choice questions* have a limited number of very specific responses (e.g., "Do you want milk or juice?" "Is that ball up or down?"). Using forced-choice questions to give choices can allow children to feel that they have some control over their world. However, the choices do not always have to be choices the child prefers. For instance, if a toddler is having a hard time making the transition to bedtime, a mother might ask, "Do you want to put on your pajamas or brush your teeth now?" The forced-choice format gives the child some control while the adult provides a scaffold of the level of control the child is allowed.

*Open-ended questions* can be answered in different ways, from a single word to short phrases. Examples of open-ended questions are "What is she doing?" or "I wonder where they are going?" Open-ended questions can be useful with most children because the adult can interpret the child's communication response to match the activity. This allows the adult to model language and expand on what the child communicates. Open-ended questions also provide the lowest level of communicative scaffold for the child. Depending on the question being asked, the variety of responses the child chooses can be infinite. For example, when Joel's mother asked him, "What do you want to do?" and Joel looked at the window, his mother modeled "Okay, you want to go outside." This allowed Joel to indicate his preference without being forced to choose between two options selected by an adult.

When open-ended questions are used in this manner, it is critically important that the adult is attentive to the child's cues and is able to interpret any communicative behavior. If the adult cannot determine the child's intent, switching to a forced-choice or yes-no question would be appropriate to help the child specify his or her response. Had Joel's mother not been sure of Joel's reply, she might have followed her question with, "Do you want to go outside?" and watched Joel to see if he looked at the window again. This use of questions also helps Joel know that his mother understood him and reinforces his attempt to communicate.

The type of question that is most appropriate depends on the circumstances of the interaction, the type of answer that is acceptable, the child's abilities, and the parent's understanding of the child's cues. Service providers can help parents move from asking yes-no questions to using choices and open-ended questions in order to help the child progress from simpler to more well-developed communication and social interaction.

## Teaching Positive Communication and Social-Emotional Skills within Routines

Skills are best learned when they are reinforced repeatedly and consistently and used in multiple routines and activities daily. Parents and caregivers should be encouraged to spend time engaging the child in social play, reading books, and having conversations every day. Opportunities for purposeful social engagement and communication can be engineered into any activity that occurs throughout the day. Some examples follow:

- Use parallel talk and talk to the child, including newborns, during all caregiving routines, such as feeding, diaper changes, dressing, and bath time. For example, label body parts by gently touching each, label food or clothing as they are presented, and describe emotions as they are displayed, such as "You are happy today."

- Offer the child a snack in a container that requires help to open and put small amounts of food or drink on plates, the spoon, or in the cup so that the child has to keep asking for more.

- Put a toy or juice cup out of reach but within sight so that the child must communicate his or her desire for the object.

- Take turns in play and use wait time to encourage the child to communicate that he or she wants the play to continue.

- For toddlers, use the child's favorite toys and familiar household objects to develop verbal turn-taking to build conversational skills.

- Pair language with gross motor play. For example, say, "wheeee" while going down the slide; say, "putt-putt-putt" while pulling a wagon; and model "up," "down," "stop," "go," and "more" while swinging on the swing.

- Open and close a door while verbally modeling "open" and "close."
- Sing songs and use simple finger plays, such as "Wheels on the Bus."

For children who are not using oral language, these activities can be modified to use the child's modes of communication such as signing, a picture communication system, a communication board or book, or a communication device. The pictures used with these should be color photographs of real objects from a child's environment. Later, the pictures can progress to smaller line drawings if needed. Even for children who are not using spoken language, words and phrases should always be paired with the child's augmentative and alternative communication (AAC) method. The use of an AAC system allows young children to communicate sooner and more effectively. AAC may immediately improve a child's functional communication while supporting the development of spoken communication (Kaiser & Roberts, 2011). Researchers have shown that using AAC does not inhibit speech development; in fact, it was shown to increase vocal and verbal output in 89% of children with disabilities (Millar, Light, & Schlosser, 2006).

Service providers should remember that not all activities have to target communication. In fact, activities that require a great deal of attention and concentration may yield little communication for many children because it can be challenging for very young children to concentrate on communication and other complicated activities at the same time. Caregivers may need to be coached on how to balance activities that focus on interaction and communication with others that focus on cognitive or motor skill development (see Chapters 6 and 7), which may produce less spontaneous communication.

## PRINCIPLES AND PRACTICES OF EARLY LANGUAGE INTERVENTION

Kaiser and Roberts (2011) proposed the following 10 principles as guidelines for quality early communication intervention when serving young children with special needs:

1. All children are communicators by signaling their state, interests, attention, and needs, regardless of age or ability level.
2. Early language impairments place children at risk for problems in social development and reading. Proactive, systematic intervention to ensure positive social and academic outcomes is needed.
3. All children with language impairments can benefit from intervention in natural environments, regardless of their developmental limitations or severity of language impairments.
4. Most children with language impairments require intervention and support to increase the rate, diversity, and complexity of their communication at every stage of development.
5. Most children with language impairments will need systematic teaching to learn, generalize, and maintain new language and communication skills across the toddler and preschool years.
6. Children's progress in using communication functionally in everyday activities should determine the methods, contexts, and duration of intervention.
7. Early communication intervention should 1) begin with supporting the social foundations of communication (e.g., joint attention, engagement, play), 2) teach prelinguistic communication skills as needed, 3) provide a mode for expressive communication, 4) build comprehension and production, and 5) continue support through the transition to spoken language.

8. A wide range of instructional strategies can improve children's language and communication skills, such as contingent responding, turn-taking, modeling in context, recasting and expanding children's communication acts, prompting, and providing meaningful feedback to children's attempts.

9. Teaching and supporting partners (parents, caregivers, family members, teachers, child care providers, and peers) are essential to successful child communication interventions. Effective early intervention depends on the participation of partners who respond to communication, who teach new forms and functions of communication in context, and who can modify how they respond and what they model as children develop new skills.

10. Full participation in learning opportunities is a critical component of early language intervention. Thus, making adaptations to promote participation and providing support and training to partners to support learning in natural environments is necessary.

Early intervention service providers of all disciplines address communication and social-emotional development as they interact with children during intervention visits. Implementing these guidelines can help ensure that all infants and toddlers have the best chances for being able to interact and communicate with those around them in ways that support learning and development.

## BEST PRACTICE HIGHLIGHTS

Progress in communication and social-emotional development is enhanced when early intervention programs offer services that do the following:

- Use all the senses, including eye contact and gaze direction, touch, smell, and movement to promote early social skills during intervention activities.
- Use coaching to show parents, caregivers, and family members how to establish joint attention, which is an essential element of communication, during caregiving routines and play. First words and object labeling are generally acquired by initiating and responding to joint attention.
- Use infants' need to be active participants in their environments to encourage those in the children's environments to effectively respond to those needs.
- Guide parents and caregivers to follow the child's lead and talk about what interests the child, what the child is doing, and what the child is feeling during routines.
- Support families as they create social foundations of communication by encouraging joint attention in play and throughout the day, teaching prelinguistic communication skills, providing a mode of expressive communication, and building comprehension and sound and language production in the child.
- Coach and support early intervention partners (parents, caregivers, family members, child care workers, peers) to encourage and appropriately respond to communication, teach new forms and functions of communication in context, use imitation and turn-taking activities, and modify how they respond and what they model as young children develop new skills.

## CONCLUSION

Communication, social interaction, and emotional development are fundamental to the human experience. Therefore, opportunities to improve functioning in these areas exist in every waking moment of every child's day. Research has demonstrated that social attention and prelinguistic communication are necessary for later language learning and use (Kaiser & Roberts, 2011). To show progress on the first OSEP child outcome, most infants receiving early intervention require communication interventions that target the range of skills acquired in infancy through toddlerhood by their typical peers. The most effective social and communicative interventions simultaneously address children and their communication partners, which tend to be their parents, other family members, and peers. Coaching parents and caregivers to use naturalistic social-communicative strategies across routines and natural environments is the most effective way to increase positive social-emotional and communicative skills.

## DISCUSSION QUESTIONS AND APPLIED ACTIVITIES

1. Describe four intervention strategies for supporting positive social-communicative skills in a 32-month-old toddler with delays in receptive and expressive language and social-emotional development. Describe how you would coach this child's 16-year-old sister to embed these strategies into the family's evening routines, which tend to involve dinner, quiet play following dinner, bath time, and the bedtime ritual. Use language and materials that would be best suited to the teenager's interests and abilities.

2. Restate the 10 principles of early communication from Kaiser and Roberts (2011) in your own words, providing an example from an intervention visit for each principle or practice.

3. Assume you have observed an intervention visit with a child who displayed significant communication delays and is just about to turn 3 years old. The physical therapist, who was serving as the family's primary service provider and service coordinator, focused on the child's cognitive, fine motor, and gross motor skills but spent little time addressing the child's communication needs. The toddler is currently using two switches to indicate a forced-choice response. If you were assigned as this family's early interventionist, identify three activities or strategies that you might share with the child's mother to promote the child's communication. Provide a rationale for why you selected each strategy and/or activity. Explain how you would begin the dialogue with the mother about embedding these strategies and activities into the family's routines.

## REFERENCES

Ainsworth, M.D.S. (1969). Object relations, dependency, and attachment: A theoretical review of the infant-mother relationship. *Child Development, 40*(4), 969–1025.

American Academy of Pediatrics. (1998). *The complete and authoritative guide to caring for your baby and young child: Birth to age 5* (Rev. ed., Vol. 1). New York, NY: Bantam Books.

Baldwin, D.A., & Moses, L.J. (2001). Links between social understanding and early word learning: Challenges to current accounts. *Social Development, 10*(3), 309–329. doi:10.1111/1467-9507.00168

Blass, E.M. (1990). Suckling: Determinants, changes, mechanisms, and lasting impressions. *Developmental Psychology, 26*(4), 520–533. doi:10.1037/0012-1649.26.4.520

Boulware, G., Schwartz, L., & McBride, B. (1999). Addressing challenging behaviors at home. *Young Exceptional Children Monograph, 1,* 29–40.

Bowlby, J. (1982). Attachment and loss: Retrospect and prospect. *American Journal of Orthopsychiatry, 52*(4), 664–678. doi:10.1111/j.1939-0025.1982.tb01456.x

Branson, D., & Demchak, M. (2011). Toddler teachers' use of teaching pyramid practices. *Topics in Early Childhood Special Education, 30,* 196–208.

Camarata, S.M., & Nelson, K.E. (2006). Conversational recast intervention with preschool and older children. In S.F. Warren & M.E. Fey (Series Eds.) & R.J. McCauley & M.E. Fey (Vol. Eds.), *Communication and language intervention series: Treatment of language disorders in children.* (pp. 237–264). Baltimore, MD: Paul H. Brookes Publishing Co.

Camarata, S., Yoder, P., & Camarata, M. (2006). Simultaneous treatment of grammatical and speech-comprehensibility deficits in children with Down syndrome. *Down Syndrome: Research & Practice, 11*(1), 9–17. doi:10.3104/reports.314

Chaiklin, S. (2003). The zone of proximal development in Vygotsky's analysis of learning and instruction. In A. Kozulin, B. Gindis, & V.S. Ageyev (Eds.), *Vygotsky's educational theory in cultural context.* Cambridge, UK: Cambridge University Press.

DeCasper, A.J., & Fifer, W.P. (1980). Of human bonding: Newborns prefer their mothers' voices. *Science, 208,* 1174–1176.

Deiner, P.L. (1997). Social development. In *Infants and toddlers: Development and program planning* (pp. 213–245). Orlando, FL: Harcourt Brace.

Dollaghan, C.A., Campbell, T.F., Paradise, J.L., Feldman, H.M., Janosky, J.E., Pitcairn, D.N., & Kurs-Lasky, M. (1999). Maternal education and measures of early speech and language. *Journal of Speech-Language and Hearing Research, 42*(6), 1432–1443.

Dunlap, G., & Fox, L. (2011). Function-based interventions for children with challenging behavior. *Journal of Early Intervention, 33*(4), 333–343. doi:10:1177105 381511429971

Early Childhood Outcomes Center. (2009). *Child outcomes handout.* Retrieved from http://projects.fpg.unc.edu/~eco/assets/pdfs/Child_Outcomes_handout.pdf

Erickson, M.F., Sroufe, L.A., & Egeland, B. (1985). The relationship between quality of attachment and behavior problems in preschool in a high-risk sample. *Monographs of the Society for Research in Child Development, 50*(1/2), 147–166. doi:10.1111/1540-5834.ep11890039

Feldman, H.M., Dollaghan, C.A., Campbell, T.F., Colborn, D.K., Janosky, J., Kurs-Lasky, M., ...Paradise, J.L. (2003). Parent-reported language skills in relation to otitis media during the first 3 years of life. *Journal of Speech-Language and Hearing Research, 46*(2), 273–287. doi:10.1044/1092-4388(2003/022)

Feldman, R., Weller, A., Eidelman, A.I., & Sirota, L. (2002). Comparison of skin-to-skin (kangaroo) and traditional care: Parenting outcomes and preterm infant development. *Pediatrics, 110*(1), 16–26.

Fenson, L., Dale, P.S., Reznick, J.S., Bates, E., Thal, D.J., & Pethick, S.J. (1994). Variability in early communicative development. *Monographs of the Society for Research in Child Development, 59*(5), 1–173.

Ferber, S.G., & Makhoul, I.R. (2004). The effect of skin-to-skin contact (Kangaroo Care) shortly after birth on the neurobehavioral responses of the term newborn: A randomized, controlled trial. *Pediatrics, 113*(4), 858–865.

Fernald, A., & Kuhl, P. (1987). Acoustic determinants of infant preference for motherese speech. *Infant Behavior and Development, 10*(3), 279–293. doi:10.1016/0163-6383(87)90017-8

Gergely, G., & Watson, J.S. (1999). Early socio-emotional development: Contingency perception and the social-biofeedback model. In P. Rochat (Ed.), *Early social cognition: Understanding others in the first months of life* (pp. 101–136). New York, NY: Psychology Press.

Gross, A.L., & Ballif, B. (1991). Children's understanding of emotion from facial expressions and situations: A review. *Developmental Review, 11*(4), 368–398.

Hoff, E. (2003). The specificity of environmental influence: Socioeconomic status affects early vocabulary development via maternal speech. *Child Development, 74,* 1368–1378.

Hoff, E., & Tian, C. (2005). Socioeconomic status and cultural influences on language. *Journal of Communication Disorders, 38,* 271–278.

Honig, A.S. (1989, Summer). Talk, read, joke, make friends: Language power for children. *Day Care and Early Education,* 14–17.

Honig, A.S. (2001, Fall). Language flowering, language empowering: 20 ways parents and teachers can assist young children. *Montessori Life,* 31–35.

Huttenlocher, J., Vasilyeva, M., Waterfall, H.R., & Vevea, J.L. (2007). The varieties of speech to young children. *Developmental Psychology, 43,* 1062–1083.

Kaiser, A.P., Hancock, T.B., & Nietfeld, J.P. (2000). The effects of parent-implemented enhanced milieu teaching on the social communication of children who have autism. *Early Education and Development, 11*(4), 423–446. doi:10.1207/s15566935eed1104_4

Kaiser, A.P., & Roberts, M. (2011). Advances in early communication and language intervention. *Journal of Early Intervention, 33*(4), 298–309. doi:10.L177./1053815111 429968

Kisilevsky, B.S., Hains, S.M.J., Lee, K., Xie, X., Huang, H., Ye, H.H., ...Wang, Z. (2003). Effects of experience on fetal voice recognition. *Psychological Science, 14*(3), 220–224. doi:10.1111/1467-9280.02435

Kuebli, J. (1994). Young children's understanding of everyday emotions. *Young Children, 49*(3), 36–47.

Lazarus, R.S., & Folkman, S. (1987). Transactional theory and research on emotions and coping. *European Journal of Personality, 1*(3), 141–169.

Lonigan, C.J. (1994). Reading to preschoolers exposed: Is the emperor really naked? *Developmental Review, 14*(3), 303–323.

McDuffie, A.S., Yoder, P.J., & Stone, W.L. (2006). Labels increase attention to novel objects in children with autism and comprehension-matched children with typical development. *Autism, 10*(3), 288–301. doi:10.1177/1362361306063287

McLaughlin, B., White, D., McDevitt, T., & Raskin, R. (1983). Mothers' and fathers' speech to their young children: Similar or different? *Journal of Child Language, 10*(01), 245–252. doi:10.1017/S0305000900005286

Messinger, D., & Fogel, A. (2007). The interactive development of social smiling. *Advances in Child Development and Behaviour, 35,* 328–366.

Mikulincer, M., Shaver, P., & Pereg, D. (2003). Attachment theory and affect regulation: The dynamics, development, and cognitive consequences of attachment-related strategies. *Motivation and Emotion, 27*(2), 77–102. doi:10.1023/A:1024515519160

Millar, D.C., Light, J.C., & Schlosser, R.W. (2006). The impact of augmentative and alternative communication intervention on the speech production of individuals with developmental disabilities: A research review. *Journal of Speech Language and Hearing Research, 49*(2), 248–264. doi:10.1044/1092-4388(2006/021)

Morisset, C.E., Barnard, K.E., Greenberg, M.T., Booth, C.L., & Spieker, S.J. (1990). Environmental influences on early language development: The context of social risk. *Development and Psychopathology, 2*(2), 127–149. doi:10.1017/S0954579400000663

National Institute of Child Health and Human Development, Early Child Care Research Network. (2000). The relation of child care to cognitive and language development. *Child Development, 71*(4), 960–980.

National Parent Technical Assistance Center. (2013). *A family guide to participating in the child outcomes measurement process.* Minneapolis, MN: PACER Center.

Neilsen, S., Olive, M., Donovan, A., & McEvoy, M. (1998). Challenging behaviors in your classroom? Don't reach—teach instead! *Young Exceptional Children, 2*(1), 2–10.

Office of Special Education Programs. (2010). *29th annual report to Congress on the implementation of the Individuals with Disabilities Education Act, 2007* (Vol. 1). Washington, DC: Author.

Pan, B.A., Rowe, M.L., Singer, J.D., & Snow, C.E. (2005). Maternal correlates of growth in toddler vocabulary production in low-income families. *Child Development, 76,* 763–782.

Pancsofar, N., & Vernon-Feagans, L. (2006). Mother and father language input to young children: Contributions to later language development. *Journal of Applied Developmental Psychology, 27*(6), 571–587. doi:10.1016/j.appdev.2006.08.003

Pancsofar, N., & Vernon-Feagans, L. (2010). Fathers' early contributions to children's language development in families from low-income rural communities. *Early Childhood Research Quarterly, 25*(4), 450–463.

Petrill, S.A., Pike, A., Price, T., & Plomin, R. (2004). Chaos in the home and socioeconomic status are associated with cognitive development in early childhood: Environmental mediators identified in a genetic design. *Intelligence, 32,* 445–460.

Qi, C.H., Kaiser, A.P., & Milan, S. (2006). Children's behavior during teacher-directed and child-directed activities in Head Start. *Journal of Early Intervention, 28*(2), 97–110. doi:10.1177/105381510602800202

Raikes, H., Luze, G., Brooks-Gunn, J., Raikes, H.A., Pan, B.A., Tamis-LeMonda, C.S., ...Rodriguez, E.T. (2006). Mother–child bookreading in low-income families: Correlates and outcomes during the first three years of life. *Child Development, 77*(4), 924–953. doi:10.1111/j.1467-8624.2006.00911.x

Raver, S., Bobzien, J., Richels, C., Hester, P., Michalek, A., & Anthony, N. (2012). Effect of parallel talk on the language and interactional skills of preschoolers with cochlear implants and hearing aids. *Literacy Information and Computer Education Journal, 3*(1), 530–538.

Rescorla, L., & Achenbach, T.M. (2002). Use of the language development survey (LDS) in a national probability sample of children 18 to 35 months old. *Journal of Speech, Language, and Hearing Research, 45,* 733–743.

Rescorla, L., Alley, A., & Christine, J.B. (2001). Word frequencies in toddlers' lexicons. *Journal of Speech, Language & Hearing Research, 44*(3), 598–609.

Robertson, S.B., & Weismer, S.E. (1999). Effects of treatment on linguistic and social skills in toddlers with delayed language development. *Journal of Speech, Language and Hearing Research, 42*(5), 1234–1248.

Rossetti, L. (1996). *Communication intervention: Birth to three.* San Diego, CA: Singular Publishing.

Rutherford, M.D., & Przednowek, M. (2012). Fathers show modifications of infant-directed action similar to that of mothers. *Journal of Experimental Child Psychology, 111*(3), 367–378. doi:10.1016/j.jecp.2011.10.012

Scarborough, H.S., & Dobrich, W. (1994). On the efficacy of reading to preschoolers. *Developmental Review, 14*(3), 245–302.

Stark, R.E. (1986). Prespeech segmental feature development. In P. Fletcher & M. Garman (Eds.), *Language acquisition* (2nd ed., pp. 149–173). New York, NY: Cambridge University Press.

Striano, T., Kopp, F., Grossmann, T., & Reid, V.M. (2006). Eye contact influences neural processing of emotional expressions in 4-month-old infants. *Social Cognitive and Affective Neuroscience, 1*(2), 87–94.

Tamis-LeMonda, C.S., Shannon, J.D., Cabrera, N.J., & Lamb, M.E. (2004). Fathers and mothers at play with their 2- and 3-year-olds: Contributions to language and cognitive development. *Child Development, 75*(6), 1806–1820. doi:10.1111/j.1467-8624.2004.00818.x

Tomasello, M., & Farrar, M.J. (1986). Joint attention and early language. *Child Development, 57*(6), 1454–1463. doi:10.1111/1467-8624.ep7252234

Visser, N., Alant, E., & Harty, M. (2008). Which graphic symbols do 4-year-old children choose to represent each of the four basic emotions? *Augmentative and Alternative Communication, 24*(4), 302–312. doi:10.1080/07434610802467339

Warren, S.F., Yoder, P.J, Gazdag, G.E., Kim, K., & Jones, H.A. (1993). Facilitating prelinguistic communication skills in young children with developmental delays. *Journal of Speech and Hearing Research, 36,* 83–97.

Weisleder, A., & Fernald, A. (2013). Talking to children matters: Early language experience strengthens processing and builds vocabulary. *Psychological Science, 24*(11), 2143–2152. doi:10.1177/0956797613488145

Widen, S.C., & Russell, J.A. (2003). A closer look at preschoolers' freely produced labels for facial expressions. *Developmental Psychology, 39*(1), 114–128. doi:10.1037/0012-1649.39.1.114

Widen, S.C., & Russell, J.A. (2008). Children acquire emotion categories gradually. *Cognitive Development, 23*(2), 291–312.

Yoder, P.J., & Warren, S.F. (2002). Effects of prelinguistic milieu teaching and parent responsivity education on dyads involving children with intellectual disabilities. *Journal of Speech, Language, and Hearing Research, 45*(6), 1158–1174. doi:10.1044/1092-4388(2002/094)

# 6 | Acquisition and Use of Knowledge and Skills

Mary Beth Bruder, Erika M. Baril, and Anne George-Puskar

This chapter discusses how infants and toddlers acquire and learn to use their newfound knowledge and skills, including the following:

- Typical cognitive development
- Piagetian theory
- Relationship between cognition, communication development, and play
- Effects of early experiences on cognitive development
- Assessment and intervention
- Practices for encouraging the acquisition and use of knowledge and skills
- The role of the early childhood special educator
- Best practice highlights

## ⚲ ⚲ ⚲ Case Study: Kayla ⚲ ⚲ ⚲

Kayla is 24 months old and has been receiving early intervention since shortly after her birth. She was found to be eligible for services due to an established condition of Down syndrome. Kayla has made great progress over the past 2 years, despite multiple illnesses and hospitalizations. She had her tonsils and adenoids removed and ear tubes placed about a month ago, but she has been healthy since then. Kayla is a funny, caring girl with an infectious smile. She has a loving, supportive family (which includes a 5-year-old sister) and close extended family. Kayla's family is concerned with Kayla's health and all areas of her development. Related to her family's priorities for Kayla's play development, her interventionist is coaching her parents and sister to help Kayla learn about stacking, aiming, controlling, and releasing her grasp on objects and figuring out how some of her toys work. They are also trying to encourage more communication.

The second Office of Special Education Programs (OSEP, 2010) child outcome, "acquisition and use of knowledge and skills, including early language and communication," addresses how a child uses thinking and reasoning, memory, problem solving, symbols, and language, as well as how a child understands his or her physical and social worlds. In essence, it focuses on how children learn how to learn. This outcome includes how children use early concepts such as symbols, pictures, numbers, classifications, and spatial relationships; use imitation for learning; display indices of early thinking, such as object permanence; use their language and communication to show what they know; and use other skills that will lead to the development of early literacy. The Early Childhood Outcomes Center elaborated on this outcome:

> Over the early childhood period, children display tremendous changes in what they know and can do. The knowledge and skills acquired in the early childhood years, such as those related to communication, pre-literacy and pre-numeracy, provide the foundation for success in kindergarten and the early school years. This outcome involves activities such as thinking, reasoning, remembering, problem solving, number concepts, counting, and understanding the physical and social worlds. It also includes a variety of skills related to language and literacy including vocabulary, phonemic awareness, and letter recognition. (2009, p. 1)

Although all OSEP child outcomes focus on learning, this outcome statement focuses on meaningful behaviors that cross developmental domains and integrates skills through functional applications that can generalize across settings, people, and activities. The outcome examines a child's functional competence in many traditional domains: fine and gross motor, cognitive, and receptive and expressive language skills. By addressing this outcome, early intervention service providers guide parents in ways to offer learning opportunities that prepare children for success in their immediate and future participation in everyday activities in their home, community, and later in school.

The specific skills referred to in this outcome relate to processes such as acquiring general knowledge, learning new vocabulary words, and using early concepts, including imitation, size discrimination, and colors. Early numeracy and literacy also emerge as foundation skills for later school learning as a child nears his or her third birthday. Last, this outcome represents the many ways children begin to exercise control over their environment and the people around them through the use of tools, such as using spoons and crayons, and engaging in symbolic play.

This outcome attempts to capture how a very young child uses thinking, reasoning, remembering, and communication to learn about the world and his or her place within it. The second OSEP child outcome attempts to answer the following questions:

- How does the child copy other people's actions or try to learn new things?
- How does the child try to solve problems?
- How does the child understand early concepts, such as "big" and "small"?
- How does the child understand [receptive language] and respond to [expressive language or some other form of communication, such as sign or gestures] directions from others?
- How does the child communicate his or her thoughts and ideas? (National Parent Technical Assistance Center, 2013)

Children learn an enormous amount of knowledge during their first 3 years of life. There are many ways children demonstrate the knowledge they have acquired as they develop. This outcome focuses on how this knowledge translates into actions that result in problem-solving across an increasingly complex range of everyday learning opportunities. As a child ages and develops more skills and competence, more of the world is available for the child to experience and experiment with; the child develops increasingly more complex skills to accommodate new learning. An understanding of typical development allows service providers to better guide family members toward embedding experiences into their routines that will immediately benefit a child.

## TYPICAL COGNITIVE DEVELOPMENT

Cognition is often thought of in terms of preacademic or school readiness behaviors, such as naming colors, identifying shapes, completing puzzles, or numeracy skills (e.g., counting, sorting by size). Cognitive skills are also traditionally considered to be literacy skills for preschool-age children, such as retelling a story in sequence or identifying sight words. These skills are frequently taught in isolation, outside of naturally occurring daily activities, such as when a caregiver attempts to teach a preschool-age child sight words by looking at flash cards. However, this narrow conceptualization of cognitive development severely negates the rich and complicated acquisition of learning and skills that precede academic mastery, occurring during the first 3 years of life. For infants and toddlers, cognitive development includes the integration of all of the sensory and physical information a child is acquiring, as well as how a child uses that knowledge to make purposeful interactions in his or her life. The consideration for how a child uses knowledge and lets others know what he or she understands emphasizes the interrelated nature of cognitive and communication development. The foundations of communication development are discussed in Chapter 5, so this chapter only discusses communication skills as they affect the expression of how a child acquires knowledge and uses it. Table 6.1 shows some of the cognitive and communication milestones typically developing children learn from birth to 3 years of age.

During their first year and a half, children primarily interact with their world through their senses and the motor explorations of parts of their bodies—eyes, mouth, hands, arms, and legs. Children use their senses to experience what their bodies have explored. Feedback from both objects and people are critical to provide the motivation for a child to continue these explorations. This is especially true for new behaviors that may be challenging to initiate and sustain because of task difficulty, such as rolling over or pulling to stand. For example, children initially look at, mouth, touch, bang, and grasp objects and people. They then begin to demonstrate problem-solving skills to control the objects and the people around them, such as when an infant drops a toy off of the highchair and waits for his or her parent to pick it up. Infants and toddlers learn how to solve simple cause-and-effect problems in their play, such as activating the buttons on noisy books, sound puzzles, or other toys. They learn to demonstrate understanding of means–ends problem solving by, for example, using a scarf to pull an out-of-reach toy to them. At the same time, they are gaining mobility as they learn to roll, crawl, and eventually walk, which increases their ability to explore and satisfy their own needs.

When a child is between 18 and 36 months old, he or she builds on learning in both complexity and variety. A child refines the ability to solve problems using cause-and-effect, means–ends, and simple tools. For example, a child can use a mallet on a musical instrument, a hammer on the ball-pound toy, a spoon or fork at meals, and crayons on paper to draw. A child discovers that a stool can help him or her climb up for something that is out of reach. With regard to spatial problem solving, a child at this age demonstrates spatial awareness and mastery by being able to place rings on and off a stacker, complete simple wooden puzzles, and insert shapes into shape sorters. A child moves from a trial-and-error approach to developing thinking and cognitive planning when solving problems. For example, a younger toddler may repeatedly try to push a square shape into different holes on a shape sorter until he or she finds the correct hole using trial and error. As children develop knowledge of spatial awareness and planning, they eventually learn to look at the shape in

**Table 6.1.**  Sequence of typical cognitive, expressive, and receptive communication development

| Age | Cognitive | Expressive communication | Receptive communication |
|---|---|---|---|
| 0–6 months | Visually recognizes parent<br>Follows toy across field of vision<br>Looks at and reaches for toy<br>Looks for dropped toy<br>Mouths objects | Has different cries<br>Laughs<br>Coos and squeals<br>Babbles | Turns toward sound or voice<br>Shows anticipatory excitement<br>Smiles at mirror |
| 6–12 months | Bangs and shakes toys<br>Holds an object in each hand<br>Transfers object between hands<br>Uncovers hidden object<br>Makes a toy move<br>Repeats actions for attention or enjoyment | Waves good-bye<br>Shouts to get attention<br>Babbles a variety of consonant sounds<br>Says "mama" or "dada" with meaning | Responds to name<br>Follows simple directions ("Come here," "Give me")<br>Stops when told "no"<br>Plays simple ritual games, such as Peekaboo<br>Looks at object when named |
| 12–18 months | Puts circle in puzzle<br>Looks at and points to some pictures in book<br>Scribbles<br>Builds tower of three to four blocks<br>Puts object in containers<br>Imitates gestures | Points and vocalizes to ask or comment<br>Uses single words with meaning<br>Says "no" | Points to named object or picture<br>Follows direction to find out-of-sight object<br>Understands about 50 words |
| 18–24 months | Names and points to body parts<br>Dumps a small container<br>Matches sounds and objects to pictures<br>Sorts objects | Uses jargon with inflection<br>Imitates and uses two-word phrases<br>Uses own name | Follows two-step directions<br>Points to pictures in book<br>Understands several prepositions (*in, on*) |
| 24–36 months | Imitates drawing lines<br>Helps put things away<br>Engages in simple pretend play<br>Understands concepts of "one" and "big/little"<br>Matches colors, pictures | Uses three- to four-word phrases<br>Uses past tense, size words, plurals<br>Asks questions | Answers questions<br>Follows three-step directions<br>Points to many pictures in books |

their hands and the shape of the holes, so they are able to insert the square into the correct hole on the first try more often.

As a child nears his or her third birthday, the child becomes more organized and goal oriented with problem solving. At this time, preacademic skills begin to emerge. A child shows the ability to match and identify common objects, shapes, and colors (by pointing or using words). He or she is able to sort objects by different attributes and begins to show an emerging understanding of the concept of quantity. Between 2 and 3 years of age, pretend play skills also develop as a child moves from functional play schemes and using toys and objects appropriately during play. The development of pretend or symbolic play is an important milestone for both cognitive and communication development because it demonstrates a child's understanding of symbols, which will be discussed later in this chapter. To comprehend the complexity of this passage from birth to the third birthday, many interventionists rely on Piagetian theory to frame early thinking.

## PIAGETIAN THEORY

The foundation of our understanding of early cognition was developed by a Swiss psychologist named Jean Piaget (1896–1980). Piaget developed his theory of cognitive development over several decades. His interest in children's cognitive development began in the 1920s, when he studied children's intelligence tests. As Piaget studied children's development, including his own children, he concluded that children constructed their own learning by acting on their world. Piaget's theory remains one of the most prominent and well-utilized theories of cognitive development today.

Piaget's theory was built around the concept of schema development. According to Piaget (1952), children develop *schemas* (i.e., units of knowledge) as ways to organize and interpret their world. Through schemas, children develop patterns of thinking and behaving in an effort to increase their understanding of new information. Schemas are considered to be "ways of looking at the world that organize our past experiences and provide a framework for understanding our future experiences" (Myers, 1992, p. 70). An example of a schema would be a young child's concept of a cat as a four-legged animal with a long tail. Thus, when the young child sees any animal with four legs and a long tail, he or she will initially refer to that animal as a "cat" as well.

As children discover and learn through experiences with peers, adults, and their environment, their schemas develop and shift. This occurs when they make new discoveries or receive new information that does not fit into their preexisting schemas. This phenomenon is known as *disequilibrium*. For example, children will learn that not all four-legged animals with long tails are cats. Some four-legged animals with long tails are dogs, others are foxes, and still others are raccoons. A child usually experiences disequilibrium when encountering a new, unfamiliar experience. When the environmental demands exceed that which is presently in a child's repertoire, the child is called upon to work a little harder to modify existing schemas. This reorganization of existing skills leads to increased sophistication in a child's ability to accommodate or understand his or her environment. This process is what Piaget referred to as *adaptation*. If environmental demands are too great, adaptation does not occur as the young child becomes frustrated. Similarly, if the demands are too small, the child does not expand his or her current repertoire; thus, disequilibrium is no longer present. It is through the experience of disequilibrium—when environmental demands are just right to challenge the child and encourage adaptation—that children initiate learning new skills and knowledge.

Children seek equilibration by learning how to adapt to their environments (Piaget, 1952). *Equilibration* is an ongoing process by which a child regulates new learning to maintain a state of internal balance or equilibrium. Children, in their quest for equilibration, regulate and adapt their behavior through the complementary processes that Piaget referred to as assimilation and accommodation. These two processes work together: One needs to assimilate in order to accommodate (Feldman, 2004). *Assimilation* is the process of adapting what one is learning to what one already knows (Dunst, 1981). For example, given the simple schema for cat, young children might assimilate by referring to all four-legged animals as cats. Eventually, however, children learn that their schema is too specific and narrow. Thus, they accommodate their learning by expanding their schema of four-legged animals with long tails to include other animals as well. It is through *accommodation* that children modify existing schemas or create new schemas, thereby learning something new.

## Piagetian Stages

Piaget's theory is built on a hierarchy of stages. According to Piaget (1952), children move through four stages of cognitive development over the course of their lives from birth to adolescence and adulthood. The impetus for this movement from one stage to the next is when schemas are altered due to a state of disequilibrium that leads to assimilation and accommodation. The four stages from birth to adolescence are sensorimotor, preoperational, concrete operational, and formal operational. Only the first two stages are discussed here because they develop or begin to develop during very early childhood. The mechanisms responsible for helping children to make the transition from one stage to the next include the four processes discussed: assimilation, accommodation, disequilibrium, and equilibration. An important criterion for movement from one stage to the next is the integration of conceptual learning of earlier stages as a child progresses through the later stages of development. That is, a child builds on what he or she has learned to move to more sophisticated learning. In this way, the earlier behaviors are embedded within higher order behaviors as a child progresses in learning.

*Sensorimotor Stage*   The sensorimotor period occurs during the first 2 years of life (Piaget, 1952; Piaget & Inhelder, 1973). As its name implies, a child learns to understand the world during this period primarily through sensory and motor interactions such as seeing, feeling, mouthing, and banging. It is important to note that all children pass through these stages in order and at their own individual pace. This stage is composed of six substages, as follows.

*1. Simple Reflexes (Birth to 1 Month)*   As its name suggests, this substage is a time when an infant is controlled by his or her early reflexes. Crying, the sucking reflex, and the grasping reflex are examples. The sucking reflex occurs when infants suck on whatever is placed near their mouth. The grasping reflex occurs when infants grab onto anything that is put it in their palm. During this stage, infants begin to coordinate their reflexes (e.g., sucking, crying, vision, grasping) as they mature.

*2. Primary Circular Reactions (2–4 Months)*   In this stage, infants tend to focus on themselves (i.e., primary) and what their bodies can do. They repeat behaviors again and again (i.e., circular), particularly those behaviors that end up resulting in pleasurable outcomes, such as thumb sucking. In this stage, events occur through chance, such as when an infant accidentally shakes a rattle placed in his or her hand. Through chance, infants begin to learn that they have some control over their world. By accidentally shaking the rattle, the infant learns that he or she can move and cause the rattle to make a pleasurable noise. This learning eventually leads to more purposeful movements, with the infant controlling the movement and sounds of the rattle, as seen in the next stage.

*3. Secondary Circular Reactions (4–8 Months)*    The learning outcome of this stage is cause and effect. Infants begin to realize that when they do something, something happens. When they drop a toy, someone picks it up. Every time they bat at a toy, it makes a noise and/or moves. When they vocalize and point to an adult, the adult reciprocates and talks back. Their repeated behaviors or actions (i.e., circular) cause something to happen (i.e., secondary). In the events occurring during the primary circular reaction stage, events provided direct sensory input to the infants, such as thumb sucking; however, in the secondary circular reaction stage, events occur that provide indirect sensory input. In this stage, the infant who accidentally shook the rattle develops an understanding that it is his or her movement that causes the rattle to make a noise.

*4. Coordination of Secondary Circular Reactions (8–12 Months)*    In this substage, infants are refining their understanding of cause and effect and developing intentionality and goal-directed behaviors. They realize that what they do directly affects their world and that they can manipulate their environment. Infants learn that their behaviors cause a response/reaction in their environment, with people as well as with objects. At this stage of development, infants are also becoming more mobile. They now are sitting, rolling, and crawling, and even cruising and walking by the end of the stage. They are able to cross midline to reach toys and objects, meaning they can reach across the middle of their bodies, and they are able to use their hands to manipulate objects. For example, they can push the buttons on a busy box on purpose because they want to see doors pop open.

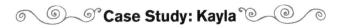

## Case Study: Kayla

Kayla was still learning how to use her hands to manipulate objects. She needed help to learn about stacking things, such as her favorite shape-sort blocks or soup cans and pudding boxes in the pantry. She was also learning to refine how she aimed and controlled her grasp so that she could put her straw in her cup. The primary service provider (i.e., the early childhood special educator on the team) was helpful in coaching Kayla's parents and her older sister, Maddy, on how to allow Kayla to practice stacking by assisting with putting groceries away in the pantry and helping to organize the cans and small boxes on the shelf. Kayla also got regular practice with her grasp by helping to set the table and putting her straw in her cup at each meal at home and at child care.

During this stage, children also develop the key concept of object permanence. *Object permanence* is the understanding that when something is out of sight, it still exists. Children demonstrate their knowledge of object permanence when they look for an object or person that is out of sight. This is the stage when children demonstrate their distress and search for a lost object or person. Infants show an awareness of the importance of their caregivers and exhibit clear attachment behaviors, such as crying when a loved one leaves; this is seen when a child experiences *separation anxiety,* which is a typical phase of early development and a demonstration of this early concept. Although Kayla did not look for her sister when she first left the room, Kayla eventually learned to vocalize, look for, and wait for her sister's return when they played the "Where's Maddy?" game. Playing Peekaboo and Hide and Seek games are natural ways to help young children develop their understanding of object permanence.

*5. Tertiary Circular Reactions (12–18 Months)*    Infants become early toddlers at this stage and demonstrate most of their learning through trial and error. They become more creative and flexible, and they are now able to expand their repertoire of what to do with objects (i.e., tertiary). For example, at the beginning of this stage, children might only push a toy car while crawling. By the end of this stage, they might push a toy car down a ramp to watch it go. Toddlers are also starting to walk and talk.

If stacking cubes were to be accomplished in this stage, the real purpose would be to allow a child to experiment with stacking many different things to demonstrate placement skills, attention and persistence, spatial awareness through aligning the objects, grasping, releasing, and problem-solving through trial and error while experimenting with many stacking schemes. Assuming a child understands this concept by merely stacking three 1-inch cubes does not provide the child with the range of experiences that are necessary to master the concepts learned in this stage. Children need to stack many different common materials, such as diapers on the shelf, plastic cups in the cupboard, and small boxes of cereal on the table.

*6. Early Representational Thought (18–24 Months)*    In this stage, toddlers move from the concrete to the abstract by developing symbolic thought. It is in this final substage of the sensorimotor period that children begin to understand the world through thought and other mental processes. One indication that toddlers are in this stage is that they are capable of *delayed imitation*. Whereas younger infants are able to imitate actions and words immediately after their occurrence, toddlers in this stage are able to imitate something that they saw or heard after some time has passed.

**Characteristics of the Sensorimotor Stage of Development**    Piaget also observed hierarchies of different types of behaviors within the stages of development he proposed. Table 6.2 provides a hierarchy of these behaviors and concepts based on Dunst (1981). These concepts rely on learning to think and learning to use communication and motor actions to express what the child knows. Each key concept and its sequence of development are described in the following sections.

*Object Permanence*    As stated, object permanence is the ability to understand that objects exist even when they cannot be seen. The sequence begins with the looking response, in which the infant attempts to visually follow objects moving in and out of the visual field. The infant subsequently turns his or her body or head to maintain visual contact with objects moving either in or out of the visual field. At the next level, the child is able to recognize an object by seeing only its component parts. Now the child is capable, for example, of securing objects that are partially hidden, such as when an infant finds her rattle peeking out from underneath her blanket. Being able to search for completely hidden objects occurs next, implying that the child understands that a disappearing object can be found by removing the specific barrier obstructing his or her view.

Further persistence is required at the next level of development, when two or more obstacles must be removed in succession in order to secure an object hidden behind or under them. For example, some cognitive assessments challenge a child's understanding of object permanence by having the child watch as a toy is covered by two small cloths. The child is expected to remove the first cloth and, upon finding that the object is still covered, persist by removing the second cloth. Until then, the child can only find disappearing objects when the displacements are visible, in the sense that the child directly observes

**Table 6.2.** Selected characteristics of the sensorimotor period

| Stages (age in months) | Domains of sensorimotor development | | | | | | |
|---|---|---|---|---|---|---|---|
| | Purposeful problem solving | Object permanence | Spatial relationships | Causality | Vocal imitation | Gestural imitation | Play |
| A: Use of reflexes (0–1) | Shows only reflexive reactions in response to external stimuli | No active search for objects vanishing from sight | No signs of appreciation of spatial relationships between objects | No signs of understanding causal relationships | Vocal contagion; cries upon hearing another infant cry | No signs of imitation of movements | No signs of intentional play behavior |
| B: Primary circular reactions (1–4.5) | Adaptations first acquired: Coordination of two behavioral schemes (e.g., hand–mouth coordination) | Attempt to maintain visual contact with objects moving outside the visual field | Reacts to external stimuli as representing independent spatial fields (e.g., visual, auditory) rather than as a spatial nexus | Shows signs of precausal understanding (e.g., places thumb in mouth to suck on it) | Repeats sound just produced following adult imitation of the sound | Repeats movements just made following adult imitation of the action | Produces primary circular reactions repeatedly in enjoyable manner |
| C: Secondary circular reactions (4.5–9) | Procedures for making interesting sights last: Repeats actions to maintain the reinforcing consequences produced by the action | Reinstates visual contact with objects by 1) anticipating the terminal position of the moving object; and 2) removing a cloth placed over his or her face; retrieves a partially hidden object | Shows signs of understanding relationships between self and external events (e.g., follows trajectory of rapidly falling object) | Uses phenomenalistic procedures (e.g., generalized excitement) as a causal action to have an adult repeat an interesting spectacle | Imitates sounds already in his or her repertoire | Imitates simple gestures already in his or her repertoire, which are visible to him or her | Repeats interesting actions applied to familiar objects |

| Stage | Means–Ends | Object Permanence | Spatial Relationships | Communication | Vocal Imitation | Motor Imitation | Play |
|---|---|---|---|---|---|---|---|
| *D:* Coordination of secondary circular reactions (9–12) | Serializes two heretofore separate behaviors in goal-directed sequences | Secures objects seen hidden under, behind, etc., a single barrier | Rotates and examines objects with signs of appreciation of their three-dimensional attributes: size, shape, weight, etc. | Touches adult's hands to have that person instigate or continue an interesting game or action | Imitates novel sounds, but only ones similar to those he or she already produces | Imitates 1) invisible movements made by self (e.g., sticking out the tongue), and 2) novel movements composed of actions familiar to him or her | During problem-solving sequences, abandons the terminus in favor of playing with the means; ritualization; applies appropriate social actions to different objects |
| *E:* Tertiary circular reactions (12–18) | Discovers "novel" means behavior needed to obtain a desired goal | Secures objects hidden through a series of visible displacements | Combines and relates objects in different spatial configurations (e.g., places blocks into a cup) | Hands an object to an adult to have that person repeat or instigate a desired reaction | Imitates novel sound patterns and words he or she had not previously heard | Imitates novel movements he or she cannot see self perform (e.g., invisible gestures) and has not previously performed | Adaptive play begins: Uses one object (e.g., doll cup) as a substitute for another (e.g., adult-sized cup) during play with objects |
| *F:* Invention of new means through mental combinations (representation and foresight) (18–24) | "Invents" means behavior, via internal thought processes, needed to obtain a desired goal | Recreates sequence of displacements to secure objects: Secures objects hidden through a sequence of invisible displacements | Manifests the ability to "represent" the nature of spatial relationships existing between objects, and between objects with him- or herself | Shows capacity to 1) infer a cause, given only its effect, and 2) foresee an effect given a cause | Imitates complex verbalizations; reproduces previously heard sounds and words from memory; deferred imitation | Imitates complex motor movements; reproduces previously observed actions from memory; deferred imitation | Symbolic play: Uses one object as a "signifier" for another (e.g., a box for a doll bed); symbolically enacts an event without having ordinarily used objects present |

From Dunst, C.J. (1981). *Infant learning: A cognitive-linguistic intervention strategy* (pp. 28–30). Allan, TX: DLM Teaching Resources; adapted by permission.

the object being hidden. The child eventually understands that objects can be found even if they are hidden through invisible displacements, meaning that the object is not hidden where the child thinks it is hidden, so the child understands to continue searching. Understanding how to find and search for hidden objects requires that the child begins to develop representational problem-solving abilities, which show that the infant has the ability to find objects independently of how they were observed to be hidden.

*Spatial Relationships*    *Spatial relationships* refer to the development of the infant's understanding of the spatial orientations and relationships between objects, persons, and oneself, and among people. Development begins with abilities such as visually locating the source of various sounds, called *sound localization,* and alternating glances between two visually presented objects. Further understanding of spatial orientations is apparent as the infant becomes capable of visually following rapidly moving objects that fall both within and outside of the immediate visual field. Further progress is achieved as the child begins to relate objects to his or her own body. For instance, the child is now able to turn a bottle around in order to place the nipple in his or her mouth.

At the next level, the child begins to relate objects to one another. At this stage, the child begins to engage in the often-observed behaviors of dropping objects into containers and building towers of blocks and other objects. Last, the child is capable of indicating where people or objects are even when they are absent, such as knowing that a favorite blanket is in the next room. With this understanding, the child is able to make complicated detours to obtain objects not directly accessible to him or her, as when a child attempts to crawl to the next room to go find the ball when asked where it is.

*Causality*    *Causality* refers to when an infant is able to assign a cause to an action. Development of causality begins with the infant's ability to engage in precausal acts such as thumb sucking and hand watching, both of which are engaged in simply for enjoyment. At the next level of development, the infant uses secondary circular reactions (e.g., shaking a rattle) and procedures, such as arm waving, body shaking, or leg kicking, as causal behaviors for inducing an adult to repeat an interesting activity or action. For example, the infant touches an adult's hand as a causal action, indicating a desire to have the adult repeat an action that the child enjoyed, such as repeating a game of Peekaboo.

More direct causal behaviors appear at the next level when an infant is provided with a toy requiring a causal action beyond his or her cognitive capabilities. At this point, the infant, instead of applying a lower form of causal action such as banging the toy, hands the toy to an adult to have it activated. Toward the end of development in this sequence, the infant actively searches for the causal behavior required to activate new toys or other mechanical devices, such as when a child presses buttons on a toy, assuming that one of them must activate it. The infant shows the capacity to infer a cause given an effect, as well as foresee an effect given a cause.

*Vocal Imitation*    *Vocal imitation* refers to repeating sounds that are heard. This sequence begins with the infant exercising the ready-made schemas of vocalizing, including both crying and cooing sounds. Repeating and experimenting with various sounds makes them highly familiar and recognizable to the infant. When hearing a sound pattern produced by an adult or another child, the infant responds by smiling or increasing his or her body movements, which are all signs of recognition. Later, the child vocalizes in response to hearing familiar sounds but generally produces different sound patterns. As these pre-imitation skills develop further, the infant attempts to more directly imitate sound patterns that are in the infant's repertoire. Upon hearing "mama," an infant at this stage might reply with a /m/ sound. The child eventually is able to imitate both familiar babbling sounds and highly familiar words; for example, the child learns to fully imitate the word *mama*.

Next, the infant attempts to imitate unfamiliar, novel sound patterns, such as "vroom vroom" when the infant hears an older sibling playing with cars. Toward the end of the sequence in the emergence of vocal imitation, the infant begins to imitate new, simple words heard in the environment. The highest attainment occurs when the infant begins to imitate models previously heard in other contexts under somewhat different conditions, which is called *deferred imitation*. Kayla's family reported that she had been imitating words from previous experiences. In fact, they shared that she said "kitty" 2 days after visiting another family who had a cat as she was looking through a picture book with her sister.

*Gestural Imitation*    Gestural imitation follows a sequence similar to that of vocal imitation. When seeing a familiar gesture performed by an adult, such as throwing a kiss, the infant often increases the rate of one or more motor actions in the child's repertoire, although not necessarily the one performed by the adult. The infant may kick or wave his or her arms in excitement. These pseudoimitative motor responses suggest that the infant may recognize that the adult's behavior is occurring. Through repeated experiences with such situations, the infant learns to more closely approximate the behaviors seen in others. At the next level, the infant combines the simple motor responses of the preceding level and is able to imitate complex motor actions composed of behaviors already in his or her repertoire. For example, up-and-down patting motions may be combined in a back-and-forth, across-the-midline action to produce clapping during a game of Pat-a-cake.

At the next level of development, the child is capable of attempting to imitate unfamiliar, visible gestures (e.g., drumming or snapping the fingers) and subsequently is able to imitate unfamiliar, invisible gestures (e.g., tapping the top of the head). Visible gestures are behaviors the child is able to see him- or herself perform, whereas invisible gestures are behaviors the child cannot see him- or herself perform without the use of a mirror. The ability to engage in deferred imitation, or imitating something the child saw performed in a different context, is the highest gestural imitative ability of the sensorimotor period.

*Play or Schemes for Relating to Objects*    *Play or schemes for relating to objects* involve the emergence of symbolic play and naming behaviors. This sequence of steps examines how the infant differentiates between objects according to the various functions they serve. At first, the child indiscriminately applies the same behaviors to all objects, with no sign of understanding the particular characteristics of the objects themselves. At this level, mouthing and passive visual inspection of objects are dominant behaviors.

As the infant's behavioral repertoire expands, simple motor responses such as shaking, banging, waving, and hitting are applied to objects more specifically. Further differentiation is noted when the infant engages in active visual examination of objects and uses complex motor actions specific to the functions of the objects themselves, such as when a child purposefully shakes a toy after seeing that it has another object inside. At the next level, the child begins to combine objects and actions in socially related sequences. Hugging a doll, drinking from a cup, and combing an adult's hair all emerge in the context of adult–child interactions. This particular behavior pattern serves as a prerequisite for the development of symbolic play abilities. Sharing, showing, and naming actions, which develop after these social actions, represent examples of the top-level landmarks in this sequence.

***Characteristics of the Preoperational Stage***    After the sensorimotor stage, around 2 years of age, children enter into a preoperational stage of development. The operational component of this stage refers to logical thinking. This is the stage at which children begin to make more symbolic sense of their world before entering into the concrete operational stage around age 7 years. (Because this book covers early childhood from birth to 3 years, anything beyond the early part of the preoperational stage of development is not covered.) During this stage, children are learning symbolic thought and language. They are learning that words represent actual objects in their world. For example, the word *ball* can now represent all balls, not just a specific ball. Some aspects or characteristics of preoperational thinking are present because children do not yet have more logistical thinking patterns.

***Egocentrism***    *Egocentrism* is defined as the child's inability to distinguish the perspectives of his or her own from the perspectives of others. This lack of perspective leads toddlers to think that the thoughts they have are the thoughts of others. For example, the child might think, "I like to play with the ball, so that must mean Mommy must like to play with the ball, too." This also relates to objects. For instance, a child might be talking on the phone with her grandmother about a toy and believe that her grandmother is also seeing the same toy.

***Animism, Irreversibility, and Centration***    Three other concepts refined and developed in the preoperational stage are animism, irreversibility, and centration (Piaget, 1952). *Animism* is when a child attributes lifelike characteristics to inanimate objects. For example, an adult might ask a child, "Why is it raining?" The young child's response may be that "the sky is sad" or "the clouds are hurting." *Irreversibility* is the inability of a child to reverse a sequence of events. For example, if a child's mother pours juice in a cup, it would not make sense to a child in the preoperational phase to pour juice that he or she did not drink back into the carton. *Centration* is focusing on one aspect, or the center, of a situation rather than being able to focus on multiple aspects of an event. For instance, a child with a juice cup might complain that she does not have enough juice when the cup is half full. If the mother were to pour the juice into a smaller cup that would appear full, the child would likely think that there is enough juice to drink. The child has focused on whether the cups appear full or not, rather than the actual amount of juice in the cups, which is the same.

***Emergence of Symbolic Thought***    Another aspect to the preoperational stage of development is the emergence of symbolic thought. A child with symbolic thought is able to use words and images that are familiar in order to make sense of and represent the world. For example, if an adult talks to a child in the preoperational stage about a book or a dog, the child is able to understand that the words apply to many objects, not just a specific book or the family's dog. The preoperational stage is a period of exploration for children when they are continually learning new symbolic words and play, but they have yet to fully understand the logistics of perspective taking and concrete operations (which is the next stage of development, occurring around age 7 years).

## RELATIONSHIP BETWEEN COGNITION AND PLAY

*Play* has been defined as spontaneous, naturally occurring activities with objects that engage attention and interest. It can be solitary or done with others, and it may or may not involve pretending (Lifter & Bloom, 1998). Play can be used as a barometer of a child's cognitive capacity, the means of communication between children and others, and the context for assessment and intervention (Lifter, Foster-Sanda, Arzamarski, Briesch, & McClure, 2011). Considering all of these functions, it is no surprise that there are differing perspectives and definitions of play. These perspectives have been delineated into two categories by Lifter, Mason, and Barton (2011): the *behavioral perspective*, which focuses on what children do, and the *constructionist perspective*, which focuses on why children do what they do and the relationship to the child's underlying cognitive processes and developmental competence. Although these perspectives differ, they can be complementary, and both perspectives lend themselves to assessment and intervention practices with infants and young children. However, it is the second perspective that aligns with the cognitive theory of Piaget.

Play skills follow a developmental progression that has been shown to be related to a child's cognitive competence (Lifter, Mason, et al., 2011). Many studies have documented and categorized the progression of play behavior, and one of the earliest was described by Parten (1932). Her work resulted in a hierarchy of social play that is still in use today, which begins with unoccupied play and progresses to solitary play, onlooker behavior, and then parallel play, associative play, and cooperative play. Children can move in and out of these stages as they develop more cognitive, communicative, and social competence. Similarly, object play has been categorized into a hierarchical progression through observational studies of children (Lifter, Foster-Sanda, et al., 2011; Pierce-Jordan & Lifter, 2005). For example, play may progress from exploratory play to relational play, then functional play, and finally pretend play (Barton, 2010). Each of these categories may be combined as new skills and competencies are developed.

Piaget assumed a strong relationship between play and cognition. He identified three categories of play, which corresponded to his cognitive stages: 1) practice play, emerging during the sensorimotor period; 2) symbolic play, emerging during the preoperational stage; and 3) games with rules, developing during the concrete stage (approximately ages 7–11 years). Two play schemes that develop in the sensorimotor stage and continue through the preoperational stage are provided as examples to illustrate this relationship: cause-and-effect play and symbolic play.

## Cause-and-Effect Play

An infant's understanding of cause-and-effect play grows out of the development of early joint attention skills. The development of joint attention, as discussed in Chapter 5, is demonstrated when children are able to focus attention on one event and readily shift attention to another. However, in the preoperational cognitive stage, children are not able to focus on more than one aspect of the event at one time (centrality).

When a child uses joint attention, it demonstrates that he or she is able to understand that there is a consequence to an event in reference to a toy. For example, an infant may use joint attention to understand that he or she can activate a toy by pressing a lever. The child attends to the lever, then to the lights that flash once the lever is pressed. An older infant who is using joint attention might get a parent's attention by verbalizing, then pointing out the window to the garbage truck going by. The child understands that by looking at the parent and pointing out the window, he or she can cause the parent to share in the same observation. When a child is able to turn a light on and off, turn a knob on a table lamp, or know that the wheels of a toy car will turn when a button is pushed down, he or she is demonstrating an understanding of cause and effect. This level of play requires a wider knowledge of an object's purpose, which expands the child's thinking beyond his or her knowledge of the toy simply as an object.

A child requires some level of exploratory play to develop an understanding of cause and effect. When children are allowed to explore toys and objects, they learn to make sense of the world with familiar objects in their natural environment. Children who are at the level of cause-and-effect play also need to display some level of imitation and joint attention skills in order to use cause-and-effect skills on their own. Children at this level of play can be both verbal as well as nonverbal and adequately master an appropriate level of cause-and-effect play. Using an object for its intended use is not needed in order to master a cause-and-effect level of play. However, the child should have a basic understanding of a consequence to a self-produced event. During this level of play, a child can also be at the parallel play stage, playing next to another child without engaging him or her, and still understand the effects of cause and effect with toys and objects.

In Kayla's case, she was able to demonstrate imitation and an early understanding of symbols as she began learning sign language as a communication tool to support her speech. She tended to explore new toys with a good deal of variety in her play, and she sought out toys that provided her with immediate feedback, such as musical books and toys with lights and sounds, which she played with over and over. She often would invite familiar people to play with her by handing the toy to them to bring them into her play.

## Symbolic Play

As described in the Piagetian stages of development, symbolism is a skill that is developed typically around 2 years of age and continues to be refined as the child matures. *Symbolic play* (also called *pretend play*) refers to a child's ability to play with an object as something other than its intended use. Kayla liked to pretend that the plastic banana from her kitchen set was a telephone and would "call" her father at work when she and Maddy played in the afternoon.

As cited by Piaget (1952), the ability to use symbolic play primarily depends on a child's ability to represent objects and situations that are both present and nonpresent. Some examples of pretend play include making "quack quack" sounds when playing with a toy duck or using a ball as a mountain for the duck to jump over during play. Another example is the ability of a child to use and manipulate a doll as well as props to set up a situation, such as feeding the doll using toy plates and utensils or giving the doll a bath using pretend water and toy bottles of soap. The most important aspect of symbolic play is that a child is able to independently understand that objects are representative of something else during a play activity. This level of play and understanding can be reached by children in the preoperational stage of development, but full understanding comes later.

Verbal language or other functional communication skills, such as using pictures, gestures, and signs, are another important aspect of symbolic play. Children express their deeper understanding of pretend actions and the use of objects by using vocabulary to explain what is occurring in a situation. Using spontaneous comments during symbolic play helps them to develop the exchange that occurs with a peer or adult during play situations. Although verbal representations are a major aspect of pretend play, this does not mean that nonverbal children are unable to pretend with objects and toys. Nonverbal does not necessarily mean noncommunicative. Nonverbal children consequently can use play to communicate and express their creativity and thinking, but adults must be more heavily reliant on behavioral observations to interpret what is occurring. A child who is nonverbal can still execute the same play skills as a verbal child; for example, the child can still play with the doll and give it a bath with pretend water and a toy bottle of soap or feed the baby a pretend toy food. Kayla loved to pretend to feed her favorite stuffed giraffe. She learned this scheme by playing with her mother and pretending to feed the animal her snacks.

## EFFECTS OF EARLY EXPERIENCES ON COGNITIVE AND COMMUNICATION DEVELOPMENT

As previously described, cognitive development progresses in a simple to complex sequence, with earlier skills being used as the foundation for later skills. As such, there are multiple threats to a child's development that can disrupt the acquisition and use of higher-order cognitive knowledge and skills. These threats may affect and delay a child's ability to develop in accordance to his or her chronological age and can be categorized as risk conditions for a typical developmental trajectory. The result is then a discrepancy between what a child is able to do and what the child's chronological age suggests that he or she should be able to do. These threats can be either biological, environmental, or both.

### Biological Risks to Cognitive and Communication Development

Children's biology predisposes them to interact with people and the environment. A biological risk can be genetic, such as Down syndrome, or the result of an adverse event in a child's life, such as in utero exposure to drugs, chronic or acute illness, or physical trauma. Kayla had both a genetic risk (e.g., Down syndrome) and adverse events (e.g., heart condition). It is important to remember that any risk the child experiences will affect the child's level of subsequent functioning. For example, a premature child who demonstrates delayed motor development will consequently have a decrease in learning opportunities to explore and act on the environment. Likewise, children with Down syndrome, such as Kayla, who have low muscle tone in their faces that affect their ability to smile, will likely have decreased opportunities for reciprocal face-to-face interactions with family members when they are infants. Finally, a child with autism spectrum disorder may be averse to experiences that require social engagement, which is needed to initiate learning and receive feedback from the environment to advance cognitive skills. In all of these examples, each child's biological makeup has the potential to adversely affect his or her ability to develop new knowledge and skills.

### Environmental Risks to Cognitive and Communication Development

Infants and young children may also experience risks from the world around them that result in delays in their cognitive development. For example, a history of trauma, such as child abuse, may result in difficulties with engaging with people and objects, thus limiting a child's ability to explore and learn. Likewise, experiences with violence or poverty may affect the range and variety of learning opportunities available to a child, through which his or her cognitive skills could have advanced. Assessment allows early interventionists to gather information about risk factors, determine where a child is currently functioning, and identify functional skills that the child needs to more effectively interact with the physical and social worlds.

## ASSESSMENT OF COGNITIVE SKILLS

Prior to any intervention, an assessment must be implemented to establish a child's skill level in all areas of development (Noonan & McCormick, 2013). Many early childhood assessments categorize the cognitive domain of development into preacademic skills only, as opposed to examining a child's behavior across and within the foundational skills of learning as described by Piaget (1952). One of the first assessments to examine cognitive development using the lens provided by Piaget was the Infant Ordinal Scales (Uzgiris & Hunt, 1987). This seminal assessment was used by many to identify the cognitive skill level of infants and young children with and without disabilities. An expansion of this model into a cognitive linguistic curriculum-referenced assessment was completed by Dunst in 1981. This curriculum addressed knowledge acquisition, organization, and use as the methods by which children applied cognitive and linguistic strategies to learn.

Two comprehensive, curriculum-referenced developmental assessments that focus on cognitive behaviors using a Piagetian framework include the Assessment, Evaluation, and Programming System for Infants and Children (AEPS®; Bricker et al., 2003) and the Carolina Curriculum for Infants and Toddlers with Special Needs (CCITSN; Johnson-Martin, Attermeier, & Hacker, 2004). The Early Learning Accomplishment Profile (E-LAP; Glover, Preminger, & Sanford, 2002) is often used as an assessment for cognitive and communication domains, but it does not follow a strict Piagetian-oriented philosophical orientation. All of these tools address the complexity, interrelatedness, and comprehensiveness of cognitive behaviors displayed by infants and young children, as described in the following sections.

## Assessment, Evaluation, and Programming System for Infants and Children

The AEPS (Bricker et al., 2003), a curriculum-referenced assessment, was designed to be used by direct services providers to evaluate the skills and abilities of infants and young children who are at risk for or who have disabilities. The assessment focuses on infants from birth to 3 years. Six curricular areas are addressed in the tool: fine motor, gross motor, adaptive, cognitive, social-communication, and social. Each domain contains multiple subdomains, representing a vertical progression of skills and behaviors. The cognitive domain contains the following Piagetian-influenced strands: sensory stimuli, object permanence, causality, imitation, problem solving, interaction with others, and early concepts. The curriculum describes the precursors to skills, explains each skill's importance, and provides related and concurrent objectives. Teaching suggestions for each skill for a home or group setting are described, as are environmental supports to elicit the skill.

## Carolina Curriculum for Infants and Toddlers with Special Needs

The CCITSN (Johnson-Martin et al., 2004), a curriculum-referenced assessment, focuses on intervention strategies that can be embedded into the daily routines of a child in a home or group setting. It covers five developmental domains: cognition, communication, social adaptation, fine motor skills, and gross motor skills, with each having multiple subdomains. The cognition domain represents a Piagetian perspective through the use of conceptual learning and behaviors indicative of the substages of the sensorimotor and preoperational stages of early development. The subdomains include attention and memory (visual/spatial), visual perception (blocks and puzzles), visual perception (matching and sorting), functional use of objects and symbolic play, problem solving and reasoning, and number concepts. The curriculum also has a cognitive/communication domain that involves concepts of vocabulary (receptive), concepts of vocabulary (expressive), and attention and memory (auditory). The CCITSN provides a guide to parents and professionals using a typical developmental progression of behaviors to frame integrated intervention activities within everyday functional routines. Adaptations are included for children with differing types of disabilities and intervention needs.

### Early Learning Accomplishment Profile

An additional criterion-referenced assessment commonly used for infants and toddlers is the E-LAP (Glover et al., 2002). The E-LAP was designed to provide a method for observing the skill development of children functioning in the birth-to-3 age range. The purpose of this assessment is to help early interventionists and parents assess a child's development, then use that information to develop the individualized family service plan (IFSP). The E-LAP is hierarchical and contains 414 developmental skills in an age-referenced and chronologically sequenced order, which is divided into six domains of development: gross motor, fine motor, cognition, language, self-help, and social-emotional. The E-LAP also contains curriculum-referenced learning activities for each item, and it has been crosswalked for use when measuring the three OSEP outcomes. For the second outcome, it is recommended that all of the cognitive items be used to measure the presence of this outcome, along with selected fine motor, social-emotional, and language skills.

## INTERVENTION SUGGESTIONS FOR PROMOTING COGNITIVE DEVELOPMENT

There has been little empirical research conducted specifically on cognitive interventions using a sensorimotor cognitive framework with infants and young children with disabilities, even though the promotion of cognitive competence is a recommended practice in early intervention (Dunst, Mahoney, & Buchan, 1996). Similarly, there is not a robust body of literature supporting evidence as to what and how to intervene in this critical learning domain. Nonetheless, the groundwork for promoting cognition was published in the 1980s and 1990s, focusing on infants and toddlers with Down syndrome, such as Kayla (Champion, 1987; Sloper, Glenn, & Cunningham, 1986). This research demonstrated that infants and young children with Down syndrome progress through the Piagetian sensorimotor stages, although at a slower pace than typically developing children. More recent research in this area of sensorimotor interventions has focused on teaching successful contingency awareness strategies to young children with disabilities to facilitate their learning about cause-and-effect skills (Dunst, Raab, Trivette, Parkey, et al., 2007; Dunst, Raab, Trivette, Wilson, et al., 2007; Dunst, Raab, Wilson, & Parkey, 2007; Raab, Dunst, Wilson, & Parkey, 2009).

The majority of cognitive intervention research with children with developmental delays or disabilities has been conducted within related developmental domains, such as language (Kaiser & Roberts, 2011), literacy (Goldstein, 2011), and play (Lifter, Ellis, Cannon, & Anderson, 2005; Lifter, Foster-Sanda, et al., 2011; Lifter, Mason, et al., 2011). Research being conducted on play and young children with disabilities has been with children who have autism spectrum disorder (Kasari, Freeman, & Paparella, 2006; Pierce-Jordan & Lifter, 2005). For example, Barton (2010) provided an overview and proposed taxonomy of pretend play for this population, as well as guidance for those wishing to develop pretend play interventions for young children with autism (Barton & Pavilanis, 2012). Most important, there is also an empirical body of evidence for teaching interventionists these techniques to successfully promote pretend play behaviors (Barton, Chen, Pribble, Pomes, & Park, 2013; Barton & Wolery, 2008, 2010), as well as a growing acceptance of play as an instructional area in intervention (Wolery & Hemmeter, 2011) and parent involvement (Childress, 2011).

## Strategies for Promoting Learning and Cognition

All infants and young children develop as a result of the experiences they have in their everyday lives. When these experiences have the potential to enhance development, they are called *activity settings*. Activity settings require the use of a variety of problem-solving skills and behaviors that facilitate early cognitive behavior (Dunst, Bruder, Trivette, & Hamby, 2005, 2006). Activity settings that occur throughout the day (e.g., vocal play, using toys that make something happen) provide learning opportunities for the child to practice emerging skills and learn new skills that promote developmental competence and a sense of mastery. Each individual child, whether typically developing or exhibiting delays, requires varying levels of support and intervention to successfully navigate new and different activity settings (Joseph & Strain, 2010; Strain & Bovey, 2011). No matter what the level of accommodations or adaptations needed, the process of learning and developing is similar for all children.

As noted before, learning begins with a child's interest. Families may describe their child's interests as activities the child likes or enjoys doing, does frequently (even if it is hard for him or her), or the child's favorite activity. When a child is interested in an activity, the child is more likely to spend a long time doing (or trying to do) that activity. Focused attention on an activity is called *engagement* and is essential to learning. When a child is engaged with an interesting activity, the child explores, manipulates, and attempts to master an activity.

This active engagement results in competence. A competent child uses his or her own abilities, and the support of the environment, to be as successful as possible despite any developmental concerns. This competence results from engaging in a variety of experiences that occur over time, resulting in the child practicing existing abilities and gaining new abilities. When a child is competent, he gains a sense of mastery ("I think I can!"). The child believes that he or she is able to succeed because the child has succeeded in the past, which opens the child up to exploring new interests, starting the circle of learning with new activities. Everyday family, child care, and other community activity settings provide multiple learning opportunities throughout the day. A very important aspect of using activity settings for learning is that caregivers (parents and others) must be the ones who identify the activity settings of most interest to the child.

According to Piaget (1952), everything a child sees, touches, and feels is a learning opportunity. The physical environment should provide rich and multiple activity settings and learning opportunities, whether it is for a young infant or older toddler. The characteristics of any environment can promote child interest and engagement.

The social environment should also be safe and responsive for infants and young children. They should have many opportunities to interact with responsive adults, beginning with consistent adult caregivers—most notably, parents. Children inherently desire to have control and predictability in their environment. They want to manipulate objects, receive social responses to their initiations, and have consistency in regularly occurring routines and activities. When children are engaged in learning opportunities, they are actively exploring, manipulating, and interacting with people, materials, and objects. These experiences provide opportunities for children to learn how their behavior influences the environment through the consequences of their actions and behavior.

All members of a child's intervention team must understand and promote a child's cognitive learning within and across activity settings. Families are integral to this process during both the identification of activity settings and the delivery of intervention strategies to ensure a child is involved in problem-solving and learning opportunities throughout the day and across physical and social environments (Bruder, 2010). Toward this end, and as with all early intervention activities, family involvement is a necessary and critical component to a child's achievement of cognitive milestones and communication competence. Effective interventions in home and child care settings require attention to the antecedents, desired behaviors, and the consequences of a child's performance.

## Antecedents: Intervention Strategies to Promote Interest and Engagement

Intervention strategies differ from one another, according to how and when assistance is provided for a child to successfully demonstrate a skill. In some instances, intervention is provided before the child engages in a desired behavior. For example, before Kayla goes to her small table, her mother places a whiteboard and markers on the table for her. The availability of this material encourages scribbling and drawing. Providing support and/or materials before an activity or routine occurs is called an *antecedent event*. Antecedent events are designed to increase the likelihood that a child will become interested in a desired activity.

### *Arranging the Social and Physical Environment*   Antecedents can include environmental arrangements and adaptations to the social and physical environment to promote child interest and engagement. Examples of social and physical arrangements include the following:

- Offering activity settings the child enjoys
- Providing opportunities for the child to initiate interactions using his or her own communication style
- Having proper positioning available so that the child can concentrate on the activity setting
- Identifying and making sure preferred toys and materials are accessible
- Ensuring that peers and siblings understand the child's communicative cues

### *Providing Assistive Prompts*   Antecedents can also involve the use of assistive prompts provided by the caregiver and interventionist. A child's characteristics determine the type of prompt that is most likely to be effective. For example, for a child with a hearing impairment, the prompts could be pointing or other gestures, as opposed to or in addition to verbal prompts. When selecting a prompt, the least intrusive prompt should be tried first, before selecting a more intrusive prompt, such as when a parent uses a verbal prompt before trying a physical, hand-over-hand prompt to help a child with self-feeding. Assistive prompts include the following:

- *Verbal prompts:* For example, asking, "Do you want juice or milk?" might facilitate a child's interest in learning to drink from a cup. The prompt provides an opportunity for the child to control the environment through choice making.
- *Tactile assistance:* An example of this prompt would be touching an infant's hand to gain the infant's attention about a toy near his or her hand, encouraging interest in the toy.
- *Physical assistance:* This strategy involves physically guiding a child through a behavior. Providing light pressure to a child's elbow to move the child's arm in an effort to encourage him or her to hit a drum is an example. This kind of physical assistance is the least intrusive manner to promote the skill of combining the use of objects in play.
- *Interrupted routines:* Daily routines such as dressing, eating, and diapering require the completion of several steps in an ordered sequence. A routine can be interrupted by

omitting a step or by completing a step incorrectly to encourage a child to engage in an activity. An example of completing a step incorrectly might be putting socks in a child's pocket rather than on his or her feet. This can make the activity interesting for the child, promoting problem solving as the child attempts to put his or her socks on, vocalizes, or interacts with the parent for help with the socks.

## Consequences: Intervention Strategies to Reinforce Interest and Engagement

Intervention strategies also can be implemented after the child performs a behavior to support learning. For example, Kayla was rewarded for making the transition into a sitting position because she was then able to reach for and attain a plastic shaker. In this instance, the reward is a consequent event, occurring after the child made the transition to sitting. Rewards or reinforcers increase the likelihood that a desired behavior will be repeated.

An important part of planning intervention strategies with families is deciding how to reinforce the child's interest and engagement. A *reinforcer* is anything (e.g., praise, attention, a pleasant sound) that results in an increase in the occurrence of the same behavior or an elaboration of the behavior. There are two types of reinforcers: naturally occurring reinforcers and learned reinforcers.

*Naturally occurring reinforcers* are the natural consequences of a child's behavior, such as signing MORE and then receiving another cookie, smiling at Dad and getting a returned smile from him, and using toys that light up and make music after the child activates them. *Learned reinforcers* also increase desired responses from a child. To help a child recognize his or her own achievements, something tangible is given, such as a sticker or a preferred toy. These more artificial reinforcers should always be paired with naturally occurring reinforcers (e.g., smiling at an infant and saying, "You got your rattle").

## Situated Learning

*Situational learning* uses antecedents and consequences to promote generalized problem solving and learning in naturalistic interventions (Dunst, 2007). Learning is contextualized and focuses on functioning in everyday activity settings to promote a child's problem solving and cognitive development. Situated learning encompasses four primary teaching/intervention methods, as described in the following sections.

**Incidental Teaching**   Incidental teaching takes advantage of unstructured, natural learning opportunities that occur throughout a family's routines. *Incidental teaching* occurs when a child initiates an interaction based on his or her interest in something, and the adult responds to the child to encourage the child to respond with an increase in a specific behavior or to change the behavior. For example, when Kayla noticed a rainbow and pointed to it while saying, "Ook!" her mother took the opportunity to use Kayla's present interest to expand her knowledge and vocabulary by saying, "Yes, a rainbow. Rainbow!"

**Contingent Responsiveness**   *Contingent responsiveness* teaches a child that his or her behavior can cause a response. The behavior–response contingency must occur often enough that the child learns the relationship. Any behavior can be considered as the child's initiation to interact, even if initially unintentional, thus opening the door to an adult response. The response can be social (e.g., a child looks at his grandmother and vocalizes "ma," and then his grandmother responds by vocalizing "ma") or nonsocial (e.g., a child drops his cup on the floor, so his father picks it up and puts it on the highchair tray). Contingent responsiveness can be planned, where the interventionist and the family determine social and nonsocial responses to a specific behavior (e.g., whenever the child vocalizes, the parent and siblings will imitate the sound), or it can result naturally (e.g., when a child drops an object, the parent picks it up). Because contingent responsiveness depends on the child beginning the interaction, child initiation is promoted. The child also learns that he or she has control over the environment.

**Response Contingent Learning**     *Response contingent learning* teaches a child that a specific behavior must be performed to produce a specific effect. For example, to get an electronic toy turned on, Kayla had to sign HELP independently. The desired response, turning on the toy, is contingent on the behavior of signing HELP. The response should be a reinforcer for the child, such as playing with the desired toy, and be based on the child's interests.

**Responsive Teaching**     Responsive teaching is based on the principles of reinforcement. It focuses on the child's current behaviors as competencies from which to promote new behaviors or competencies. The child becomes interested and engaged in a learning opportunity through antecedents that already exist in the activities the child likes to do, or they are created through environmental arrangements or prompts. When a child is engaged, responsive teaching uses natural or learned reinforcers to promote behaviors the child can already accomplish. The child's current competencies are reinforced. By reinforcing these behaviors, the child becomes interested and engaged in practicing the behavior until it is mastered. The child also becomes interested in attempting new behaviors related to the current behavior.

For example, a toddler crawls over to his mother's desk to interact with her (interest). To get his mother's attention, the child pulls to a standing position (current behavior). While he stands holding onto the desk with two hands, his mother smiles and speaks to him (reinforcement). The child then squats down and then pulls to stand again (practicing current behavior). His mother reinforces his behavior with smiles and talking. This time,. however, she also lifts one hand off her keyboard and waves at the child. The child smiles, squats down, and pulls to stand again. His mother again smiles, speaks, and waves. This time, the toddler lifts one hand off the desk and waves. The child's mother attended to the child's interests and abilities, maintained the child's engagement, reinforced the current competency, and provided an opportunity to learn a new behavior through elaborating or adding to the child's behavior by waving during their interaction.

## INTERVENTION CONTENT

Rather than teach the item a child missed on an assessment tool, such as block stacking, it is recommended that service providers coach families and child care providers on ways to create learning opportunities that address cognitive concepts and skills in naturally occurring home and community activity settings using the methods described in this chapter (Buchanan, 2009). For example, the activity settings that occurred in Kayla's home included a full range of learning opportunities:

- Family routines (cooking, cleaning, animal care)
- Parenting routines (child's bedtime and bath time)

- Child routines (brushing teeth, dressing, eating, playing before and after dinner)
- Literacy activities (looking at books, listening to stories, "reading")
- Play activities (lap games, playing with toys)
- Physical play (roughhousing, sibling's T-ball games, swimming)
- Entertaining activities (dancing, singing, watching television)
- Family rituals (family talks, spiritual readings, weekly trips to the grocery store)
- Family celebrations (holiday dinners, birthdays, decorating the house for holidays)
- Socialization activities (having friends over, family picnics, visiting neighbors)
- Gardening activities (outside walks, planting flowers, growing vegetables)
- Child care routines (story reading, snack time, center play)

Any or all of these activity settings can be used as the context in which cognitive intervention can be embedded. To assess which activity settings were most appropriate for Kayla, her parents talked with the service provider about the times of the day that were difficult for them and times that seemed to go well. Together, the parents and the early interventionist discussed these settings (including new ones), the skills that Kayla could learn during each activity, and why these skills and behaviors were important to the family. Then, they listed this information on a planning form, which was used when developing Kayla's IFSP and planning intervention activities. Figure 6.1 shows what the family developed. The interventions were selected because they were functional, fun, and developmentally appropriate for Kayla; they could be accomplished without overwhelming her already busy family; and each intervention focused on several outcomes.

## ADAPTATIONS

The availability and arrangement of materials, equipment, furniture, and space influence how and what children participate in and learn. So, too, does the appropriateness of interactions with others. For many infants and young children with disabilities, interventions must be adapted to enhance their active engagement in cognitive learning. These adaptations must occur in both their social and physical environments, in all the settings where the child and family participate.

### General Adaptations

Families have been known to be extremely creative in finding ways for their child to participate in activity settings that are important to them. For an adaptation to be useful and facilitate learning, it should share the following characteristics.

***Allow the Child to Participate in an Activity Setting Valued by the Child and Other Family Members***    Adaptations and supports should be useful within the activity settings identified by the family so that the goal can be to foster participation and learning. For example, Kayla's family wanted her to participate more at her child care center with the other toddlers. With the help of Kayla's child care teacher, her parents identified water play as a play context that interested her. With the assistance of the early intervention service provider, the family identified sensorimotor skills Kayla needed to learn and discussed how they could be easily embedded into this activity. This plan was shared with Kayla's child care teacher and used each time the children engaged in water play. Figure 6.2

| Intervention activity setting recording form | | | | |
|---|---|---|---|---|
| Parent's name: *Jessica* | | Date: *10/1* | Child's name: *Kayla* | |
| Location | Activity setting | Frequency | Learning opportunity | Why is this important |
| *Kitchen table* | *Eating meals* | *Daily* | *Use utensils to eat* *Use signs to get more and different foods* | *Our family can eat together.* |
| *Mall* | *Walking and playing* | *Every 2 weeks* | *Exploring all the halls and child interactive or play areas* | *Kayla can explore her world and make new friends.* |
| *Community pool* | *Swimming* | *Weekly* | *Splashing and playing in the water with objects and toys* | *She enjoys swimming.* |
| | | *3 times per week* | *Playing with other children* | |
| *Morning child care program* | *Using the learning materials, following directions, initiating play* | *3 times per week* | *Problem solving* | *Kayla can learn to use new toys and learn to make friends.* |
| *Family room* | *Playing with her sister* | *2–3 times per day* | *Tell her sister what she wants* | *Kayla can communicate and interact with Maddy.* |
| *Family room* | *Playing with toys* | *Daily* | *Playing with toys and learning independently* | *Kayla can learn to play by herself for about 10 minutes.* |
| *Neighborhood* | *Going for walks and stroller rides* | *3–5 times per week* | *Meeting others and interacting with neighborhood families* *Using tools (signs and vocalizations) to get needs met* | *Kayla can get outside for neighborhood walks to meet more children.* |
| *Car* | *Family outings or trips* | *Weekly* | *To participate in community activities, such as the library story hour* | *Kayla can be included in the community.* |
| *Restaurants* | *Eating out* | *Once per week* | *Eating with utensils and communicating wants and needs* | *We can go out to dinner as a family.* |

**Figure 6.1.** Kayla's opportunities to learn and use knowledge and skills.

shows how the family determined that they could embed important sensorimotor skills for Kayla into her swim class and child care routines. For adaptations and supports to be considered successful, the child's participation in the activity setting should increase.

| Routine: | *Water play at swim class and child care center* | | |
|---|---|---|---|
| Materials: | *Pool, tub, sink, or water table and water buckets, water smocks, cups, bottles, straws* | | |
| Activity description: | *Toddlers will be able to pour water from one container to another, have the cups float, and blow in the water with straws. The parent or caregiver will comment on the children's play and elicit interactions between the children.* | | |

| Target | Antecedent | Behavior | Consequence |
|---|---|---|---|
| Response to sensory stimuli: Responds to tactile stimulation | *The parent or another child will pour cold water over the child's arm.* | *Kayla will pull away arm, look at her arm, vocalize, or laugh.* | *The parent comments on the event (i.e., "Cold?").* |
| Object permanence: Maintains search for objects until found; searching more than one place | *The parent will ask the child to find a boat that is not readily seen.* | *Kayla will search around the room until she finds it.* | *Kayla gets to play with the boat in the water.* |
| Imitation: Imitates words approximately | *The parent will blow soap bubbles, point to them, and say "bubbles."* | *Kayla signs BUBBLES and/or vocalizes.* | *Kayla gets to blow bubbles.* |
| Causality: Following event by a mechanical toy, produces motion that activates action | *The parent or other child activates a toy fish to swim.* | *Kayla will look at the fish until it stops and imitate the movement needed to activate the fish to swim again.* | *Fish will swim.* |
| Means–ends: Uses tools to obtain objects | *The boat is at other end of the water table.* | *Kayla will use a straw to get the boat over to her side of the water table.* | *Kayla gets to play with the boat.* |
| Object differentiation: Child pretends in play with objects | *Kayla will be offered a cup by a friend during water play.* | *Kayla will use the cup as a boat.* | *Kayla will play with the cup/boat.* |
| Classification: Groups by one common attribute/ on same dimension | *The parent will tell the child to put away the water toys.* | *Kayla will put straws into a small container and cups into a large container.* | *The parent and Kayla get to play games with different-sized objects.* |

**Figure 6.2.**   Sensorimotor activity in Kayla's swim class and child care setting.

**Promote Development and Competence**    Adaptations and supports should facilitate the achievement of learning objectives and increase a child's independent participation in an activity setting that is appropriate for the child's age. For example, the use of a communication board can lead to the learning opportunity of interacting with others, whereas the use of a nonskid foam rubber kitchen liner on a highchair tray will keep the child's bowl in place while scooping food with a spoon, decreasing the likelihood that his or her caregiver will need to hold the bowl.

**Facilitate Participation in Age-Appropriate Activities**    An adapted activity should support a child in doing the things other children the same age are doing. For example, if a child requires support for sitting while his or her peers are sitting independently, an inflatable U-shaped ring could support the child's independent sitting during an infant music group.

**Promote Acceptance by Peers**   When recommending adaptations and supports, care should be taken to have the adaptation look as ordinary and attractive as possible. Many times, everyday household objects can be adapted, such as taping down boxes on a busy box that a child has not learned yet. As another example, communication devices that "talk" when the child presses a button are very popular with all toddlers.

**Promote Generalization**   Adaptations and supports should increase the child's functioning across existing and desired activity settings. Therefore, the adaptive equipment must be available to the child across activity settings. Family members and possibly community providers should be involved in selecting and using the adaptations and supports so that the child learns how to perform a skill in all settings with all people.

## Adaptations to the Social Environment

Adaptations of the social environment can focus on providing the control and predictability that a child with disabilities requires. Social adaptations may include any of the following:

**Identify and Respond to Subtle Communicative Cues**   As discussed in Chapter 5, consistently recognizing and responding appropriately to these cues affords the opportunity for reciprocal communication that every child requires for social-emotional development. During peer interactions, an adult can support the interaction by identifying a child's subtle communication cues for a peer so that the peer can respond and the interaction is continued.

**Provide Opportunities for the Child to Try Activities Independently or to Initiate Asking for Assistance**   The child should be able to try to figure out activities by him- or herself when the activities are interesting and appropriately challenging. Adults can support the child by demonstrating a positive affect toward the child's attempts, regardless of success. The child's persistent efforts should not be disturbed unless the child becomes frustrated or asks for help using his or her own communication style. When a child is given the opportunity to ask for help instead of having help thrust upon the child, the child begins to learn a sense of control.

**Extend Wait Time Before Initiating Interactions or Facilitating Interaction Turns**   Some children need more time to initiate an interaction or respond to another's initiation. A child who is slower to respond to an interaction would be interrupted, and therefore unsuccessful, if a typical interaction pace was used. Slowing the pace of interaction, or waiting longer for a child's response, provides an opportunity for the child to participate in, and share control of, the interactional environment.

## Adaptations to the Physical Environment

Infants and young children with disabilities often benefit from adaptations to their physical environment, which can be an unobtrusive method for supporting independent participation in activity settings. The physical environment can be adapted in a variety of ways. Two examples are described in the following sections.

***Change the Way a Space Is Arranged***    The design of the physical environment should consider the mobility and sensory abilities of a child. For example, a toddler mattress can be placed on the floor instead of on the bed frame so that the child who commando crawls for mobility can climb into bed. This simple adaptation provides the learning opportunities of independence and motor planning during the bedtime routine. At the same time, the child's sense of competence is increased as he or she is successful and independent.

***Plan a Child's Surroundings to Promote Engagement with Materials***    A child's engagement with materials is increased when materials are interesting and available to the child. Increasing a child's interest occurs by providing materials that are responsive based on the child's sensory strengths (e.g., lights, sounds) and can be obtained by the child independently (e.g., low shelves, easy-to-grab objects and containers). In addition, providing furniture and other supports that facilitate positioning can promote engagement because the child is stable and can concentrate on the materials available. By observing a child functioning in specific activity settings, adaptations can usually be easily identified and developed.

## Curriculum Adaptations

For young children with disabilities to successfully participate in the activity settings occurring in group settings, such as child care or a toddler play group, curriculum adaptations to daily routines and learning activities may be required. There are several ways to adapt curriculum, including the following three.

***Develop Related Goals***    The goal of a group activity can be adapted so that all children are participating in the same activity setting, but with different outcomes. For example, for one child, the goal of an art activity may be to give objects to a peer (grasp and release, turn-taking), whereas the goal for another child might be to use language to ask for a paintbrush and grasp it with an adapted handle (initiate request, grasp).

***Add Goals***    Some young children may benefit from additional intervention goals in areas not addressed by a program's curriculum. For example, learning opportunities may need to be added for a child with a cognitive delay or disability who is functioning at a younger stage of cognitive development to address goals such as turn taking and initiating interactions.

***Adapt Materials***    Materials can be modified and simplified to increase a child's participation and facilitate a child's success. For example, taping down the cardboard jacket of a board book will make it easier to turn pages so that the child can participate in book reading. While creating an art project, a child can use markers instead of crayons so that less pressure is needed to successfully color. In addition, knobs can be glued onto puzzle pieces so that they are easier to manipulate. These adaptations allow the child to fully participate in the same activity as others, eliminating environmental barriers.

## PRACTICES FOR ENCOURAGING THE ACQUISITION OF KNOWLEDGE AND SKILLS

Experiences that enhance the development of knowledge and skills provide opportunities for children to learn how their behavior influences the environment. As children understand that their behaviors create effects, they gain a sense of mastery. General strategies that use this process for cognitive learning include the following five characteristics.

### Identify and Use a Child's Strengths and Interests

A child's interest leads to engagement, which is a necessary characteristic for learning. Focusing on what the child is currently able to do (strengths)—and is interested and engaged in—provides opportunities to reinforce behaviors that enhance the child's development. When behaviors are reinforced, the child is more likely to try elaborations of the behavior or new behaviors, both of which result in learning and competence.

### Follow the Child's Lead and Arrange the Environment for Child Control

Activities that interest and engage a child most are the ones that the child initiates or controls. Intervention strategies should focus on providing the child these opportunities by reinforcing the behaviors the child currently has available. For example, responding to a child's communicative attempts, regardless of how subtle, reinforces the child's use of these cues, increasing the likelihood the child will use the cue again and try other means of communication. Adapting a toy so that a child can create an effect without adult assistance reinforces the independent behavior the child can do. When less adult direction is provided, the child has more opportunities to encounter the natural consequences of his or her actions, such as when an infant touches a mobile and the mobile moves and makes music.

### Promote Generalization of Skills

For a behavior to be learned, the child must use the behavior across any activity settings in which the behavior may be used. Providing opportunities for the child to practice new and emerging behaviors across activity settings, using a variety of materials with different peers and adults, promotes generalization. For example, when different friends, family members, and community providers reinforce a child's attempt to request desired objects with gestures in numerous activity settings (e.g., playing in the family room, picnicking, playing music in the toddler music class), the child is more likely to learn the behavior to the point of mastery.

### Support a Child Becoming More Independent

The strategies discussed (e.g., arranging the social and physical environment for access, assistive prompts, situated learning, response contingent learning) facilitate a child's independence and ability to participate in activity settings. These strategies might involve offering physical assistance during mealtimes, prompting the correct response to complete a puzzle, or providing Velcro shoes so that the child can put on his or her shoes independently.

## Target Several Skills in One Activity Setting

As stated, a child uses a variety of cognitive skills to participate in an activity setting. The key is to find ways to address multiple skills within an activity setting so that learning occurs in natural contexts and family members are more easily able to embed these learning activities into their lives.

## EARLY CHILDHOOD SPECIAL EDUCATOR

A misconception in the field of early intervention is that the early childhood special educator on the team is responsible for supporting a child's cognitive development. It is commonly thought that other specialists are more easily assigned to domains aligned with their training and expertise as well, such as assuming that a physical therapist must serve a child with motor developmental delays (which is also a misconception). In many instances, the early childhood special educator serves as an integration specialist for all the disciplines providing services to a child and family, although program variations exist (Cochran et al., 2012). Early childhood special educators must be knowledgeable about all areas of development and can be resources to the early intervention team for finding ways to integrate intervention strategies and outcomes across developmental domains and across family activities.

In Kayla's situation, the early childhood special educator consulted with the other team members to integrate all of Kayla's developmental needs into a cohesive learning plan that optimized Kayla's participation in many family-identified activity settings. This team approach seemed to serve Kayla's and her family's needs well.

## BEST PRACTICE HIGHLIGHTS

Progress in cognitive and communication development is enhanced when early intervention programs offer services with the following best practices:

- Use everything a child sees, touches, and feels as a learning opportunity that may be adapted, supported, or modified to promote cognitive and communication learning (Piaget, 1952).
- Coach families to use antecedents, such as arranging a child's social and physical environments to promote problem solving, reasoning, and interaction.
- Help families learn to identify and use consequences, such as naturally occurring reinforcers and learned reinforcers, to encourage a child's knowledge and learning throughout the day.
- Encourage families to use situated learning, contingency responsiveness, and responsive contingent learning to guide children in how to make sense of their world.
- Support family members and community programs, such as child care centers, in using adaptations to the physical space, materials, curriculum, and how adults interact with a child to increase participation and independence in infants and toddlers with special needs.
- Encourage families to structure home and community settings to facilitate engagement, turn-taking, communication, and learning.
- Promote a child's acquisition of knowledge and skills by using a child's strengths and interests, arranging all environments for increased control by the child, and addressing multiple skills within one activity or routine.

## CONCLUSION

Cognitive development is a foundation area for all learning and development. Successful learners are provided frequent and varied learning opportunities from the moment they are born. These learning opportunities allow children to experience appropriate and consistent feedback about the effect their actions have on the social and physical worlds around them. It is during these learning opportunities that cognitive development and the acquisition of knowledge and skills occur, and competence and mastery follow.

## DISCUSSION QUESTIONS AND APPLIED ACTIVITIES

1. You have been assigned a family whose child just came home after spending his first 4 months of life in a neonatal intensive care unit environment. The child was born at 27 weeks gestation at less than 2,500 grams. Describe three things you would say to these parents when explaining your first priority as an early interventionist in helping the family help their infant learn.

2. Describe the interrelationships of the cognitive concepts learned during the sensorimotor period and how, as a service provider, you would embed each into a learning opportunity for the following two children:

   • A 10-month-old child with mild developmental delays

   • A 25-month-old child with no evidence of cognitive or communication delays but who has a moderate visual impairment, meaning that the child has been classified as having low vision.

3. Observe a child under the age of 3 years during a play session with the child's parent for 30 minutes. Record all the opportunities provided to the child to demonstrate his or her cognitive competence using Piagetian schemes and stages.

## REFERENCES

Barton, E.E. (2010). Development of a taxonomy of pretend play for children with disabilities. *Infants and Young Children, 23,* 247–261.

Barton, E.E., Chen, C.-I., Pribble, L., Pomes, M.P., & Park, Y.A. (2013). Coaching pre-service teacher to teach play skills to children with disabilities. *Teacher Education and Special Education, 36,* 330–349.

Barton, E.E., & Pavilanis, R.L. (2012). Teaching pretend play to young children with autism. *Young Exceptional Children, 15,* 5–17.

Barton, E.E., & Wolery, M. (2008). Teaching pretend play to children with disabilities. *Topics in Early Childhood Special Education, 28,* 119–125.

Barton, E.E., & Wolery, M. (2010). Training teachers to promote pretend play in children with disabilities. *Exceptional Children, 77,* 85–106.

Bricker, D., Capt, B., Johnson, J., Pretti-Frontczak, K., Slentz, K., Straka, E., & Waddell, M. (2003). *Assessment, Evaluation, and Programming System for infants and children (AEPS®): Curriculum for birth to three years* (2nd ed.). Baltimore, MD: Paul H. Brookes Publishing Co.

Bruder, M.B. (2010). Early childhood intervention: A promise to children and families for their future. *Exceptional Children, 76*(3), 339–355.

Buchanan, M. (2009). The home play of toddlers with disabilities: Context and maternal perspectives. *International Journal of Disability, Development, and Education, 56*(3), 263–283.

Champion, P. (1987). An investigation of the sensorimotor development of Down's syndrome infants involved in an ecologically based early intervention programme: A longitudinal study. *British Journal of Mental Subnormality, 33,* 88–99.

Childress, D.C. (2011). Play behaviors of parents and their young children with disabilities. *Topics in Early Childhood Special Education, 31,* 112–120.

Cochran, D.C., Gallagher, P.A., Stayton, V., Dinnebeil, L., Lifter, K., Chandler, L., & Christiansen, K. (2012). Early childhood special education and early intervention personnel preparation standards of the division for early childhood: Field variation. *Topics in Early Childhood Special Education, 32*(1), 38–51. doi:10.1177/0271121412436696

Dunst, C.J. (1981). *Infant learning: A cognitive-linguistic intervention strategy.* Allan, TX: DLM Teaching Resources.

Dunst, C.J. (2007). Early intervention with infants and toddlers with developmental disabilities. In S.L. Odom, R.H. Horner, M. Snell, & J. Blacher (Eds.), *Handbook of developmental disabilities* (pp. 161–180). New York, NY: Guilford Press.

Dunst, C.J., Bruder, M.B., Trivette, C.M., & Hamby, D.W. (2005). Young children's natural learning environments: Contrasting approaches to early childhood intervention indicate differential learning opportunities. *Psychological Reports, 96,* 231–234.

Dunst, C.J., Bruder, M.B., Trivette, C.M., & Hamby, D.W. (2006). Everyday activity settings, natural learning environments, and early intervention practices. *Journal of Policy and Practice in Intellectual Disabilities, 3*(1), 3–10.

Dunst, C. J., Mahoney, G., & Buchan, K. (1996). Promoting the cognitive competence of young children with or at risk for developmental disabilities. In S. Odom & M. McLean (Eds.), *Early Intervention/Early Childhood Special Education: Recommended Practices* (pp. 159–196). Austin, TX: PRO-ED.

Dunst, C.J., Raab, M., Trivette, C.M., Parkey, C., Gaetens, M., Wilson, L.L., ...Hamby, D.W. (2007). Child and adult social-emotional benefits of response-contingent child learning opportunities. *Journal of Early and Intensive Behavior Intervention, 4,* 379–391.

Dunst, C.J., Raab, M., Trivette, C.M., Wilson, L.L., Hamby, D.W., Parkey, C., ...French, J. (2007). Characteristics of operant learning games associated with optimal child and adult social-emotional consequences. *International Journal of Special Education, 22*(3), 13–24.

Dunst, C.J., Raab, M., Wilson, L.L., & Parkey, C. (2007). Relative efficiency of response-contingent and response-independent stimulation on child learning and concomitant behavior. *Behavior Analyst Today, 8,* 226–236.

Early Childhood Outcomes Center. (2009). *Child outcomes handout.* Retrieved from http://projects.fpg.unc.edu/~eco/assets/pdfs/Child_Outcomes_handout.pdf

Feldman, D.H. (2004). Piaget's stages: The unfinished symphony of cognitive development. *New Ideas in Psychology, 22*(3), 175–231.

Glover, M., Preminger, J., & Sanford, A. (2002). *Early Accomplishment Profiles for Young Children* (E-LAP). Lewisville, NC: Kaplan Press.

Goldstein, H. (2011). Knowing what to teach provides a roadmap for early literacy intervention. *Journal of Early Intervention, 33*(4), 268–280.

Johnson-Martin, N., Attermeier, S., & Hacker, B. (2004). *The Carolina Curriculum for Infants and Toddlers with Special Needs* (3rd ed.). Baltimore, MD: Paul H. Brookes Publishing Co.

Joseph, G.E., & Strain, P.S. (2010). Teaching young children interpersonal problem-solving skills. *Young Exceptional Children, 13*(3), 28–40.

Kaiser, A.P., & Roberts, M.Y. (2011). Advances in early communication and language intervention. *Journal of Early Intervention, 33*(4), 298–309.

Kasari, C., Freeman, S., & Paparella, T. (2006). Joint attention and symbolic play in young children with autism: A randomized controlled intervention study. *Journal of Child Psychology and Psychiatry, 47,* 611–620.

Lifter, K., & Bloom, L. (1998). Intentionality and the role of play in the transition to language. In S.F. Warren & J. Reichle (Series Eds.) & A.M. Wetherby, S.F. Warren, & J. Reichle (Vol. Eds.), *Communication and language intervention series: Vol. 7. Transitions in prelinguistic communication* (pp. 161–195). Baltimore, MD: Paul H. Brookes Publishing Co.

Lifter, K., Ellis, J.T., Cannon, B.O., & Anderson, S.R. (2005). Developmental specificity in targeting and teaching play activities to children with pervasive developmental disorders. *Journal of Early Intervention, 27*(4), 247–267.

Lifter, K., Foster-Sanda, S., Arzamarski, C.A., Briesch, J., & McClure, E. (2011). Overview of play: Its uses and importance in early intervention/early childhood special education. *Infants & Young Children, 24*(3), 1–21.

Lifter, K., Mason, E.J., & Barton, E.E. (2011). Children's play: Where we have been and where we could go. *Journal of Early Intervention, 33*(4), 281–297.

Myers, D.G. (1992). *Psychology* (3rd ed.). New York, NY: Worth Publishers.

National Parent Technical Assistance Center. (2013). *A family guide to participating in the child outcomes measurement process.* Minneapolis, MN: PACER Center.

Noonan, M.J., & McCormick, L. (2013). *Teaching young children with disabilities in natural environments* (2nd ed.). Baltimore, MD: Paul H. Brookes Publishing Co.

Office of Special Education Programs. (2010). *29th annual report to Congress on the implementation of the Individuals with Disabilities Education Act, 2007* (Vol. 1). Washington, DC: Author.

Parten, M.B. (1932). Social participation among preschool children. *Journal of Abnormal Social Psychology, 27,* 243–269.

Piaget, J. (1952). *The origins of intelligence in children.* New York, NY: International Universities Press.

Piaget, J., & Inhelder, B. (1973). *Memory and intelligence.* London: Routledge & Kegan Paul.

Pierce-Jordan, S., & Lifter, K. (2005). The interaction of social and play behaviors in preschoolers with and without pervasive developmental disorders. *Topics in Early Childhood Special Education, 25*(1), 34–47.

Raab, M., Dunst, C.J., Wilson, L.L., & Parkey, C. (2009). Early contingency learning and child and teacher concomitant social-emotional behavior. *International Journal of Early Childhood Special Education, 1*(1), 1–14.

Sloper, P., Glenn, S.M., & Cunningham, C.C. (1986). The effect of intensity of training on sensori-motor development in infants with Down's syndrome. *Journal of Mental Deficiency Research, 30,* 149–162. doi:10.1111j.1365-2788.1986.tb01307.x

Strain, P.S., & Bovey, E.H. (2011). Randomized, controlled trial of the LEAP model of early intervention for young children with autism spectrum disorders. *Topics in Early Childhood Special Education, 31,* 133–154.

Uzgiris, I.C., & Hunt, J. (1987). *Infant performance and experience: New findings with the ordinal scales.* Urbana: University of Illinois Press.

Wolery, M., & Hemmeter, M.L. (2011). Classroom instruction: Background, assumptions and challenges. *Journal of Early Intervention, 33*(4), 371–380.

# 7 | Using Appropriate Behaviors to Meet Needs

Toby M. Long

This chapter discusses how infants and toddlers gradually become more independent by learning how to manage some of their personal needs, including the following:

- Gross and fine motor development
- Adaptive development
- Service delivery models
- Assessment practices
- Assistive technology
- Best practices highlights

## Case Study: Serena

Serena is an 8-month-old girl who was born at 24 weeks' gestation, weighing only about 1 pound. She had many problems while she was in the neonatal intensive care unit, where she stayed for close to 4 months. Her mother, who has some cognitive limitations, dropped out of high school at 15 years of age and now, at 22, is attending a program for adults with developmental disabilities. Currently, at the corrected age of 4 months, Serena attends an Early Head Start program during the day while her mother attends her program. Serena's mother describes her daughter as doing well developmentally, although she also describes her as "fussy" and sensitive to loud noises. Her primary child care provider at the Early Head Start program, however, has many concerns. She thinks Serena is small for her age and describes bottle feeding her as very difficult. She also describes Serena as having a flat affect and says that she often cries uncontrollably after hearing a loud sound. Serena, according to her child care provider, responds easily to comforting by an adult, although she prefers to be held rather than being placed on a mat, floor, or in a portable play yard (Pack 'n Play).

Serena's development has been generally slow. She is able to hold her head up when supported by an adult. She can roll from her side to her back. She has difficulty keeping her head up and eyes focused when held in sitting. She is beginning to make some noises when lying on her back. She will respond to her name by looking at you briefly. She is also beginning to recognize her mother and will move her arms and legs when her mother approaches her. However, her movements are stiff, and she seems tense when she tries to move around.

The third Office of Special Education Programs (2010) child outcome is phrased this way: "Using appropriate behaviors to meet their needs." This outcome involves measuring improvements in a child's fine and gross motor skills, personal-social skills, and cognitive and communication development. The Early Childhood Outcomes Center further described the outcome in this way:

> As children develop, they become increasingly more capable of acting on their world. With the help of supportive adults, young children learn to address their needs in more sophisticated ways and with increasing independence. They integrate their developing skills, such as fine motor skills and increasingly complex communication skills, to achieve goals that are of value to them. This outcome involves behaviors like taking care of basic needs, getting from place to place, using tools (such as forks, toothbrushes, and crayons), and, in older children, contributing to their own health, safety, and well-being. It also includes integrating motor skills to complete tasks; taking care of one's self in areas like dressing, feeding, grooming, and toileting; and acting on the world in socially appropriate ways to get what one wants. (2009, p. 2)

The third outcome of the child outcomes measurement process focuses on the child becoming more independent in taking care of him- or herself and using what he or she knows to meet needs. The child should be learning to use movement functionally by using tools and utensils, moving around independently, and taking care of developmentally appropriate personal needs, such as dressing, feeding, and personal hygiene. The third child outcome attempts to answer the following questions:

- How does the child get from place to place?
- What does the child do when he or she wants something? What if it is difficult to reach?
- What does the child do when help is needed?
- What does the child do when hungry?
- How does the child help with dressing, undressing, using the bathroom, and brushing his or her teeth?
- Can the child feed him- or herself?
- What does the child do without help? (National Parent Technical Assistance Center, 2013)

To prepare infants and toddlers to accomplish these skills, early interventionists need a sound foundation in typical motor and adaptive development.

## TYPICAL FINE AND GROSS MOTOR AND ADAPTIVE DEVELOPMENT

The development of efficient motor and adaptive skills is important for the development of other skills in areas such as cognition, social-emotional, and communication (Iverson, 2010). Moving helps an infant or toddler explore his or her environment, which is helpful for immediate and later learning. Developing adaptive skills allows a child to assist with and eventually be independent with activities such as self-feeding, dressing, and toileting. Children with physical disabilities or delays in motor or adaptive development may have difficulty moving for successful interaction with objects and people and may become dependent on others to anticipate their needs.

Although each child develops a bit differently, key developmental milestones emerge in an orderly sequence. There are variations to this sequence, and the rate that each child moves through the sequence can vary. Gross motor skills require the coordination of the large muscles of the arms, legs, and trunk. Gross motor skills are important as infants learn to roll over, sit, crawl, and eventually walk. For toddlers, gross motor skills include learning to climb, balance on one foot, carry large objects, and begin to run. These skills are the foundation skills used in many games and sports when the child is school age. Fine motor skills include reaching, grasping, and dexterity when picking up small objects. These skills are important for learning to use utensils such as spoons, writing implements, and other tools such as computers. Adaptive skills are self-help skills, such as feeding, dressing, and personal hygiene.

Table 7.1 describes some of the major developmental milestones in the gross motor, fine motor, and adaptive areas of development. Professionals need a firm understanding of this typical developmental sequence in order to make recommendations for a child that are developmentally appropriate. The only way to determine how a child is presently functioning in these areas is through assessment.

**Table 7.1.**   Sequence of typical fine motor, gross motor, and adaptive development

| Age | Gross motor | Fine motor | Adaptive |
|---|---|---|---|
| 0–6 months | Pushes up on hands and looks around<br>Rolls from stomach to back and back to stomach<br>Sits with support | Brings hands to mouth<br>Looks at hands<br>Swipes at an object | Brings hands to mouth<br>Sleeps 10–12 hours/night with night waking<br>Naps 2–3 times/day |
| 6–12 months | Crawls on all fours<br>Pulls to stand<br>Moves sideways along furniture<br>Walks with support | Reaches out and grabs an object<br>Bangs two blocks together<br>Transfers objects from one hand to the other | Holds own bottle<br>Begins to take solid foods<br>Finger feeds<br>Feeds self a cracker<br>Naps twice daily |
| 12–18 months | Walks independently<br>Climbs up and down stairs | Turns pages of a book<br>Isolates index finger to point | Holds cup handle<br>Removes socks<br>Removes hat<br>Holds spoon |
| 18–24 months | Carries a toy when walking<br>Throws a ball<br>Stands on one foot momentarily | Imitates motor activities<br>Scribbles | Drinks from a cup<br>Takes off shoes<br>May be dry for several hours<br>Scoops with spoon |
| 24–36 months | Runs<br>Kicks a ball<br>Jumps up and forward | Imitates vertical and horizontal lines<br>Strings beads<br>Snips with scissors | Turns doorknobs<br>Uses spoon and fork<br>Puts on shoes<br>Pulls pants up and down<br>Begins to use the toilet |

## ASSESSMENT PRACTICES

Assessment of children with atypical or delayed motor development, as for all typically developing children, may be completed to determine the existence of a developmental delay and plan for the child's intervention. Early intervention service providers most often assess a child's development in preparation for writing the individualized family service plan (IFSP). These assessment purposes are discussed in the following sections.

### Eligibility for Service

Tools used to help teams make a diagnosis or to determine eligibility for early intervention services often compare a child to others the same age. Most standardized, global diagnostic instruments provide information about whether a child has achieved motor milestones as well as milestones in other developmental domains. Table 7.2 describes the commonly used tools for determining developmental status in the sensorimotor area of development. A motor-specific tool commonly used by physical and occupational therapists is the Peabody Developmental Motor Scales 2 (PDMS-2; Folio & Fewell, 2000), which is a norm-referenced, standardized tool that assesses both fine and gross motor skills in children from birth to 6 years of age.

However, different tools may be used based on the particular assessment questions the team has about a child. Serena, from the case study, is a good example. Because of Serena's birth history and her caregivers' concerns, she was evaluated by the local early intervention program's multidisciplinary team. They decided to use the Bayley Scales of Infant and Toddler Development, Third Edition (Bayley, 2006). Serena was found to have a delay in her gross motor skill development, even considering her degree of prematurity. The team was also concerned about her oral-motor skills and the stiffness they felt in her arms and legs. Because of her mother's and teacher's concern about Serena's sensitivity to loud noises and

**Table 7.2.**    Tools commonly used by physical and occupational therapists for team assessments

|  | Bayley Scales of Infant Development, Third Edition (Bayley, 2006) | Battelle Developmental Inventory, Second Edition (Newborg, 2004) | Infant/Toddler Sensory Profile (Dunn, 2002) |
|---|---|---|---|
| Purpose | Identify developmental delay; monitor developmental progress | Identify developmental delay; monitor developmental progress | Determine the effect of sensory processing and sensory modulation difficulties on behavior and social interactions; classify child's sensory profile |
| Age | 12–42 months | Birth to 7 years | Birth to 36 months |
| Areas assessed | Gross motor, fine motor, expressive language, receptive language, cognition, social-emotional, adaptive | Adaptive, cognition, personal-social, communication, motor | Auditory, visual, tactile, vestibular, oral sensory, multisensory |
| Time to administer | 25–60 minutes | 30–60 minutes | 15–20 minutes |

difficulties calming herself, the evaluation assessment team assisted Serena's mother in completing the Infant/Toddler Sensory Profile (Dunn, 2002). The profile indicated that not only was Serena sensitive to loud noises, but changes in routines that were difficult and quick, as well as jostling movements such as those used when picking her up or changing her diaper, were also uncomfortable for her.

## Intervention Planning

As part of the early intervention team, physical therapists and occupational therapists are often involved in the assessment of motor and adaptive skills, as well as with developing IFSPs. Functional skills, rather than developmental milestones, are generally stressed in intervention plans. Routines-based assessments help therapists and team members identify the capabilities of a child within everyday activities and help families identify activities and routines that they find challenging (McWilliam, 2010). These capabilities and challenges are used to help teams develop functional outcomes and determine appropriate services. For example, a single mother of triplet toddlers told a service provider that she finds the bedtime routine difficult because the children are unable to crawl up the stairs, so the mother has to carry each one. To help this mother, the provider would want to observe the child and family within this routine to determine any barriers to success.

Developing intervention plans based on a routines-based assessment process helps service providers (including therapists) with the following:

1. Determining how a child's sensorimotor skills are affecting his or her functional abilities
2. Developing outcomes that are meaningful to parents, caregivers, and child care providers
3. Creating activities and intervention strategies that are practical, take little time, and do not disrupt important ongoing family activities

In addition, observing a child and caregiver within a routine shows how they interact and solve problems, which is useful when individualizing interventions.

During the development of Serena's IFSP, her mother and child care provider agreed that feeding was a challenge, so they decided that they would like the early intervention team to focus attention on this area. The occupational therapist (OT) explained that Serena had difficulty keeping her lips closed around the bottle when being fed and, because of the stiffness in her arms, had difficulty holding her own bottle. She explained how these barriers to efficient feeding would be addressed during intervention visits. By adding occupational therapy to the IFSP as a consulting service, the OT was able to train the family's primary service provider on how to address these issues. The service provider then coached both the caregiver and Serena's mother on how to improve the feeding experience.

Because children use a variety of developmental domains to solve problems and interact with their worlds, interdisciplinary assessments provide a comprehensive picture of the child that no single service provider could do alone. Many tools gather information from the individuals who see a child perform target skills on a regular basis, such as parents, interventionists, and other caregivers. The Routines-Based Interview (McWilliam, 2010) and the Measure of Engagement, Independence, and Social Relationships (McWilliam & Younggren, 2007) have been shown to be helpful in developing family-directed IFSPs (McWilliam, Casey, & Sims, 2009). Regardless of the tools used, the assessment process must provide a detailed description of a child's strengths and needs to develop appropriate therapeutic interventions (Long & Sippel, 2000).

## INTERVENTION CONSIDERATIONS AND MODELS

Current practices promote the acquisition of functional movement and the importance of incorporating treatment into naturally occurring family activities and routines (Long, 2013). The focus of early therapeutic intervention is the child's participation in everyday activities and routines. Therefore, services take place within these natural environments, such as in the child care setting, in the home, at playgroups, and in other community settings. Therapeutic strategies and interventions are embedded into routines, rather than offered only in individual therapy sessions.

A number of models stress this type of therapeutic intervention. Activity-Based Motor Intervention (Valvano & Rapport, 2006), for instance, uses structured practice and repetition of functional actions to teach, facilitate, and use motor skills within a relevant and functional context. All routines-based models require service providers to collaborate with families to identify which activities and routines are going well or not so well; then, family members and other caregivers are coached in how to use strategies to promote successful participation in the routines that the family determined to be priorities. Interventionists use a variety of strategies including exercise, assistive technology, splinting, bracing, remediation, and teaching specific skills to help children participate. All of these strategies, however, are presented playfully and are embedded into ongoing regular family routines.

### Approaches to Intervention

Early intervention service providers design intervention strategies to meet the specific needs of a child and the desired outcomes determined by the child's family and team. Depending on a child's needs, a provider will most often use a variety of approaches and expect to change approaches as the needs of a child change. For many children, a physical therapist (PT) or OT may be the most appropriate team member to address motor and adaptive needs. However, this is not always the case. As mentioned elsewhere in this book, the determination of which service provider is most appropriate is made based on the provider's knowledge and skills and the outcomes written on the IFSP. When an OT or PT is part of a child's intervention team, he or she may use any of the following four general approaches to intervention.

The *remedial approach,* which is the most familiar to therapists, attempts to correct impairments that interfere with attaining typical motor skills. Therapists identify performance impairments and try to resolve them by promoting age-appropriate sensorimotor and adaptive abilities. Although this approach may be how many therapists were trained to address developmental delays or disabilities, it is not the approach that is most aligned with best practices in early intervention due to its impairment focus.

The goal of the *compensation approach* is to provide an alternative method of accomplishing a function when impairment prevents the skill or function from occurring. Assistive technology, adaptive equipment, or other devices are used to allow a child to perform a skill when the child is unable to perform it without assistance, or when the child has yet to master a skill. Compensation strategies help prevent further impairment or disability, such as tight muscles or scoliosis. Compensation strategies are also used to promote development. For example, providing a child who has little or no movement with a power-drive wheelchair encourages the child's independent exploration and supports the child's social development.

The purpose of the *prevention approach* is to avoid the development of secondary impairments or disabilities in children with known difficulties. For instance, proper positioning of a young child with cerebral palsy is used to help prevent scoliosis, joint contractures, deformities, or stiff joints that may occur as the child grows older.

Consistent with the framework of current early intervention practice, therapists using a *promotion approach* embed therapeutic interventions into natural activities and routines. The objective is to ensure that every activity a child participates in throughout the day is accomplished in a way that is beneficial, therapeutic, and functional for the child. This is the preferred approach for engaging infants and toddlers in intervention to support their motor and adaptive development.

## Supports to Therapy

Because of the complexity of motor disabilities, therapists use a variety of supports to help young children move more efficiently or functionally. *Assistive technology*—materials used to encourage appropriate movement—may include a wheelchair. *Adaptive equipment,* such as cushions and bolsters, and *orthotics,* or braces (e.g., ankle-foot orthoses) and splints, are frequently used. Children with spina bifida, for example, tend to be fitted with appropriate orthotics around 8–12 months of age, when they are beginning to stand and attempting to walk. Children with significant neuromuscular disabilities, such as cerebral palsy, may receive medications such as botulinum toxin (Botox) and baclofen, undergo neurosurgery to reduce spasticity or rigidity, or undergo orthopedic surgeries to lengthen muscle tendons. Today, due to expanding resources, many professionals and families are able to select a variety of services. Therapists play an important role in helping team members examine the effectiveness of available treatments.

## Service Delivery

As with all early intervention services, once the family and team decide on the outcomes that the family would like accomplished, the discussion moves to deciding on the appropriate services to meet those outcomes and the most effective, efficient service delivery method. All team members, including therapists who may be on the team, contribute to this decision making, taking into consideration the outcomes identified by the team and family, the strengths and needs of the child, and the family's priorities.

Campbell (2011, 2013) divided intervention service delivery strategies into two categories, which are further divided into three levels. The first category requires an adult to implement. The strategies are often physical guidance or specific skill training, such as hand-over-hand feeding or strength-building exercises. The second category focuses on adapting or modifying the environment and using assistive technology. For example, the service provider may provide a variety of assistive devices or alternate strategies to foster feeding independence rather than the hand-over-hand approach. The provider also may design a variety of developmentally appropriate activities that can be embedded in the family's daily routines, which require the child to build muscle strength in contrast to doing exercises with the child. Often, these two categories are used together.

These two strategy categories are further divided into three levels: 1) universal, 2) specialized, and 3) custom strategies. *Universal strategies* are used with all children, such as using a highchair, encouraging a 12-month-old to walk, or practicing ball throwing with a young toddler. *Specialized strategies* may be used with same-age peers but not always in the same way. For example, some children use a battery-operated car as a toy or fun activity. A child with a physical disability may use this same car as a mobility device. *Custom intervention strategies* usually require the early interventionist or parent to deliver the intervention. Using a gait trainer to promote walking or using a specific passive exercise to relax tight muscles are examples of customized services.

When deciding what strategies or services to use with a child and family, service providers consider evidence of the strategy's appropriateness and effectiveness. Evidence-based practices take into account well-designed research studies as well as policy and experiential knowledge. Interventionists use the evidence available, taking into consideration the sources of evidence, the rigor of the research, the cost–benefit analysis of specific strategies, and the appropriateness for the individual child and family.

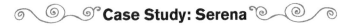

## Case Study: Serena

Based on Serena's and her mother's needs, the early intervention team decided that a combination approach to intervention would be most helpful. The team suggested that to improve Serena's participation in mealtime feedings, the physical therapist, as the primary service provider, would coach both Serena's mother and her child care provider during regularly scheduled feeding times. The therapist would coach them about how to use strategies to improve lip closure around the nipple and promote efficient sucking and swallowing of the formula. The therapist also would demonstrate activities to relax Serena's arm and leg muscles, preventing further tightness and promoting holding her own bottle. The PT decided to coach the family and child care provider on how to use some specialized techniques, such as oral-motor massage, and also suggested environmental changes to limit distractions during feeding. In addition, the therapist made universal suggestions regarding movement, play, and positioning to reduce Serena's fussiness.

## ROLE OF THE PEDIATRIC PHYSICAL OR OCCUPATIONAL THERAPIST

The functional use of movement to meet a child's needs is an important precursor to language development, cognitive development, and successful participation in all of life's activities and routines. Physical and occupational therapists play a critical role in enhancing a child's use of his or her motor abilities by actively participating as a collaborating member of a child's and family's team, being a child's primary service provider, or consulting with a child's primary provider on a regular basis.

Serving children and families under Part C of the Individuals with Disabilities Education Improvement Act (IDEA) of 2004 (PL 108-446) requires that PTs and OTs have skills and knowledge in the principles of family-centered and community-based services and supports. Training, in addition to the therapist's professional preparation education, may be needed to effectively participate in early intervention. Both the American Physical Therapy Association's Section on Pediatrics (Chiarello & Effgen, 2006) and the American Occupational Therapy Association (2009) have created competencies and/or other training materials to assist therapists in obtaining appropriate knowledge and skills. Early intervention teams and families should expect therapists to possess the skills and knowledge to implement early intervention services and support using existing activities and routines as the natural context for learning. According to Rush and Shelden (2011, 2012), an early intervention practitioner (including an OT and PT) should be an evidence-based practitioner, competent in providing parenting support, and able to coach or mediate a parent's or caregiver's ability to support a child's learning and development. As seen in Serena's case study, OTs and PTs may act as the primary service provider and/or a consultant to the family and team. Each role is discussed here.

## Primary Service Provider

As explained in Chapter 1, the primary service provider provides early intervention services for the child and family with consultation, support, and/or coaching from other team members. Any member of the team, including the PT or OT, can be the primary service provider. Once the outcomes are determined, the team decides which member of the team would best serve the family as the primary service provider. Rush and Shelden (2012) recommended that teams consider the characteristics of the parent and family, child, environment, and practitioner when deciding on which team member would act in this role. OTs or PTs are often considered as primary service providers for children with a primary motor disability or delay or for very young infants to promote the acquisition of developmental skills. OTs and PTs should be able to collaborate with other service providers to develop comprehensive, integrated intervention sessions that support all aspects of an infant's development.

## Consultant

If they are not the primary service provider, OTs and PTs may be expected to consult with the primary service provider and other team members, ensuring that the child and family receive appropriate and effective intervention. As a consultant, the therapist may make an occasional visit to the child and family, usually with the assigned primary service provider. Like all team members, the OT and PT attend regular program meetings and provide and receive colleague-to-colleague consultation, ensuring that the child and family are making progress toward all IFSP outcomes. At times, the primary service provider may bring a video of the child and family to a team meeting to receive input from other team members.

For example, during the IFSP meeting, it was decided that the physical therapist would be Serena's primary service provider. The physical therapist had expertise in feeding, so she was the most appropriate team member to see Serena. However, the team was very concerned with Serena's social development and supporting her mother's ability to engage Serena in social interaction and maintain that interaction. Because of that concern, the team decided that the team's psychologist would consult with the PT on a regular basis and that the PT would bring videos of the child and mother playing to team meetings to obtain advice as needed. The occupational therapist, who had expertise in sensory processing, agreed to provide the PT with suggestions regarding Serena's fussiness, as well as to provide simply written parent information tips to share with Serena's mother. As Serena's case study demonstrates, there are many strategies professionals may use to address skills that a child needs to learn. There are also many ways to present interventions to families.

## GENERAL INTERVENTION STRATEGIES

Service providers, including OTs and PTs, use a variety of strategies and approaches to maximize a child's motor and adaptive development and functioning and to help the child and family meet the IFSP outcomes.

## Positioning

Children with motor impairments often need to be positioned (and repositioned) to promote function and symmetrical body alignment, thus preventing further disability. Therapists show caregivers and other service providers how to position children in ways that promote learning and social interactions with others. For example, children should always sit at eye level with other children. Sometimes, a chair must be adapted or modified to achieve this. The creative use of blankets and rolled towels when a child is placed in *prone* (stomach lying), *supine* (back lying), or sidelying position can help a child maintain a position while playing with toys or people.

Although a child may be placed in a position to help relax tight muscles, positioning is most often used to promote independent, functional skills. Infants, especially those born prematurely, may be positioned in ways to counteract some of the atypical positions they assume. Figure 7.1 shows the appropriate positioning of an infant in prone, supine, and sidelying positions.

Older infants and toddlers with significant motor impairments may need more extensive positioning adaptations to promote independence or movement exploration. Figure 7.2 shows the use of specialized equipment and adaptations to a standard highchair for a child with a motor impairment.

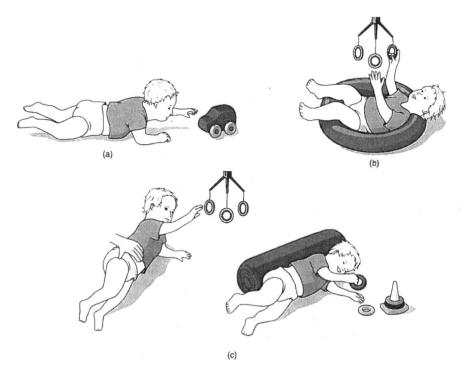

(a)

(b)

(c)

**Figure 7.1.**   Activities for promoting symmetrical body alignment and functional skills in infants in prone, supine, and sidelying positions: (a) to increase weight bearing on upper extremities; (b) to promote flexion and reaching against gravity; and (c) to promote reaching and grasping. (From Baker, C., & Long, T. [1989]. *Tips for tots: A resource guide for your infant and toddler* [pp. 1–2]. Palo Alto, CA: VORT. Copyright © 1989 by Toby Long. As reprinted in Raver, S.A. [2008]. *Early childhood special education—0 to 8 years: Strategies for positive outcomes* [p. 187]. Upper Saddle River, NJ: Pearson.)

Positioning a toy in relation to the child may increase the child's ability to use the toy more appropriately and efficiently. Play gyms, which allow toys to be suspended, often increase the child's interaction and exploration with the materials. A child with significant motor impairments may need to be placed in a supported sidelying position to promote accessibility. For some children, using an easel or other vertical surface is helpful in strengthening the whole arm and hand.

## Case Study: Serena

After 3 months of intervention, Serena was bottle feeding without difficulty, was starting to eat from a spoon when placed in her infant seat, and was ready to begin finger feeding and sitting in a highchair. Serena was still quite small for her age, and her sitting posture was not stable. The PT helped Serena's mother create lateral supports for Serena from towel rolls. These rolls were placed on each side of Serena's hips when she was placed in the highchair (see Figure 7.2). These towel rolls gave her just the right amount of support to sit upright in the highchair. Serena's arms were then in an ideal position to finger feed. With Serena in her highchair, Serena's mother was able to fix meals and talk to Serena at the same time. Serena really enjoyed being with her mother while she made meals.

**Figure 7.2.** Ways to support trunk alignment in infants and toddlers with significant motor dysfunction using support in a highchair. (From Raver, S.A. [2009]. *Early childhood special education—0–8 years: Strategies for positive outcomes* [p. 192]. Upper Saddle River, NJ: Pearson. Illustrated by Rachel Brady, D.P.T., M.S., P.T., Research Associate, Georgetown University Center for Child and Human Development, Washington, D.C.; reprinted by permission.)

## Motor Performance Activities

Actively participating in motor games strengthens children's muscles, builds their coordination, and prepares them for playing games and sports when they are older. Play is an ideal context for movement exploration and motor improvement (Menear & Davis, 2007). Creative movement activities are ideal for toddlers to not only promote motor development, motor coordination, and movement efficiency but also language development (Iverson, 2010). Play-oriented activities increase the pleasure, engagement, and motivation of a child, the child's parents, and professionals, and the activities are easily embedded into most interactions in natural environments.

***Promoting Gross Motor Skills***    The foundation for many games and sports-related activities for young children is the development of gross motor skills. Children who have difficulty performing gross motor skills smoothly and efficiently are often frustrated by motor games and may shy away from participation. However, service providers and family members can structure activities that promote foundational motor skills, regardless of a child's abilities (Menear & Davis, 2007). The following are developmentally appropriate activities at particular stages of development.

*Activities for Infants from Birth to 18 Months*    The following activities are appropriate for infants (birth to 18 months):

- Although infants should sleep on their backs, when awake and supervised, they should be placed on their stomachs for tummy time to encourage pushing up on their forearms and, eventually, their hands (American Academy of Pediatrics, 1992). Placing a mirror or toy in front of a child will encourage the child to look up. Sometimes, lying down while facing the child will encourage her or him to push up to play. (This activity is especially effective with children with visual and/or hearing impairments.) Placing a towel roll under the child's chest and arms can also encourage this position. This activity provides important sensory feedback for building body awareness in the arms and hands (Chizawsky & Scott-Findlay, 2005).

- During diapering, help the infant see his or her feet by rolling his or her hips, thighs, and feet up toward the chest. The child's bottom will come off the surface, but the low back should stay flat on the surface. This will help infants develop flexibility around their hips.

- When an infant is on his or her back, play Peekaboo with his or her feet.

- Gently tie a ribbon with a bell on it around the infant's ankle, or use ankle or wrist rattles. These will encourage kicking, leg lifting, and arm movements.

- Begin playing Pat-a-cake by passively bringing the baby's hands together. This game helps the child learn to bring his or her hands together in midline (to the middle of the chest).

- To help improve sitting balance, sit the infant on an adult's knees and gently bring one knee up and the other down. Bringing your heels up and down will move your knees up and down. The infant will need to catch his or her balance as the adult moves. As the child gets older and more stable, the adult's movements can be faster.

- To build up strength in a child's shoulders and hips, have him or her crawl around, under, and through furniture or set up an obstacle course with boxes and pillows.

- Have the beginning walker hold onto a hula hoop with an adult to practice walking.
- Encourage walking over uneven surfaces at home, in the backyard, at the park, in the sandbox, and at the beach.

*Activities for Toddlers from 19 to 36 Months*    As children become toddlers, they are eager to start playing games. The following activities can be easily adjusted to the ability, motor needs, and age of individual children. Some can be easily incorporated into activities involving communication, cognitive development, or preliteracy and literacy learning. Most of these games can be used with a group.

- An adult slowly wriggles a rope on the floor like a snake. The older toddler jumps over it, trying not to touch the rope. If the child touches it, he or she is "bitten by the snake."
- A child lies on his or her belly on a scooter while holding a rope with both hands. If a child cannot hold the rope with two hands, tie the rope around the child's torso. An adult pulls the child around by the rope. Encourage the child to hold his or her head up. If the child's head falls, stop pulling until the head is upright again. (This is a fun activity with toddlers with more significant disabilities.)
- Tape several cardboard shapes (1' × 1') close together on the floor. A child attempts to step from one shape to the next without stepping off a shape.
- A child gets on his or her hands and knees like a dog, then waves a front "paw" while remaining balanced on the other three "paws."
- Other common early childhood games that help promote gross motor skills include Tug of War, Tag, Duck-Duck-Goose, Simon Says, and Hot Potato.

**Promoting Fine Motor Development**    The development of fine motor skills is interconnected with the development of gross motor skills. Skilled hand use requires infants and toddlers to bear weight on their arms, explore their environment by touching, and manipulate a variety of materials with one or both hands. Activities that promote foundational fine motor skills prepare very young children for the more refined skills needed in school, such as tying shoes, cutting with scissors, and eventually writing.

*Activities for Infants from Birth to 18 Months*    The following activities are appropriate for infants from birth to 18 months:

- Offer a variety of small infant toys to the infant to explore, such as rattles, blocks, cars, books, or plastic animals, that have different shapes, colors, sounds, and textures. This will help a child learn to adjust his or her grip and explore ways to make the toys move or produce noise. A good rule of thumb is that small toys should not fit inside a toilet paper tube; if they do, they may be choking hazards and should not be given to infants or toddlers. Be sure to supervise infants and toddlers when playing with any small toys.
- Offer two different toys at the same time, holding them apart from each other. Encourage the infant to choose one of them. As the child gets a bit older, encourage holding a toy in each hand.
- Dangle a toy in front of the infant or suspend it from a baby gym. Encourage the child to swipe at the toy and grasp it.
- To promote reaching with both arms, place a washcloth on an adult's or sibling's head or face and have him or her lean in close to the infant. By playing Peekaboo, the play

partner can encourage the child to reach up and pull the washcloth off. For children who have difficulty reaching, passively move their hands to the adult's face or washcloth and have the child touch it.

- When spoon feeding the infant, give the child a spoon to hold onto. The adult could also give the child a teething ring to hold. Dip it in the child's baby food so that the child can try feeding him- or herself that way, too.

*Activities for Toddlers from 19 to 36 Months*    The following activities are appropriate for toddlers (age 19–36 months):

- Older infants and toddlers enjoy filling containers and dumping them. They are learning and practicing grasping, releasing, and problem solving. A variety of everyday items, such as balls, blocks, lids from small containers, and other nonbreakable objects, are good for filling plastic containers.
- Creating opportunities for children to use both hands together is very important for functional hand use. Simple activities to encourage using both hands include opening and closing containers, holding and stabilizing paper while coloring, holding one toy while trying to retrieve another with the other hand, stringing beads, and building and taking apart interconnecting blocks and beads.
- To promote body awareness and to strengthen shoulder muscles, have children push and pull large boxes and weighted containers around the floor or outside. Show children that, by working together, they can push and pull heavier items.
- Have children "paint" with whipped cream, pudding, or Jell-O to encourage tactile exploration. This may be beneficial for children who are reluctant to touch a variety of materials or textures. Messy play helps children learn how different materials feel and increases their tolerance.
- To prepare a 2- to 3-year-old child for cutting with scissors, have him or her use tongs to move small objects from one container to another. When introducing scissors (at around 30 months), encourage the child to place the thumb in one loop while the middle, ring, and small fingers are positioned in the larger loop. The index finger is used to stabilize the blade of the scissors. Guide the child to approach the paper in a thumbs-up position, encouraging the child to cut in a forward direction.
- Lacing macaroni on yarn is a fun activity that requires a child to use both hands. A 2- to 3-year-old child can make macaroni necklaces using large macaroni.
- To strengthen the small muscles of the hands, 2- to 3-year-old children can imitate finger movements, such as Itsy Bitsy Spider, play with finger puppets, trace designs in sand, and make shapes with playdough.

**Promoting Adaptive Skills**    Children develop independence in self-care activities gradually. Typically developing children have established basic self-care skills by the time they enter kindergarten. Children with disabilities often have more difficulty developing these skills and may need assistance. Therapists and other service providers may advise caregivers and professionals in ways to adapt or modify tasks to assist a child. Depending on a child's needs, modifications may need to be made to a task or to the child's environment. Feeding, dressing, and personal hygiene skills are discussed.

*Feeding*    Infants and toddlers with motor disabilities, especially cerebral palsy, or other motor delays frequently have oral-motor problems that lead to feeding difficulties.

Atypical motor patterns, such as difficulty controlling the lips, tongue, and facial muscu-lature, may make feeding challenging. Feeding problems may be due to difficulties with oral-motor, sensory, or feeding processes. Many infants and toddlers served by the early intervention system have a combination of these difficulties.

The first intervention to consider to promote efficient feeding is proper positioning. An infant should be positioned in a slightly reclined position, face to face with the caregiver and with his or her head and trunk supported. Toddlers who have difficulty maintaining a sitting position with trunk alignment may need external supports. These children may require supports placed in the highchair, may need to use a feeder chair, or may need to use a wheelchair or other adapted seating system, such as the one shown in Figure 7.2.

Some children will have specific problems with the muscles around the mouth. Ther-apists may coach parents and other caregivers in ways to hold the child or support the mouth during feeding to promote ease and efficiency of oral feeding, especially for young infants or those born prematurely.

Many infants and toddlers are hypersensitive to touch around or in the mouth; as a consequence, they may avoid certain foods and textures (Eicher, 2013). These infants may feed better if fed in a quiet environment with few distractions. Specific desensitization techniques, such as oral massage or placing food on the top half of the tongue (which may be less sensitive than the back of the tongue), may be shown to parents and caregivers. Some older infants and toddlers will chew better if food is placed on the sides of the child's mouth.

Older infants and toddlers should be encouraged to finger feed in preparation for self-feeding. Providing support with rolled towels placed in a child's highchair offers the trunk support that is needed for efficient arm use and self-feeding. Because mealtime is an opportunity for families to socialize, it is critical that young children be fed during that time. Service providers will always consider this routine when coaching families about key oral-motor and feeding strategies. When a toddler is ready to be at the table with his or her family, modifying or adapting the environment may be needed. Ideally, the child should be positioned so that the table is at mid-chest level to encourage an upright posture. Most children will not need a specialized chair, but an armless chair may not provide adequate lateral support. Using a chair with arms or placing an infant or toddler into a standard highchair may provide the needed support.

In addition to proper positioning during mealtimes, a wide variety of utensils may be helpful to increase independence in self-feeding. Built-up handled utensils are easier to grasp, spoons or forks that are bent are easier to scoop with, and straps can be used to maintain the proper position of a child's wrist. Bowls and plates are available with built-up sides or detachable food guards, making it easier for a child to scoop food onto a spoon. Some bowls and plates have suction cups that adhere to the table or tray to stabilize them.

Learning to self-feed is a complex process requiring a stable trunk position, efficient use of the arms and hands, and control around the mouth. Consider the following in devel-oping specific feeding programs:

1. The unique characteristics of the child (e.g., oral-motor strengths and weaknesses, food preferences)
2. The environment (e.g., distractions during feeding, time of day)
3. The caregiver's level of comfort
4. The feeding equipment used (e.g., adapted bottle, chair) when attempting to design an effective feeding program for a child and family

*Dressing*    As toddlers reach their second birthday, they are often ready to help with dressing and undressing. Dressing includes putting on and taking off clothes, as well as manipulating fasteners such as snaps, buttons, and zippers. Children may acquire dressing skills at different rates, depending on a family's routine and cultural views on the importance of these skills. In general, toddlers are able to remove loose clothing around 2 years of age. They can put on loose clothing around 3 years of age. Toddlers who have difficulty using their muscles may find these rudimentary dressing skills challenging.

The following general strategies can be used to encourage toddlers to participate in dressing:

- Be patient. Helping a child learn to dress him- or herself takes time. Allow the child ample opportunities to put on and take off clothes.
- Use loose-fitting clothing without fasteners, such as elastic waistbands, which are easier for the child to put on independently.
- If the child has a disability that affects one side of the body more than the other, put clothes on the affected side first.
- Children with poor balance may need to sit while dressing.
- If dressing is challenging or tiring for a child, especially during the early-morning rush, it may be best to advise caregivers to have the child help with only one or two items.
- Some children may need additional help and creative ways to differentiate back from front, left from right, or outside from inside. Color coding the backs and fronts of garments may help a child avoid putting clothes on backwards.

Dressing can be challenging for young children with motor delays. Parents should be coached to make the activity fun and to praise children for personal successes. Incorporating dress-up games and dressing and undressing dolls are other motivating ways to help children learn the skills that are necessary for dressing.

*Personal Hygiene*    As children approach their third birthday and are ready to make the transition from early intervention, the team may provide anticipatory guidance to the family to begin to prepare them for toileting, bathing, and toothbrushing skills. Personal hygiene skills, such as toileting, bathing, and oral care, may require input from PTs and OTs. Therapists commonly offer the team suggestions for compensating for missing skills or when a child has difficulty performing activities because of muscular concerns, such as muscle tightness or decreased flexibility.

Bath chairs and benches provide stability and increase safety for a child who is unable to sit independently or feel secure without support. Special commode seats are available to improve a child's ability to transfer onto the toilet and remain stable while seated. An upright sitting posture with feet placed firmly on the floor will assist the child with bowel movements. Simple clothing with few fasteners is also helpful.

The bathroom's environment may also need to be changed to ease physical access to the tub, sink, and commode, especially if the child uses a mobility device such as a walker or wheelchair. Simple suggestions, such as providing a step stool so that children can reach the sink, may be helpful. Children with poor balance or those who feel insecure may need to have a step stool with arm supports.

For children with weak grasps or wrist and forearm movement limitations, built-up handles on toothbrushes and hairbrushes may be easier to manage. A battery-operated toothbrush is more efficient for children with joint limitations, tight muscles, or weakness.

There are many commercial devices designed to assist with grooming. OTs and PTs can assist the team, and ultimately the family, with a selection of appropriate tools.

## ASSISTIVE TECHNOLOGY

*Assistive technology* (AT) for infants and toddlers is underused, despite mandates to consider how it can be used to help a young child meet his or her outcomes. Current best practices in early intervention suggest that AT should be available for children of all ages and abilities, be considered during the development of every child's IFSP, and be available for daily use. In addition, training and technical assistance should be provided to the family, caregivers, and all team members as needed to help the child use AT. Funding information should be readily available and provided to families and professionals.

AT is defined as any tool or item that helps a child with a disability to perform a task that he or she desires to do or is expected to do, including sitting up, walking, speaking, singing, drawing, playing, building towers, enjoying books, or blowing bubbles. This definition includes both low-technology and high-technology devices, such as those listed in Table 7.3.

Some toys may need to be manipulated and adapted to make them functional for a child with motor delays or limitations. Basic adaptations can increase the appropriateness of play materials. Materials may need to be stabilized, enlarged, or made more familiar. Changing the switch mechanism that controls the toy may allow the child to operate the toy independently. For example, if Serena's stiffness continues as she gets older, it may be difficult for her to play with toys without making some adaptations. If her limited dexterity continues, putting masking tape or a cushion around a toggle switch on a battery-operated toy when she is a toddler, or changing a toggle switch to a large button switch if she needs to use her full hand to hit the switch, will allow Serena to have more independent play. Some toys may need to be made less distracting by removing extraneous parts or cues. Taping sections of the toy not being used or making the toy more inviting by adding sounds to its action may make the toy more engaging and appropriate for a child.

**Table 7.3.**  Examples of low-technology and high-technology assistive technology for infants and toddlers

| Low technology | Mid-technology | High technology |
|---|---|---|
| Readily available devices, off-the-shelf, low-cost, little training required | Usually electronic devices that are available commercially but can be used in a specialized way | Specialized devices designed for disability, more costly, training required |
| Slant boards, page turners | Switch-adapted toy | Corner chair |
| Inflatable balls | Battery interrupter | Adaptive seating and walking equipment |
| Large nonroll crayons | Single-message communication device | Multilevel communication device |
| Booster chair | Computer software with touchscreen | Therapeutic swing, stroller |
| Photographs/pictures on a choice board | iPad cause–effect application | Mobile seating systems |
| Car seat insert | Electronic storybook systems | Sit-to-stand standers |
| Reactive touch toy | | Gait trainers |
| Curved handle spoon | | Specially adapted toys |
| Scoop bowl | | Adapted reading devices |
| Reclining bath seat | | |
| Wedges, rolled towels | | |
| Velcro, nonslip materials | | |

Part C of IDEA stresses the importance of AT. Teams writing IFSPs must discuss the need for AT in meeting the needs of a child, and this consideration must be documented. Many systems have specific AT teams or AT specialists available to assist early intervention teams with the correct selection of technology and to train professionals and families in appropriate AT use. Once the team selects a device, it is imperative that training and support is offered to the child, the family, and all professionals serving that child. As the needs of a child change over time, reassessment of AT will be necessary.

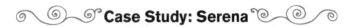

## Case Study: Serena

The physical therapist on Serena's team provided weekly coaching sessions to Serena's mother and primary child care provider at the Early Head Start program. As the family's primary service provider, she consulted with the psychologist and occasionally arranged a joint visit with the team's occupational therapist. This arrangement continued for 6 months. Serena and her mother made slow but steady progress in her feeding skills. Serena's mother, however, made significant positive changes in how she interacted with Serena, and it was clear that they had a warm, loving relationship.

When Serena's 6-month IFSP review took place, it was noted that Serena's motor skill development was affected by her tight muscles. At 14 months of age, she was still unable to sit up by herself or hold herself in a sitting position when placed. The towel rolls placed in her highchair were not enough support as she got bigger and more active. The highchair itself was also not very stable. During the IFSP review, the PT asked for a consultation from the OT on the team to determine if an adaptive seating system would be of benefit. The team wanted to be able to introduce more tabletop-type activities and improve Serena's finger feeding. The team thought a more supportive seating system would help her to sit upright and maintain a better functional position. The team also discussed introducing some sort of mobility device to help Serena move around her environment by herself. Her Early Head Start teacher communicated that she would like Serena to move around on her own so that she had a better chance to play with the other children.

## GENERAL RECOMMENDATIONS

Movement is an essential component of infant and toddler development. Social interactions and play between a child and caregiver or professional offer the perfect context for intervention. Children with motor disabilities, delays, or atypical motor development need toys and activities that build on the child's strength and promote the functional use of motor skills. All team members should incorporate movement into their intervention sessions and should coach families to incorporate movement in their interactions with their infants and toddlers. The suggestions described throughout this chapter are easy to incorporate into daily activities. Key to these suggestions are the following points:

- Use the child's favorite toys and people as motivation to move.
- Offer the child opportunities to play in different positions throughout the day, every day.
- Teach adaptive and independence skills within the routine in which the skills are needed.

- Use materials within each home or the child's other natural environments whenever possible to support the development of motor and adaptive milestones.
- Balance the use of hands-on intervention with coaching families as they support their child's development and independence.
- Professionals should look for natural opportunities to encourage a child to practice motor and adaptive skills and help families seize these opportunities as well.
- *Remember:* All intervention should be FUNctional!

## BEST PRACTICE HIGHLIGHTS

The following best practice highlights are grounded in early intervention evidence-based practices:

- Use appropriate, individualized intervention for children with motor disabilities or delays to promote active movement, functional skills, and community integration, as well as to prevent impairment.
- Depending on a child's needs, physical therapists and occupational therapists use a remedial, compensation, promotion, and prevention approach—or a combination of these—to design intervention plans for children.
- Physical and occupational therapists may effectively serve as primary service providers or team consultants as needed to help a child and the child's family meet family-identified outcomes.
- Assessment of children with atypical or delayed motor or adaptive development may be conducted for screening and/or intervention planning purposes.
- Intervention planning requires therapists and other service providers to collect information about a child's use of abilities, strengths, and interests using a variety of authentic methods, including routines-based assessment.
- Use positioning and repositioning to promote function and symmetrical body alignment and to prevent further disability in children with severe motor impairments.
- Consider the use of low- and high-technology assistive technology to maximize a child's functional skills and interactions with his or her world.
- Employ creative movement games and activities to promote appropriate gross and fine motor skills in an engaging way for any child with motor delays or difficulties.
- Depending on an individual child's needs, modify tasks or modify the environment to assist a child in learning dressing, feeding, and personal hygiene skills.

## CONCLUSION

All intervention should be integrated and embedded into a child's daily activities and routines. Like all service providers, PTs and OTs use a collaborative consultation model of service delivery, in which they assume the responsibility of training and coaching family members and their colleagues in ways to manage and implement therapeutic activities with children with motor and adaptive disabilities or delays. Whatever model of teamwork or service delivery may be employed, PTs and OTs continue to pursue their principal goal of promoting effective movement and personal independence in very young children.

## DISCUSSION QUESTIONS AND APPLIED ACTIVITIES

1.  Describe three reasons why a routines-based assessment may be more helpful in intervention planning for a toddler with significant disabilities than a traditional developmental test.

2.  A 28-month-old child with cerebral palsy uses a baby walker to move around her home and child care center. When she is in the walker, she is on her toes and is bent over the top of it. The child's parents would like her to practice walking with the walker. However, the physical therapist on the team believes that the child is not ready to walk because her leg muscles continue to be very tight and she needs to develop better weight-bearing abilities. The therapist also knows that baby walkers are not recommended for infants by the American Academy of Pediatrics; particularly for children with cerebral palsy, walkers can make issues such as toe walking worse. Using a family-centered approach, role-play how this conflict might be resolved.

3.  For her second birthday, Diana, who does not walk and is exhibiting global delays, was given a motorized car that she uses to drive herself around the backyard. Discuss how you think the family might be able to use this toy functionally for Diana during an upcoming trip to the zoo.

## REFERENCES

American Academy of Pediatrics, Task Force on Infant Positioning and SIDS. (1992). Positioning and SIDS. *Pediatrics, 89*(6), 1120-1126.

American Occupational Therapy Association. (2009). *Guidelines for supervision, roles, and responsibilities during the delivery of occupational therapy services.* Retrieved from https://www.aota.org/-/media/Corporate/Files/Practice/OTAs/Supervision/Guidelines%20for%20Supervision%20Roles%20and%20Responsibilities.pdf

Bayley, N. (2006). *Bayley Scales of Infant and Toddler Development, Third Edition (Bayley III).* San Antonio, TX: Harcourt Assessment.

Campbell, P.H. (2011). Addressing motor disabilities. In M. Snell & F. Brown (Eds.), *Instruction of students with severe disabilities* (7th ed., pp. 340–376). Upper Saddle River, NJ: Pearson.

Campbell, P.H. (2013). Occupational and physical therapy. In M.L. Batshaw, N.J. Roizen, & G.R. Lotrecchiano (Eds.), *Children with disabilities* (7th ed., pp. 599–612). Baltimore, MD: Paul H. Brookes Publishing Co.

Chiarello, L., & Effgen, S. (2006). Updated competencies for physical therapists working in early intervention. *Pediatric Physical Therapy, 18,* 148–167.

Chizawsky, L.L.K., & Scott-Findlay, S. (2005). Tummy time! Preventing unwanted effects of the "Back to Sleep Campaign." *AWHONN Lifelines, 9,* 382–387.

Dunn, W. (2002). *Infant/Toddler Sensory Profile.* San Antonio, TX: Harcourt Assessment.

Early Childhood Outcomes Center. (2009). *Child outcomes handout.* Retrieved from http://projects.fpg.unc.edu/~eco/assets/pdfs/Child_Outcomes_handout.pdf

Eicher, P.S. (2013). Feeding and its disorders. In M.L. Batshaw, N.J. Roizen, & G.R. Lotrecchiano (Eds.), *Children with disabilities* (7th ed., pp. 121–140). Baltimore, MD: Paul H. Brookes Publishing Co.

Folio, M.R., & Fewell, R.R. (2000). *Peabody Developmental Motor Scales–2.* Austin, TX: PRO-ED.

Individuals with Disabilities Education Improvement Act (IDEA) of 2004, PL 108-446, 20 U.S.C. §§ 1400 *et seq.*

Iverson, J.M. (2010). Developing language in a developing body: The relationship between motor development and language development. *Journal of Child Language, 37,* 229–261.

Long, T. (2013). Early intervention. In M.L. Batshaw, N.J. Roizen, & G.R. Lotrecchiano (Eds.), *Children with disabilities* (7th ed., pp. 547–557). Baltimore, MD: Paul H. Brookes Publishing Co.

Long, T., & Sippel, K. (2000). Screening, evaluating, and assessing children with sensorimotor concerns and linking findings to intervention planning: Strategies for pediatric occupational and physical therapists. In The Interdisciplinary Council on Developmental and Learning Disorders (Eds.), *Clinical practice guidelines: Redefining the standards of care for infants, children, and families with special needs* (pp. 185–213). Bethesda, MD: ICDL Press.

McWilliam, R.A. (2010). *Routines-based early intervention: Supporting young children and their families.* Baltimore, MD: Paul H. Brookes Publishing Co.

McWilliam, R.A., Casey, A.M., & Sims, J. (2009). The Routines-Based Interview: A method for assessing needs and developing IFSPs. *Infants & Young Children, 22,* 224–233.

McWilliam, R.A., & Younggren, N. (2007). *Measure of engagement, independence, and social relationships.* Retrieved from http://www.siskin.org/downloads/MEISR_Instrument-NEW-1-1-1.pdf

Menear, K.S., & Davis, L. (2007). Adapting physical activities to promote overall health and development: Suggestions for interventionists and families. *Young Exceptional Children, 10,* 11–16.

National Parent Technical Assistance Center. (2013). *A parent guide to participating in the child outcomes measurement process.* Minneapolis, MN: PACER Center.

Newborg, J. (2004). *Battelle Developmental Inventory–2*. Itasca, IL: Riverside Publishing.

Office of Special Education Programs. (2010). *29th annual report to Congress on the implementation of the Individuals with Disabilities Education Act, 2007* (Vol. 1). Washington, DC: Author.

Raver, S.A. (2009). *Early childhood special education—0–8 years: Strategies for positive outcomes.* Upper Saddle River, NJ: Pearson.

Rush, D., & Shelden, M. (2011). *The early childhood coaching handbook.* Baltimore, MD: Paul H. Brookes Publishing Co.

Rush, D., & Shelden, M. (2012). Worksheet for selecting the most likely primary service provider. *CASEinPoint, 6*(3), 1–9.

Valvano, J., & Rapport, M.J. (2006). Activity-focused motor interventions for infants and young children with neurological conditions. *Infants & Young Children, 19,* 292–307.

# IV

# Supporting Children with Diverse Abilities

# 8 | Infants and Toddlers with Autism Spectrum Disorder

Dana C. Childress, Lori E. Meyer, and Hedda Meadan

This chapter discusses strategies and supports for young children with autism spectrum disorder (ASD) and their families, including the following:

- Myths, prevalence, and etiology
- Early signs and symptoms
- Screening, evaluation, and diagnosis
- Intervention approaches, strategies, and considerations
- Specific intervention activities
- Best practice highlights

## Case Study: Colin

Colin is a rambunctious toddler who loves tractors and is the joy of his family's life. When Colin was around 14 months old, his parents, Ronnie and Lisa, became concerned because Colin did not point to things that he wanted and would rarely go to adults for comfort when he was frustrated or tired. He liked to keep to himself and was not socializing like his older sister had at the same age. Colin was also not using any words to communicate. He did make sounds, though, and could often be heard humming during the day. When Ronnie and Lisa were asked to think back on Colin's development, they realized that he did not respond to his name or seem to understand many words.

When Lisa took Colin in for his 18-month wellness checkup, she expressed the family's concerns about Colin's development to his pediatrician. The pediatrician conducted a screening that confirmed risk factors for ASD and recommended a referral to a developmental pediatrician who specialized in autism at the local children's hospital. After a series of evaluations, Colin received the diagnosis of ASD. The developmental pediatrician discussed the importance of early intervention with Ronnie and Lisa and referred Colin's family to the local program.

Within the next month, Colin's individualized family service plan (IFSP) was developed and services began, including service coordination, special instruction (provided by an early childhood special educator with training in working with toddlers with ASD), and speech therapy. Colin's family members worked closely with their early intervention service providers to address their goals for Colin, which included helping him learn to use sounds and words with intent, socially engage others, and purposefully play with his toys.

## WHAT IS AUTISM SPECTRUM DISORDER?

An increasing number of infants and toddlers who have or are suspected of having ASD are being served in early intervention programs. It is well documented that early and appropriate treatment for children who have or may have ASD is associated with more positive developmental and academic outcomes (Bruder, 2010; Woods & Wetherby, 2003). Because of this, efforts to identify these children as early as possible are also on the rise. Young children do not need to have a diagnosis of ASD to be eligible for early intervention because they often qualify due to a developmental delay in areas such as communication or social-emotional development. Identifying these children early and addressing their strengths and needs through family-centered planning and evidence-based practices increases their chances for a positive developmental trajectory and is an important goal of early intervention (Childress, Conroy, & Hill, 2012).

*Autism spectrum disorder* is a neurodevelopmental disorder that appears during early childhood and affects a child's ability to communicate and interact with other people and the environment. According to the *Diagnostic and Statistical Manual of Mental Disorders, Fifth Edition* (American Psychiatric Association, 2013), children with ASD demonstrate social and communication impairments as well as display restricted and repetitive behaviors. In infants and toddlers who have ASD, social-communication impairments may look like developmental delays in social-emotional and communication development—difficulty with making eye contact, difficulties with engaging and responding to others, and a tendency for the child to appear isolated or in his or her "own world."

Restricted and repetitive behaviors in infants and toddlers might include spinning wheels on toys, opening and closing cabinets over and over, playing with toys in the same repetitive patterns (e.g., lining toy cars up along the windowsill in a particular order), hand flapping or body rocking, or becoming extremely upset when a familiar routine is changed. Toddlers without ASD may exhibit any of these behaviors as well; however, a pattern of atypical behavior that interferes with a child's ability to socially interact and communicate with others is cause for concern. When a concern is identified, it is imperative that early intervention begins as soon as possible to achieve the best possible outcomes (Boyd, Odom, Humphreys, & Sam, 2010; National Research Council, 2001; Webb & Jones, 2009; Woods & Wetherby, 2003).

### Myths About Autism Spectrum Disorder

Autism was first identified by Leo Kanner (1943), a psychiatrist at The Johns Hopkins University, who coined the phrase *early infantile autism*. Since then, diagnostic criteria, risk factors, and a variety of treatments for ASD have been identified. With these advances also came the dispelling of many myths and misunderstandings about autism that had developed over time. Among the earliest myths was the idea that autism was caused by "frigid" mothers or mothers who did not show their children enough affection. It is now known that autism is a brain-based disorder that likely has a genetic component (Boyd et al., 2010) and is generally not caused by poor parenting (with the exception of conditions of extreme neglect, which could lead to developmental delays and symptoms resembling ASD).

Another common myth about ASD states that children with this diagnosis do not make eye contact and do not speak or communicate. While making and sustaining eye contact is challenging for many individuals with ASD, some infants and toddlers do make eye contact, particularly with their parents, but their eye contact is typically fleeting. Even for children with significant communication impairments, communication can happen using body language and behavior, as well as early sounds, so it is important that the child's communication partners, such as parents, siblings, child care providers, and interventionists, learn to read and respond to the child's early communication attempts. All children, regardless of ability, communicate through their behaviors and actions. Infants and toddlers with ASD do communicate and may learn to communicate in multiple ways, such as through speech, sign language, communication devices, and/or pictures.

Some children with ASD develop early expressive language but appear to regress around 18 months of age, losing the early sounds and words they previously said. It is a myth that all toddlers with ASD will experience such a period of developmental regression and lose skills, such as speaking simple words, making eye contact, or engaging socially. Reported rates of regression in young children with ASD vary between 15% and 30% (Boyd et al., 2010), with some literature reporting regression rates as high as 49% (Webb & Jones, 2009). Some children are believed to experience slow development between the ages of 1 to 2 years, which could appear as if their development was regressing. Based on what is known from retrospective studies in which researchers examine home videos of young children who later received an ASD diagnosis, it appears that many infants were actually showing atypical development prior to 18 months of age, so they may not have been developing typically prior to the apparent regression (Matson, Wilkins, & Gonzalez, 2008).

Another myth that bears mentioning is that vaccinations, specifically the mumps, measles, and rubella (MMR) vaccine, may cause autism. According to the Autism Science Foundation (ASF; 2013), this myth began in 1998 when a study was published that reported a link between autism and the MMR vaccine. After years of other researchers being unable to replicate these findings, it was discovered that the study's author had a financial investment in the study he published, having planned to develop a rival vaccine. The author later retracted his paper and was consequently barred from practicing medicine. Scientists continued to study this issue and found no causal link between the MMR vaccine and autism. The relationship between the MMR vaccine and autism is considered to be coincidental in that the MMR vaccine is typically administered when children are around 18 months of age, which is also the time when many of the symptoms of ASD become more notable or when regression occurs in some children. Because of this myth, some parents have chosen to withhold the MMR vaccine or have it administered on a slower schedule, but research has found no differences in the rate of ASD diagnosis among children who receive the vaccine and those who do not receive it or who do so at a later time. Examining studies regarding the relationship between vaccines and ASD led the American Academy of Pediatrics (AAP, 2013) to note that "these studies do not show any link between autism and MMR vaccine, thimerosal, multiple vaccines given at once, fevers or seizures" (p. 1).

Table 8.1 presents these and other myths about autism in very young children and provides information dispelling these myths. Familiarity with these myths is very useful for early interventionists as they answer questions about autism from families and caregivers who are new to the diagnosis.

**Table 8.1.**  Common myths about autism spectrum disorder (ASD)

| Myth | Fact |
|---|---|
| Children with autism never make eye contact. | Eye contact is often fleeting or it looks like the child is looking just above or to the side of the other person. Some children do make eye contact, especially when looking at the parent, when the child needs something, or when the child is engaged in a motivating activity. |
| Progress means that a child no longer has autism. | Children with autism do experience positive developmental changes. This is not necessarily evidence of an incorrect diagnosis, but rather an indication of maturation and appropriate interventions. |
| Autism can be cured or outgrown. | There is currently no cure for autism and children do not outgrow the symptoms. The cause of autism has not yet been established, but it is generally believed to have a strong genetic component. |
| Children with autism do not communicate or speak. | All children communicate, including children who are nonverbal. It is estimated that more than half of children with ASD will develop at least a single-word vocabulary. |
| Autism is caused by poor mother–child attachment. | Because autism is believed to be neurobiological in nature, it is now known that parents do not "cause" autism. |
| Children with autism are not affectionate and do not give or receive hugs. | Some children with ASD are affectionate with their parents and may give and receive hugs. Others may find being hugged or kissed difficult and may resist, likely due to sensory differences. Many children do well with firm hugs or show affection in different ways, such as by leaning on the parent or playing with his or her hair. |
| Children with autism do not interact with other people. | Very young children with ASD often demonstrate fleeting interactions with others and more extensive interactions with a particular caregiver. They may use their motor skills to interact by climbing, pushing, or leaning on others. They may use their bodies to interact by taking the parent by the hand and leading him or her to where the child needs to go, such as pulling the parent to the kitchen to communicate the need for a drink. |
| Signs of autism do not appear until a child is a preschooler or older. | Although the age for first diagnosis is typically between 4 and 5 years old, some signs of ASD appear in children as early as the first year of life. These signs might include gaze aversion, difficulties with feeding, and difficulties with attachment and interaction. |

## Prevalence and Etiology

Although once considered to be a low-incidence disorder, ASD is now known to be one of the most common developmental disabilities in children (Boyd et al., 2010). ASD is diagnosed in approximately 1 in 68 children, according to ongoing monitoring studies conducted by the Centers for Disease Control and Prevention (CDC)'s Autism and Developmental Disabilities Monitoring Network (ADDMN; 2014). Furthermore, the CDC (2013) published data based on parent reports, which estimated that 1 in 50 U.S. children may have autism. ASD is three to four times more common in boys, appearing in approximately 1 in 42 boys and 1 in 189 girls (ADDMN, 2014; Webb & Jones, 2009). It is believed that the symptoms of ASD are more severe in girls (Webb & Jones, 2009). The prevalence of ASD is generally consistent across cultural and socioeconomic groups, but the age of initial diagnosis appears to differ, occurring later for children of minority families or families with lower incomes (Boyd et al., 2010).

There is no universally accepted single cause of ASD. Rather, due to the heterogeneous nature of ASD and the variations in individual expression of the disorder, it is thought to be likely that there are multiple causes (Landa, 2007). In the vast majority of cases, no cause can be identified. Certain risk factors have been identified that increase a child's chances of being diagnosed with ASD, such as being born prematurely or having low birth weight, having an older sibling or identical twin with ASD, having older parents, or having a co-occurring disorder with symptoms associated with ASD (CDC, 2013; Schendel & Bhasin, 2008; Webb & Jones, 2009). In 5%–10% of cases, ASD appears as a comorbid condition secondary to a primary disability, such as fragile X syndrome, Down syndrome, or Rett syndrome (Boyd et al., 2010; Johnson & Myers, 2007). Other causes that have been suggested include exposure to triggers in the environment, but scientists have yet to definitively identify any such triggers. The only cause that has been accepted by the field is the role of genetics in autism (AAP, 2012). Based on twin and sibling studies, there appears to be clear evidence for a genetic link with the diagnosis of ASD (ASF, 2013; Johnson & Myers, 2007).

## EARLY SIGNS AND SYMPTOMS OF AUTISM SPECTRUM DISORDER IN INFANTS AND TODDLERS

Although researchers have not yet clearly identified the causes of autism, much work has been done in identifying early signs and symptoms to aid in early identification. Most of what is known about the early characteristics of ASD has been learned from the retrospective studies mentioned previously. Prospective studies, or studies that follow younger siblings of children with ASD to see if they develop the disorder, have also provided information on what is known about the development of children with ASD. Two areas of development appear to be most commonly affected in very young children with ASD: communication and social interaction.

### Communication and Language Development

The abilities to effectively express and understand communication are usually significantly affected in children with ASD. In fact, language delays are some of the most commonly reported concerns from parents of toddlers who are suspected of having ASD (Boyd et al., 2010; Webb & Jones, 2009). Early communication competence has been linked to a child's abilities to develop relationships (Woods & Wetherby, 2003), manage his or her own behavior, and learn from others and the environment. Woods and Wetherby (2003) noted that the development of fluent speech by the age of 5 years has been found to predict later IQ, as well as language, adaptive, and academic development. Because of the predictive nature of early communication abilities and what is known about the positive effects of well-designed communication interventions, many interventions focus on increasing the capacity of young children with ASD to communicate and respond to the communication of others.

*Infancy* Early language and joint attention development have been found to be important predictors of later communication and social development (Siller & Sigman, 2002). Similarly, early verbal imitation skills appear to be related to later language comprehension and expression (Landa, 2007; Levy, Kim, & Olive, 2006). Social communication is particularly difficult for infants with ASD, as evidenced by fewer early communicative gestures and less initiating and responding to joint attention bids. Not using or responding to pointing by 9–12 months of age is considered to be a developmental red flag that is indicative of possible impairments in joint attention, which has been identified as a pivotal skill in early development.

During the first year of life, infants with ASD show less attention to faces and voices and display less complex babbling, with less variety in the sounds the children make (Webb & Jones, 2009). The onset of first words is also often delayed. In young children who experience a developmental regression, early words may be lost before the child's second birthday. Receptive language development is also delayed, as seen in infants who fail to respond when their name is called or when spoken to. Parents often initially express concerns that their babies are not hearing them; ruling out a hearing issue is an important first step when determining the cause of such developmental delays.

**Toddlerhood**    Toddlers with ASD continue to show similar characteristics, which begin to be recognized by many parents as concerns for early language development during the second year of life. These children typically show less vocal imitation and use fewer words or phrases to communicate with others. They may also show gaze aversion or difficulties with making and sustaining eye contact. They continue to show delays in their understanding of language, appearing to ignore simple commands or failing to show an understanding of labels for familiar people and objects. Their reduced attention to speech and tendency to engage in less vocal imitation is especially important because these differences result in fewer opportunities to learn how to use and understand language; a child must attend to and practice using speech in order to develop successful communication skills.

The communication of toddlers with ASD is also marked by difficulties with the pragmatic use of language. *Pragmatics* involves the social aspects of language and communication. When some toddlers with this diagnosis use their first words, the words are often nouns that the children use to label familiar items (e.g., *ball* or *book*), but not words to engage others with the item (i.e., to play with the ball or look at the book). Many toddlers with ASD appear to be able to make requests and protest as frequently as toddlers with typical development, but they struggle with integrating the use of vocalizations, gestures, affect, and eye gaze to make what they are communicating clear to the parent or caregiver (Webb & Jones, 2009; Woods & Wetherby, 2003). This struggle to communicate can result in challenging behavior for some toddlers with ASD and in what appears to be a lack of communication in others. For example, a toddler with typical development might point to his cup, which is up on the counter, look at his mother, and say, "juice," to get something to drink. A thirsty toddler with ASD might simply cry while looking at the cup or take his mother's hand and pull her to the kitchen. His communication is less specific, making it difficult for his mother to know what he wants. When his need is not met, he might walk away without the drink or have a tantrum. Determining what the child is trying to communicate and helping him develop more refined communication skills would be an important functional focus of early intervention with this child and his family.

It is not uncommon for toddlers with ASD to say their first meaningful words around 18–24 months of age, which represents a developmental delay of at least 6 months. Toddlers who gain language tend to use their words for the purposes of labeling, requesting, and protesting and show delays in learning to use language for social-communication purposes (Koegel, 2000). It is estimated that approximately one quarter of children with ASD will remain nonverbal. In those who do learn to talk, many will engage in *echolalia,* or the immediate or delayed repetition of language the child heard (Woods & Wetherby, 2003). A toddler with ASD might repeat phrases he or she heard on a favorite cartoon or commercial, sing a favorite song repeatedly, or repeat back the last word he or she heard during a conversation. Many children with typical development also go through a period of echolalia as they are learning and trying out new language; however, for children with ASD, the use of echolalia can last longer and interfere with their development of language.

Delays and atypical development of expressive and receptive language in very young children with ASD also affect their ability to interact with others. Poorer social-communication skills make it significantly more difficult for them to learn from others and get their needs met. It is impossible to tease out difficulties in communication without also considering the challenges to social-emotional development that occur as a result of having ASD.

## Social-Emotional Development

Impairments in social and emotional development are among the core impairments in ASD. Infants and toddlers with ASD show delayed development in this area, particularly in social smiling, social referencing, attending to faces, and responding to social bids from others (Boyd et al., 2010). The same difficulties with developing joint attention that negatively affect communication also play an important role in this domain of development. These children have difficulty coordinating their attention between people and objects and are much less likely to engage in shared interactions or humor than their peers with typical development (Williams, 2003).

*Infancy*    Infants with autism may show a general lack of social interest in others by averting their gaze and failing to attend to the faces and voices of others. Their social affect tends to be more flat and their expression of positive emotion reduced (Webb & Jones, 2009). Because they are less likely to imitate others, both verbally and physically, they are also less likely to engage in turn-taking during play. Impairments and delays in imitation and turn-taking affect all areas of development for these children. Infants and toddlers with ASD have fewer typical opportunities to learn cognitive, adaptive, and motor skills that are usually learned through social imitation.

*Toddlerhood*    A marked tendency for isolation is a hallmark of young children diagnosed with ASD. Toddlers may be reported to be extremely "good," meaning that they can entertain themselves for hours without the interference of others (Webb & Jones, 2009). Compare this to a toddler with typical development who can entertain himself for about 5 minutes before needing social attention. This is a significant difference and one that, although not necessarily indicative of ASD, should trigger further screening or evaluation when reported by parents. How frequently a child initiates social interaction appears to be linked with intervention outcomes. That is, children who initiate social interactions with others more often prior to intervention tend to show the greatest gains in development following intervention (Koegel, 2000). The opposite is also true: Children with fewer social initiations are less likely to have positive outcomes.

Toddlers with ASD are also reported by parents to be challenging to play and interact with, often avoiding or ignoring social engagement attempts by others. Parents of young children with ASD appear to try to engage their children as frequently as do parents of children with typical development, but the interaction is often more difficult to establish and is briefer in duration (Siller & Sigman, 2002). In group situations with peers, toddlers with ASD are also often seen to play by themselves or wander around the environment, perhaps on the periphery or through the group without an apparent purpose. Peers often find it challenging to engage the child, which can result in the child being left alone or excluded from play due to his or her apparent lack of interest. Despite this, it is consistently reported in the literature that the quality of parent–child and peer interactions plays a key role in the development of social-communication for very young children with ASD (Rocha, Schreibman, & Stahmer, 2007).

## Play Development

Parents and other partners have an important role in the development of play in infants and toddlers with ASD. The challenge comes with engaging these children and sustaining a shared play activity because their play tends to lack imitation and shared interaction. They also show little to no turn-taking during play. This lack of imitation and turn-taking is critical because it affects the child's ability to learn from others and expand his or her attention span. As noted with communication and social skills, difficulties with attending to and imitating others also have a significant impact on early play development and should be a key focus of early intervention.

Manipulative play development in infants and toddlers with ASD tends to be less complex and less purposeful, involving, for example, simple motor activities such as holding and dropping an object, knocking objects down or off a table, or rolling or spinning objects. Play often centers on single objects and involves a single step, rather than the typical play of older infants and toddlers that involves multiple steps, such as combining objects to put shapes in a shape sorter or pretending to feed and dress a doll. The exception to this might be a toddler who is skilled at spatial tasks, such as putting puzzles together or constructive play, which have been reported to be strengths for young children with ASD (Woods & Wetherby, 2003). The play of toddlers with ASD may be marked by an interest in the parts of objects, rather than the whole object, and in simple cause-and-effect play, including repetitive activities such as opening and closing a door on a toy car, spinning the wheels on a truck, or repeatedly pressing the same button on a musical toy (Landa, 2007).

Another area of play development that is consistently affected in toddlers with ASD is symbolic play. These children often do not engage in symbolic play, which may be a sign of their lack of symbolic understanding. Symbolic understanding is important not only for pretend play but also for communication development. In children with typical development, a burst in language and play skills is seen around 24 months of age, when children's understanding of symbols leads them to use and understand more words (which are symbols for the actual objects) and to engage in more pretend play (e.g., pretending a plastic banana is a telephone, pretending to feed a baby doll from an empty spoon). Developing and enhancing symbolic play is another important goal of early intervention because of the positive impact the skills will have across a child's development.

***Restricted, Repetitive Behavior and Play***    Toddlers, more so than infants, may begin to engage in restricted and repetitive behaviors, which are also hallmarks of the ASD diagnosis, before the age of 3 years. These behaviors are often seen in the child's play, with a tendency for narrow play interests and repetitive play routines, such as lining up toys or playing with them using the same routine. For example, Colin liked to entertain himself by lining up his toy tractors along the edge of the table then pushing one tractor off at a time. When all of the tractors were off the table, he restarted the routine and lined them up again. He would play this game for hours if his parents let him. Another example might be a toddler who picks up and drops his blocks over and over rather than attempting to build something with them. Young children with ASD like predictable play routines such as these and may protest when these routines are changed or interrupted, making engaging them in interactive play challenging.

Restricted and repetitive behaviors may also include motor behaviors such as rocking, spinning, or hand flapping (Boyd et al., 2010). These behaviors are problematic when they interfere with a child's ability to explore his or her environment, interact with others, and play. A child who is flapping his hands or who carries puzzle pieces in his hands all day is unable to use his hands for other playful exploration. These stereotypical behaviors may serve a purpose for the child, such as self-soothing or self-stimulation, and should not be completely discouraged. When they interfere with development, however, they should be decreased by redirecting the child to some other playful activity.

## Sensory Development

Retrospective studies of children with ASD have revealed that as many as 42%–88% of children have sensory processing differences during very early childhood (Filipek et al., 2000). One of the most common sensory differences is being *hypersensitive,* or extremely sensitive, to sound, which may be why some toddlers with ASD cover their ears or cry when they hear certain sounds, such as the vacuum cleaner. Children may be hypersensitive to some sounds and *hyposensitive,* or less sensitive, to others, such as voices (Johnson & Myers, 2007). In addition, toddlers with ASD may show sensitivities to tactile stimulation (touch), as seen with resistance to wearing certain fabrics, irritation with tags or seams in clothing, seeking out textures such as fur to rub on the face, or a tendency to mouth nonedible objects. A resistance to eating foods with certain textures is not uncommon and can lead to a limited diet. Sensitivities to movement might be present in toddlers who like to spin, walk in their toes, slam their bodies into things such as the couch, or crave movements such as climbing or swinging.

Toddlers with ASD often show hyper- and hyposensitivity in multiple sensory areas or different forms of sensitivity in a single area, as with the example of sensitivity to sound. As with any of the possible developmental characteristics discussed thus far, demonstrating any one or two of these symptoms does not automatically mean that a young child has ASD or sensory processing differences; rather, it is a pattern of behaviors and reactions that impairs a child's ability to engage with the environment that may be indicative of a problem.

## Other Developmental Differences

Other differences noted with infants and toddlers with ASD include behavior problems and differences with motor development, such as poor coordination, atypical muscle tone, and delayed motor milestones (Landa, 2007). Difficulties with motor development are not seen in all children with this diagnosis, and in fact is an area of relative strength for many, as they may be skilled climbers, runners, and motor problem solvers. Some children show differences in *motor planning* (i.e., the ability to plan and execute motor activities to accomplish a task), such as building a tower of blocks or using utensils to self-feed. Toddlers with fine motor planning difficulties find activities that require refined eye–hand coordination difficult and may throw objects or push them away rather than coordinate an intended activity. Feeding and sleep difficulties are also common in this population. Differences in head growth and circumference are also being studied, with physicians noting a period of rapid head growth during the first 2 years, which may indicate abnormal brain development (Boyd et al., 2010).

Early interventionists should become familiar with these early signs and symptoms of ASD because the diagnosis appears to be on the rise. Because many of these symptoms can be identified very early, they can be among the first indicators to families and pediatricians that there may be a developmental difference that warrants further screening and evaluation. Service providers cannot actually make the diagnosis of ASD, but they can be a part of the team that assesses children's functional development and links families to specialists who can rule out or confirm the disorder. A list of red flags related to ASD is presented in Box 8.1.

## SCREENING, EVALUATION, AND DIAGNOSIS OF AUTISM SPECTRUM DISORDER

Early screening and evaluation is recommended whenever symptoms of the disorder appear during infancy or toddlerhood. Although very young children with these symptoms may be able to receive early intervention without being diagnosed (i.e., if they exhibit associated developmental delays), they may be more likely to receive appropriate intervention if the IFSP team, including the family, has a clear understanding of the etiology of the child's developmental differences.

### Importance of Early Identification and Screening

Early identification and diagnosis of ASD has been associated with earlier access to appropriate intervention and better long-term outcomes (Matson et al., 2008). Although some symptoms are apparent before the age of 1 year, most symptoms are recognized during the second and third years of life. Researchers have found that approximately 30% of parents identified concerns related to ASD prior to 1 year of age (Webb & Jones, 2009), 80% recognized characteristics by age 2, and 93% noted these concerns by age 3 (Matson et al., 2008). Most families express their initial concerns to the pediatrician by the 18-month wellness checkup (Landa, 2007). The majority of parents expressed concerns for their child's limited language development or behavioral issues during this appointment. The American Academy of Pediatrics (2012) recommends early, regular developmental screening as well as autism-specific screening at 18 and 24 months.

---

**BOX 8.1.        Red flags that may signal autism spectrum disorder in the first 2 years of life**

- Lack of joint attention
- Gaze aversion or fleeting use of gaze
- Delayed expressive and receptive communication
- Lack of response to name by 9–12 months of age
- Reduced use or lack of early communicative gestures, such as pointing
- Tendency for isolation
- Restrictive and repetitive play
- Lack of symbolic play
- Repetitive behaviors, such as rocking or hand flapping
- Sensory processing differences
- Loss of language or social skills

There have been significant efforts to raise awareness of early identification of autism spectrum disorder and to encourage early monitoring and screening. Challenges with early identification persist, however, because of several factors. The natural variability in achieving developmental milestones, the reluctance of physicians and families to seek a diagnosis when a child is so young, the presence of other conditions or challenging behaviors that may be more primary concerns, and the tendency to "wait and see" if the child's developmental trajectory changes can complicate the identification process. Once a screening is completed, parent follow-up is necessary, whether it is for further evaluation or initiation of early intervention services. Parents may choose to wait or decide not to take the next step, especially when the child is showing fewer symptoms, when other children or family members showed similar delays, or when children are younger when first identified (Webb & Jones, 2009). At the point when concerns arise on a developmental screening, it is important that families are made aware of their choices and understand the next steps, such as how to access an evaluation and intervention services, so that they can make informed decisions for their child and family.

Screening tools are now available that allow for developmental surveillance of very young children who are suspected of having ASD. One of the most widely recommended screening tools is the Modified Checklist for Autism in Toddlers–Revised, with Follow-Up (M-CHAT-R/F). The M-CHAT-R/F has been validated for use with toddlers between the ages of 16 and 30 months and is used by many pediatricians and early intervention professionals. The M-CHAT-R/F is available online as a free download, or it can be completed and scored online (https://m-chat.org/). This instrument is a 20-question screening that helps parents and professionals determine when a child should be referred to a specialist to evaluate for ASD (Robins et al., 2014). Not all children who fail the screening will have ASD. However, the M-CHAT-R/F has been shown to be sensitive to identifying children who need further evaluation due to markers for the disorder.

## Evaluation and Diagnosis

A comprehensive evaluation for ASD is a multicomponent process. When a child is suspected of having ASD, the pediatrician will likely refer the child for audiological testing to rule out a hearing loss and genetics testing to rule out other conditions that may be associated with the disorder. A physical examination is conducted, as well as developmental testing to determine if the child is showing delays. Diagnostic testing for ASD includes the diagnostician taking medical histories (including health, development, and behavior), gathering information from the family, and completing standardized assessments of the child's development and functioning using tools such as the Autism Diagnostic Observation Scale (ADOS-2; Johnson & Myers, 2007). The ADOS-2 is considered to be the criterion standard of autism assessment tools, with strong predictive validity. It must be completed by trained professionals, uses a semistructured format, and takes less than 1 hour to administer. There is a toddler module that is appropriate for children ages 12–30 months who are not yet using phrases to communicate. The results of the ADOS-2 toddler module are provided using ranges of concern rather than a formal diagnosis to help determine when continued monitoring is needed. As children age beyond 30 months, other modules can be used to determine a more formal diagnosis, as appropriate.

Despite the push for earlier identification, the age of initial diagnosis for ASD continues to be during the preschool years. The Centers for Disease Control and Prevention (CDC, 2013) reported that more children are being diagnosed before age 3 years, but most children receive their initial diagnosis between the ages of 4 and 5 years. This delay between when parents first express concerns (by age 18 months) and when children receive the diagnosis is likely to be influenced by the same challenges noted with early screening. Another reason for this delay could be that some physicians are uncomfortable with labeling such a young child. When diagnosis is conducted by qualified professionals with training in evaluating infants and toddlers with ASD using appropriate evaluation tools, diagnosis can be reliably made for many children as young as 2 years old (Boyd et al., 2010; Woods & Wetherby, 2003). Although early diagnosis is very important, a formal ASD diagnosis is not necessary for young children to receive early intervention services. Young children who are suspected of having ASD can receive supports and services if they qualify for early intervention, depending on their state's eligibility criteria and the extent of their developmental delay(s).

The diagnostic process takes time and should include information from multiple sources. Observation of the child is also important, as is the use of clinical judgment to interpret the findings. Once the diagnosis is made, the child's development should be monitored over time to see if maturation or intervention cause changes in the child's presentation of the disorder (Matson et al., 2008). Appropriate intervention has been found to change a child's developmental trajectory (Childress et al., 2012). Therefore, whether a toddler receives a formal diagnosis or not, a referral for early intervention services is highly recommended when a child shows symptoms of ASD (Strain, Schwartz, & Barton, 2011).

## INTERVENTION APPROACHES, STRATEGIES, AND CONSIDERATIONS

Due to the increased understanding and awareness of red flags associated with ASD, young children are starting to receive intervention services for ASD earlier than ever before. Along with the increased ability to identify infants and toddlers with ASD, recommendations guiding the provision of targeted treatments have been developed. One such form of guidance has come from the National Research Council (NRC, 2001), which provided the following eight recommendations regarding intervention services and supports for children with ASD:

1.  Intervention should begin as soon as ASD is suspected.
2.  Developmentally appropriate and systematically planned interventions should be intense, occurring for approximately 25 hours per week (with the caveat that specificity of intervention intensity is ultimately dependent on the needs of the child and family).
3.  Interventions should be individualized to meet children's needs and could include a variety of delivery formats (e.g., one-to-one and small-group instruction).
4.  Children's progress should be monitored and instructional programs should be modified if positive responses to the interventions are not observed.
5.  Children should receive instruction in settings in which interactions with typically developing peers are possible as appropriate for children's individualized goals.
6.  Prioritized intervention objectives should include functional communication, social skill instruction, play skills, cognitive development, and positive behavior as appropriate to children's individual needs.
7.  All interventions should be age appropriate and individually appropriate, and instruction should be delivered in natural environments in which the skills will be used to the maximum extent possible.

8.  Attention should be paid to children's stage of learning, with adjustments made to instructional practices as necessary (e.g., different teaching strategies should be used when children are learning new skills versus learning to generalize the skills to new settings, people, or materials).

In addition to these guidelines, an important goal in the field of early childhood intervention has been to ensure that families and children with ASD are provided with supports and services that are supported by scientific evidence. Although many interventions for autism exist, only some have been shown to be effective through scientific research. These interventions are considered to be *evidence-based practices* (EBPs).

As implied from the label, ASD is a spectrum disorder, which includes young children with different abilities and needs. The process of identifying effective interventions should include the following steps:

1.  Assessing the child's and family's strengths and needs
2.  Developing goals for both the child and the family
3.  Identifying EBPs that fit the child's and family's characteristics and needs
4.  Developing a plan for implementing the EBPs
5.  Monitoring progress and making adjustments as needed

EBPs provide a framework for selecting effective interventions, but the unique characteristics, strengths, and needs of each child and family should guide the team in identifying the best interventions. The determination of which evidence-based interventions are most appropriate ties in closely with the development and implementation of the IFSP.

## Effective Interventions for Autism Spectrum Disorder

Researchers have conducted systematic reviews of interventions for individuals with ASD, with the goal of identifying EBPs for this population. Two national centers, the National Standards Project at the National Autism Center and the National Professional Development Center on ASD, undertook the task of reviewing autism intervention studies for this purpose. Between these two centers, specific intervention strategies and comprehensive intervention models were identified as having a level of evidence that shows they are effective for infants, children, or youth with ASD (Wong et al., 2013).

In general, the types of ASD interventions can be divided into two broad categories: 1) medical and alternative interventions and 2) behavioral interventions. Medical and alternative interventions include strategies such as medications, supplements, special diets, sensory integration, and massage. A number of these interventions, such as diets, vitamins and supplements, and sensory integration therapy, do not have supportive evidence to suggest their effectiveness in addressing the core symptoms of ASD. These approaches may alleviate some issues experienced by young children with ASD, such as sleep irregularity and gut and bowel abnormalities. However, these interventions may not work for all young children with ASD. Parents eager to help their children may turn to these interventions, regardless of a limited evidence base. In some cases, parents may inadvertently put their children at risk for harm by using interventions associated with dangerous outcomes, such as chelation therapy—a treatment to remove heavy metals from the body. When working with families who are considering the use of medical or alternative interventions, service providers should encourage the family to find out as much information as possible about the intervention, support their search for evidence about associated outcomes or risks, and urge them to talk to other professionals, such as their child's pediatrician, who may offer expert advice on the treatment.

Because both the National Autism Center and the National Professional Development Center on ASD did not include medical and alternative interventions in their reviews, only behavioral interventions are described in this chapter. Behavioral interventions include strategies such as changing the physical and social environments and teaching a child specific skills. However, other interventions need additional scientific support and are not currently identified as EBPs but could help some young children with ASD. Identifying which specific practices are effective for which children is an individualized process. Early intervention service providers who are knowledgeable about the variety of practices available for very young children can assist families by providing information and support so that families can make careful decisions about which interventions to try with their children.

## Behavioral Interventions

Many behavioral interventions are based on applied behavior analysis. *Applied behavior analysis (ABA)* has been defined as the scientific study of behavior (Cooper, Heron, & Heward, 2007). The main goal when studying behavior, according to principles of ABA and the behavioral theory of learning (Skinner, 1938, 1953), is to reveal cause-and-effect relationships between environmental events and behavior, using systematic direct observations of behavior. A three-part cycle, known as the ABCs of behavior, is used to study and describe this relationship:

- *Antecedent,* or the environmental events or stimuli that precede a behavior
- *Behavior,* or what the child will or does display
- *Consequence,* or the environmental events or stimuli that follow a behavior

For young children, the first part of the learning cycle, the antecedent, can be anything that triggers a behavior. Antecedents could be favorite toys, companions, snacks, or a natural event that occurs in the environment. For example, when Colin's older sister sang to him, he would begin to smile in response to the experience. Colin's smile represents the second part of the learning cycle, which is the behavior or response. Behavioral responses can take multiple forms, such as facial expressions, gestures, and vocalizations. The last part of the learning cycle, which is the consequence, could increase the chance that the child will repeat the same behavior (i.e., reinforcer) or decrease the chance the child will repeat the same behavior (i.e., punisher).

Going back to the example, after Colin smiled, his sister rubbed his back, which he enjoyed. Because the back rub was something Colin liked, it could serve as a reinforcer. With this reinforcer, it would be very possible that the next time the older sister sang, Colin would smile at her again. In contrast, if his older sister yelled at him and left the room when Colin smiled (i.e., something that would scare Colin and serve as a punisher), the chances are that Colin would not smile again when his older sister sang. Examining each part of the learning cycle is key to the ABA approach to intervention.

When studying behaviors, the antecedent and type of consequence are examined to determine causes of behaviors. They can also be manipulated to change behavior. Individuals who provide early intervention services should be familiar with ABA principles and use the ABCs to help children learn appropriate behavior. Additional training is also available for service providers who wish to specialize in ABA and work with children with ASD, such as training that leads to the board-certified behavioral analyst (BCBA) credential. It is important to note, however, that others who do not have this specialized training, such as parents, siblings, and child care providers, can deliver many of the EBP behavioral strategies used in ABA interventions effectively after receiving appropriate training, coaching, and support (Meadan, Ostrosky, Zaghlawan, & Yu, 2009).

**Behavioral Strategies**    Behavioral interventions are described as either focused or comprehensive. Focused interventions are individual strategies, used alone or in combination, to address specific skills or behaviors. Comprehensive interventions are a set of procedures or programs designed to address a broad array of skills or behaviors. The following are descriptions of some of the common behavioral intervention strategies used with young children with ASD.

*Environmental Arrangement*    Environmental arrangements, environmental modifications, or antecedent-based interventions include modifications of stimuli or events that typically precede the occurrence of a target behavior. The changes in the environment are used to increase the likelihood that a target behavior will occur, such as when a preferred toy is placed in a child's view but out of reach to increase the likelihood that the child will initiate communication, or reduce the likelihood of a problem behavior, such as when highly preferred activities are used during intervention to increase interest level and reduce challenging behavior (Ostrosky & Meadan, 2010). Environmental arrangement is often used with other EBPs, such as extinction and reinforcement, which will be described later.

For example, Colin's mother learned how to embed opportunities to teach Colin how to sign EAT within the family's everyday routines and activities. During his afternoon snack time, Lisa gave Colin a small portion of his favorite crackers. When he wanted more to eat, Lisa showed him the cracker box (environmental arrangement) and prompted Colin to sign EAT by using the sign herself and saying the word. Each time Colin wanted another cracker, he had to get her attention and sign EAT. This strategy was easy to repeat during snack times and mealtimes and resulted in Colin quickly learning to use the sign to get what he wanted.

*Prompting*    Prompting is another behaviorally based antecedent teaching strategy. Early interventionists and parents can teach a child a new skill by providing help or assistance through prompts, as Colin's mother did after showing him the box of crackers. *Prompts* are systematic strategies used to increase the likelihood that a child will correctly complete a task or give an appropriate response (Ault & Griffen, 2013; Meadan, Ostrosky, Santos, & Snodgrass, 2013). There are different types of prompts, including 1) gestural or nonverbal prompts, 2) verbal prompts, 3) visual prompts, 4) modeling, and 5) physical prompts. Table 8.2 shows examples of each type of prompt.

Several types of prompts are often used during one activity to help children learn communication and play behaviors. For example, while playing with puzzles, which was a favorite activity, sometimes Colin needed help requesting puzzle pieces. During a recent intervention visit, Colin's service provider showed his mother how to use verbal and physical prompting during puzzle play to help Colin request what he needed and to place pieces appropriately. The interventionist coached Lisa, Colin's mother, how to wait a few seconds for Colin to independently request a puzzle piece. When Colin did not make a request, Lisa learned to say, "Colin, do you want a puzzle piece?" (a *verbal prompt*). When Colin made eye contact with Lisa, she gave him a piece. If Colin struggled to find the right place to put the puzzle piece, Lisa held Colin's hand—while he held the piece—and led it to the correct spot on the puzzle (a *physical prompt*). This simple activity encouraged Colin to interact with Lisa and helped him learn during an activity that he already enjoyed.

**Table 8.2.**  Examples of different types of prompts

| Gestural or nonverbal prompt | Pointing to a toy to encourage the child to reach for it |
| --- | --- |
| | Holding out a hand to signal for the child to give an object |
| Verbal prompt | Providing a verbal model for a word, sound, or phrase that matches an activity a child is performing, then waiting for the toddler to imitate it |
| | Asking a child a question such as "What do you want?" |
| Visual prompt | Using pictures of favorite toys or activities to help the child learn to make choices |
| Modeling | Demonstrating how to complete a puzzle |
| | Video recording a modeled activity, having the child watch the video, and then asking the child to do what he or she saw |
| Physical prompt | Using hand-over-hand guidance to help a child learn how to perform a task, such as scribbling with a crayon or opening a snack box |

In addition to the different types of prompts, there are different types of prompting procedures. These procedures guide the adult in how to provide prompts in a systematic and intentional way to prevent the child from making mistakes while learning a new skill, otherwise known as *errorless learning*. When using least-to-most prompting procedures, the adult gradually increases the level of help, or prompts, to support the child in successfully learning or completing the activity. When using most-to-least prompting procedures, the adult provides progressively less assistance as the child achieves his or her goals (Meadan et al., 2013). For instance, a parent who wants his daughter to learn to feed herself using a spoon may begin by teaching the child by using hand-over-hand guidance, or a physical prompt. The father wraps his hand around the child's hand, scoops the food, then brings the spoon to the child's mouth. Over time, the father would gradually remove his hand, perhaps by helping his daughter scoop the food then removing his hand so she can finish feeding herself. The father would eventually only provide a verbal prompt, such as "Eat your mashed potatoes," to encourage the child to use her spoon. Once the child has mastered this skill, she will no longer need the physical or verbal prompt and will be able to feed herself independently. Although effective, prompts may need to be used for a good deal of time with some children before the child is able to perform the skill independently.

Another prompting procedure that was identified as an EBP for children with ASD is time delay. *Time delay* is a practice that focuses on fading the use of prompts while teaching. Time delay is always used with other prompting procedures, such as least-to-most prompting. In time delay, a brief delay is provided between the initial direction or cue to complete a task and any additional prompts. While Colin was learning to request a puzzle piece, his mother also learned to wait about 5 seconds after each prompt she gave so that he would have time to respond. For example, after asking Colin, "What do you want?" Lisa waited 3–5 seconds (time delay) to see if Colin responded or if he needed more support. If more support was needed, the family's service provider coached Lisa to use another form of support, such as modeling and signing the word *more* for Colin to repeat. Waiting several seconds allowed Colin time to process what his mother said and to respond. After practicing using time delay, Lisa noticed that Colin would attempt to imitate *more* by making the /m/ sound. When he made this sound, she praised him and gave him the puzzle piece, understanding that over time he would learn to more closely approximate that word.

*Reinforcement*   Reinforcement is a behaviorally based consequence teaching strategy. In contrast to prompting, which is used before the behavior occurs, reinforcers are presented after a behavior occurs. *Positive reinforcement* occurs when a behavior is followed immediately by the presentation of a stimulus or event that increases the likelihood of the behavior to occur. Examples of positive reinforcers include edible (e.g., cookies, crackers), social (e.g., hugs, tickles), and verbal (e.g., praise such as "nice talking!") reinforcers. Positive reinforcers are chosen based on what the child enjoys. For young children with ASD, verbal praise may not be as effective as it is for other same-age children because of their difficulties with attending to and processing the speech of others, so other positive reinforcers may need to be identified. *Negative reinforcement* occurs when a behavior is followed by the termination or removal of a stimulus, which causes the frequency of the behavior to increase in the future. Colin's mother used positive reinforcement when she praised Colin for approximating *more* by saying, "You asked for more puzzle pieces, Colin! Way to go!" She also handed him the puzzle piece as soon as he made the /m/ sound for *more,* which was another natural positive reinforcer.

Interventionists can identify positive reinforcers by interviewing family members about the child's favorite foods or activities and/or by conducting a preference assessment. A *preference assessment* for a young child with autism typically includes several items or activities that family members have identified as motivating to the child. The service provider presents various items to the child in pairs and keeps track of which items the child chooses most often. Once the interventionist has an idea of which items are most preferred, they can be used as reinforcers during intervention activities as well as throughout the time between intervention visits. Another way to determine a child's preferences is to observe which activities the child enjoys doing when other options exist. Observation also works well with children who are nonverbal. For example, if a child always chooses to play in the block center during play time at a child care center, the interventionist can deduce that playing with block center materials, such as dinosaurs or trains, could be used as a reinforcer.

A specific type of EBP related to reinforcement is called *differential reinforcement.* When adults use this strategy, they reinforce a desired or appropriate behavior while ignoring an inappropriate behavior. The goal in using this strategy is to increase the likelihood that the child will engage in a desired behavior, such as pointing to a preferred toy that is out of reach, and decrease the likelihood the child will use the inappropriate behavior, such as crying when she or he cannot reach the toy. Parents can be easily coached to use differential reinforcement throughout the day once a behavior is identified that the family wishes to change.

*Extinction*   Extinction is a behavioral strategy that is used to reduce or eliminate unwanted behavior. *Extinction* involves withdrawing or terminating the positive reinforcer that maintains an inappropriate behavior. This withdrawal results in the decrease or stopping of behavior.

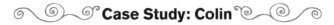
## Case Study: Colin

Every time Colin was buckled into his carseat, he would squirm and cry. When Lisa shared this concern with the service provider, they talked about how Lisa typically responded. Lisa reported that she would take Colin out of the carseat to try to calm him down and to see if he was uncomfortable. He would calm down but would quickly resume crying when placed back in the carseat. This behavior was becoming so problematic that the family was trying to avoid taking Colin out in the car. The interventionist shared that Lisa's behavior of removing Colin from the carseat could be a reinforcer for Colin's crying because he appeared to want to be removed from it. To eliminate or decrease the crying, it was suggested that Lisa ignore Colin's crying, as long as he was safely buckled in, and not take him out of the carseat. The interventionist advised Lisa that Colin's crying may get worse before it got better, while he learned that crying would not get him what he wanted. She also suggested that this strategy should be used with other strategies, such as reinforcing Colin when he was not crying and providing him with favorite toys or music while in his carseat. At the next intervention visit, Lisa reported that it had been difficult to ignore Colin's crying; however, after several trips in the car, Colin was now crying less and seemed to be distracted by playing with a musical toy that she saved for car trips.

Although extinction has been found to be an effective strategy, many researchers argue that the most effective methods of prevention of and intervention for challenging behavior in young children with ASD involve indirect practices. *Indirect practices* are those that are implemented when challenging behaviors are not occurring, such as teaching alternative communication and social skills and arranging the environment to prevent the unwanted behavior (Dunlap, Strain, & Ostryn, 2010). An example of preventing unwanted behavior is avoiding letting the child see a toy that he or she always cries for until it is given to the child. By not making that toy available before the child can have it, the outburst is prevented.

*Visual Supports*    *Visual supports* are any tool presented visually that provides support for children with ASD. Visual supports for toddlers might include, but are not limited to, real objects, pictures, line drawings, and symbols. Meadan, Ostrosky, Triplett, Michna, and Fettig (2011) found that several types of visual supports were effective for young children, including visual schedules, visually structured environments (e.g., pictures on toy shelves to illustrate what toys were stored there), visual scripts, and visual rule reminders. These types of visual supports are often used in preschool classrooms, but they can also be employed successfully by parents in their homes.

For young children with ASD, instructional prompts that include visual supports may be more helpful than verbal prompts alone. For instance, prompting a child to say "ball" while also showing the child his favorite ball during a game of toss is more likely to help the child learn the word and its meaning than simply asking the child, "What is this?" In addition, visual supports can help create predictable routines and activities, something young children with ASD prefer.

*Behavioral Programs*    The following sections describe some common behavioral programs used with young children with ASD.

*Discrete Trial Training*    *Discrete trial training* (DTT) is a one-to-one instructional approach used to teach skills in a planned, controlled, and systematic manner. The interventionist uses antecedents and consequences to increase the likelihood the child will be motivated to participate in the training activities. DTT is used when a child needs to learn a skill best taught in small, repeated steps. Positive reinforcers, such as praise and favorite toys or food, are often used during instruction. Each trial or teaching opportunity has a definite beginning and end—hence the descriptor *discrete trial*. Each skill that the child needs to learn is broken down into small steps and taught one step at a time. Each trial within the intervention is completed quickly and can be repeated many times to provide many opportunities for the child to practice the new skill.

The structure of DTT is very formal because it is intended to help children make the connection between their response to instruction (i.e., the *stimuli* or *antecedent*) and the positive reaction that results (i.e., the *consequence*). The formal setup of DTT includes an interventionist or parent seated at a small workspace, which for young children might include a highchair or child-size table. When DTT is delivered at home, a room or other small space is designated for intervention purposes only. On the table are the materials needed for the skill or task being taught. The adult leading the trial would verbally prompt the child to do something and may provide prompts or supports to help the child successfully engage in the desired behavior (e.g., model the action, such as waving a hand while saying, "Wave your hand," to foster receptive language and motor imitation). If the child correctly responds, a positive reinforcer is provided. After brief enjoyment of the reinforcer, another instructional trial begins. Once a skill is learned, instruction is embedded in natural daily routines and activities to promote generalization of the skill to more natural situations.

*Naturalistic Intervention*    *Naturalistic intervention* is embedded instruction that occurs within the daily routines and activities of families and children. Naturalistic instruction goes by many names, such as incidental teaching and enhanced milieu teaching. It includes effective strategies, such as modeling (the adult models the target behavior), mand models (the adult asks the child a question or gives a direction, then if the child does not respond, a model is provided), and time-delay procedures. Naturalistic interventions are based on children's interests and are more child orientated than adult directed. The adult builds on the child interests by intentionally arranging the physical and social environments to increase the likelihood the child will engage in target behaviors, such as requesting an item or requesting help. When the child is engaged in the target behavior, the adult elaborates and expands on the behavior to help the child learn.

## Case Study: Colin

Colin's mother found that using naturalistic intervention techniques fit easily into her day. She used them with their snack time routine as well as when she was teaching Colin to take turns and use simple words in play. One game that Colin enjoyed was putting his blanket on his mother's head and then watching it fall off. He would giggle and make fleeting eye contact when the blanket fell. With the service provider's coaching, Colin's mother expanded on this game to add simple words, such as *1–2–3, uh-oh,* and *fell down*. She would say, "1–2–3" as the blanket was getting ready to fall, then exuberantly say, "Down!" as it fell off. Colin eventually began imitating her model and saying, "down," as the blanket fell to the floor. This fun game was often played in the evenings before bath time and by other family members as well.

*Pivotal Response Training*    *Pivotal response training* (PRT) emphasizes instructing skills that are considered fundamental to learning in a variety of developmental areas. These pivotal skills include 1) motivation, 2) responsivity to multiple cues, 3) self-management, and 4) self-initiation (Koegel & Koegel, 2012). PRT is an intervention that incorporates elements familiar to early childhood educators, such as providing young children with opportunities to make choices and engaging children in conversations to encourage independent initiations of language. PRT also includes elements familiar to special educators, such as using reinforcers and direct instruction. PRT is especially helpful for young children learning communication, language, play, and social skills.

## Comprehensive Treatment Models

Comprehensive treatment models (CTMs) contain many of the strategies listed above and have been packaged and evaluated for their efficacy for supporting positive outcomes for young children with ASD. CTMs can be distinguished from one another by examining their conceptual or theoretical frameworks, procedures, level of intensity, length of intervention, and targeted outcomes (Wong et al., 2013).

There are a number of comprehensive treatment models that are designed to meet the needs of infants and toddlers with ASD (Odom, Boyd, Hall, & Hume, 2010). Some of these models are built upon the framework of ABA, such as Project DATA (Developmentally Appropriate Treatment for Autism; Schwartz, Sandall, McBride, & Boulware, 2004) and the Lovaas model (Lovaas Institute, 2014). Others are built upon developmental and relationship-based theories, such as the Early Start Denver model (Dawson et al., 2010), the Developmental, Individual Difference, Relationship-based/Floortime model (Greenspan & Wieder, 2006), and the Relationship Development Intervention (Gutstein & Sheely, 2002). Other models might include a mix of many frameworks, such as the TEACCH model (Treatment and Education of Autistic and Related Communication Handicapped Children; TEACCH Autism Program, 2014). Of the CTMs currently available to families residing in the United States, those based on developmental and relationship-based theories have the least amount of scientific evidence to demonstrate efficacy or to be considered evidence based.

When reviewing possible intervention approaches, early intervention service providers should remember that many CTMs, such as the ones identified above, require interventionists to receive specialized training and/or certification prior to delivering them in a formal way. However, many of these CTMs are composed of EBPs that any interventionist can learn to deliver. Although CTMs may be successful in addressing the needs of very young children with ASD, they are not the only method for delivering effective services. Early interventionists can create responsive IFSPs and intervention programs for very young children with ASD using a combination of the EBPs described in this chapter (Odom, Hume, Boyd, & Stabel, 2012).

## Supporting Early Learning with Specific Intervention Strategies

Service providers can consider a number of other specific intervention strategies as they assist families with embedding interventions for young children with ASD into everyday routines and activities. These strategies can be taught to family members who can use them throughout the day to promote social, communication, and play development. As with any intervention strategy, it is essential that the service provider collaborate with the parent to determine how the strategy can be implemented in the family's unique routines. Although these strategies are helpful in supporting the development of children with ASD, they are also useful for many of the other children served in early intervention. How the following strategies will be used in practice differs for each child and family.

***Fostering Engagement***   For children with ASD, fostering engagement is key to supporting development across domains. Early intervention service providers should ask families about what activities during the day are most engaging for the child, including activities that the child most enjoys and activities the parent and child enjoy together. Extending these activities by making them more interactive and embedding simple communication prompts and opportunities to learn and use new words are natural ways to contextualize intervention. It is important for the service provider to remember to coach the family during these activities, rather than engage the child in a provider-led interaction, so that the family can continue fostering engagement throughout the week.

**Using Physical and Object-Based Play**     Young children with ASD are more likely to engage during physical play (e.g., playing tickle games, chasing, jumping on the bed) or object-based play (e.g., playing with balls, toy trains, bubbles, or other favorite objects) than they are during purely social games (Doussard-Roosevelt, Joe, Bazhenova, & Porges, 2003; Williams, 2003). Service providers can help families use physical and object-based games to build their child's social-communication and cognitive understanding by embedding opportunities to communicate and problem-solve in these activities. Colin's game of putting his blanket on his mother's head is an example of how communication and engagement strategies can be embedded into such a play routine.

**Using Structured and Repetitive Activities**     All children benefit from structure and repetition as they learn and practice new skills. Using or creating structure through repetition and use of familiar play and caregiving routines can be very effective. Service providers can help parents create activities that involve repeating actions or phrases during play or caregiving routines, such as making dots and lines with the child while scribbling on paper or saying, "Ready, set, go!" while rolling toy trains along a track. These routines become predictable for the child and can make it easier for him or her to imitate actions, sounds, and words. When a child is already engaging in repetitive behavior, such as spinning a bowl on the floor, the parent can learn how to turn these solitary games into opportunities for social engagement by joining the child's play, imitating the child, and introducing turn-taking. For example, the adult can take a turn spinning the bowl while saying, "Go!"

**Teaching Turn-Taking**     Embedding frequent opportunities for turn-taking during play and other routines can help infants and toddlers learn the purpose of social communication and the benefits of engaging others. Simple turn-taking games can be built around any child interest. For example, when Colin played by himself by pushing his tractors along the table, his parents learned to become part of this activity by taking a turn catching the tractors, then giving them to Colin. They also took turns pushing a tractor along the edge of the table. Communication was embedded in this activity as well, with the parents modeling words and phrases, such as "Go tractor" or "My turn ... your turn."

**Using High-Intensity Interactions and Anticipatory Phrases**     Interactions that use exuberant language and an expressive face and voice can help a child with ASD attend to and engage with the speaker (Doussard-Roosevelt et al., 2003). These interactions can draw the child in and help maintain the interaction. Using wide eyes, big smiles, and anticipatory phrases, such as "Ready, set, go!" or "Up, up, and away," when playing also makes the activity more enjoyable for the child. Anticipatory phrases can be used repetitively during play or other routines; eventually, pausing can be introduced to give the child the opportunity to fill in the missing word. Colin's parents and sister used "Ready, set, go!" as the tractors moved along the table and began to fall. Colin became excited when he heard this phrase and eventually learned to say, "Go!" just before the tractor fell.

***Using Pausing and Narration***     Embedding purposeful pauses, such as those used during time delay, to facilitate communication and play allows the child time to process and respond to the communication bid or play request. Some children may need longer pauses than others, but waiting in silence and with an expectant look on the adult's face can offer the child a prompt that it is his or her turn in the activity. Narration is also extremely useful but can be challenging for parents who are not used to talking during daily activities. Service providers can model how to narrate daily activities and play using self-talk and parallel talk, as discussed in Chapter 5. Using narration offers children a low-stress opportunity to hear language and associate meaning without the demand to engage or communicate (Siller & Sigman, 2002).

***Creating Expectations***     Service providers should help parents create expectations that the child engage and communicate throughout the day. For instance, a parent can learn to expect the child to help with dressing by pausing and talking the child through putting his or her arm in the shirt sleeve. The parent can create the expectation that the child use eye contact or a sound to request more juice, instead of accepting the child bringing the cup to the parent as a request. When discussing daily routines, parents and service providers can identify opportunities when an additional expectation can be embedded so that the child is more actively engaged. It is important to remember, though, to expect the child to do something that he or she can already do, rather than stressing the child by expecting something beyond his or her current abilities. For Colin, his mother knew he could use the /m/ sound, so prompting him to use it as an approximation of *more* was appropriate. Had she held out for him to enunciate the actual word, both she and Colin would have likely become frustrated.

***Planning for Generalization and Maintenance***     Because generalization of learned skills and abilities to new people, materials, and contexts can be challenging for children with ASD, it is important for service providers to purposefully plan with families how children will practice what they are learning with different people, in different places, and in different activities within their routines (Kashinath, Woods, & Goldstein, 2006). Helping families plan for how a child will practice a new skill during the week increases the likelihood that the child will maintain the behavior and use it with intention in other situations. For example, after a child learns to say, "bye-bye," to his sister in the morning before school, he could practice this skill when his father leaves for work, by saying good-bye to the cashier at the supermarket, and by telling his toy figures "bye" when he and his mother have them drive away during play.

These specific intervention strategies can be useful for enhancing development in any child. However, when used intentionally and consistently with children with ASD, they can help build early abilities that are pivotal to development. All of these strategies should be used in such a way that the child enjoys intervention and learns that engaging, communicating, and playing with others is motivating and fun. Although these strategies are likely to be embedded within the treatment models discussed, service providers and families make decisions about which models to use and which strategies to try based on the strengths and needs of the child and family, the family's priorities, the service provider's knowledge and training, and the outcomes developed in the IFSP. Careful consideration when making these decisions is a collaborative family–professional effort.

## Making Decisions About Intervention

When working within a team to create an IFSP and determine intervention approaches, service providers must always remember that all children are unique. This is especially true for infants and toddlers with ASD. Intervention approaches that work for one child will not work for all children with ASD. Avoiding the assumption that one strategy will work for all children allows team members to focus on the family's priorities for their child's development and the child's strengths, interests, and needs.

When considering which EBPs might address a family's priorities and a child's needs, it can be very helpful to share details with the family about what those strategies would look like in practice. In other words, describe the characteristics of the recommended strategy, offer examples of when the strategy could be implemented within daily routines, and identify the skills needed to implement the strategy. Sharing this information with families during the decision-making process is crucial to identifying strategies that appeal to family members. Strategies chosen by family members will aid the coaching process as interventionists work alongside families to help them learn to deliver EBPs within everyday routines and activities.

The decision about the frequency of early intervention services for infants and toddlers who have or who are suspected of having ASD is an important one that teams make based on the individual needs of the child and family, as well as what supports the family needs to address their goals for the child. With the NRC (2001) recommendations that intervention must be intense and occur at least 25 hours per week, some people in the field have interpreted this to mean that early intervention services must be provided at this frequency. However, if service providers are using a family-centered, routines-based approach to intervention that employs coaching, collaborative practices, and the use of EBPs for young children with ASD, then they are helping families learn how to engage their children throughout the week during daily life.

A decision about intensity of services should be based on the needs of the child and the support needs of the family (Strain et al., 2011). When parents are confident about using the strategies discussed and are able to adapt them to their routines with their child, then the child will be receiving much more intervention than 25 hours per week. This level of intensity does not necessarily require a professional when families are well prepared to support their child's development every day.

## BEST PRACTICE HIGHLIGHTS

The following best practices should guide service providers as they engage with young children who have or who are suspected of having ASD and their families during early intervention:

- Young children with ASD may show signs of the disorder during infancy and toddlerhood. A sign by itself does not indicate ASD; rather, a pattern of symptoms is indicative of the need for further evaluation.
- Service providers should be aware of the myths, signs, and symptoms of ASD so that they can support families in seeking appropriate screening, evaluation, and diagnosis.

- Every child with ASD is unique. The intervention strategies and approaches that will be effective depend on the child's strengths and needs, the family's priorities and preferences, and the knowledge and skills of the service provider and other members of the early intervention team.

- Behavioral treatments and strategies have the strongest evidence base for use with children with ASD. Although there are formal treatment models that require specific training, many of the EBPs in these models can be learned and implemented by any service provider and all family members.

- Behavioral strategies for young children with ASD include modifications to environmental arrangements, prompting, reinforcement, extinction, and visual supports.

- Many specific intervention strategies should be part of the service provider's repertoire when supporting young children with ASD, such as fostering engagement, using physical and object-based play, using structured and repetitive activities, teaching turn-taking, using high-intensity interactions and anticipatory phrases, using pausing and narration, creating expectations, and planning for the generalization and maintenance of learned skills.

- Making decisions about appropriate intervention approaches, strategies, and frequency of services is a team decision based on the child's and family's strengths and needs, the family's priorities and preferences, the outcomes on the IFSP, and what the family needs to feel confident and competent with embedding intervention into their everyday lives.

## CONCLUSION

Ravet (2011) described ASD as a "unique and distinct way of thinking, communicating and interacting" (p. 676) that affects a child's development. Scientific advances in screening and evaluating very young children who experience these distinctive patterns in their social, communicative, and cognitive development are leading to ASD diagnoses at earlier ages than ever before. Along with a deeper understanding of EBPs, teams supporting these children and their families are capable of developing distinctive and unique IFSPs and intervention programs to best meet the needs of very young children diagnosed with ASD in developmentally appropriate ways within the child and family's natural environments.

## DISCUSSION QUESTIONS AND APPLIED ACTIVITIES

1.  As the evidence base for practices and interventions related to supporting young children with ASD grows, describe three ways that early interventionists can stay up to date with current research findings.

2.  Providing young children with ASD appropriate early intervention services does not always mean more hours of intervention. In no longer than one page, write how you would explain this concept to parents of infants and toddlers suspected to have or diagnosed with ASD.

3.  What type of family supports are there in your community for families of young children diagnosed with autism? Identify the available supports and services and create a list of all of the opportunities and resources for the families you may eventually serve.

# REFERENCES

American Academy of Pediatrics. (2012). *Prevalence of autism spectrum disorders.* Retrieved from http://www.aap.org/en-us/about-the-aap/aap-press-room/pages/Prevalence-of-Autism-Spectrum-Disorders.aspx

American Academy of Pediatrics. (2013). *Vaccine safety: Examine the evidence.* Retrieved from http://www2.aap.org/immunization/families/faq/vaccinestudies.pdf

American Psychiatric Association. (2013). *Diagnostic and statistical manual of mental disorders* (5th ed.). Washington, DC: Author.

Ault, M.J., & Griffen, A.K. (2013). Teaching with system of least prompts: An easy method for monitoring progress. *TEACHING Exceptional Children, 45*(3), 46–53.

Autism and Developmental Disabilities Monitoring Network. (2014). Prevalence of autism spectrum disorder among children aged 8 years—Autism and developmental disabilities monitoring network, 11 sites, United States, 2010. *Morbidity and Mortality Weekly Report, 63*(2). Retrieved from http://www.cdc.gov/mmwr/pdf/ss/ss6302.pdf

Autism Science Foundation. (2013). *Autism and vaccines: History of the vaccination issue.* Retrieved from http://autismsciencefoundation.org/autismandvaccines.html

Boyd, B.A., Odom, S.L., Humphreys, B.P., & Sam, A.M. (2010). Infants and toddlers with autism spectrum disorder: Early identification and early intervention. *Journal of Early Intervention, 32,* 75–98. doi:10.1177/1053815110362690

Bruder, M.B. (2010). Early childhood intervention: A promise to children and families for their future. *Exceptional Children, 76*(3), 339–355.

Centers for Disease Control and Prevention. (2013). *Autism spectrum disorders (ASDs): Data & statistics.* Retrieved from http://www.cdc.gov/ncbddd/autism/data.html

Childress, D.C., Conroy, M.A., & Hill, C.F. (2012). *Supporting young children with autism spectrum disorders and their families: Infant & toddler connection of Virginia guidance document.* Richmond: Partnership for People with Disabilities at Virginia Commonwealth University.

Cooper, J.O., Heron, T.E., & Heward, W.L. (2007). *Applied behavior analysis* (2nd ed.). Upper Saddle River, NJ: Pearson.

Dawson, G., Rogers, S.J., Munson, J., Smith, M., Winter, J., Greenson, J., ...Varley, J. (2010). Randomized, controlled trial of an intervention for toddlers with autism: The Early Start Denver Model. *Pediatrics, 125,* 17–23. doi:10.1542/peds.2009-0958

Doussard-Roosevelt, J.A., Joe, C.M., Bazhenova, O.V., & Porges, S.W. (2003). Mother–child interaction in autistic and nonautistic children: Characteristics of maternal approach behaviors and child social responses. *Developmental and Psychopathology, 15,* 277–295. doi:10.1017/S0954579403000154

Dunlap, G., Strain, P., & Ostryn, C. (2010). Addressing challenging behaviors of young children with autism spectrum disorders. In H.H. Schertz, C. Wong, & S.L. Odom (Eds.), *Young exceptional children monograph 12: Supporting young children with autism and their families* (pp. 54–65). Missoula, MT: Division for Early Childhood.

Filipek, P.A., Accardo, P.J., Ashwal, S., Baranek, G.T., Cook, E.H., Dawson, G., ... Volkmar, F.R. (2000). Practice parameter: Screening and diagnosis of autism: Report of the quality standards subcommit-

tee of the American Academy of Neurology and the Child Neurology Society. *Neurology, 55*(4), 468–479. doi:10.1212/WNL.55.4.468

Greenspan, S.I., & Wieder, S. (2006). *Engaging autism: Using the Floortime approach to help children relate, communicate and think.* Boston, MA: Da Capo Press.

Gutstein, S.E., & Sheely, R.K. (2002). *Relationship-based intervention: Social and emotional development activities for Asperger syndrome, autism, PDD and NLD.* London, UK: Jessica Kingsley.

Johnson, C.P., & Myers, S.M. (2007). Identification and evaluation of children with autism spectrum disorders. *Pediatrics, 120*(5), 1183–1215. doi:10.1542/peds.2007-2361

Kanner, L. (1943). Autistic disturbances of effective contact. *Nervous Child, 2,* 217–250.

Kashinath, S., Woods, J., & Goldstein, H. (2006). Enhancing generalized teaching strategy use in daily routines by parents of children with autism. *Journal of Speech, Language, and Hearing Research, 49,* 466–485. doi:10.1044/1092-4388(2006/036)

Koegel, L.K. (2000). Interventions to facilitate communication in autism. *Journal of Autism and Developmental Disorders, 30*(5), 383–391. doi:10.1023/A:1005539220932

Koegel, R.L., & Koegel, L.K. (2012). *The PRT pocket guide: Pivotal response treatment for autism spectrum disorders.* Baltimore, MD: Paul H. Brookes Publishing Co.

Landa, R. (2007). Early communication development and intervention for children with autism. *Mental Retardation and Developmental Disabilities Research Reviews, 13,* 16–25. doi:10.1002/mrdd.20134

Levy, S., Kim, A., & Olive, M.L. (2006). Interventions for young children with autism: A synthesis of the literature. *Focus on Autism and Other Developmental Disabilities, 21*(1), 55–62. doi:10.1177/10883576060210010701

Lovaas Institute. (2014). *The Lovaas approach.* Retrieved from http://www.lovaas.com/approach-method.php

Matson, J.L., Wilkins, J., & Gonzalez, M. (2008). Early identification and diagnosis of autism spectrum disorders in young children and infants: How early is too early? *Research in Autism Spectrum Disorders, 2,* 75–84. doi:10.1016/j.rasd.2007.03.002

Meadan, H., Ostrosky M.M., Santos, A., & Snodgrass, M. (2013). How can I help? Prompting procedures to support children's learning. *Young Exceptional Children, 16,* 32–40. doi:10.1177/1096250613505099

Meadan, H., Ostrosky, M.M., Triplett, B., Michna, M., & Fettig, A. (2011). Using visual support with young children with autism spectrum disorder. *TEACHING Exceptional Children, 43*(6), 28–35.

Meadan, H., Ostrosky, M., Zaghlawan, H., & Yu, S. (2009). Promoting the social and communicative behavior of young children with autism spectrum disorders: A review of parent-implemented intervention studies. *Topics in Early Childhood Special Education, 29*(2), 90–104. doi:10.1177/0271121409337950

National Research Council. (2001). *Educating children with autism.* Washington, DC: National Academies Press.

Odom, S.L., Boyd, B.A., Hall, L.J., & Hume, K. (2010). Evaluation of comprehensive treatment models for individuals with autism spectrum disorders. *Journal of Autism and Developmental Disorders, 40,* 425–436. doi:10.1007/s10803-009-0825-1

Odom, S.L., Hume, K., Boyd, B., & Stabel, A. (2012). Moving beyond the intensive behavior therapy vs. eclectic dichotomy: Evidence-based and individualized program for students with autism. *Behavior Modification, 36*(3), 270–297. doi:10.1177/0145445512444595

Ostrosky, M.M., & Meadan, H. (2010). Helping children play and learn together. *Young Children, 65*(1), 104–110.

Ravet, J. (2011). Inclusive/exclusive? Contradictory perspectives on autism and inclusion: The case for an integrative position. *International Journal on Inclusive Education, 15*(6), 667–682. doi:10.1080/13603110903294347

Robins, D.L., Casagrande, K., Barton, M., Chen, C.-M.A., Dumont-Mathieu, T., & Fein, D. (2014). Validation of the Modified Checklist for Autism in Toddlers, Revised with Follow-up (M-CHAT-R/F). *Pediatrics, 133*(1), 37–45. doi:10.1542/peds.2013-1813

Rocha, M.L., Schreibman, L., & Stahmer, A.C. (2007). Effectiveness of training parents to teach joint attention in children with autism. *Journal of Early Intervention, 29*(2), 154–172. doi:10.1177/105381510702900207

Schendel, D., & Bhasin, T.K. (2008). Birth weight and gestational age characteristics of children with autism, including a comparison with other developmental disabilities. *Pediatrics, 121*(6), 1155–1164. doi:10.1542/peds.2007-1049

Schwartz, I., Sandall, S., McBride, B., & Boulware, G. (2004). Project DATA (Developmentally Appropriate Treatment for Autism): An inclusive school-based approach to educating young children with autism. *Topics in Early Childhood Special Education, 24*(3), 156–168. doi:10.1177/02711214040240030301

Siller, M., & Sigman, M. (2002). The behaviors of parents of children with autism predict the subsequent development of their children's communication. *Journal of Autism and Developmental Disabilities, 32,* 77–89. doi:10.1023/A:1014884404276

Skinner, B.F. (1938). *The behavior of organisms: An experimental analysis.* New York, NY: Appleton-Century.

Skinner, B.F. (1953). *Science and human behavior.* New York, NY: Simon & Schuster.

Strain, P.S., Schwartz, I.S., & Barton, E.E. (2011). Providing interventions for young children with autism spectrum disorders: What we still need to accomplish. *Infants & Young Children, 33,* 321–332. doi:10.1177/1053815111429970

TEACCH Autism Program. (2014). *TEACCH approach.* Retrieved from http://teacch.com/about-us/what-is-teacch

Webb, S.J., & Jones, E.J.H. (2009). Early identification of autism: Early characteristics, onset of symptoms, and diagnostic stability. *Infants & Young Children, 22,* 100–118. doi:10.1177/0271121409337950

Williams, E. (2003). A comparative review of early forms of object-directed play and parent-infant play in typical infants and young children with autism. *Autism, 7*(4), 361–377. doi:10.1177/1362361303007004003

Wong, C., Odom, S.L., Hume, K., Cox, A.W., Fettig, A., Kucharczyk, S., …Schultz, T.R. (2013). *Evidence-based practices for children, youth, and young adults with autism spectrum disorder.* Chapel Hill: The University of North Carolina, Frank Porter Graham Child Development Institute, Autism Evidence-Based Practice Review Group.

Woods, J.J., & Wetherby, A.M. (2003). Early identification of and intervention for infants and toddlers who are at risk for autism spectrum disorder. *Language, Speech, and Hearing Services in Schools, 34,* 180–193. doi:10.1044/0161-1461(2003/015)

# 9 | Infants and Toddlers with Sensory Disabilities

Tanni L. Anthony (vision section), Mallene P. Wiggin (hearing section),
Christine Yoshinaga-Itano (hearing section), and Sharon A. Raver

This chapter discusses issues relating to serving children with sensory disabilities and their families, including the following:

- Causes of visual and hearing impairments
- Impact of visual impairment or hearing loss on child development
- Best practice highlights for children with visual and hearing impairments

## Case Study: Tony

Tony is an 18-month-old child who recently mastered walking. His early intervention team members, including his parents, child care providers, and professionals trained in visual impairments, are thrilled with this new accomplishment. Achieving this outcome is the result of deliberate and ongoing support provided to Tony by his family and the team as they guided Tony's sensory, cognitive, and motor development. Tony is blind due to a condition called retinopathy of prematurity (ROP), which resulted in retinal detachment in both eyes. He was born early at 24 weeks' gestation and had three surgeries in the first few months of his life to try to prevent the resulting retinal detachment that can be associated with this eye condition. Tony's twin sister, Sara, has low vision as a result of ROP. Despite their early birth, they both are now healthy children with easy dispositions. Like other children who delight in the rewards of independent walking, Tony is now on a mission to explore his environment.

The roles of vision and hearing in the early development of infants and toddlers are indisputable. When an infant is born with vision or hearing loss, it is critical that professionals on the early intervention team are well prepared to support the child's family in understanding the cause and characteristics of the sensory loss, as well as how to best address the potential impact of the sensory loss on their child's development. Although vision and hearing serve different roles as the two primary near and distance learning senses, their individual and combined influence on development can be significant on incidental learning, concept acquisition, mobility, and nonverbal and verbal communication skill development. This chapter discusses the causes, terminology, and the potential developmental impact of a visual or hearing impairment on a very young child. Furthermore, suggestions for supporting optimal development in each of these cases are addressed. The first part of the chapter presents information about infants and toddlers with visual impairments and blindness, whereas the second part discusses issues related to very young children with hearing loss.

## INFANTS AND TODDLERS WITH VISUAL IMPAIRMENTS

Early identification of any type of visual challenge is paramount in the early years of life. The role of vision in a child's development is so critical that eye examinations are recommended to begin at a child's birth and continue at all subsequent well-child visits, according to the American Academy of Pediatrics, the American Association of Pediatric Ophthalmology and Strabismus, and the American Academy of Ophthalmology (2003) in their joint position statement. Furthermore, the American Optometric Association (2002) recommended that all infants have their first comprehensive vision examination by an eye care specialist at 6 months of age, with additional vision examinations by age 3 years and just before the child enters first grade.

There are a number of different types of vision problems. A vision problem may involve poor eye alignment (called *strabismus*), refractive errors that require the need for glasses, and/or *amblyopia* (commonly called "lazy eye"). Concerns about eye alignment should always be reported to an eye care specialist for further evaluation because an eye deviation may indicate an ocular muscle imbalance or a more serious condition that permanently affects the child's vision. Children do not outgrow an eye that turns in, out, up, or down. *Refractive errors* may include nearsightedness, in which a child sees best at a near distance; farsightedness, in which a child sees best at a far distance; and/or *astigmatism,* in which the vision is blurred due to atypical curvature of the cornea. Refractive errors can be present at birth or occur at any time throughout one's lifetime; they can usually be corrected with prescriptive lenses. Amblyopia is most often caused by a persistent uncorrected eye alignment problem, extreme unequal acuity in both eyes, and/or the unilateral (i.e., one eye) obstruction of vision. In many cases, amblyopia can be prevented or treated when the child has received early eye care attention.

Visual problems are not uncommon in young children, affecting as many as 1 of every 20 children (Schor, 1990). The rate of vision problems is higher in children with disabilities. Disabilities related to genetic syndromes, neurological damage, and/or prenatal infections are likely to have an associated vision problem (Menacker & Batshaw, 1997).

Infancy and toddlerhood is the optimal time to prevent or minimize visual problems (Schor, 1990). Without treatment, the child's development is at risk and/or the visual problem may manifest into a permanent visual impairment. The earlier a vision problem is detected, the better are the chances that treatment—such as glasses, eye patching, and/or surgical procedures—will improve outcomes (Whetsell, 1996).

To foster proactive and optimal eye care, it is important that early interventionists talk with families about pursuing a medical examination for their child if there are any concerns about the child's visual performance. This is especially true for children with multiple disabilities. With this group, professionals may fail to recognize or may underestimate the impact of the vision challenges due to more obvious or medically acute conditions (Teplin, Greeley, & Anthony, 2009). All children benefit from observant professionals who are stewards of optimal eye health and visual performance.

There are several definitions associated with the term *visual impairment,* which is an overarching category of uncorrectable and permanent visual loss that affects day-to-day visual functioning. A child who is considered to have a visual impairment may be totally blind or have varying degrees of reduced visual performance. Visual performance may stay consistent or fluctuate throughout the child's day.

A visual impairment may be *static,* meaning that the degree of vision loss remains the same over the course of the person's lifetime, or it may be *progressive,* meaning that the visual performance will decrease over time, sometimes to total blindness. For example, a child diagnosed with Usher syndrome will experience vision and hearing loss over time. The child will be born deaf (Usher type 1), born hard of hearing (Usher type 2), or present with an early-onset progressive hearing loss (Usher type 3) and will manifest the symptoms of retinitis pigmentosa as early as infancy or within the first 20 years of life. *Retinitis pigmentosa* refers to a group of inherited disorders that lead slowly to blindness due to abnormalities of the retinal photoreceptors. In all three of the scenarios with Usher syndrome, the vision loss will be progressive due to retinal deterioration.

As mentioned, the diagnosis of a visual impairment may be accompanied by other medical and/or developmental challenges. Some visual impairment conditions will have secondary visual loss complications, such as the occurrence of *cataracts* (a clouding of the lens of the eyes) or *glaucoma* (increased ocular pressure), which will further compromise the child's visual abilities. Finally, a visual impairment may be just one of the constellation effects of a syndrome or condition where other disabilities are present, such as hearing loss, cerebral palsy, seizure disorder, other health impairment, and/or intellectual disabilities. The vast majority of children with visual impairment have at least one other concomitant disability (Teplin et al., 2009).

When an early-onset visual challenge involves a permanent visual impairment, early identification is critical to ensure that all needed medical interventions are available to the child. Some eye conditions will result in the infant having one or more surgeries designed to restore or preserve some level of visual functioning, such as with Tony in the case study. Tony had three surgeries to prevent full retinal detachment in both eyes, but without success. His sister, Sara, had the same condition but with less effects of vision loss. Sara had one surgical procedure to preserve her sight, which was successful. Besides receiving appropriate early medical care, infants and toddlers with visual impairment will benefit from the services of an early intervention program to address the impact of vision loss on the child's general development. Early-onset blindness or visual impairment can have a significant effect on the developing child, as well as the child's family.

## Methods for Early Identification

Early-onset visual impairment is diagnosed at an average age of 4.9 months in the United States, according to one large exclusive database of children with pediatric visual impairments (Hatton, Ivy, & Boyer, 2013). Early diagnosis is usually the result of three factors: the infant's birth circumstances, the appearance of the eyes, and definitive visual performance skills that are obvious in the first 6 months of life. One or more of these factors may signal the family or a medical or educational professional that an infant does not have typical visual functioning.

Birth circumstances such as prematurity, a difficult birth, and/or the overt presence of a syndrome or other medical condition should alert hospital personnel to be vigilant about determining the status of any newborn's eye health and visual status. Infants born prematurely are at increased risk for visual complications that may result in permanent visual impairments, as was the case with Tony and Sara. A traumatic birth that involved a period of *anoxia* (lack of oxygen) to the infant may also result in early-onset brain-based visual impairment. Furthermore, a syndrome or other medical condition that is associated with a visual impairment, such as CHARGE syndrome or oculocutaneous albinism, would alert medical professionals to give the infant a thorough visual evaluation. *CHARGE syndrome,* a genetic condition, is characterized by sensory, health, and/or intellectual development challenges. *Oculocutaneous albinism,* also a genetic condition, involves a lack of the pigment melanin in the eyes, skin, and hair and results in low vision.

Visual conditions that affect the appearance of the child's eyes may include congenital cataracts or *anirida,* in which the pupil (the dark center of the eye) or iris (colored portion) of the eyes have a cleft or keyhole notch. *Micro-ophthalmia,* a condition that produces abnormally small eyes, or *anophthalmia,* a condition in which the child is born without eyes, may occur. Some visual impairment conditions will not be physically noticeable at birth. For example, only by 6–8 weeks of age is *sensory nystagmus* evident. This involuntary shaking movement of the eyes is indicative of early-onset poor vision in both eyes.

A final method that parents and intervention professionals may use to identify early-onset vision challenges is observation of the infant's visual performance skills. During the first weeks of life, the infant will orient his or her gaze to another person's face. Eye contact and fixation on objects becomes more consistent and sustained over the course of the first 3 months. In addition, the child's eye movements will become steadily more coordinated with improved tracking, which means he or she can follow a slowly moving target, shift gaze, or look at one target and then another. The beginnings of eye–hand coordination will be evident as the child first randomly, and then more purposefully, bats at and then grasps objects. Global developmental checklists detailing cognitive and fine motor developmental milestones will assist the early intervention team in determining whether there are suspicions of a vision challenge due to poor or absent demonstration of these early visual skills. Some causes of visual impairment have been discussed. However, there are other eye conditions that service providers are likely to encounter.

## Prevalence and Causes of Early-Onset Visual Impairment

Considered to be a low-incidence disability, congenital or early-onset blindness/visual impairments occur in approximately 1–3 per 10,000 children (birth to 15 years) in developed countries (Teplin et al., 2009). The three leading rank-order causes of early-onset visual impairment in the United States are *cortical visual impairment* (CVI), ROP, and *optic nerve hypoplasia* (ONH) (Hatton, 2001; Hatton, Schwietz, Boyer, & Rychwalski, 2007). Each of these may produce a range of vision abilities in children who have the condition, from blindness to low vision. Key characteristics of each condition are presented in the following sections.

***Cortical Visual Impairment*** CVI occurs when there is congenital or acquired damage to the posterior visual pathways, the visual cortex, or both areas of the brain (Jan & Groenveld, 1993). It involves visual impairment due to neurological compromise. Frequent causes of CVI are oxygen deprivation, head trauma, and/or infections of the central nervous system (Good et al., 1994). Because CVI involves a history of neurological compromise, the child may also have cerebral palsy, a seizure disorder, and/or intellectual disability. Of the three leading pediatric causes of visual impairment, children with CVI are often diagnosed the latest (at an average age of 7.6 months), according to one national database of 2,150 children with pediatric visual impairments (Hatton et al., 2007).

***Retinopathy of Prematurity***    The second leading cause of pediatric visual impairment in the United States is ROP, although it appears to have been decreasing in recent years (Hatton, Ivy, & Boyer, 2013). Children with ROP are often diagnosed early, at approximately 3.4 months of age (Hatton et al., 2007). ROP is the diagnosis that Tony and Sara received. For Tony, the ROP resulted in blindness. In contrast, for Sara, the ROP resulted in vision loss, which is described as low vision. Premature infants, especially children with low birth weights (less than 1,000 grams), are at significant risk for a variety of vision concerns, including strabismus, mild to severe refractive error, and retinal compromise leading to permanent and serious visual impairments, including blindness (Keith & Doyle, 1995; Menacker & Batshaw, 1997; Teplin et al., 2009). In addition, children with ROP often have additional disabilities (Hatton et al., 2013).

***Optic Nerve Hypoplasia***    The incidence of ONH, a congenital condition characterized by an underdeveloped optic nerve in one or both eyes, appears to be growing across the United States (Hatton et al., 2007; Patel, McNally, Harrison, Lloyd, & Clayton, 2006). The optic nerve is responsible for transmitting visual signals from the retina to the brain for interpretation of the visual image. In individuals diagnosed with ONH, however, there are considerably fewer optic nerve fibers. The result can be significantly reduced vision. Optic nerve hypoplasia can occur in isolation or in combination with a myriad of functional and anatomic central nervous system abnormalities, including growth hormone needs (Borchert & Garcia-Filion, 2008). Children with ONH should be followed closely for endocrine problems and educational needs specific to a possible additional diagnosis of autism spectrum disorder.

In addition to these conditions, children may be born with visual impairment due to a variety of other ocular disorders, some of which have been discussed. Each eye condition has its own unique characteristics and implications for reduced or absent sight. Young children with visual impairment may display a range of visual skills and have a range of learning needs.

## Characteristics of Visual Impairment

A vision impairment may be first recognized by a medical professional, who then communicates the noted concerns to the family, or by the family, who then alerts the medical community. In either sequence, confirmation of the diagnosis of a visual impairment will need to be made by a pediatric eye care specialist through a clinical vision examination. Once diagnosed, one of the primary roles of the certified teacher of children with visual impairments (TVI) on an early intervention team will be to explain specific information about the child's medical diagnosis and its functional implications to the parents and other colleagues on the team. A TVI is a university-trained special educator with specific expertise in the instructional needs of children who have visual impairments. He or she is trained to interpret eye care reports, identify and address the effects of vision loss on a child's early development skills and later academic school experience, assess for and procure needed specialized equipment, and provide specialized intervention and instruction unique to children with visual impairments, such as braille and low-vision device training. A TVI has been prepared to work with learners with visual impairments from birth to 21 years of age. All service providers need to have foundational information about the broad functions of visual acuity and the visual field as they relate to each child's unique visual impairment.

***Visual Acuity***    *Visual acuity* describes the clarity of the visual image, with 20/20 being the standard notation for normal vision. As the bottom number of the visual acuity equation increases (e.g., 20/40, 20/200, 20/400), a person's visual acuity decreases. The larger the denominator, the more significant the vision loss will be. Someone with a visual acuity of 20/400 would have more compromised vision than a person with 20/200 visual acuity in a comparable environment, such as when the levels of lighting and visual contrast are the same. All newborns are typically born with very low visual acuities, in the 20/200 range. Visual acuity improves markedly over the course of the first year of life. By 3 years of age, a child with typically developing vision will have close to adult-like acuity of 20/30 to 20/40 vision.

It is important to note that all children are at risk for refractive errors, as identified in the previous section. This also includes children with a permanent visual impairment, who may benefit from glasses due to a refractive error. In these situations, the glasses cannot correct the poor vision related to the actual cause of the visual impairment, but they will improve any "add-on" visual clarity problems caused by the child also being nearsighted, farsighted, and/or having astigmatism. For example, a child born prematurely may have significant nearsightedness that can be corrected with glasses and still have uncorrected visual impairment due to retinal compromise. Visual acuity is often used to label the level of visual impairment for a variety of purposes, including functional considerations, such as how a child sees in everyday situations; program eligibility requirements for early intervention and/or special education school-based services; and/or legal definition purposes tied to adult services or government programs. A child may be described as having low vision (visual acuity at 20/70 to 20/200) or being legally blind, which involves possessing visual acuity of 20/200 or worse in the best corrected eye. Sara, Tony's twin, has low vision due to ROP. Even with glasses to correct her high level of nearsightedness, her vision is estimated to be 20/400 in both eyes. This means that Sara sees best at near distances. As people and objects are increasingly farther away, she is less likely to be able to identify the person or object or even know that something is there (depending on the object's size, color, and contrast with the background environment). In comparable lighting conditions, what a person with 20/20 vision sees at 400 feet is what a person with 20/400 sees from 20 feet away. For example, Andrew, Sara's older brother with typical vision, may see the neighbor's dog coming across their yard from 400 feet, yet Sara does not notice the dog until it is 20 feet away from her.

When an acuity loss is so significant that it cannot be quantified with numbers, the visual impairment may be referred to in one of the following four categories: 1) light perception (ability to detect light), 2) light projection (ability to determine the source of light), 3) hand motion (ability to detect a hand wave at close range), or 4) object or form perception (the ability to detect but not recognize an object or person). Close to 40% of very young children with visual impairment have a visual acuity impairment that falls into the legal blindness category (Hatton et al., 2007).

Visual acuity provides information about both the gestalt and the detail of a visual display or scenario. Visually locating a dropped piece of cereal on the highchair tray or spying the ladybug in a children's book are examples of functional near-range visual acuity tasks. Distance visual acuity allows a child to spot a favorite toy from 10 feet away or recognize that his parent just entered the child care center from across the room. When a child's visual acuity is permanently compromised due to a condition beyond the benefit of prescriptive lenses, it is likely that distance vision will be the most compromised. The child may be able to compensate for reduced near vision by leaning closer to a picture book to find the ladybug, but the child will not recognize a parent from across the room unless the child hears the familiar voice when the parent greets the child care staff. As a child matures, low-vision magnification devices for both near and distance vision tasks may be prescribed. Such devices may include free-standing or handheld magnifiers for close view-ing or a monocular (telescope) for distance spotting tasks, such as reading a math equation off the white board across the room or a street sign when traveling in a new location.

**Visual Field**    *Visual field* is defined as "the extent in which objects are visible to a stationary eye" (Leat, Shute, & Westall, 1999, p. 245). Everyone uses his or her visual field to gather information in front, to the side, above, and below. Visual field is measured with the head in a stationary position and the eyes looking ahead. A normal visual field extends approximately 180 degrees from one side of the head to the other side. The top of the visual field is slightly above one's head (50 degrees) and the bottom field parameter is below the chin (70 degrees). Legal blindness specific to field loss occurs when a person has a field restriction in the better eye of less than 20 degrees, typically manifesting in what might be called tunnel vision.

Visual field assists with getting a full-spectrum picture of a near-range visual display, such as multiple banana pieces scattered across a highchair tray, an array of objects or pic-tures on a communication board, or a distance-based visual scenario, such as the kitchen down the hall with the refrigerator on one side of the room and the table on the other side of the room. The amount of vision in both eyes contributes to one's visual field abilities or restrictions. Visual field loss can present in a number of ways, including 1) tunnel vision (peripheral or side vision is unavailable); 2), absent or compromised central vision (the straight-ahead best-viewing vision used for high-focus tasks, such as making eye contact or reading, is affected), 3) missing quadrants or spots of vision (*scotomas* or blind spots) or the opposite where there are just islands of vision ("swiss cheese" vision), and/or 4) *hemianopsia* (loss of half the vision field in each eye). A child with hemianopsia may miss informa-tion, such as the pieces of banana that are scattered to the far side of the highchair tray. A child with blind spots in his lower field may trip over an object on the floor while walking toward the bedroom because of a lower-field loss. In addition to visual acuity and/or visual field complications, a child with visual impairment may also experience challenges with *photophobia* (light sensitivity), poor eye teaming, and/or reduced depth perception. The degree and functional characteristics of each child's visual impairment will influence the progress of young children's development.

## Impact of Visual Impairment on Development

Vision has been credited as the main avenue for learning in the first years of life, as well as being the leading sense to invite a child's curiosity, integrate information, and entice exploration (Teplin et al., 2009). Vision also serves as a confirmation sense to auditory information as the child looks to see what is making a sound in his or her environment. No other sense provides such automatic and complete information. As such, early-onset visual impairment has the potential to affect every domain of the infant's development. The impact, however, will be highly individualized based on the age of onset, severity of the vision loss, the presence of any other concomitant disabilities or health conditions, and, perhaps most important, the available supports to the family to address the child's needs.

While listening and touch are primary or even strong secondary learning modalities, the developmental path of an infant or toddler with visual impairment will likely follow a unique course. Early intervention personnel are cautioned not to assume the validity of a strict comparative model between milestone norms founded on children with typical sight and the developmental status of a child who has a visual impairment. Instead, service providers need to keep an open mind about how the child learns and progresses. Each developmental domain is reviewed here for possible impacts, and recommended strategies to encourage optimal development are provided.

**Cognition and Play**    Blindness and visual impairment will affect *how* a child learns, not *what* a child learns (Ferrell, 1997). Although this notion will continue to be true throughout the child's lifetime, it is especially salient in the first years of life. Three factors need to be understood and deliberately addressed during infancy and toddlerhood:

1.  The child will have reduced incidental learning and imitation opportunities.
2.  The child will need time to develop the characteristics of part-to-whole learning.
3.  The child will face additional challenges with highly visual experiences and concepts.

Much of what is learned in the early years and throughout one's lifetime comes through incidental learning. *Incidental learning* involves the process of observing one's environment and the activities occurring away from one's body and learning from it. Incidental learning is responsible for much of an infant's or toddler's understanding about people, objects, settings, and activities. Children with visual impairments are at risk for developing fragmented concepts due to the lack of opportunities to either visually or physically experience the full sequence of an activity (Anthony, Bleier, Fazzi, Kish, & Pogrund, 2002).

To illustrate the profound value of incidental learning, envision an older infant in a highchair watching his older sister prepare a snack for him. He observes the sister moving to the kitchen counter by the refrigerator, where she takes a peach out of a bowl with many different types of fruit in it, opens a drawer across the room to retrieve a silver knife, cuts off the fuzzy peel and puts the peel remnants into the garbage can located under the sink, uses the knife to slice small pieces of the peach, and then walks back to her brother, where she offers him the peach pieces. He watches his sister pick up a slice and bring it to her mouth to eat. Within these few minutes of silent observation, the child has information about where certain items are kept within the kitchen, what a peach looks like before and after it is peeled and sliced, that a knife is used for cutting, and that his sister eats food just like he does—and, as a matter of fact, so does the dog when a peach slice is dropped accidentally to the floor. For a child who does not have the visual advantage of such incidental learning, a peach may seem to just appear on the highchair tray and may exist only in its peeled and sliced form. A child with significant visual impairment loses thousands and thousands of hours of incidental learning opportunities that fuel concept development about the everyday activities of his or her family and others, as well as the layout and general contents of each room in his home or other locations (Teplin et al., 2009).

Auditory information alone in the first years of life is not as helpful as visual information in creating a connection between the sounds associated with the activities occurring nearby the young child (Fazzi & Klein, 2002). The rattles of drawers being opened and closed, the knife clanking against the other silverware, or the soft plop of a peach hitting the highchair tray cannot provide the child with the full picture of the scenario just described, nor does the steady verbal narrative of his sister's voice describing what is being done. This is particularly true before the child has a conceptual framework to apply the vocabulary of *peach, bowl, knife, sharp, cutting* and other terms associated with the snack activity. Furthermore, incidental learning fosters a child's imitation of other's facial expressions, body movements, and actions with objects. As a mother smiles and raises her hands for a "sooo big" interaction, so will the baby. The toddler playing next to other children will imitate his or her peers' actions with toys or the adult's hand movements when he or she waves good-bye. The child observing his brother putting his clothes on in the morning has a model for performing the same actions with his own shirt and pants. Imitation is also important for imaginary play as the older toddler begins to display pretend play with familiar objects, such as taking a pretend sip from an empty cup and then offering his mother a taste from an empty spoon. Imitation provides both an incentive and instruction for the execution of gross motor skills, such as skipping, hopping, and climbing.

When vision can be used for learning, the child is able generally to get the "big picture" of his or her world and its contents. Objects can be viewed in their totality first and then explored for individual parts later. When vision is compromised as a viable learning vehicle, the child will have to use other sensory information to understand the world. When the primary sense is tactile, a child's learning will be part to whole. Part-to-whole learning will take more time and requires the child to build a whole concept from examining an item piece by piece only (Ferrell, 2000). In the early years, as a child is creating an understanding of his or her world based on first-time experiences, part-to-whole learning may be best described as putting together a jigsaw puzzle without first seeing the completed picture (Ferrell, 1997). As a child matures, part-to-whole learning can be better actualized with language assistance and an internal inventory of already developed concepts.

The last factor that affects concept development includes the wide range of concepts that cannot be tactually experienced or that are highly abstract in nature for the child's current conceptual understanding. This includes colors, butterflies, birds or airplanes flying overhead, images in a book or on a computer screen, or wild or extinct animals represented in storybooks. In the early years, it is important that early interventionists coach families so that they focus on concrete, hands-on, fully sequenced experiences to support a child's concept development. As the child builds a deeper experiential repertoire of concepts, this information can be used to explain more abstract notions.

***Social-Emotional Development***    As has been stated in previous chapters, all infants benefit from predictable routines and responsive caregivers. The first 6 months is a time to "get acquainted" (Ferrell, 2011, p. 13). When an infant is blind or has a significant visual impairment, bonding and attachment may proceed without much challenge, or the visual impairment may present some possible difficulties. For some children, one such challenge may be a long hospitalization due to prematurity and/or other early health-related circumstances, which may significantly affect predictable routines and attachment activities with caregivers. Another challenge may involve the early communication cues that are so closely tied to positive social-emotional development. Early social-emotional and communication behaviors are nurtured typically through a combination of eye contact reciprocity, predictable and comforting touch and movement (e.g., holding and rocking), and the caregiver's tone of voice. The infant will respond with returned eye gaze, contented facial expressions, and increased body movements indicating his or her excitement at seeing and interacting with others. The adult, in turn, reads the infant's nonverbal cues to determine what to continue or change to keep the child calm, increase his or her attention, and/or maintain the child's interest in the activity.

When an infant has a significant visual impairment, it is important to work with the family to identify the subtle or unique social-communication signals the infant is sending, which may be different from a child who is sighted (Teplin et al., 2009). For example, the infant who is blind or who has significant visual impairment will often grow quiet, "stilling" his face and body when he is listening or in anticipation of the next step of a caregiving routine (Fraiberg, 1977). Other behavioral indicators of the child's self-consolation or interest in an activity may include ear and/or head tilting toward the sound, head lowering, shutting eyes, and/or altered breathing (J.C. Greeley, personal communication, December

10, 2010). This body quieting may be misinterpreted as passivity or even a lack of interest, when it actually may indicate the exact opposite—the infant is communicating that he or she is engaged in the interaction. Conversely, an infant may startle and cry because of an unexpected touch that he or she could not see coming. Caregivers and other family members must be coached to provide preparatory cues, such as talking to the infant while approaching and then touching the child's chest to confirm their presence. With Tony's blindness, his parents learned early on to talk to him before touching him to prevent startling him with an unexpected touch or movement. Other touch cues can help to signal the child to what will be happening, such as a tap to the side of the hip for a diaper change or gentle pressure under one shoulder to indicate that the baby is about to be lifted, while using the words to describe what is about to happen. As the child gets older, language becomes even more important in providing information about what is coming next. Language is also the primary tool for describing how other children are playing and where they are in relation to the child with limited sight.

**Communication and Language Development**     In general, there may not be many issues with language development in a child who is blind with no other disabling conditions (Bigelow, 1987; Brambring, 2007; Hatton, Bailey, Burchinal, & Ferrell, 1997). Nonetheless, Rowland (1983) showed that infants with significant visual impairments may demonstrate fewer vocalizations during or after an adult's vocalizations than their sighted peers. Rather than conclude that the infants in her study had an early language impairment, however, Rowland noted, "Listening may be so critical to the interpretation of the distal (distant) environment that it would be maladaptive for the blind infant to clutter the auditory environment with her own vocalizations" (p. 127). This interpretation has been supported anecdotally. Although adult language and environmental sounds are key to the young child's language development and understanding of the surrounding environment, it is important that these sounds do not compete with the active learning of a child in play. Caregivers should consequently not provide a continual flood of narration of what is occurring around the child, but they should pay attention to when new language information will advance the child's knowledge of and/or interest in an object or play situation.

A slight delay in the acquisition of the first meaningful words has been reported with children with significant visual impairments, but there is evidence that most children overcome this delay quickly (Bigelow, 2005; Brambring, 2007). Toddlers with visual impairments may be delayed in the use of single words and two-word combinations (McConachie, 1990; McConachie & Moore, 1994). Other reported issues may include longer periods of *echolalia* (repeating words or phrases), a period of incorrect use of pronouns (e.g., *me, I, him, her*), differences in the use of spatial prepositions (e.g., *on, off, under*), and the extensive use of questions (Anderson, Dunlea, & Kekelis, 1984; Bigelow, 1987; Brambring, 2006a, Urwin, 1984). Without visual cues from facial expressions and gestures that accompany turn-taking between the speaker and listener, a child might be confused about how to classify personal pronouns correctly (Brambring, 2006b). It has been explained that vision also plays a role in confirming the spatial features of objects within the environment. The extensive use of questioning has been linked to how often adults use questions in their conversation with the child. Language development is closely tied to what is modeled to the child. As such, adults need to take care not to pepper their conversations with an overabundance of questions. Simple questions can be restated. For example, the statement "Do you want to get down from the highchair?" may be replaced with "Let's get you down from the highchair."

In addition, when a child has a visual impairment, it will be especially important to ensure that the child has hands-on interaction opportunities with the objects being discussed to confirm the meaning of the words attached to the object or experience. Involving the child in full-bodied experiences from beginning to end is key to the child understanding where objects are kept, how they feel in their original form (e.g., the peach with its fuzz before it is peeled and sliced), and how people respond to one another (e.g., "I am smiling at you. You make me so happy.").

***Gross and Fine Motor Development***    Visual impairment in early life may affect how quickly a very young child achieves gross motor milestones, how well the milestones are executed, the quality of movement, and possibly the sequence in which motor skills are mastered (Ferrell, 1998, 2011). Movement-based milestones, such as crawling or independent walking, often occur later than the range of sighted norms (Brambring, 2006b; Fraiberg, 1977; Sonksen, Levitt, & Kitsinger, 1984; Tröster, Heckler, & Brambring, 1994). The greatest gross motor delays may involve shifting positions in open space without the benefit of holding-on supports, cruising around furniture, independent walking, and walking up and down the stairs (Brambring, 2006a).

Several factors can influence the acquisition of gross and fine motor skills. Three possible single or overlapping challenges may occur in a child who is blind or who has significant visual impairment (Anthony, 2012):

1.  There may be a lack of (or reduced) visual reinforcement for movement.
2.  Low postural tone may be present.
3.  There may be a delay of object permanence, which may influence ambulation or walking skills.

It is important for the child, and the child's family, to have guidance from an occupational therapist, a physical therapist, or personnel trained in blindness, such as a TVI or a certified orientation and mobility specialist (COMS), to support the development of fine and gross motor skills. A COMS is a university-trained related services professional who specializes in the movement and travel skills of individuals who are blind or have a visual impairment; this is the only professional who should recommend and oversee the introduction of and instruction for a long cane for a child who has a visual impairment.

These professionals will need to work closely together to best address the child's motor needs from both a body mechanics and a visual impairment viewpoint. An important early function of vision is to provide the incentive for the child to change body positions or move toward a person or an object of interest. Vision is typically the lure for an infant to lift his or her head while in a prone position (on the tummy). If an infant does not lift the head when in the prone position around 3 months of age, this could be a sign of motor delay in infants who are blind. The action of an infant lifting his or her head activates and strengthens muscles in the neck, shoulders, and upper trunk. This strength is needed to gradually build a child's ability to propel a hand forward to play in this position, roll over, and, ultimately, push him- or herself into a sitting position.

When visual reinforcement cannot be the lure, it will be necessary to use tactile feedback to encourage the infant to raise the head in a prone position. One strategy is to place the infant on the chest of a supine (on the back) or semireclining adult (Cutter, 2007; Stokes, 2002). The adult then can angle his or her body position to help the baby with this action. A more upright position will give the infant the benefit of gravity pulling the head up off the adult's chest. When Tony was an infant, he could be enticed to lift his head in prone to feel a nuzzle or get a kiss on the top of his head from one of his parents. His parents also placed Tony on his tummy on a firm, flat surface with a light blanket underneath so that he could work against the firm surface. The service provider had shown his mother how to position herself on the floor facing Tony and to offer kisses and praise to encourage him to lift his head. Brightly colored, high-contrast, and/or illuminating objects were used to entice Sara, Tony's sister, because she has low vision and could see the objects. First, she was guided to raise her head in prone, and then she was invited to reach toward objects while in this position. The importance of these activities on later fine and gross motor development cannot be overstated.

Vision has further ties to the development of *postural tone,* which has been described as the tension in the body's muscles that provides "motoric readiness for movement" (Rosen, 2010, p. 175). Postural tone also provides a support base for independent sitting and mobility skills, such as rolling, crawling, and walking. Infants with significant visual impairment have been found to have a high incidence of *hypotonicity,* or low postural tone (Brown & Bour, 1986; Jan, Robinson, Scott, & Kinnis, 1975; Rosen, 2010). The presence of hypotonia with young children who are blind or have a visual impairment and who do not have cerebral palsy or another motor-related diagnosis may be the result of a combination of factors. A common theory involves the lack of "visual tutoring" of the vestibular, proprioceptive, and kinesthetic senses (Brown & Bour, 1986; Prechtl, Cioni, Einspieler, Bos, & Ferrari, 2001). Without visual feedback from the infant's first random body movements, there is less reinforcement for the infant to deliberately move his or her arms, hands, legs, and feet. As such, there are reduced opportunities for experiencing the proprioceptive awareness of moving parts of the body and developing postural tone (Rosen, 2010).

Low postural tone can affect the age at which milestones in motor development are reached (Brown & Bour, 1986; Jan et al., 1975). Low muscle tone appears to have more of an impact on milestones that do not involve movement, such as maintaining an independent sitting position, as opposed to movement milestones, such as crawling or walking (Brambring, 2006b). Children with hypotonia often have decreased endurance in motor activities, reduced trunk strength, and out-toeing (i.e., turning the feet outward to assist with widening the base of gravity).

## Case Study: Tony

The physical therapist, the TVI, and the COMS have all been beneficial to Tony, his family, and the infant-toddler program. Tony's first independent steps were made using an adapted mobility device (AMD) made out of polyvinyl chloride (PVC) pipe, which was designed by the COMS. The AMD served both as an orthopedic tool for postural support to help Tony maintain his upright balance as he pushed the device forward across the floor and as an adapted "cane," which gave Tony information about the ground surface just in front of him. Now that Tony has more postural stability and is walking, the plan is to ultimately provide him with a long cane. His parents are excited about his new mobility skills and see the long cane as the next step for his independence as a person who is blind. All of these professionals have collaborated during the first year and a half of Tony's life to coach his family in ways to embed exercises and activities into their days. The attention has paid off, with Tony developing trunk strength despite his low postural tone. One of the exciting outcomes of this team effort has been watching Tony chase after his sister Sara.

The quality of a child's movement may be affected by low postural tone. The child may use postural adjustments called "fixing" to support movement or sustain a posture (Rosen, 2010). *Postural fixing* may offer short-term stability, but it will limit mobility and the development of true postural stability (Brown & Bour, 1986). Examples of postural fixing in the sitting position include keeping the legs far apart for a wider base of support, sitting with a rounded back to lower the center of gravity, or keeping the hands on the floor to support an upright sitting posture.

A third factor that may affect motor development in infants and toddlers with visual impairment is actually a cognitive milestone. Object permanence (discussed in Chapter 6) plays an important role in self-initiated locomotion. It signals that the child understands that objects and people exist beyond the child's body, which in turn invites the child toward objects that are out of reach (Bigelow, 1986; Fraiberg, Siegel, & Gibson, 1966). There is an age range for when object permanence acquisition occurs for children who are blind (Fraiberg et al., 1966; Rogers & Puchalski, 1988). The median age at which a child who is blind and has no other disabilities will search for a removed object has been found to be 13.4 months (Ferrell, 1998). There appears to be no difference in the timetable for beginning to search for a sounding or a silent object for the child who is blind, as both tasks require the concept of object permanence (Fraiberg et al., 1966). The sound of the nearby object does not appear to encourage a child to search for it before he or she has attained object permanence. This is an important finding because it demonstrates that sound is not a substitute for sight in the very early months of the development of a child who is blind.

The acquisition of object permanence occurs typically around 9 months of age in sighted children. Both sighted children and those with vision loss appear to acquire the concept of object permanence through a comparable cognitive process (Bigelow, 1986). The important difference is that, although sighted children do not reach for a hidden object prior to the onset of object permanence, they have abundant opportunities to experience the practice of reaching toward objects when they are in view. With visual reinforcement, the sighted child learns to lean forward or to the side to stretch, reach, and ultimately move to objects of interest that they see, even though the objects are not located within touching distance. Sighted children will reach consistently for a visible object at 6–7 months, but children with significant visual impairments do not develop that ability until 10 months or later, when they demonstrate true object permanence (Fraiberg et al., 1966). As such, children who are blind or who have significant visual impairments often have significantly fewer experiences with reaching out to touch and explore objects. Until they have the conceptual understanding that people and objects exist beyond what they can touch—that is, until they have the concept of object permanence—these children will have restrictions in the development of self-initiated crawling or walking. Reaching out in space is the critical link to self-propelled movement for a child who is blind; crawling and walking often follow shortly after the child begins to reach for objects (Fraiberg, 1977). The act of reaching is essential because it is one of the first self-initiated contacts that a child who is blind makes with his or her external world (Bigelow, 1986).

***Adaptive Development***    The lack of incidental learning and imitation in children with significant visual impairment will play a role in their development of daily living skills. Without visual models of how to bring a spoon to one's mouth, put an arm out for a sleeve, or sit on the potty chair, the child will need physical guidance for most adaptive skills. In particular, feeding may present challenges because low postural tone can influence the organization of food in the mouth. The parents, a feeding specialist (e.g., speech-language therapist, occupational therapist), and a TVI should work together closely to address the feeding needs of each child. There may be very specific recommendations about the child's position, the use of adaptive equipment (e.g., specific bottle nipples, suction bowls or plates, adapted cups and spoons), information about the consistency of food, and/or ideas about how the child is cued to take another bite that will make eating more enjoyable for both the child and his or her parents. The child will need a steady introduction to variation in the texture and smell of food given so that the child becomes more tolerant of new food and eating experiences.

The biggest possible obstacle for mastering most age-appropriate adaptive development skills for a child who has a visual impairment is the low expectations of others. Although there may be a need for extra time to learn a task, with intentional instruction and hands-on modeling of the actions involved with self-care tasks, most children are very capable of learning how to use a spoon, drink from a cup, undress, dress, and become toilet trained. It is best to work on these skills within the child's daily routines and in consistent locations for the tasks.

## Assessment Considerations

Most children suspected of having a disability will have a vision screening as a part of their Child Find activities. Vision screening is important to identify whether a child requires further evaluation of his or her vision and is an opportunity to exclusively address a child's visual development skills separate from other developmental domains. Most developmental assessment tools do not have a separate section that teases out visual milestones from cognitive and fine motor assessment items. Before any developmental assessment is completed for a young child with a suspected or diagnosed visual impairment, it is critical to first gather information about the child's sensory abilities and limitations. This information will inform what assessment tools should be used, determine how objects are presented to the child, and lead to more accurate interpretation of the assessment results. The participation of a TVI is key to completing any needed sensory assessments before developmental assessments and will assist the early intervention team in completing an appropriate developmental assessment of the child.

The type of sensory assessment(s) will depend on the visual abilities of the child. When a child has usable vision, the TVI will complete a *functional vision assessment* (FVA) to determine the child's visual abilities, preferences, and support needs to best use his or her vision as an avenue of learning. An FVA is designed to supplement the clinical vision examination performed by an eye care specialist. An FVA is completed by gathering evidence of the day-to-day visual skills of the child and to identify what helps or hinders a child's visual performance during daily activities (Anthony, 2000). The FVA of an infant or toddler with a visual impairment will provide information on the following:

- Appearance of eyes
- Visual reflexes
- Visual responsiveness to light, color, and shape
- Ocular muscle balance
- Eye preference
- Eye movement behaviors
- Visual field
- Depth and figure–ground perception
- Light sensitivity and lighting preferences
- Near- and distance-range functional visual acuity
- Visual–motor or eye–hand coordination
- Visually based cognitive skills, such as visual imitation, object recognition, and naming

The TVI will work with the child's caregivers to gather and interpret the child's medical records, conduct observations of the child in his or her home or other care settings, talk to the people who know the child best, and engage the child in developmentally appropriate functional vision assessment tasks. Medical information will provide details as to the diagnosis and prognosis of the visual impairment, the presence of other disabilities or health concerns, and the need for any prescribed procedures or medicines. Information about prescribed medicines is important because some drugs have side effects that can alter a child's visual performance, such as extreme light sensitivity, significant fatigue, or double vision. An FVA report reviews the assessment findings and details recommendations designed to support the child's visually based learning, with attention to the child's positioning and the size, focal distance, color/contrast, and field presentation details of the visual target. Box 9.1 describes common strategies used to enhance the visual functioning of a young child with some vision.

It is also recommended that the TVI work with service providers to complete an Individual Sensory Learning Profile (Anthony, 2004) to ascertain the overall sensory abilities and preferences of the young child with visual impairment (Anthony et al., 2002). An Individual Sensory Learning Profile offers a more appropriate assessment for a child who is blind, such as Tony, and who would not benefit from the traditional FVA. This kind of assessment assists in gaining a full picture of the functional sensory abilities and distinct preferences of the child who has limited usable vision and who may or may not have additional disabilities. For example, questions such as the following are asked:

---

**BOX 9.1.    Strategies to enhance visual efficiency in infants and toddlers with visual impairments**

- *Positioning of the object and the child:* Confirm the following: 1) how close the object or visual display should be from the child based on the size, contrast, and familiarity of the object or visual display; 2) the best position of the object to ensure that it is within the visual field of the child; and 3) the positioning needs of the child to maintain a supported viewing posture. For example, can the child sit independently or does the child need to be in a supported sitting position so that the child's energy is expended primarily in looking and interacting with the object and not working to maintain an upright posture?
- *Size and distance:* Increase the magnification of objects by bringing them closer or by increasing the size. As long as it is safe to do so, allow the child to bring materials as close as needed and allow the child to be close to the adult, materials, or activities.
- *Color:* Use specific colors to increase the child's visual interest in an activity. For example, children with cortical visual impairment often respond best to objects that are red or yellow.
- *Contrast:* Pay attention to the contrast between the presented object and the background of where the object is situated. Background contrast should be provided with a solid color that is considerably darker or lighter than the objects being used. For example, a light-colored toy should be placed on a dark surface to enhance its visibility to the child.
- *Lighting:* Consider the child's illumination needs. What is the child's need and preference for types and location of lighting? This will be very individualized based on the type of visual impairment. As a general rule, lighting should fall over the child's shoulder as opposed to having the child face the lighting source. It will be important to control for unnecessary glare in the environment.
- *Visual clutter:* Simplify the viewing environment of a particular task to avoid possible difficulties with too much visual information at one time. When choosing a toy for play, multiple objects crowded together present a figure–ground challenge for many children with low vision or cortical visual impairment. Reduce the amount of items in the visual display.
- *Familiarity of objects:* Use consistent objects in daily routines. Visual interpretation of the environment is a highly cognitive function. Visual awareness and recognition of objects are often dependent on the child's direct experience and understanding of them.

*Sources:* Anthony (2008); Brown (2003).

- Does the child still or show visible body movements when a soft rattle is shaken nearby or when he or she hears a sibling's voice from across the room?
- Does the child have preferences for a visual display of objects of a certain color or background contrast and/or lighting level(s)?
- Does the child respond favorably or adversely to certain types of touch?

Knowing the status of the child's sensory skills will provide information about the calming, alerting, and sensory overload influences of noise and lighting, the potential need for prescriptive optical or listening devices, and the child's individual learning style. Information from a sensory assessment will assist the team in identifying possible motivators for listening, learning, communicating, exploring, and moving (Anthony, 1998).

In addition to completing separate sensory assessments, a TVI will work with the early intervention team to identify authentic and appropriate developmental assessment tools for a child who has a visual impairment. The goal will be to find a tool(s) that allows for adaptations of testing materials and procedures to accommodate to the needs of the child. The assessment must be reviewed to determine whether each test item has the following characteristics (Friedman & Calvello, 1989):

- No need to make an adaptation because vision is not required to complete the task
- Requires adaptation to ensure accessibility for the child (e.g., change in contrast, ease in grasp, time for part-to-whole exploration)
- Cannot be adapted because the task is a purely visual task (e.g., identifies self in mirror, names a color)

Items that are solely visually based cannot be readily substituted with a tactile task. That is, it is not the same developmental construct for a child to identify a photograph of his or her mother as it is for a child with a visual impairment to identify his or her mother's shoe.

The final role of the TVI will be to assist the team with interpreting the results of the developmental assessment. There will be times when the sequence or the rate of a developmental skill may be appropriately different for a child with a significant visual impairment. Together, the team can examine the assessment findings to address intervention strategies that are most appropriate for each child and family. Once the early intervention professionals have completed the sensory and development assessments, they will determine the next step outcomes for the child, with input from the family. Family priorities and routines are the guideposts for determining how to tailor these activities. In addition, suggestions for how to embed outcomes should be guided by general intervention strategies and considerations that are specific to young children with visual impairments.

## BEST PRACTICE HIGHLIGHTS FOR INFANTS AND TODDLERS WITH VISUAL IMPAIRMENTS

As mentioned, service providers spend time discussing family schedules and activities to jointly identify activities that coincide with caregiver-identified outcomes for their child. The following are strategies and suggestions to consider as activities are collaboratively designed:

- Implement the recommendations of the child's functional vision assessment and Individual Sensory Learning Profile so that learning situations can be customized for low vision (e.g., size, color, contrast, lighting), listening, and/or touch needs. This will include paying attention to how best to position the child and objects within the child's daily care and play routines for optimal accessibility.

- Use the TVI to assist the family with providing any needed specialized equipment, such as a lightbox (table-like box with a lighted surface) or braille writer.
- If the child has prescribed glasses, they should be worn during all waking hours.
- Take care not to overload the child with too much sensory information at one time. This includes visual, auditory, and tactile input. Too much auditory information may include ongoing verbal information from another person. If the child is actively engaging in a social, motor, or play task, sit back and observe the child's learning. As the child pauses, add information such as new words, give verbal confirmation of what he or she is doing, and/or model a next step to elevate the demands of the task. Carefully observe the child's cues of engagement to know when the child is ready for more information and when the adult may need to pull back just a bit.
- In coaching parents, model for and encourage them to use verbal and physical cues or prompts before moving or manipulating the child. For example, they can say, "I'm going to help you find your cookie" or "Get ready, I'm going to pick you up." Provide simple auditory descriptions for a task without verbal overload, which will cause the child to tune out the information. Give information and then pause, allowing the child time to process the information and respond.
- Provide the child with hands-on experiences with the real objects involved in daily care or play routines. Allow the child ample time to explore new objects, which he or she will do by using all available senses (e.g., touch, smell, sound). Be sure to give the child the wait time that he or she needs to explore. Provide time to move to the next new play routine.
- Ensure that the child has opportunities for repetition. Learning is cemented through repetition and practice, whether it is motor skills such as batting a toy, winding up a toy, or going through the sequence of scooping the spoon with a bite of food and bringing the spoon to the mouth. A TVI can assist the team, including the family, by providing shallow trays or adapted playboards that keep toys contained in one space for increased interaction opportunities.
- Select play items that are developmentally appropriate and engaging to the child. Avoid toys that are simply "plastic blobs" to a child or that are passive noisemakers. Play tools may be everyday objects, such as pots, pans, whisks, and measuring spoons. The goal for play is that the child is engaged in practicing existing play schemes such as banging and swatting, and then gradually expanding to new actions with toys, such as putting objects into a container or shapes into a puzzle. Toys that an infant or toddler must activate help with learning early cause-and-effect skills.
- Work from behind the child so that the child can feel the natural movements of a task, such as holding a bottle, pulling a brush through his or her hair, or stacking tuna cans. The adult should put his or her hands underneath the child's so that the child can feel the adult's actions. This is called a *hand-under-hand approach* and has been reported by many parents, teachers, and individuals who are blind or have visual impairment to be a preferred way of learning something new. Many report that this strategy is preferred to having their hands physically guided and moved in a task. Pay attention to what works with each individual child.
- Keep toys, materials, and personal items in predictable places to enable the child to use a combination of spatial memory, functional vision, and/or touch to locate books, toys, and self-care objects. For instance, the child may not be able to see a favorite toy

across the room but will learn to move to the bookshelves where it is kept. Once within visual range—perhaps 3–4 feet—the child can scan and locate the object visually if he or she has that ability.

- When choosing a toy for play, multiple objects crowded together present a figure–ground challenge for children with low vision. Reduce the number of toys and personal items to just a few—often no more than two to three objects. Position objects in a predictable storage area in individual baskets on shelves or an established toy box.

- Because infants and toddlers with blindness or visual impairment cannot profit from incidental learning and imitation, most skills must be taught intentionally at about the same time that those skills are learned by children with sight.

- Provide early age-appropriate literacy experiences that include daily reading to the child. Work with the TVI to determine the child's need for books in braille and, if so, how to add braille to commercial print books and/or how to order books with braille labels. Provide storybook manipulatives and props to bring the content of the story to life, such as having real mittens for a story that involves mittens. The TVI can also provide a braille writer for the home when the child learns to scribble in braille, just as sighted learners use crayons to practice making marks and "writing."

- Provide ongoing support for motor development and early ambulation skills by providing adapted mobility devices (AMDs) as needed. Work with a COMS to determine the child's need for early orientation and mobility services.

## SUMMARY

Like all children, infants and toddlers with visual impairments are individuals with personal preferences, likes, dislikes, abilities, and challenges. The first goal of early intervention personnel should be to understand the child's visual impairment and determine which senses are viable avenues of learning. Personnel trained in visual impairment, such as a TVI and COMS, will be valuable additions to the team in the completion of appropriate developmental assessments and the identification and implementation of next-step strategies for promoting optimal development in each child.

## INFANTS AND TODDLERS WITH HEARING LOSS

 **Case Study: Sammy**

Sammy was born full term after an uncomplicated pregnancy. Before Sammy left the hospital with his parents, Samantha and David, he received a newborn hearing screening. Sammy did not pass his screening in both ears. The technician administering the screening encouraged the family to follow up with another screening in a few days. Sammy's parents followed up with a pediatric audiologist and learned that he was born with moderate sensorineural hearing loss. This was devastating news for them. Samantha and David did not have a family member with hearing loss, nor had they ever met a person with one.

A service coordinator with expertise in early childhood deafness met with the family in their home and initiated the early intervention process when Sammy was 3 weeks old. At that time, the family was having a difficult time with the diagnosis and was grieving. As a resource to the family, a deaf role model who had a similar degree of hearing loss as Sammy came to their home. This meeting helped the family feel a bit better about the possibilities for Sammy's future.

A pediatric audiologist fit Sammy with hearing aids at 3 weeks of age. She sent him home with loaner hearing aids until his personal hearing aids arrived. The family could not afford hearing aids, even though they had insurance, so the audiologist and the early intervention program helped secure funding through a community organization to pay for them. Sammy began attending child care at 12 weeks old. His parents were very concerned about sending the hearing aids to child care. They were worried because the hearing aids were expensive, even though they had been told he needed to wear them during all waking hours. Because Sammy pulled at the hearing aids frequently, his parents worried that it seemed like a large burden to put on the child care workers to manage his care. Sammy's mother also reported that she felt embarrassed having Sammy wear the hearing aids because they made him look different from the other infants.

Due to early identification, advances in technology, and improvements in intervention, children with hearing loss are showing very positive outcomes. Many children with hearing loss who do not have secondary disabilities are achieving age-appropriate speech, language, and auditory skills (National Institutes of Health, 2006). Service providers can help support these outcomes by encouraging families to be aggressive in audiological management, be consistent about amplification, and seek specialty intervention when appropriate. When working with families who have a young child with hearing loss, it is important to be knowledgeable about hearing loss, amplification, auditory development, communication modality choices, and specific strategies that support each communication modality. It is also important to know that there are many specialized professionals who work with this population; they can join the early intervention team to maximize outcomes for the child and family.

Because children with hearing loss are being identified in the first few months of life as a result of universal newborn hearing screening, the presence and identification of additional disabilities may not yet be known at the time of screening. The early interventionist is often the first professional to suspect a secondary or additional disability as a result of monitoring the anticipated performance and developmental progress of children who are deaf and hard of hearing (Yoshinaga-Itano, Sedey, Coulter, & Mehl, 1998). Sammy's case demonstrates how a team approach can support a child and the child's family through some of the difficult decisions that have to be made in the first years of the child's life.

The experience of Sammy and his family is not uncommon for children with hearing loss. However, some infants who fail their newborn screening do not receive early follow-up care, perhaps because the family did not receive the information about the results of the screening or the family chose not to follow up with additional testing. Early identification and early intervention from professionals who are knowledgeable about early childhood deafness and hearing loss are critical to maximizing the best outcomes for young children with hearing loss (Holt & Svirsky, 2008; Nicholas & Geers, 2006).

Most children with *congenital hearing loss*—hearing loss that is present at birth, like Sammy—are identified through universal newborn hearing screenings by 3 months of age. Early identification in infancy is vital so that services can begin in the first year of life, during the critical period for speech and language development. Early identification and intervention can make the difference between a young child with hearing loss entering the educational system with significant speech and language delays or functioning with age-appropriate language (Moeller, 2000; National Institutes of Health, 2006; Yoshinaga-Itano et al., 1998). Service providers and hearing professionals need to have specialized knowledge about language and communication, both visual and spoken. If the parents have a goal of spoken language, knowledge about the acoustics of spoken language and its interaction with amplification technology is critical for the development of optimal listening and spoken language skills.

## Definitions and Prevalence of Hearing Loss

It is estimated that 1–2 per 1,000 infants are born with hearing loss (Centers for Disease Control and Prevention, 2011). Children may acquire hearing loss after birth or have a progressive hearing loss that is not identified at birth. Hearing loss is described by the timing of onset, degree of hearing loss, and the cause. The timing of hearing loss can be *prelingual* (before learning speech and language) or *postlingual* (after speech and language have developed). The degree of hearing loss can range from mild to profound and is documented on an audiogram, which is conducted by an audiologist.

The initial audiograms from the follow-up appointment after the universal newborn hearing screening are based on physiological thresholds for pitch and loudness, or the intensity of sound. Early intervention service providers can assist the audiologist by providing behavioral information to supplement the physiological testing findings. This information helps the audiologist adjust amplification to assure that the sounds are loud enough for the child to hear across the speech frequencies (Yoshinaga-Itano & Sedey, 2000). The audiogram is an important educational tool that helps service providers and families understand what a child hears with amplification (*aided hearing*) and without amplification (*unaided hearing*).

**Degree of Hearing Loss**    The degree of hearing loss is measured in decibels (dB HL), which are units representing loudness or intensity (American Speech-Language Hearing Association, 2014). A child with a *minimal hearing loss* (15–25 dB HL) will have difficulty hearing soft speech or distant speech, responding to subtle cues during conversation, detecting grammatical markers, and keeping pace in quick conversational exchanges (Northern & Downs, 2002; Tharpe, 2006). A child who has *mild hearing loss* (25–40 dB HL) and is unamplified will have difficulty hearing speech signals, overhearing, or listening in during conversations and may appear to be "tuning out" conversation (Northern & Downs, 2002). *Moderate hearing loss* that is untreated will cause a child to miss 50%–100% of conversation in a noisy environment (Mueller & Killion, 1990), and the child will have speech impairments, syntax impairments, and limited vocabulary (Northern & Downs, 2002). A child with *moderately severe hearing loss* (55–70 dB HL) who is not amplified or is inappropriately amplified will miss 100% of speech in a noisy environment, and all areas of speech and language will be affected (Northern & Downs, 2002). A child with a *severe hearing loss* (70–90 dB HL) or *profound hearing loss* (90 dB HL or greater) who does not wear amplification will display speech, spoken language, and auditory development that is significantly affected (Northern & Downs, 2002). In addition, hearing loss can be *unilateral* (one ear) or *bilateral* (both ears). It can also be conductive (i.e., damage to outer or middle ear), *sensorineural* (i.e., damage to inner ear), or *mixed* (i.e., a combination of conductive and sensorineural hearing loss).

Any degree of hearing loss warrants the use of amplification, even when a child with a hearing loss is initially able to respond to speech without hearing aids. Amplification, via either hearing aids or cochlear implantation, is necessary for all degrees of hearing loss for parents who have a goal of listening and spoken language for their child. This is the only way for children with hearing loss to have the opportunity to learn spoken language through audition (hearing) that is commensurate with their same-age peers.

***Audiological Assessment Options***   Audiologists have many options for assessing the hearing of infants and toddlers. In fact, newborns do not leave the hospital without having their hearing screened using otoacoustic emission testing (OAE) or automated auditory brainstem response (AABR). OAEs and AABRs are performed while the infant is asleep and are fast and comfortable procedures. As children get older, the audiologist will use behaviorally based measures that are specifically designed for testing young children, such as having a child look toward sounds emitted from different sides of the room. The audiologist's role on the early intervention team is critical for ensuring that the child's family receives accurate and current information about the child's hearing needs. Specifically, audiologists make sure that the child has appropriate assistive devices (e.g., hearing aids, cochlear implants) and interventions necessary to hear sounds in order to learn, as well as that the team is aware of skills that may be affected by impairments in the child's hearing.

## Causes of Hearing Loss

There are many causes of hearing loss. *Congenital hearing loss* (a loss that is present at birth) presents prior to the full development of speech and language. This kind of hearing loss may be caused by internal, genetic, or external factors. If hearing loss is genetically dominant, the child has a 50% chance of developing hearing loss. If hearing loss is recessive and both parents are carriers, the child will have a 25% probability of having hearing loss (Canalis & Lambert, 2000). Congenital hearing loss may occur as a result of the following (Northern & Downs, 2002):

- Connexin 26, which is found on chromosome 13 and has been identified as causing genetic nonsyndromic hearing loss
- Syndromes such as Usher, Pendred, Waardenburg, Crouzon, Alport, and Treacher Collins, which co-occur with hearing loss
- *Anoxia,* a lack of oxygen before, during, or shortly after birth
- Prematurity
- Maternal diabetes
- Intrauterine infections

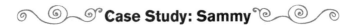

## Case Study: Sammy

Sammy's parents decided to pursue genetic testing to try to determine the cause of his hearing loss. They were a bit nervous about going through the process because they did not want one parent to feel responsible for the hearing loss. The results of the testing indicated that there was no genetic cause for his hearing loss. During their meeting with the geneticist, Sammy's parents learned that approximately 90% of all children born with permanent hearing loss are born to two hearing parents (Mitchell & Karchmer, 2004).

Hearing loss can also be acquired after birth due to a variety of reasons, including the following:

- Infections, such as mumps, measles, influenza, cytomegalovirus (CMV), or meningitis
- Ototoxic damage from receiving high doses of certain drugs, such as mycin drugs or aspirin
- Noise exposure
- Head injury

*Otitis media,* otherwise known as a middle ear infection, may cause conductive hearing loss, which will reduce hearing sensitivity for a child with typical hearing and compound the impact of the loss for a child with a diagnosed hearing loss. Some of these causes of hearing loss may have other associated disabilities. For example, children born with CMV may have additional cognitive impairments (Ramirez Inscoe & Nikolopoulos, 2004).

Regardless of the cause of a hearing loss or the presence of comorbid disabilities, receiving appropriate amplification and intervention for the type and degree of loss is critical for the development of speech, spoken language, and listening skills. Many children who receive appropriate services from skilled staff are able to demonstrate age-appropriate progress (Geers, Moog, Biedenstein, Brenner, & Hayes, 2009).

## Effects of Hearing Loss on Development

Hearing loss without secondary disabilities (e.g., cerebral palsy), with early appropriate amplification and intervention, does not necessarily have an impact on cognition, social communication, motor development, or adaptive development. However, untreated hearing loss that leads to impaired language can have a significant impact on the development of cognitive, social, and communication skills.

The major impact of hearing loss is its effect on language skills. A child who is born deaf and raised in a family that uses American Sign Language (ASL) to communicate will likely have typically developing cognitive, social, communication, motor development, and adaptive development. This is because the child is able to develop typical language skills using the family's chosen visual language. A child who does not have full access to language through amplification or visual communication, such as ASL, will have delayed and/or impaired social, communication, and higher level cognitive skills. Motor development and adaptive development are less likely to be affected, even if a child has impaired language skills due to hearing loss. Hearing loss can influence auditory development, which is the foundation for speech and spoken language development.

Auditory skills are necessary to develop the ability to listen and understand speech and environmental sounds in different environments. Delayed auditory development will affect the development of speech and spoken language, especially when the child does not receive appropriate amplification and intervention as soon as a diagnosis is received. Auditory development follows a continuum of specific skills (Erber, 1982), beginning with *sound detection,* or the ability to respond to the presence or absence of sound. *Discrimination* is the ability to hear the difference between sounds or speech stimuli. *Identification* is the ability to label the stimulus that is presented. For example, when the child hears his daddy's car in the driveway and says, "I hear daddy's car," the child is labeling the auditory stimulus. The highest level of auditory development is *comprehension,* or the ability to understand the meaning of speech. Auditory checklists detail specific skills within each step of the continuum and assist interventionists in planning developmentally appropriate intervention sessions with a child and family. The early intervention provider will find it helpful to keep a detailed auditory checklist available for reference during visits with the family. Figure 9.1 provides an example of an auditory checklist.

Date of visit: _____    Name: _____

Amplification device and date: _____    Date of birth: _____

*Key:* S = has skill; D = doesn't have skill; E = emerging skill.

## Detection

| Does your child... | History | Observation |
|---|---|---|
| 1. Wear the amplification device during his or her waking hours? | | |
| 2. Use body language to indicate when something is heard (e.g., turns head, eyes widen, quiets, stops action, changes facial expressions)? | | |
| 3. Show awareness (turns to the sound source, alerts or quiets in response to loud sound) of loud environmental sounds (e.g., dog barking)? | | |
| 4. Show awareness of soft environmental sounds (e.g., microwave bell, clock ticking)? | | |
| 5. Show awareness of voices, spoken at typical loudness levels? | | |
| 6. Detect the Ling-6 sounds (/a/, /i/, /o/, /s/, /sh/, and /m/)? | | |
| 7. Detect the speaker's voice when background noise is present? | | |
| 8. Search to find out where a sound is coming from? | | |
| 9. Localize correct sound source (to the direction the sound is coming from)? | | |

## Discrimination

| Does your child... | History | Observation |
|---|---|---|
| 10. Discriminate the voice of a speaker talking and sounds in his or her environment? | | |
| 11. Discriminate different types of environmental sounds (e.g., dog barking versus a telephone ringing)? | | |
| 12. Discriminate a speaker using a soft voice (whisper) and a loud voice (conversational level)? | | |
| 13. Discriminate a person singing (e.g., "Happy Birthday") from a person having a conversation? | | |
| 14. Discriminate family members' voices (e.g., Dad's voice versus Mom's voice versus a sibling's voice)? | | |
| 15. Discriminate minimal pair words (similar sounding words such as *pat, bat,* and *mat*)? | | |
| 16. Discriminate similar sounding phrases and sentences (e.g., "How old are you?" versus "How are you?")? | | |

## Identification

| Does your child... | History | Observation |
|---|---|---|
| 17. Identify his or her name when called? | | |
| 18. Identify an item with an associated sound (e.g., a train goes "choo-choo")? | | |

| | | |
|---|---|---|
| 19. Identify one-syllable words versus two- and three-syllable words (e.g., *ball* versus *hotdog* versus *computer*)? | | |
| 20. Understand if the speaker is happy, angry, or surprised by the change in their vocal tones? | | |
| 21. Identify or recognize commonly used words (varies from child to child)? | | |
| 22. Identify the Ling-6 sounds (/a/, /i/, /o/, /s/, /sh/, and /m/)? | | |
| 23. Identify familiar songs (e.g., "Happy Birthday," "Itsy Bitsy Spider")? | | |

**Figure 9.1.**  Sample auditory skills checklist. (From Choo, D., Creighton, J., Meinen-Derr, J., & Wiley, S. [2005]. *Auditory skills checklist.* Cincinnati, OH: Cincinnati Children's Hospital Medical Center, Center for Hearing and Deaf Research; reprinted by permission.)

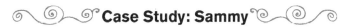

## Case Study: Sammy

Sammy's parents learned about auditory development during an early intervention visit from their service provider, who was an educator and a hearing specialist. Sammy's parents began to understand that consistent use of the hearing aids was necessary to help them reach their stated goal of having Sammy attend a mainstream kindergarten at their neighborhood school. As part of early intervention services, the educator met with the child care providers to educate them about the use and importance of Sammy's hearing aids. As noted on Sammy's individualized family service plan (IFSP), the educator continued to see Sammy at the child care center once each month to support his success in that environment.

## Developmental Assessment

It is critical that assessment of infants and toddlers with hearing impairment involve professionals who have specialized training in hearing loss. To find a specialist in hearing impairment, early intervention professionals may need to contact a child's audiologist for a referral. This professional, who usually has a master's degree in speech pathology or deaf education, may work in the early intervention program, a children's hospital, private practice, auditory-verbal therapy clinic, cochlear implant center, or other facility. This specialist must have extensive experience with very young children with hearing loss to assist the rest of the assessment team in determining what elements of the child's needs are due to the hearing loss and what elements may be due to a secondary disability or developmental delay. This professional should also be knowledgeable about resources, services, family support organizations, and specialists who serve children with hearing loss in the area.

***Assessment Tools for Birth to 3 Years***  Most assessment tools used with children with hearing loss are appropriate for all children in this age range. It is important to compare children with hearing loss to their age-matched peers. Many assessments for children who are birth to 3 years old are criterion-referenced instruments, meaning that these tools offer information about a child's approximate developmental age using an age-based standard. It is recommended to also include norm-referenced tests in the assessment battery to give the family and the service provider a realistic picture of how the child is performing compared to age-matched peers. Box 9.2 presents a brief list of assessments that are appropriate for infants and toddlers with hearing loss.

---

**BOX 9.2.    Examples of assessment instruments used with infants and toddlers with hearing loss**

Global developmental assessments

- Child Development Inventory (Ireton, 1992)

Language assessments

- Receptive Expressive Emergent Language 3 (Bzoch, League, & Brown, 2003)
- Preschool Language Scale, Fifth Edition (Zimmerman, Steiner, & Pond, 2011)
- Reynell Developmental Language Scales (Reynell & Gruber, 1990)

Speech assessments

- Conditioned Assessment of Speech Production (Ertmer & Stoel-Gammon, 2008)
- Arizona Articulation Proficiency Scale (Fudala & Reynolds, 2000)
- Goldman Fristoe Test of Articulation 2 (Goldman & Fristoe, 2000)

Auditory assessments

- Infant-Toddler: Meaningful Auditory Integration Scale (Zimmerman-Phillips, Osberger, & Robbins, 2000)
- Functional Auditory Performance Indicator: An Integrated Approach to Auditory Skill Development (Stredler-Brown & Johnson, 2004)
- Early Listening Function Test (Anderson, 2007)

---

Auditory assessments are not typically part of the general early intervention assessment protocol, but these assessments are critical to monitor the development of speech and spoken language skills in young children. These assessments can be obtained from a speech pathologist or educator who specializes in hearing impairment. The pediatric audiologist may also have these assessments available. Auditory assessments will ask questions such as the following:

- Does the child detect quiet sounds?
- Can the child localize to a sound source in the room?
- Can the child discriminate the difference between words such as *pat* and *mat*?

It is recommended that a child with hearing loss receive a comprehensive auditory assessment from a hearing loss specialist every 6 months while receiving early intervention. This hearing assessment may be conducted in addition to the annual evaluation of the IFSP required under Part C of IDEA. Auditory assessment should include consideration of the child's hearing, speech, language, pragmatic (i.e., the social usage of language), and cognitive development. If a child has no secondary disabilities and the family provides ongoing developmental support, it is expected that a child with hearing loss will achieve milestones at the rate of his or her typically developing peers (Moeller, 2000; Robinshaw, 1995).

***Adapting Assessment Tools for Hearing Loss***    There are two ways to approach assessment for children with hearing loss. The appropriate approach will be determined by the goal of the assessment. The first approach is to not adapt the assessment tool. This will allow a professional to determine how the child is performing when compared to same-age peers without hearing loss. An interventionist may use this information to help qualify a child for services or provide information to a family about the child's current level of functioning. Although some service providers might consider this to be unfair, it is critical information for the provider and family. This approach allows professionals to determine how the child's skills compare to same-age peers and which needs are directly related to the hearing loss.

Developmental expectations for children with hearing loss who have normal cognitive development should be the same as for children with normal hearing or typical development. Therefore, it is not appropriate to tell parents that their child is doing well for a child who is deaf or a child with a hearing loss. Instead, the service provider should determine if a child is performing within the average range and compare the child to his or her same-age peers.

If service providers work with a child who was identified late or who received a cochlear implant, it can be helpful to consider a child's hearing age, in addition to his or her chronological age, when interpreting test results for children who are developing spoken language. *Hearing age* is the duration of time the child has accessed sound through amplification. It can be calculated by subtracting duration of deafness from the child's chronological age. For example, consider a child who was born profoundly deaf and who received a cochlear implant at 12 months of age. At a chronological age of 18 months, the child will have a hearing age of 6 months. This age can be used when interpreting test results, keeping in mind that test results should have a child performing at or above his or her hearing age.

The second approach is to modify an assessment, taking into consideration whether a child uses sign language and whether he or she has access to auditory information. Some assessments can be used for a family who uses sign language without significantly affecting the scores. For example, the Child Development Inventory (Ireton, 1992) can be modified to include whether a child says or signs the item. Other assessments, such as the word structure subtest of the Clinical Evaluation of Language Fundamentals–Preschool 2 (Wiig, Secord, & Semel, 2004), are not appropriate for a child who uses sign language because the grammatical markers are indicated differently in ASL. When modifying an assessment, it is important to indicate this in the report and explain to the family that the scores cannot be used to compare the child to other children. The scores can only be used to document progress over time for the same child. The report should indicate the specific modifications so that the test can be administered in the same way during future testing.

As with any child, assessment information should provide insights into the child's functional abilities in his or her everyday routines and activities. This information is then used during the development of the IFSP to plan outcomes, determine appropriate services, and choose service providers who can best support families in deciding on communication options and other interventions for their child.

## Intervention for Hearing Loss

There are a number of professionals who specialize in interventions with children with hearing loss and their families. The most appropriate providers will be determined by the communication and amplification choices made by the family; options for communication and amplification will be discussed later in this chapter. Using a team approach, these professionals can serve as a resource to other early intervention team members. Possible team members include the following:

- *Early intervention hearing specialists/providers:* These professionals have specialized training in early childhood deafness and hearing loss, such as teachers of the deaf, aural rehabilitationists with professional certification in audiology, and/or speech-language pathologists.

- *Audiologists:* Audiologists with specific knowledge and skills in pediatric audiologic evaluation and amplification may be part of the early intervention team. They are critical for keeping the team aware of hearing changes in the child and informed about appropriate accommodations.

- *Sign language instructors:* Instructors should have fluency in American Sign Language (ASL) to assist families that have selected a total communication or ASL approach to communication.

- *Listening and spoken language specialists:* A specialty certification is available through AG Bell Organization to deaf educators, speech pathologists, and audiologists who complete additional training, supervised clinical experiences, and continuing education related to developing listening and spoken language. Parents participate in therapy sessions, and the therapist supports the family in seeking inclusion school placements. Credentials will be indicated by LSLS Cert AVEd or LSLS Cert AVT and assure a high level of skills and experience. These specialists will serve families who want to develop listening and spoken language skills in their child. These specialists provide direct treatment and consultation.

- *Cochlear implant center team:* Cochlear implant programs may have social workers, speech pathologists, and deaf educators who specialize in working with children accessing sound through cochlear implants. All cochlear implant centers will have audiologists and otolaryngologists or otologists.

- *Parent professionals:* Parent professionals are trained to provide information and/or advocacy to other parents for parent-to-parent support.

- *Deaf and hard-of-hearing professionals:* Deaf and hard-of-hearing professionals have specialized training to provide information to parents about the impact of hearing loss on daily life, growing up, and family interactions. If the family requests, they can collaborate with the early intervention team to provide the family with coordinated ideas for supporting the child's development.

All of these professionals are assets to early intervention programs and can assist them in accomplishing positive outcomes for the child and the child's family. When children have multiple disabilities including hearing loss, there may be other providers that are necessary to create the ideal intervention team. For example, a child with hearing impairment and autism may benefit from a speech-language pathologist and/or occupational therapist who specializes in autism spectrum disorder. This additional disability may have a greater impact on outcomes for the child as compared to the impact of the hearing loss.

**Amplification**    With the support of appropriate professionals and advancements in technology, the majority of infants and toddlers with hearing loss are able to access sound through hearing aids, cochlear implants, or bone conduction amplification. Rare cases, such as a malformed or absent cochlea, may prevent a child from accessing sound through one of these technologies.

A hearing aid is used to treat minimal to severe sensorineural hearing loss and is the most common form of amplification. A *hearing aid* is a small device that fits in or on the ear and amplifies sound. Children wear hearing aids that fit behind the ear with an ear mold that directs sound to the ear canal and helps hold the aids in place.

A *cochlear implant* is used to treat severe to profound sensorineural hearing loss. A cochlear implant is a surgically implanted device that is placed under the skin behind the ear with electrodes that extend into the cochlea. The individual wears an external sound processor behind the ear that picks up the sounds in the environment.

*Bone conduction amplification* is used to treat unilateral hearing loss, single-sided deafness, and all degrees of permanent conductive hearing losses. This is a surgically implanted abutment, or bridge, which allows for direct conduction of sound to the inner ear by bone vibration of the skull and inner ear. Young children can wear bone conduction devices on a soft headband before they are old enough for the surgical procedure.

Hearing aids, cochlear implants, and bone-anchored hearing aids do not correct hearing loss. These devices allow the child to access sound through technology. The child will only be able to hear at the level of their unaided hearing when the technology is removed.

All three personal amplification systems can be connected to frequency modulation (FM) systems. An *FM system* is an assistive listening device that amplifies the voice of the primary speaker. This system helps to reduce the impact of distance from the primary speaker and background noise. There are different types of FM systems, including personal systems that only amplify the speaker for the person with hearing impairment and sound field systems that amplify the speaker over a group of listeners.

The early interventionist can learn to work with the child's amplification by finding information available on each manufacturer's website, meeting with the child's audiologist, and/or collaborating with a hearing specialist. A hearing specialist is a professional who has been trained to provide intervention specifically to children with hearing loss. A hearing specialist typically will have a degree in speech pathology, audiology, or deaf education. The hearing specialist may have particular expertise in one type of amplification or modality of communication but should be able to provide the family with unbiased information about the range of options available for the child.

Families can choose whether or not to pursue amplification for their child. Some families decide not to use amplification because they prefer to use ASL to communicate. Other families may choose to have their child wear hearing aids even when the child has a significant hearing loss that warrants a cochlear implant. It is important to respect each family's choice but to also provide appropriate education and information to the family to ensure that the family's choice is consistent with that family's goals for the child.

### Encouraging Infants and Toddlers to Wear Amplification

As Sammy's parents and child care workers found out, it is challenging to keep hearing equipment on infants and toddlers. Infants may pull out the hearing aids or cochlear implant equipment, put them in their mouths, and throw them. This does not mean that hearing aids are hurting the child or that the child does not like the amplification. It may mean that the child has not yet adjusted to the equipment or that the child is uncomfortable. When Sammy continued to remove his hearing aids, his family returned to the audiologist, who confirmed that Sammy's hearing aid had the appropriate settings and fit. She also checked to make sure Sammy did not have an ear infection. The audiologist provided suggestions to the family to help Sammy adjust, including having him wear a light cap that covered his ears to help prevent him from removing his hearing aids.

It is critical that infants or toddlers wear amplification during all waking hours so they have an opportunity to learn to listen to their world. Some infants may initially respond best to gradually increasing the amount of time they wear their hearing aids, until they are able to tolerate them all day. After discussing their concerns, the hearing specialist and the early intervention service provider were able to help Sammy's family understand the importance of using his amplification to ensure opportunities for speech, language, and auditory development. His mother made sure he wore his hearing aids all the time at home and collaborated closely with his caregivers at child care so that he wore them there as well.

There are supports to help keep the amplification on a child. Using toupee tape on the inside of the hearing aid can help secure the amplification to the child's head. A critter clip can be supplied by the audiologist to attach the hearing aids to the child's clothing. When the hearing aids are removed, they will still be attached to the child's clothing. The audiologist can also provide huggies to help keep the hearing aids in place. *Huggies* are a plastic loop that fits around the front of the child's ear and helps snugly hold a hearing aid or cochlear implant to the ear. As suggested with Sammy, pilot caps or hats with ear flaps or that cover the ears can keep the child from physically being able to reach the amplification. Pilot caps that are lightweight and tie underneath the chin are very effective in keeping amplification on a child's ears. The thin fabric also does not significantly reduce sound input. Figure 9.2 shows a sample pilot cap.

In addition to amplification options, families also often must sort through options for the child's communication modality. The child's audiologist and other early intervention team members can be resources to the family by providing unbiased information and linking parents with resources in the community.

## Communication Choices

Another early decision that families encounters after learning their child has a hearing loss is deciding what communication option is the best match for their child and their family. As professionals, there is value in understanding each individual communication option. Figure 9.3 describes these modality options. Communication modality options range from entirely auditory to entirely visual.

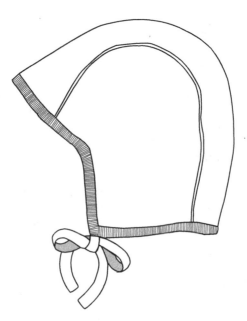

**Figure 9.2.** A pilot cap for keeping amplification devices on an infant's or a toddler's head.

|  | American Sign Language<br>VISUAL APPROACH | Auditory-Verbal<br>AUDITORY APPROACH | Cued Speech<br>COMBINED APPROACH | Auditory-Oral<br>COMBINED APPROACH | Simultaneous<br>Communication<br>COMBINED APPROACH |
|---|---|---|---|---|---|
| Definition | A bilingual approach, which includes the development of both ASL and English. ASL is a natural, visual/manual language totally accessible to children who are deaf, that has its own grammar and linguistic principles. The acquisition of English is addressed through the use of teaching strategies for English as a second language. | An approach emphasizing spoken language development through listening. Child develops spoken language through one-on-one therapy and use of residual hearing with optimal amplification. Strives to make the most of a child's ability to learn through listening; therefore, the child does not rely on visual cues. | An auditory-visual communication approach combining a system of hand cues with the natural mouth movements of speech, specifying each sound (phoneme) of spoken language clearly. A hand shape (consonant groups) at a location (vowel groups) cues a syllable. This integration provides clear access to all the phonemes (sounds) as parents coo, babble, and talk. | An approach that teaches a child to use his/her remaining hearing through amplification and the use of speechreading/natural gestures/visual cues to aid the child's understanding of language. The use of any form of sign language communication is not encouraged. | An educational philosophy that uses spoken language and sign language simultaneously. Uses an English-based sign language system, which can include speech, speechreading, fingerspelling, natural gestures, and the use of residual hearing. |
| Primary Goals | To acquire an age-appropriate internal language as a basis for learning a second language and opportunities for academic achievement. To develop a positive self-image and cultural identity providing access to the Deaf community. To provide a basis for learning written and, when possible, spoken English as a second language. | To develop spoken language through listening by following the stages and sequence of typical development. To develop the skills necessary for successful mainstreaming in school and integration into the hearing community. To promote a positive self-image through natural family and social interactions using spoken language. | To provide clear communication in the spoken language of the home. To develop the phonemic language base to achieve full literacy in conversation, reading, and writing. To support speechreading, speech, and auditory skill development. | To develop spoken language through listening and visual cues. To develop spoken language and communication skills necessary for school success and integration into the hearing community. | To provide a bridge to the development of spoken language in the very young child. To provide spoken communication between the child and his/her family, teachers, and peers using sign language. To support integration into both the hearing and the Deaf communities. |

**Figure 9.3**   Descriptions of communication choices for children with hearing loss. (From BEGINNINGS for Parents of Children Who Are Deaf or Hard-of-Hearing. [2014]. *Communication approaches chart.* Raleigh, NC: Author. Retrieved from http://ncbegin.org/reference-chart/; reprinted by permission.)

*(continued)*

Figure 9.3 *(continued)*

| | American Sign Language VISUAL APPROACH | Auditory-Verbal AUDITORY APPROACH | Cued Speech COMBINED APPROACH | Auditory-Oral COMBINED APPROACH | Simultaneous Communication COMBINED APPROACH |
|---|---|---|---|---|---|
| Language Development (Receptive) | The child develops early language concepts as well as higher order cognitive skills by utilizing the visual nature of ASL. | The child develops understanding of spoken language through early and consistent intervention that emphasizes learning through listening in a developmentally appropriate sequence. Optimal listening opportunities require the use of appropriate hearing technology. | The child absorbs language through early, consistent, clear communication using Cued Speech, speechreading and hearing. Cueing boosts auditory awareness, discrimination, and understanding. | The child develops internal language through early, consistent listening experiences and developmentally appropriate therapy, which includes speechreading and the use of hearing technology. | The child develops language through speechreading, listening, and exposure to a combination of speech and sign-based systems in English order. |
| Expressive Language | ASL fluency and written English. Ability to code switch from ASL to English (signed, spoken or written as needed). | Spoken and written English. | Cued, spoken and written English or other languages (60+ cued languages). | Spoken and written English. | Spoken English using sign language in English word order, and written English. |
| Hearing | Encourages individual decision about amplification. Amplification may provide access to spoken language and allow the child more opportunity to become bilingual. | Early, consistent and appropriate use of hearing technology (hearing aids, cochlear implant[s], FM system) is critical to this approach. Requires ongoing auditory management. | Early, consistent, and appropriate use of hearing technology (hearing aids, cochlear implant[s], FM system) is important with this approach. Requires ongoing auditory management. | Early, consistent and appropriate use of hearing technology (hearing aids, cochlear implant(s), FM system) is important with this approach. Requires ongoing auditory management. | Consistent and appropriate use of hearing technology (hearing aids, cochlear implant[s], FM system) is strongly encouraged. |
| Family/Primary Caregiver Responsibilities & Guidance | Parents are committed to learning and using ASL consistently. Families emphasize literacy in the home. Families provide opportunities for interaction with the Deaf community to help ensure a future independent and fulfilled Deaf citizen. ASL is learned through classes, media, websites, and interaction with members of the Deaf community. | Parents are expected to actively participate as partners in sessions with therapist(s) in order to learn strategies and techniques that promote the auditory learning of goals. Families need to carry over the goals established in therapy into the child's daily routines and play activities. Parents learn to create an optimal "listening" learning environment. Parents must also provide a language-rich environment, to make learning through listening a meaningful part of all experiences. | Parents are expected to learn to speak-and-cue at all times in order for children to absorb the phonemes critical to language and reading readiness. Families need to provide consistent use of cues and speech during daily routines and play activities. The system is taught in less than 20 hours through multi-media, classes, and Family Cue Camps. Consistent daily use and practice leads to conversational ease within a year. | Families are expected to provide appropriate carry-over of goals, strategies and techniques from the child's classroom setting and/or individual therapy sessions into daily routines and play activities. Parents need to work with the child's teacher(s) and/or therapist(s) to learn strategies and techniques for developing listening, speechreading and speaking skills in an oral learning environment. | Families are expected to learn and consistently use the chosen English-based sign language system. Parents need to work with the child's teacher(s) and/or therapist(s) to learn strategies that promote language expansion. |

*Auditory-verbal* and *auditory-oral* communication approaches use only spoken language. *Cued speech* uses hand gestures indicating speech sounds used simultaneously with speech. The hand cues help the child differentiate speech phonemes that are *visemes,* or sounds that look similar on the lips, such as /b/ and /p/. *Total communication* is a philosophy that includes the use of multiple methods, such as sign language, gestures, and other visual aids to support spoken language. *Simultaneous communication* is communication with the simultaneous use of speech and sign language. The communication partner may use sign language in a variety of forms, such as Signed English with no morphological endings, Signing Exact English (SEE 2), Seeing Essential English (SEE 1), or Linguistics of Visual English (LOVE). Manually coded English is a type of sign language that uses English word order to support aspects of English that are not auditorially or visually available through speechreading.

*Bilingual-bicultural approaches* use ASL for conversational interaction between conversational partners and use written English to teach English for academic learning. *Bimodal bilingualism* is the use of spoken English for some classroom instruction during the day and the use of ASL for the remaining instruction. The instructor does not use ASL when teaching in spoken English and does not speak when using ASL. Half of the day may be in one language and the other half in the other language. ASL is the native language of the Deaf culture in the United States. When working with a deaf family, it is important to be sensitive to cultural differences in the Deaf community.

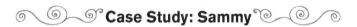

## Case Study: Sammy

Sammy's family received information on communication modality choices from the early intervention service coordinator who specialized in children with hearing loss. Sammy's mother also called the parent-to-parent support mentor that she had been put in touch with for advice. The parent mentor encouraged Sammy's mother to make the right choice for her family. She also cautioned Sammy's mother that people may say very biased things to them about communication modality choices, such as "If you sign with your child, he will never speak" or "If you do not sign with your child, he will be angry with you for not introducing him to Deaf culture." These statements are not based on facts and can be very hurtful to a family sorting through communication options. It was very helpful for Sammy's mother to have other parents to talk to as she and her husband made their decision.

Sammy's parents ultimately selected an auditory-oral communication approach. The family did not know anyone who was deaf and felt overwhelmed by trying to learn a new language. They also wanted Sammy to learn to listen and talk so that he could communicate with the neighborhood children and his family members. However, they also decided to learn a small set of signs just in case it might be helpful when Sammy was not wearing his hearing aids, such as in the bathtub or swimming pool.

As Sammy's parents' decision illustrates, children and families do not necessarily fit neatly into categories of individual communication approaches. Information about communication options should be presented in an unbiased manner that allows family members to make the best choice for their child and family at that time. It should also be communicated that this decision is not permanent. Families can change their communication modality choice over time as new audiological or developmental information emerges about their child.

Although a family can change communication modalities over time, it is important to keep the critical window of language development in mind. The first 5 years of life are sensitive periods for speech and auditory development (Sharma & Dorman, 2006; Sharma, Dorman, & Spahr, 2002). If families want their child to speak, a communication modality that incorporates auditory and speech skills is required. If families want their child to be able to communicate with deaf adults, the communication modality needs to include sign language.

Early intervention service providers can best support families by listening to them and supporting the choice of communication modality that they have selected for their child and family. Encouraging family members to pursue other options if they express discomfort with their choice and assisting them with integrating the new communication choice into their everyday life are also important ways to provide support during the implementation of early intervention services.

## BEST PRACTICE HIGHLIGHTS FOR INFANTS AND TODDLERS WITH HEARING IMPAIRMENT

An early interventionist can use many strategies to promote social, speech, language, and cognitive growth in young children with hearing loss. The following strategies and recommendations should be shared with parents and caregivers for use during the family's daily routines with their child and followed during all intervention visits. All of these strategies are consistent with the recommendations set forth by the Joint Committee on Infant Hearing for Early Intervention for Children Who are Deaf or Hard of Hearing (Muse et al., 2013).

- Check amplification at the beginning of each intervention visit. With the family's approval, the early interventionist could attend an audiological appointment to learn how to help the parents check amplification if the child uses unfamiliar technology.
- Encourage the family to ensure that the child is wearing his or her hearing aids during all waking hours. Support the family in finding ways to keep amplification on the child.
- Teach the parents to troubleshoot amplification and empower parents to do this on their own.
- Teach parents to conduct a Ling-6 sound test daily to determine whether the technology is functioning appropriately and/or to detect changes in hearing loss, such as progression of hearing loss. This test involves presentation of six sounds that verify the child is hearing across all speech frequencies (Ling, 2002). The six sounds are: /a/ ("ah"), /i/ ("ee"), /o/ ("oo"), /s/, /sh/, and /m/. A seventh "sound" of silence can also be presented to monitor for false-positive responses from the child. These sounds should be presented in an auditory-only condition at a normal volume. Document the child's responses and the distance at which the sounds were presented in contact notes. Encourage the family to check daily and provide the family with a log to document responses.
- Provide continual information to the family on developmentally appropriate skills for the child based on the child's chronological age and hearing age. Have high expectations for development of auditory, speech, and language skills.
- Teach the caregiver to point to his or her ear and say, "I heard that," when a very young child is first learning to listen. This will help the child become aware of sounds in the environment and that sound is important. Discontinue this strategy as the child spontaneously alerts to sound.

- Encourage parents to use auditory cues before moving or manipulating the child. Always use auditory spoken language cues first, prior to reliance on visual and physical cues.
- Use the "auditory sandwich": Present information through sound, present the same information through sound with visual support, and repeat the information again through sound alone.
- Use coaching to teach the family to narrate the child's day. The parent should continually describe what the child is doing, how the child is feeling, and what the child might be thinking. Narrating events in the environment immerses the child in opportunities to learn language.
- Conduct intervention visits in quiet areas, unless the goal of the activity is to complete it with background noise. Help the family reduce background noise in the home to support the child's development of listening skills.
- During intervention visits, the parent and interventionist should sit within a few feet of the child, unless the goal of the activity is to complete it with distance.
- Speak in a natural voice. Check the child's hearing equipment if he or she is not responding.
- Talk with families about their communication preferences and integrate their choice into intervention sessions. If family members choose to use sign language, help them find sign language classes and a native and fluent sign language instructor. Use resources such as board books that have a picture of a person signing key vocabulary words or online signing dictionaries, which parents can use to help learn how to sign.

The following general guidelines will increase productivity in visits that incorporate sign language:

- Use signs next to pictures when looking at books. The family may need help positioning the child to use sign language during storytime. Suggest that the parent sit the child in front so that the child can see the book, hands, and facial expressions of the parent. An infant could be seated in a car seat, highchair, or feeding seat to achieve the desired positioning. The family may need to adjust positioning depending on the height and neck control of the infant.
- Play in positions that encourage auditory input first but also allow for visual support if necessary. Many children who use sign language have adequate access to spoken language and do not need to be physically manipulated to view the adult's face and hands.
- Continually challenge the auditory skills of the child. It is expected that children will learn to alert to all speech and environmental sounds within months after receiving their amplification.
- Do not use toys that vibrate or light up to teach cause-and-effect or auditory skills. Instead, determine a sound that the child consistently responds to hearing. Use that sound to teach this concept.
- Use coaching to teach the family how to use communication temptations (Wetherby & Prizant, 1989) throughout the day. *Communication temptations* create opportunities in the environment that tempt a child to communicate. An example would be handing a container of bubbles to a child that he or she cannot open. The child will want the bubbles and so will be tempted to communicate with the adult to request opening the container.

- Encourage the family to make experience books or keep a journal to talk about things that have happened, or will be occurring, in the child's life.
- The child should be expected to use auditory skills and spoken language skills in each interaction. This is true even when sign language is used, unless the family selected an ASL approach to communication. The parents should be coached on what to expect at the child's continually changing developmental levels.

These suggestions should aid service providers in offering services that are developmentally appropriate for a child, as well as tailored to satisfying the family's stated priorities and goals for the child.

## SUMMARY

For infants and toddlers with hearing loss to become strong communicators in their chosen communication modality, they need immersion in that system from the time of first diagnosis. Because of the role of neural plasticity in language and communication development, it is critical that a child be identified and fit appropriately with amplification, as well as provided with immediate early intervention services from a service provider who is knowledgeable about early childhood deafness and hearing loss. It is possible for children with hearing loss who do not have additional disabilities to develop language and communication skills commensurate with their hearing peers. However, this can only be achieved if families have timely access to appropriate technology, work with the most knowledgeable and experienced of professionals, and develop the skills necessary for supporting their child. If quality services and supports are not provided before the child's third birthday, the same strategies used at a later age will yield significantly poorer results (Yoshinaga-Itano et al., 1998).

## DISCUSSION QUESTIONS AND APPLIED ACTIVITIES

1. Talk to a parent who has a child who is blind or has a visual impairment to learn more about the family's experience. No matter the age of the child, the family will have many important insights to share. Ask the following questions:
   - What were the most helpful and least helpful specific information and/or guidance given to your family when your child was under the age of 3?
   - What would be your advice now to other parents?
   - When your child was an infant or toddler, what toys or objects were most motivating to him or her?
2. Identify five potential challenges that infants and toddlers with visual impairments may encounter and describe one intervention suggestion to address each.
3. Using Figure 9.3, discuss the different communication modality options available for a child with hearing loss and the family's responsibilities for each communication modality.
4. You are a service provider working in a rural area. One family in your caseload has gone to see an audiologist who primarily sees adult patients in your community. She tells the family to come back in 3 months for more testing before they order hearing aids.

   - What are the problems with this recommendation?
   - What other professionals can help you support this family?
   - How might you counsel this family right now?

## RECOMMENDED RESOURCES FOR PROFESSIONALS

### Blindness and Visual Impairment

Take a free correspondence course from the Hadley School for the Blind (http://www
.hadley.edu/) addressing the early years, braille, or another topic pertinent to very young
children who have visual impairments.

Use available professional resources from the American Foundation for the Blind (http://
www.afb.org), the American Printing House for the Blind (http://www.aph.org), and
the National Federation of the Blind (http://www.nfb.org) to learn more about early
intervention with children with blindness or visual impairments.

### Hearing Impairment

Cole, E.B., & Flexer, C. (2007). *Children with hearing loss: Developing listening and talking birth
to six.* San Diego, CA: Plural Publishing.

Estabrooks, W. (2006). *Auditory-verbal therapy and practice.* Washington, DC: Alexander
Graham Bell Association for the Deaf and Hard of Hearing.

## RECOMMENDED MATERIALS AND CURRICULA

### Blindness and Visual Impairment

American Foundation for the Blind's Family Connections (http://www.familyconnect.org/
parentsitehome.aspx)

Texas School for the Blind/Visually Impaired (http://tsbvi.edu/)

### Hearing Impairment

Cochlear Americas. (2003). *Listen, learn, and talk.* Retrieved from http://hope.cochlearamer
icas.com/listening-tools/listen-learn-talk

Cole, E.B., Carroll, E., Coyne, J., Fill, E. & Paterson, M. (2005). *The SKI-HI curriculum.*
Logan, UT: Hope.

Rossi, K. (2005). *Let's learn around the clock: A professional's early intervention toolbox.* Washington, DC: Alexander Graham Bell Association for the Deaf and Hard of Hearing.

Wilkes, E.M. (1999). *Cottage Acquisition Scales for Listening, Language & Speech.* San Antonio,
TX: Sunshine Cottage School for Deaf Children.

## REFERENCES

American Academy of Ophthalmology. (2003). Eye
examination in infants, children, and young adults by
pediatricians: Organizational principles to guide and
define the child health care system and/or improve the
health of all children. *Ophthalmology, 110,* 860–865.

American Optometric Association. (2002). *Pediatric eye
and vision examination.* Retrieved from http://www.aoa
.org/documents/optometrists/CPG-2.pdf

American Speech-Language Hearing Association. (2014).
*The audiogram.* Retrieved from http://www.asha.org/
public/hearing/Audiogram/

Anderson, E.S., Dunlea, A., & Kekelis, L.S. (1984). Blind
children's language: Resolving some differences. *Journal of Child Language, 11,* 645–664.

Anderson, K. (2007). ELF—*Early Listening Function Test.*
Somerset, NJ: Oticon.

Anthony, T.L. (1998). Sensory learning: A framework of early O&M skill development. In E. Siffermann, M. William, & B.B. Blasch (Eds.), Conference proceedings: The ninth international mobility conference (pp. 279–280). Atlanta, GA: Rehabilitation Research and Development Center.

Anthony, T.L. (2000). Performing a functional low vision assessment. In C. Farrenkopf & F.M. D'Andrea (Eds.), Looking to learn: Promoting visual efficiency skills in students with low vision (pp. 32–83). New York, NY: American Foundation for the Blind.

Anthony, T.L. (2004). Individual Sensory Learning Profile. Chapel Hill: University of North Carolina, Chapel Hill, Frank Porter Graham Child Development Institute, Early Intervention Training Center for Infants and Toddlers with Visual Impairments.

Anthony, T.L. (2008). Strategies for working with children with visual impairments. In T. Linder (Ed.), Transdisciplinary play-based intervention (pp. 163-181). Baltimore, MD: Paul H. Brookes Publishing Co.

Anthony, T.L. (2012). Early childhood development: Play and movement in early childhood. In L.J. Lieberman, P.E. Ponchilla, & S.V. Ponchilla (Eds.), Physical education, sports, and recreation for people with visual impairments or deafblindness: Foundations of instruction (pp. 159–186). New York, NY: American Foundation for the Blind.

Anthony, T.L., Bleier, H., Fazzi, D.L., Kish, D., & Pogrund, R.L. (2002). Mobility focus: Developing early skills for orientation and mobility. In R.L. Pogrund & D.L. Fazzi (Eds.), Early focus: Working with young children who are blind or visually impaired and their families (2nd ed., pp. 326–404). New York, NY: American Foundation for the Blind Press.

BEGINNINGS for Parents of Children Who Are Deaf or Hard of Hearing. (2014). Communication approaches chart. Raleigh, NC: Author. Retrieved from http://ncbegin.org/reference-chart/

Bigelow, A. (1986). The development of reaching in blind children. British Journal of Developmental Psychology, 4, 355–366.

Bigelow, A. (1987). Early words of blind children. Journal of Child Language, 14(1), 47–56.

Bigelow, A.E. (2005). Blindness and psychological development of young children. In B. Hopkins (Ed.), Cambridge encyclopedia of child development. Cambridge, UK: Cambridge University Press.

Borchert, M., & Garcia-Filion, P. (2008). The syndrome of optic nerve hypoplasia. Current Neurology and Neuroscience Reports, 8(5), 395–403.

Brambring, M. (2006a). Early intervention with infants and preschoolers who are blind. Bielefeld Observation Scales (BOSBLIND). (J. Harrow, Trans.). Wurzburg, Germany: Edition Bentheim.

Brambring, M. (2006b). Divergent development of gross motor skills in children who are blind or sighted. Journal of Blindness & Visual Impairment, 100(10), 620–634.

Brambring, M. (2007). Divergent development of verbal skills in children who are blind or sighted. Journal of Blindness & Visual Impairment, 101(12), 749–762.

Brown, C. (2003). Recommendations to enhance visual and visual efficiency with the physical environment. Chapel Hill: University of North Carolina, Chapel Hill, Frank Porter Graham Child Development Institute, Early Intervention Training Center for Infants and Toddlers with Visual Impairments.

Brown, C., & Bour, B. (1986). Volume V-K: Movement analysis and curriculum for visually impaired preschoolers. Tallahassee: Florida Department of Education, Bureau of Education for Exceptional Students.

Bzoch, K.R., League, R., & Brown, V. (2003). Receptive-Expressive Emergent Language Test (3rd ed.). Austin, TX: PRO-ED.

Canalis, R.F., & Lambert, P.R. (2000). The ear: Comprehensive otology. Philadelphia, PA: Lippincott Williams & Wilkins.

Centers for Disease Control and Prevention. (2011). Summary of 2011 national CDC EHDI data. Retrieved from http://www.cdc.gov/ncbddd/hearingloss/2011-data/2011_ehdi_hsfs_summary_a.pdf

Choo, D., Creighton, J., Meinen-Derr, J., & Wiley, S. (2005). Auditory Skills Checklist. Cincinnati, OH: Cincinnati Children's Hospital Medical Center, Center for Hearing and Deaf Research.

Cutter, J. (2007). Independent movement and travel in blind children: A promotional model. Charlotte, NC: Information Age Publishing.

Erber, N.P. (1982). Auditory training. Washington, DC: Alexander Graham Bell Association for the Deaf and Hard of Hearing.

Ertmer, D.J. & Stoel-Gammon, C. (2008). The Conditioned Assessment of Speech Production (CASP): A tool for evaluating auditory-guided speech development in young children with hearing loss. The Volta Review, 108, 59–80.

Fazzi, D.L., & Klein, M.D. (2002). Cognitive focus: Developing cognition, concepts, and language. In R.L. Pogrund & D.L. Fazzi (Eds.), Early focus: Working with young children who are blind or visually impaired and their families (2nd ed., pp. 107–153). New York, NY: American Foundation for the Blind Press.

Ferrell, K.A. (1997). What is it that is different about a child with blindness or visual impairment? In P. Crane, D. Cuthbertson, K.A. Ferrell, & H. Scherb (Eds.), Equals in partnership: Basic rights for families of children with blindness or visual impairment (pp. v–vii.) Watertown, MA: Hilton/Perkins Program of Perkins School for the Blind and the National Association for Parents of the Visually Impaired.

Ferrell, K.A. (1998). Project PRISM: A longitudinal study of the developmental patterns of children who are visually impaired: Executive summary: CFDA 84.0203C: Field-initiated research HO23C10188. Greeley: University of Northern Colorado.

Ferrell, K.A. (2000). Growth and development of young children. In M.C. Holbrook & A.J. Koenig (Eds.), Foundations of education: Vol. 1. History and theory of teaching children and youths with visual impairments (2nd ed., pp. 111–134). New York, NY: AFB Press.

Ferrell, K.A. (2011). Reach out and teach: Helping your child who is visually impaired learn and grow. New York, NY: AFB Press.

Fraiberg, S. (1977). Insights from the blind: Comparative studies of blind and sighted infants. New York, NY: Basic Books.

Fraiberg, S., Siegel, B., & Gibson, R. (1966). The role of sound in the search behavior of a blind infant. Psychoanalytical Study of the Child, 21, 327–357.

Friedman, C.T., & Calvello, G. (1989). Developmental assessment. In D. Chen, C.T. Friedman, & G. Calvello (Eds.), Parents and visually impaired infants. Louisville, KY: American Printing House for the Blind.

Fudala, J., & Reynolds, W. (2000). *Arizona Articulation Proficiency Scale* (3rd ed.). Los Angeles, CA: Western Psychological Services.

Geers, A.E., Moog, J.S., Biedenstein, J.B., Brenner, C., & Hayes, H. (2009). Spoken language scores of children using cochlear implants compared to hearing age-mates at school entry. *Journal of Deaf Studies and Deaf Education, 14*(3), 371–385.

Goldman, R., & Fristoe, M. (2000). *Goldman-Fristoe Test of Articulation* (2nd ed.). San Antonio, TX: Pearson.

Good, W.V., Jan, J.E., DeSa, L., Barkovich, A.J., Groenveld, M., & Hoyt, C.S. (1994). Cortical visual impairment in children. *Survey of Ophthalmology, 38*(4), 351–364.

Hatton, D.D. (2001). Model registry of early childhood visual impairment: First-year results. *Journal of Visual Impairment & Blindness, 95*(7), 418–433.

Hatton, D.D., Bailey, D.B., Burchinal, M.R., & Ferrell, K.A. (1997). Developmental growth curves of preschool children with vision impairments. *Child Development, 68,* 788–806.

Hatton, D.D., Ivy, S.E., & Boyer, C. (2013). Severe visual impairments in infants and toddlers in the United States. *Journal of Visual Impairment & Blindness, 107*(5), 325–336.

Hatton, D.D., Schwietz, E., Boyer, B., & Rychwalski, P. (2007). Babies count: The national registry for children with visual impairments, birth to three years. *Journal of American Association for Pediatric Ophthalmology and Strabismus, 11*(4), 351–355.

Holt, R.E., & Svirsky, M.A. (2008). An exploratory look at pediatric cochlear implantation: Is earliest always best? *Ear & Hearing, 29*(4), 492–511.

Ireton, H. (1992). *Manual for the Minnesota Child Development Inventory.* Minneapolis, MN: Behavioral Science Systems.

Jan, J.E., & Groenveld, M. (1993). Visual behaviors and adaptations associated with cortical and ocular impairment in children. *Journal of Visual Impairment & Blindness, 87*(4), 101–105.

Jan, J., Robinson, G., Scott, E., & Kinnis, C. (1975). Hypotonia in the blind child. *Developmental Medicine and Child Neurology, 17,* 35–40.

Keith, C.G., & Doyle, L.W. (1995). Retinopathy of prematurity in extremely low birth weight infants. *Pediatrics, 95,* 42–45.

Leat, S.J., Shute, R.H., & Westall, C.A. (1999). *Assessing children's vision: A handbook.* Oxford, England: Butterworth-Heinemann.

Ling, D. (2002). *Speech and the hearing impaired child* (2nd ed.). Washington, DC: Alexander Graham Bell Association for the Deaf and Hard of Hearing.

McConachie, H.R. (1990). Early language development and severe visual impairment. *Child: Care, Health, and Development, 16,* 55–61.

McConachie, H.R., & Moore, V. (1994). Early expressive language of severely visually impaired children. *Developmental Medicine and Child Neurology, 36,* 230–240.

Menacker, S.J., & Batshaw, M.L. (1997). Vision: Our windows to the world. In M.L. Batshaw (Ed.), *Children with disabilities* (4th ed., pp. 211–239). Baltimore, MD: Paul H. Brookes Publishing Co.

Mitchell, R.E., & Karchmer, M.A. (2004). Chasing the mythical ten percent: Parental hearing status of deaf and hard of hearing students in the United States. *Sign Language Studies, 4*(2), 138–163.

Moeller, M.P. (2000). Early intervention and language development in children who are deaf and hard of hearing. *Pediatrics, 106*(3), e43.

Mueller, H.G., & Killion, M.C. (1990). An easy method for calculating the articulation index. *The Hearing Journal, 43*(9), 1–4.

Muse, C., Harrison, J., Yoshinaga-Itano, C., Grimes, A., Brookhouser, P.E., Epstein, S., ...Martin, B. (2013). Supplement to the JCIH 2007 position statement: Principles and guidelines for early intervention after confirmation that a child is deaf or hard of hearing. *Pediatrics, 131*(4), e1324–e1349.

National Institutes of Health. (2006). *Fact sheet: Newborn hearing screening.* Washington, DC: U.S. Department of Health and Human Services.

Nicholas, J.G., & Geers, A.E. (2006). Effects of early experience on the spoken language of deaf children at 3 years of age. *Ear & Hearing, 27*(3), 286–298.

Northern, J.L., & Downs, M.P. (2002). *Hearing in children* (5th ed.). Baltimore, MD: Lippincott Williams & Wilkins.

Patel, L., McNally, R.J., Harrison, E., Lloyd, I.C., & Clayton, P.E. (2006). Geographical distribution of optic nerve hypoplasia and septo-optic dysplasia in northwest England. *Journal of Pediatrics, 148*(1), 85–88.

Prechtl, H.F., Cioni, G., Einspieler, C., Bos, A.F., & Ferrari, F. (2001). Role of vision on early development: Lessons from the blind. *Developmental Medicine and Child Neurology, 43,* 198–201.

Ramirez Inscoe, J.M., & Nikolopoulos, T.P. (2004). Cochlear implantation in children deafened by cytomegalovirus: Speech perception and speech intelligibility outcomes. *Otology & Neurotology, 25,* 479–482.

Reynell, J.K., & Gruber, C.P. (1990). *Reynell Developmental Language Scales* (U.S. ed.). Los Angeles, CA: Western Psychological Services.

Robinshaw, H.M. (1995). Early intervention for hearing impairment: Differences in the timing of communicative and linguistic development. *British Journal of Audiology, 29,* 315–334.

Rogers, S., & Puchalski, C. (1988). Development of object permanence in visually impaired infants. *Journal of Visual Impairment & Blindness, 82,* 137–142.

Rosen, S. (2010). Kinesiology and sensorimotor functioning for students with vision loss. In W.R. Wiener, R.L. Welsh, & B.B. Blasch (Eds.), *Foundations of orientation and mobility, Vol. I: History and theory* (3rd ed., pp. 138–172). New York, NY: AFB Press.

Rowland, C. (1983). Patterns of interaction between three blind infants and their mothers. In A.E. Mills (Ed.), *Language acquisition in the blind child: Normal and deficient* (pp. 114–132). Kent, UK: Croom Helm.

Schor, D.P. (1990). Visual impairment. In J.A. Blackman (Ed.), *Medical aspects of developmental disabilities in children birth to three* (2nd ed., pp. 269–274). Rockville, MD: Aspen Publications.

Sharma, A., & Dorman, M. (2006). Central auditory development in children with cochlear implants: Clinical implications. *Advances in Otorhinolaryngology, 64,* 66–88.

Sharma, A., Dorman, M., & Spahr, A. (2002). A sensitive period for the development of the central auditory system in children with cochlear implants: Implications for age of implantation. *Ear and Hearing, 23,* 532–539.

Sonksen, P.M., Levitt, S., & Kitsinger, M. (1984). Identification of constraints acting on motor development in young visually disabled children and principles of remediation. *Child Care, Health, and Development, 10,* 273–286.

Stokes, B. (2002). *Amazing babies: Essential movement for your baby in the first year.* Allenwood, NJ: Move Alive Media.

Stredler-Brown, A. & Johnson, C.D. (2004). *Functional auditory performance indicators: An integrated approach to auditory skill development.* Retrieved from http://www.cde.state.co.us/cdesped/sd-hearing.htm

Teplin, S.W., Greeley, J., and Anthony, T.L. (2009). Blindness and visual impairment. In W.B. Carey, A.C. Crocker, W.L. Coleman, E.R. Elias, & H.M. Feldman (Eds.), *Developmental-behavioral pediatrics* (4th ed., pp. 698–716). Philadelphia, PA: Elsevier.

Tharpe, A.M. (2006). *The impact of minimal and mild hearing loss on children.* Paper presented at the Fourth Widex Congress of Paediatric Audiology, Ottawa, Canada.

Tröster, H., Heckler, W. & Brambring, M. (1994). Longitudinal study of gross-motor development in blind infants and preschoolers. *Early Childhood Development and Care, 104,* 61–78.

Urwin, C. (1984). Communication in infancy and the emergence of language in blind children. In R. Schiefelbusch & J. Picklar (Eds.), *The acquisition of communication competence* (pp. 479–524). Baltimore, MD: University Park Press.

Wetherby, A., & Prizant, B. (1989). The expression of communicative intent: Assessment issues. *Seminars in Speech and Language, 10,* 77–91.

Whetsell, W.O. (1996). Brain development and early stimulation. *Kennedy Center News, 34,* 1–2.

Wiig, E.H., Secord, W.A., & Semel, E. (2004). *Clinical Evaluation of Language Fundamentals–Preschool* (2nd ed.). Toronto, Canada: Harcourt.

Yoshinaga-Itano, C., & Sedey, A. (2000). Speech development of deaf and hard-of-hearing children in early childhood: Inter-relationships with language and hearing. In C. Yoshinaga-Itano & A. Sedey (Eds.), Language, speech and social-emotional development of children who are deaf or hard of hearing: The early years [Monograph]. *Volta Review, 100*(5), 181–211.

Yoshinaga-Itano, C., Sedey, A., Coulter, D., & Mehl, A. (1998). Language of early- and later-identified children with hearing loss. *Pediatrics, 102*(5), 1161–1171.

Zimmerman, I.L., Steiner, V.G., & Pond, R.E. (2011). *Preschool Language Scales* (5th ed.). San Antonio, TX: Pearson.

Zimmerman-Phillips, S., Osberger, M.J., & Robbins, A.M. (2000). *Infant-Toddler: Meaningful Auditory Integration Scale.* Sylmar, CA: Advanced Biotics.

# 10 | Infants and Toddlers with Cognitive and/or Motor Disabilities

Jonna L. Bobzien, Dana C. Childress, and Sharon A. Raver

This chapter discusses issues regarding providing services to infants and toddlers with cognitive and/or motor delays and disabilities, including the following:

- Causes, prevalence, and types of associated disorders and disabilities
- Medical interventions
- Roles of medical and early intervention professionals
- Assessment tools and strategies
- Intervention strategies
- Best practice highlights

## Case Study: Jennifer

Jennifer is 28 months old and has multiple disabilities, including significant cognitive delays and cerebral palsy (CP). Jennifer was born 12 weeks premature via cesarean section following a routine ultrasound, during which the obstetrician noticed the umbilical cord was wrapped around her neck. Following her delivery, Jennifer spent 8 weeks in the neonatal intensive care unit. As a result of the lack of oxygen in utero and the resulting complications of a premature delivery, Jennifer displays developmental delays in all domain areas. Jennifer has mixed CP, which means the muscles in her lower extremities are very tight (spastic) and she displays slow and uncoordinated (athetoid) movements in her upper extremities. The motor impairments in her lower extremities affect her ability to move about independently, and those in her upper extremities affect her ability to complete everyday activities, such as playing with toys.

Since her birth, Jennifer has received early intervention services in her home. She is seen weekly by a physical therapist (PT), who acts as the primary service provider. Jennifer's PT consults with an occupational therapist (OT) once each month and brings information about intervention strategies from the OT to the family during intervention visits. These visits focus on increasing Jennifer's ability to move independently and improving the functioning in her upper extremities so she can play with her older brother, eat with a spoon, and assist with dressing. To facilitate her mobility, the PT fitted Jennifer with a pair of ankle-foot orthotics and showed her mother multiple stretches to use with Jennifer every day during their regular routines to reduce her muscle tightness.

Jennifer and her family are visited twice a month by a speech-language pathologist (SLP). The speech therapist also communicates regularly with the OT for guidance on ways to promote oral-motor control because Jennifer has a difficult time swallowing. The speech therapist integrates suggestions offered by the PT and OT to focus on improving Jennifer's expressive and receptive language by using proper body positioning and embedding games that practice the production of sounds and words that are needed daily (e.g., *eat, drink, play, go, more, no,* and *yes*).

Jennifer and her family have experienced success with these interventions. At the last team meeting, Jennifer's parents expressed that they were also concerned about their daughter's ability to play with other children her age. To encourage social interaction and play skills, Jennifer's parents have enrolled her in a local church playgroup, which she attends two mornings a week with her mother. An individualized family service plan (IFSP) review meeting was held to add an outcome to Jennifer's plan to promote her social-emotional development. The location of services was also reconsidered. As a result, both of her service providers have increased their focus on play as the basis for working on the skills that Jennifer needs. The team then decided that intervention visits will alternate between the home and the playgroup to provide support for Jennifer and her family in both settings.

Infants and toddlers with cognitive disabilities and/or motor delays or impairments often display unique developmental differences that require intervention with different kinds of services. Determining service(s), how often a service will be provided, and which strategies and interventions will be used must always be tailored to the individual needs of the child. Often, children like Jennifer, who demonstrate both cognitive and physical impairments, exhibit significant delays in multiple domain areas (e.g., motor, adaptive behavior, communication, social-emotional, cognition), which could have a pervasive impact on their overall development. Because the presence of moderate to severe cognitive and/or motor delays are frequently evident at birth or are detected within the first 6 months of life, early identification is common. This early detection opens the door to early initiation of appropriate medical and developmental interventions for the children and their families (Bruder, 2010; Giannoni & Kass, 2012).

## IMPORTANCE OF EARLY IDENTIFICATION

Overall, approximately 7.2% of infants and toddlers receiving early intervention services qualified specifically due to the existence of a cognitive delay. Likewise, approximately 17.5% of infants and toddlers receiving early intervention services needed these services because of motor impairment (Hebbeler et al., 2007). However, the number of children under the age of 3 years who are receiving services for disorders that have the potential to result in cognitive and/or motor impairment comes closer to about 43% (Hebbeler et al., 2007). Due to the potentially large number of children with delays, disorders, and/or diseases related to these impairments, it is crucial that parents and practitioners strive to identify concerns early so that intervention can begin as quickly as possible.

Unfortunately, when seeking assistance, difficulties often arise because families may become overwhelmed by the number of required or recommended services and therapies for an infant or toddler with these needs. Most families will also have recently received devastating medical diagnoses or information about their child that will require time to process. Therefore, to best serve the child and family, early interventionists must strive to understand the family's emotional perspective while organizing specialized supports and services based on the child's unique strengths and needs.

## CAUSES OF COGNITIVE AND/OR MOTOR DELAYS OR DISABILITIES

When working with these infants and toddlers, service providers must be knowledgeable about the potential causes of a child's needs to create an intervention plan that addresses those needs appropriately. The most common causes of cognitive and motor impairment are biologically based. Approximately 75% of such disabilities can be linked to a specific biological origin, and nearly all of the triggers for these delays occur during the *prenatal* (in utero), *perinatal* (during birth), or *postnatal* (shortly after birth) periods (see Table 10.1). As in the case of Jennifer, the majority of incidences of cognitive or motor impairment can be linked to some type of brain disorder or injury.

Several factors can lead to abnormal brain development. For example, some infants and toddlers display impairments related to brain dysgenesis. *Brain dysgenesis* is a term used to define brain development that was abnormal from conception. In other words, there was no period of typical brain development. Brain dysgenesis is different from *brain damage,* which is defined as an insult or injury that alters the structure or function of a brain that had been developing normally up until the point at which the damage occurred. Brain damage is often the result of fetal or infant exposure to environments with extremely low levels of oxygen, referred to as *hypoxia,* or to environments that have an absence of oxygen, known as *anoxia.* Additional potential triggers for intellectual and/or motor impairments include chromosomal, genetic, or metabolic abnormalities, as well as exposure to viruses, bacteria, environmental agents, and/or teratogens, such as drugs or radiation from x rays (Coleman, 2006).

Because the specific impairments and characteristics exhibited by an infant or toddler are directly related to the origin of the disability, it is necessary to become familiar with the most common disorders associated with cognitive and/or motor delays. Neuromotor, chromosomal, genetic, metabolic, and endrocrine disorders; infectious diseases; environmental influences; and orthopedic and musculoskeletal disorders are discussed in the following sections.

**Table 10.1.**  Causes of cognitive and motor impairments before, during, and after birth

| Prenatal | Perinatal | Postnatal |
|---|---|---|
| Chromosomal abnormalities | Lack of oxygen | Infections |
| Viral infections | Physical injury to the brain | Traumatic brain injury |
| Drug/alcohol intake | Contracted infections | Heavy metal poisoning |
| Malnutrition | | Reactions to medications |
| Physical trauma to the mother | | Environmental conditions |

## Neuromotor Disorders

There are many types of neuromotor disorders. Two of the most common, cerebral palsy and neural tube defects, are discussed.

***Cerebral Palsy***    Many infants and toddlers with cognitive and/or motor impairments, such as Jennifer, are diagnosed as having the neurological disorder known as *cerebral palsy (CP)*. CP is a group of nonprogressive disorders characterized by the inability of the brain to control muscles in a normal fashion. This lack of muscle regulation by the brain leads to impairments in voluntary movement and posture. CP results either from abnormal brain development or from brain injury or damage that occurs before birth, during birth, or within the first few years of life. Four situations increase the chances of CP occurring: 1) periods of inadequate oxygen supply, either prenatally or during delivery; 2) maternal infection during pregnancy; 3) infections of the infant's brain; or 4) head trauma (Nelson, 2008). According to the Centers for Disease Control and Prevention (CDC, 2013), approximately 4 out of every 1,000 children born have some degree of CP, making it the most common cause of motor impairment in children. In addition, nearly 15% of infants born prematurely will develop CP (Kirby et al., 2011).

Infants and toddlers with CP will display a diverse range of impairments in voluntary movement, balance, and coordination ranging from barely noticeable involvement to significant involvement in all aspects of functioning. Because CP is the result of brain dysfunction and not impairments in the spinal cord or peripheral muscle system, the impairments displayed will depend on the extent and location of the brain damage (Accardo & Whitman, 2011; Coleman, 2006). Based on the area of the brain affected, CP is classified into four main types, as described in the following sections: spastic CP, dyskinetic CP, ataxic CP, and mixed CP.

*Spastic Cerebral Palsy*    *Spastic CP* accounts for approximately 60% of all incidences of CP and is characterized by extreme tightness in muscle groups, which limits movement (Krägeloh-Mann & Cans, 2009). Spastic CP is a result of damage to the portion of the brain known as the pyramidal system, which houses the nerve cells and pathways that transmit motor impulses from the brain to the spinal cord. Children with spastic CP exhibit stiff and jerky movements as well as difficulty moving from one position to another. They also have difficulty grasping and releasing objects. Spastic CP is often further classified based on the location of the affected muscle groups. In *hemiplegic spastic CP,* only one side of the body is affected. In *diplegic spastic CP,* either the upper half or the lower half of the body is affected. Individuals with *quadriplegic spastic CP* have both the upper and lower extremities affected, as well as the trunk and face.

*Dyskinetic Cerebral Palsy*    The second most common form of CP, accounting for approximately 20% of cases, is dyskinetic CP. *Dyskinetic CP* is characterized by either involuntary or jerking movements (*chorea*) or slow writhing movements (*athetoid*) of the arms, legs, head, and/or trunk. These involuntary movements are the result of damage to the basal ganglia area of the brain, which is responsible for making movement smooth and controlled. Therefore, a child with dyskinetic CP will have difficulty with skills that require coordinated movements such as feeding, speaking, sitting, and walking.

*Ataxic Cerebral Palsy*    Children who have damage to the cerebellum are classified as having ataxic CP. *Ataxic CP,* which accounts for only about 1% of all cases, is characterized by low muscle tone, poor coordination of movement, and a lack of timing of motor activities, which prevents the smooth progression from one muscle movement to the next. This form of CP affects balance and depth perception, making walking unsteady. These children will typically place their feet unusually far apart when walking. In addition, as the child ages, he or she will have difficulty with movements that require a great deal of hand, arm, and shoulder control, such as writing.

*Mixed Cerebral Palsy*   The final category of CP is known as mixed CP. Children with *mixed CP* display impairments associated with more than one type of CP due to multiple areas of damage to the brain. The most common type of mixed CP is a combination of spastic and dyskinetic CP (CDC, 2013; Coleman, 2006). Jennifer was diagnosed with mixed CP because she displayed high muscle tone, or spasticity, in her lower extremities and jerky movements in her upper extremities.

Although official diagnosis and classification of CP relies on brain imaging tests such as magnetic resonance imaging (MRI), cranial ultrasound, or x-ray computed tomography (CT scan), parents may be the first to suspect that a developmental difference is present (National Institute of Neurological Disorders and Stroke [NINDS], 2013). Although early signs of CP vary from child to child, many cases of CP are diagnosed before a toddler's second birthday because the child fails to reach age-appropriate motor milestones. For example, an infant younger than 6 months may display a head lag when pulled to sitting, may overextend his or her back and neck when held, or may scissor his or her legs when picked up. Infants between the ages of 6 and 10 months may fail to roll over, bring their hands together at midline, or keep their hands fisted. Infants older than 10 months may have difficulty crawling, standing, and/or walking (CDC, 2013; NINDS, 2013). Nevertheless, if a child's symptoms of CP are mild, diagnosis may not occur until the child is older. Regardless of the age of initial diagnosis, the existence of associated impairments may become apparent as the child ages. *Comorbid diagnoses* of cognitive delay, seizure disorder, communication delays, swallowing and feeding difficulties, and visual and/or auditory impairments are common (Accardo & Whitman, 2011).

**Neural Tube Defects**   Another group of neuromotor impairments that result in significant motor and/or cognitive impairments are neural tube defects. During the embryonic stage of prenatal development, the neural folds come together to form the neural tube, which will develop into the spinal cord, brain, and vertebrae (Accardo & Whitman, 2011). If the neural tube fails to close completely, the structures and membranes of the spinal cord or brain may be exposed. Neural tube defects can cause a variety of impairments, including learning disabilities, as well as medical problems such as paralysis. The effects of a neural tube defect vary greatly and depend primarily on the location of the defect and the degree to which the spinal cord and/or brain is exposed. Neural tube defects are categorized into three diagnoses known as spina bifida, encephalocele, and anencephaly.

*Spina Bifida*   *Spina bifida* occurs when one or more vertebrae that make up the spinal column fail to close completely during prenatal development. Spina bifida can occur along any part of the spinal column, with the location greatly affecting the level of impairment an infant will display. If the area of the gap is located in the lower regions of the spinal column (i.e., sacral or lower lumbar), the resulting impairment may be minimal and isolated to the lower extremities. If the location of the gap is located in the upper regions of the spinal column (i.e., thoracic or upper lumbar), the resulting impairments tend to be more severe and affect both upper and lower extremities.

In addition to the location of the opening, the severity of spina bifida also depends on whether the opening is isolated to the bone or if it results in a corresponding protrusion of spinal membranes, spinal cord, and/or cerebrospinal fluid. For example, an infant who has spina bifida occculta has no protrusion of spinal material, so this defect often goes undetected. The most common impairment associated with spina bifida occulta, which affects approximately 10% of the general infant population, is the appearance of a dimple, mole, or hairy patch on the skin covering the gap in the vertebrae (Accardo & Whitman, 2011). Likewise, infants who have spina bifida with a meningocele (an area where the membranes surrounding the spinal cord protrude out through an opening) require surgical repair; however, the infant typically does not exhibit any functional or developmental problems.

Conversely, an infant with spina bifida with an accompanying myelocele (protrusion of spinal membranes and spinal cord) or myelomeningocele (protrusion of spinal membranes, spinal cord, and cerebrospinal fluid) may exhibit significant motor and cognitive delays. Approximately 40% of infants born with a myelomeningocele will have some level of cognitive disability and some degree of paralysis or loss of sensation, depending on the location of the protrusion (Accardo & Whitman, 2011). Additional concerns for infants born with spina bifida include *hydrocephalus* (excess fluid in the brain), curvature of the spine (*scoliosis* and *kyphosis*), foot anomalies (e.g., clubfoot and congenital rocker-bottom foot), visual impairments, seizures, and chronic medical problems affecting the heart, kidneys, intestines, and bladder.

*Encephalocele and Anencephaly*    Although spina bifida is the most commonly occurring neural tube defect, there are two additional rare types of neural tube defects that have a significant impact on an infant's development when present. A neural tube defect that results in the malformation of the skull allowing a portion of the brain and *meninges* (membranes surrounding the brain) to protrude is called *encephalocele*. Encephalocele typically occurs in the occipital lobe, which is located in the back, lower portion of the brain. Because a portion of brain tissue is exposed, the result is usually moderate to severe brain damage, which causes cognitive involvement, motor impairment, and/or seizure disorder.

The most severe neural tube defect that can occur is anencephaly. *Anencephaly* occurs when the malformation of the brain and skull are so significant that there is a lack of brain development above the brainstem. Although the brainstem controls all primitive functioning, such as respiration, circulation, and digestion, most infants born with anencephaly will not survive the newborn period. Those who do survive will have profound multiple disabilities.

Although the precise cause of neural tube defects is not known, physicians believe there are many contributing factors, including low amounts of maternal folic acid. Therefore, it is recommended that women who are pregnant or intend to become pregnant should have adequate daily intake of prenatal vitamins with folic acid to prevent the development of these anomalies (Coleman, 2006).

## Chromosomal, Genetic, Metabolic, and Endocrine Disorders

Several specific chromosomal, genetic, metabolic, and endocrine disorders can lead to cognitive and/or motor impairments in infants and toddlers. Many of these conditions can be linked directly to genetic disorders in which either too many or too few chromosomes are present in cells, or when chromosomes themselves have extra pieces, missing pieces, or pieces from neighboring chromosomes. Other conditions are associated with inborn or inherited errors in metabolism, known as metabolic disorders, or with hormone deficiencies resulting from endocrine disorders. Impairments associated with disorders such as Down syndrome, fragile X syndrome, phenylketonuria (PKU), and congenital hypothyroidism vary from mild to severe, making infants with chromosomal, genetic, and metabolic disorders a very heterogeneous population.

**Down Syndrome**  *Down syndrome* is one of the most common chromosomal syndromes associated with the development of intellectual impairment and chronic medical conditions. The average occurrence of Down syndrome is approximately 1 in 691 children. Risk factors for having a child with Down syndrome increase with maternal age, as demonstrated by data that indicates the incidence at approximately 1 in 1,500 for mothers younger than 30 and 1 in 25 for mothers older than 45 years (Parker et al., 2010). Down syndrome is the result of the existence of one extra chromosome at the 21st position. Typically developing infants have 46 total chromosomes, or 23 pairs. However, infants with Down syndrome have a total of 47 due to the extra 21st chromosome.

Infants and toddlers with Down syndrome will demonstrate a wide range of needs. In general, they will display low overall muscle tone (*hypotonia*), which leads to joint hyperflexibility, short stature and fingers, flat facial profile and flattened back of the head, small ears, an upward slant to the eyes, and a speckling of the iris (the colored part of the eye). In addition, children with Down syndrome typically exhibit delays in motor development, communication, and adaptive skills. They display intellectual abilities ranging from average to severe impairment. Finally, children with Down syndrome have significantly higher incidences of chronic medical conditions. For instance, approximately 60% of children will have hearing impairments, 45%–50% will have congenital heart disease, 60% will have visual impairments, and up to 90% will have thyroid or endocrine abnormalities (Long, Eldridge, Galea, & Harris, 2011; Roizen & Patterson, 2003; van Trotsenburg, Heymans, Tijssen, de Vijlder, & Vulsma, 2006).

**Fragile X Syndrome**  *Fragile X syndrome,* also known as Martin-Bell syndrome, has been recognized as one of the most commonly inherited genetic disorders causing cognitive disability. Fragile X syndrome is the result of a partially broken or fragile site on the *FMR1* gene of the X chromosome. Although both males and females may inherit fragile X, it is more common in males, with an approximate occurrence of 1 in every 3,600 males and 1 in every 4,000–6,000 females. Furthermore, because this disorder is linked directly to the X chromosome, the impairments associated with fragile X syndrome are more significant in males.

Of female children who inherit fragile X, approximately 30% will display a mild learning disability. The remaining 70% will not demonstrate any impairments related to the syndrome (Coleman, 2006). Conversely, male children who inherit fragile X display weak social and communication skills; engage in stereotypical behaviors (e.g., hand-flapping, body rocking); and exhibit tactile defensiveness, inattention, and hyperactivity. In addition, 80% of male children with fragile X have cognitive impairments that range from mild to severe. Fragile X is often misdiagnosed as autism spectrum disorder (ASD) because the impairments associated with ASD and fragile X are very similar. However, because fragile X is a genetic disorder, it is possible to identify the existence of this condition through a series of blood tests, whereas the etiology of ASD remains unknown.

**Phenylketonuria**  *Phenylketonuria* (PKU) is an inherited metabolic disorder that results in the deficiency of an enzyme called phenylalanine hydroxylase, which allows an amino acid called phenylalanine to build up in the body. Too much phenylalanine in the body can lead to a variety of disorders, including cognitive delay, behavioral and social problems, seizure disorder, hyperactivity, and stunted growth. Although PKU is considered a rare condition in the United States, affecting approximately 1 in every 10,000 infants, it is crucial that newborns are screened immediately following birth. If PKU is suspected and the infant is placed on a specialized diet right away, the impact of the disorder will be dramatically decreased.

**Congenital Hypothyroidism**    The endocrine system is responsible for the production and regulation of a variety of hormones that are crucial to early growth and the development of the central nervous system. One of the main hormones associated with early development is the thyroid hormone. *Congenital hypothyroidism* is a fairly common hormone deficiency that affects approximately 1 in every 3,000 infants (Batshaw, Roizen, & Lotrecchiano, 2013). Early identification and subsequent treatment using thyroid hormone replacement drastically reduces the likelihood of long-term difficulties. If left untreated, affected infants will have severe growth problems and abnormal brain development, which results in significant cognitive and motor impairments (Fingerhut & Olgemöller, 2009; Pass & Neto, 2009).

## Infectious Diseases

Infectious diseases are considered a class of diseases that are derived through exposure to biological agents, such as viruses, bacteria, and parasites (Horn, Chambers, & Saito, 2009). Infants and toddlers are more susceptible to infectious diseases because their immune system has not fully developed. Exposure to an infectious disease that occurs prenatally because the mother passes the disease to the fetus is classified as a *congenital infection,* whereas diseases acquired after birth are classified as *acquired infections.* Infectious diseases account for approximately 3% of congenital malformations observed during the first year of life (Brent, 2004). Several infectious diseases, such as meningitis, toxoplasmosis, and cytomegalovirus (CMV), can result in significant cognitive and/or motor impairments if contracted during the early stages of development, as discussed in the following sections.

**Meningitis**    *Meningitis* is defined as an inflammation of the meninges, the membrane lining the spinal cord and brain. It is caused by either a viral or bacterial infection, such as streptococcus or *E. coli*. Although the development of viral meningitis is usually mild, with the infected infant suffering no long-term brain damage, bacterial meningitis is more severe and requires prompt medical attention. In some instances, infants with bacterial meningitis experience significant and permanent effects, including CP, vision or hearing loss, developmental delay, and seizures.

**Toxoplasmosis**    Toxoplasmosis is a common parasitic infection caused by contact with raw meat, cat feces, or the eggs of animals infected by the microorganism *Toxoplasma gondii*. Although exposure to the infection and subsequent development of toxoplasmosis is harmless to those with intact immunology, the infection can be transmitted from mother to fetus. Transmission of the infection in this manner is known as *congenital toxoplasmosis* and is estimated to occur in 1 of every 1,000 live births (Accardo & Whitman, 2011; Gilbert-Barness, 2010). Overall, approximately 40% of infants with affected mothers will develop symptoms such as brain damage, hydrocephalus, blindness, seizures, *microcephaly* (abnormally small head), and cognitive involvement. In extreme cases, such as infection early in pregnancy, congenital toxoplasmosis can be fatal (Coleman, 2006).

***Cytomegalovirus***    Congenital cytomegalic inclusion disease, also known as *cytomegalovirus* (CMV), is one of the most common intrauterine infections, with an estimated 1% of all newborns being infected during the prenatal period (Fowler & Boppana, 2006). Although an estimated 90% of instances of congenital CMV infection are *asymptomatic* (without symptoms), rare incidences of prenatal CMV exposure can result in low birth weight and poor overall growth. This 10% of infected infants may develop severe illness and congenital anomalies, such as cognitive limitations, microcephaly, hearing loss, anemia, liver damage, and spleen damage (Dollard, Grosse, & Ross, 2007).

## Environmental Influences

Approximately 1 in 250 newborns has physical impairments or structural anomalies that are a result of exposure to an environmental teratogen (Gilbert-Barness, 2010). A *teratogen* is defined as any environmental agent that causes permanent damage in structure, function, or growth during the prenatal period. The most common environmental teratogens responsible for congenital malformations have remained consistent so far in the 21st century: prenatal exposure to alcohol, illegal drugs such as heroin and cocaine, tobacco smoke, heavy metal exposure, and x-ray radiation (Brent, 2004; Ujházy, Mach, Navarová, Brucknerová, & Dubovický, 2012).

The harm caused by exposure to environmental teratogens varies based on the specific element involved, the dose or amount of exposure, and whether there was exposure to several negative environmental teratogens at once. That is, heavy caffeine use during pregnancy can be linked to miscarriage, low birth weight, and higher neonatal heart rates, and tobacco use can lead to miscarriage, prematurity, or impaired heart rate. The use of both prescription drugs, such as antidepressants, and nonprescription drugs, such as aspirin, can lead to low birth weight, cognitive impairment, poor motor development, and birth complications (Woolfolk & Perry, 2012). In addition, the use of illegal drugs, such as cocaine or heroin, often results in premature birth, low birth weight, respiratory issues, physical defects, or infant death. Unfortunately, 10%–11% of all newborns were exposed to prenatal substance abuse (Young et al., 2009). Similar to drug use, if a pregnant woman consumes alcohol, this could lead to the development of *fetal alcohol syndrome,* which results in a wide range of physical, mental, and behavioral impairments. Finally, exposure to radiation (e.g., x rays) or to high levels of heavy metals, such as lead and mercury, can cause miscarriage, underdeveloped brains, physical deformities, and slow physical growth (Gilbert-Barness, 2010; Woolfork & Perry, 2012).

## Orthopedic and Musculoskeletal Disorders

In rare cases, and often as a result of a neuromotor disorder or exposure to environmental toxins, infants can be born with orthopedic or musculoskeletal disorders. An infant born with a myelomeningocele may also have a spinal curvature, whereas an infant whose mother used illegal drugs may have limb differences. In addition, an infant with significant brain abnormalities may experience muscle imbalance and joint or bone abnormalities (Batshaw et al., 2013). Orthopedic and musculoskeletal disorders can lead to conditions such as subluxation or dislocation of joints.

When muscle tone is imbalanced, muscles attached to bone that allow for voluntary movement may remain in a state of constant *flexion* (tightness) or constant relaxation (may feel floppy) rather than making the transition between those states as necessary for proper movement. If this occurs, the point at which bones meet and articulate (joints) will be affected. *Subluxation* occurs when there is partial contact between the articulating components of a joint, and dislocation occurs at a joint when there is no contact between articulating surfaces of a joint. Both subluxation and dislocation can result in discomfort and can impede an infant's ability to engage in activities, such as sitting, walking, and eating.

If orthopedic or musculoskeletal disorders are significant, the result may be a deformity in which a body part or limb is permanently fixed into an abnormal position. There are several orthopedic or musculoskeletal disorders, such as torticollis, club foot, and curvature of the spine, that require immediate intervention to reduce potentially negative outcomes affecting typical motor development. For these reasons, PTs and OTs are essential members of early intervention teams. They are able to coach family members in ways to embed stretches and other movement interventions into their unique daily activities to increase the likelihood that the child will receive frequent intervention throughout the day.

Torticollis is a condition that occurs in approximately 1% of infants. *Torticollis* results in an infant's head being tilted and/or turned to one side. This abnormal neck position is the product of muscle spasms in the neck that, if left untreated, can result in the permanent shortening of neck muscles (Accardo & Whitman, 2011). An infant may develop torticollis in utero, and it is more common in infants who are in the breech position. Torticollis can also be acquired if there is damage to the neck muscles during a birth trauma. Treatment typically involves immediate intervention including physical therapy and, depending on severity, bracing of the neck. In 5%–10% of severe cases, surgery is required to reduce the likelihood that permanent muscle shortening will occur (Cheng et al., 2001).

Clubfoot, also known as talipes equinovarus, is another relatively common congenital abnormality, occurring in about 1 of every 1,000 births. *Clubfoot* is so named because the foot of the infant will be twisted into an abnormal position, which often results in only the outer sole of the foot being able to touch the ground (Flynn et al., 2004). There is no single cause of club foot; however, there appears to be an inherited component because the larger the rate of occurrence within a family, the greater the likelihood it will reoccur with increasing severity (Accardo & Whitman, 2011). Clubfoot has also been linked to disorders such as CP, spina bifida, and a variety of generic disorders (Accardo & Whitman, 2011; Flynn et al., 2004). Therapy and treatment with *orthotics,* which are braces and support appliances used to align targeted muscles, should begin immediately to reduce long-term negative implications.

Approximately 6 million people have conditions that result in *curvature of the spine.* Although most cases are acquired and occur as a person ages, typically beginning around age 10, some infants are born with congenital curvature of the spine (National Scoliosis Foundation, 2013). For these infants, this group of abnormalities occurs as the result of abnormal development of the vertebrae in the spinal column. Curvature of the spine is classified into three conditions based on the presentation of the curve. Infants with *scoliosis,* the most common type of curvature, have a spine that curves to the left and/or right, creating either a C-type or S-type curve. *Lordosis* is a condition in which the infant has an inward curvature of the spine, so the lower back looks concave. Finally, *kyphosis* is the term used to define a forward curvature of the spine, which results in a humped back (Batshaw et al., 2013). Regardless of the type of curvature, the long-term effects will depend on the degree of the curve. In other words, the more pronounced the curve, the more significant the potential impact. Most children with curvature of the spine will be treated with therapy; the use of a thoracic, lumbar, and sacral orthotic that wraps around the body; and/or surgery to correct the curve. If this condition is left untreated, it may eventually interfere with sitting, walking, and breathing (Fernandes & Weinstein, 2007).

When an infant has orthopedic or musculoskeletal disorders, they frequently are severe enough to negatively affect the child's learning. They require physical accommodations such as positioning and supportive devices, as well as assistive technology, to enhance the child's participation at home and in the community (Westling & Fox, 2009). Practical suggestions for embedding therapeutic exercises and positioning into daily care activities are shown in Figure 10.1.

## INFANTS AND TODDLERS WHO ARE MEDICALLY FRAGILE

In some instances, the presence of several medical and/or health concerns may render an infant or toddler at risk for the development of cognitive and/or motor delays. These children are often referred to as being medically fragile. A *medically fragile* infant or toddler is one whose health status is unstable, limiting the child's ability to participate in normal activities, often due to extended hospital stays and/or the necessity for surgical procedures (Coleman, 2006). In addition, some infants who are medically fragile develop musculoskeletal impairments, such as skeletal deformation, muscle shortening, and restricted joint mobility, which can result from the restrictive positions they are placed in while in the hospital (Long et al., 2011). Examples of infants who may be classified as medically fragile include those who were born premature or with low birth weight and are displaying developmental delays, as well as those with chronic lung or congenital heart disease (Batshaw et al., 2013).

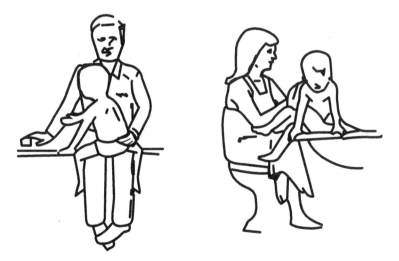

**Figure 10.1.**   A father positioning materials to encourage trunk rotation and a mother incorporating movement and rotation in towel drying for tone reduction.

Approximately 13% of all infants are born *premature,* which means they were born before the pregnancy reached 37 weeks. Another 2% of infants are considered *very preterm* because they were born at 32 weeks or earlier. In the United States, premature birth remains the foremost cause of infant mortality and morbidity and is responsible for roughly one half of all incidences of neonatal-onset neurodevelopmental disabilities, including CP (Nelson, 2008; Woolfolk & Perry, 2012). Furthermore, neurodevelopmental impairments that occur as a result of prematurity tend to persist into middle childhood, with 15% having a diagnosis of CP and 50% exhibiting cognitive, motor, or behavioral problems (Orton, Spittle, Doyle, Anderson, & Boyd, 2009). The cause of premature birth varies greatly and includes factors such as maternal toxemia, high blood pressure, drug use, rupture of the embryonic sac, abnormal placenta development, or multiple pregnancies.

Infants who are born premature are at greater risk for low birth weight. An infant who is considered to have *low birth weight* weighs less than 5.5 pounds; those classified as having *very low birth weight* weigh less than 3.3 pounds. Regardless of whether an infant with low birth weight is born premature or not, he or she is still more likely to have CP, major neurological challenges, speech and language delays, cognitive delays, and/or vision and hearing loss (Cole et al., 2002). In addition, Rosenberg, Zhang, and Robinson (2008) reported that, of the approximately 1.3% of infants born with very low birth weight that they studied, 4.8% displayed moderate to severe cognitive delays at 9 months old and 6.5% demonstrated significant motor delays. As these infants aged to 24 months old, the numbers grew larger: 6.8% demonstrated moderate to severe cognitive delays and 7.6% exhibited significant motor delays.

Approximately 8% of premature infants and 16% of very premature infants are diagnosed as having birth defects (Woolfolk & Perry, 2012). Common birth defects in premature infants include central nervous system and cardiovascular impairments, as well as respiratory disorders. Although approximately 8 of every 1,000 infants will have congenital heart disease (CHD), it is two to three times more likely to occur in premature infants (Reller, Strickland, Riehle-Colarusso, Mahle, & Correa, 2008; Wren et al., 2012). Premature infants who have CHD that is severe enough to warrant surgery are at risk for cognitive and motor delays, as well as musculoskeletal impairments, such as muscle shortening and scoliosis (Long et al., 2011). Although prematurity can result in multiple difficulties, respiratory disorders tend to have the most significant impact on the infant. Because the lungs of a premature infant do not have enough *surfactin* (a coating that prevents the lungs from collapsing), the infant may experience *respiratory distress syndrome* (RDS). When an infant has RDS, the air sacs of the lungs cannot stay open and the infant is unable to breath without oxygen and ventilator support (Wirbelauer & Speer, 2009).

## MEDICAL INTERVENTIONS FOR CHILDREN WITH DIVERSE DISABILITIES

When an infant or toddler displays substantial cognitive and/or motor delays, the child will likely need specialized medical interventions and mobility accommodations. These interventions and accommodations will vary from simple and unobtrusive, to complex and permanent surgical solutions. There are a multitude of possible interventions and accommodations available, with each depending on the specific physical and/or medical needs of each child. For example, an infant born with spina bifida may present with hydrocephalus. One of the most effective treatments for hydrocephalus is the surgical implantation of a *ventriculoperitoneal (VP) shunt.* Implanting a VP shunt involves placing plastic tubing, with a one-way valve, just under the skin that connects the area in the brain containing excess fluid to the child's abdominal cavity. This tubing diverts excess cerebral spinal fluid from the brain to the abdominal cavity, where it can be more easily absorbed by the body (Batshaw et al., 2013; Sandberg, 2008).

Despite the variety and invasiveness of the interventions or accommodations that may be offered to a child, most revolve around providing nutritional support, respiratory support, and mobility assistance for the child and training for the family in how to manage these supports at home, as discussed in the following sections.

## Nutritional Support

Infants and toddlers with CP or other neuromotor or musculoskeletal conditions often have limitations that affect their ability to take in nutrition by mouth. Limitations in eating and/or drinking by mouth are most often due to oral-motor impairments, gastroesophageal reflux, or refusal by the child to eat or drink. Jennifer is a good example. She had difficulty eating by mouth because she displayed significant athetoid movements that affected her ability to keep her head in a stable position to induce swallowing. Because Jennifer was not receiving an adequate amount of nutrition by mouth, the family's physician recommended nutritional support through the temporary use of a *nasogastric (NG) tube*. An NG tube was inserted into one of Jennifer's nostrils and passed through the esophagus directly into her stomach (Batshaw et al., 2013). This tube allowed Jennifer to receive the supplemental nutrition that she needed. If Jennifer continued to struggle with low nutritional intake, the family was told that other surgical interventions may become necessary.

Many children undergo surgical procedures to place temporary or permanent feeding tubes. The most common feeding tube is a *gastrostomy tube* (G-tube), which goes from outside the abdomen through the abdominal wall, directly into the stomach (Coleman, 2006). A G-tube is typically used when the child has a weak or damaged esophagus due to neuromotor or musculoskeletal conditions. Similarly, if a child experiences severe gastrointestinal or nutrient reflux while eating, the surgical implantation of a *jejunostomy tube* (J-tube) may be warranted. A J-tube is inserted from outside the abdominal wall and runs directly into the jejunum section of the intestines (Batshaw et al., 2013). Both of these feeding tubes allow for supplemental or replacement nourishment if the child is unable to maintain an appropriate level of nutrition.

## Respiratory Support

Young children born premature or who display musculoskeletal abnormalities, such as kyphosis, may experience difficulty with breathing, which requires respiratory support. The type of support required depends on the specific nature of the condition, ranging from simple oxygen supplementation to lung function assistance to alternative airway creation. Similar to nutritional supports, respiratory supports can be delivered using simple techniques, such as nasal cannula and continuous positive airway pressure (CPAP), or through techniques that require surgical intervention, such as tracheostomy. The simplest oxygen supplementation technique is the delivery of an oxygen/air mix directly to the child via a tube connected to either plastic prongs placed in the nose (*nasal cannula*) or a face mask.

For children who have more significant respiratory problems or *apnea* (a pause in breathing that lasts 20 seconds or more), the use of CPAP may be necessary. Like supplemental oxygen, CPAP provides the child with a mixture of oxygen and air through a face mask, but the air is delivered under continuous pressure, which prevents the alveoli of the lungs from collapsing between breaths. The use of supplemental oxygen and/or CPAP is quite effective in most cases of respiratory disorder. However, in extreme cases that involve damage to or disruption of the trachea, surgical intervention may be necessary. A *tracheostomy* is a surgical intervention in which a slit is made through the throat and into the trachea. A specialized tube, called a tracheal tube, is inserted into the slit to form an airway through which the child is able to breath. A child who has a trachea tube will either be able to breathe room air or still require assistance from supplemental oxygen delivery, the use of a CPAP, or a ventilator that provides mechanical breaths (Montagnino & Mauricio, 2004).

Because respiratory disorders can result in severe consequences, including death, it is crucial to monitor these conditions carefully. Many infants with respiratory disorders will have monitoring or surveillance devices that provide early warning of potential problems. An *apnea monitor* is a device that sounds an alarm if a child experiences an episode of apnea. Apnea monitors are frequently used with infants who are at risk for chronic respiratory distress, such as infants who were born prematurely. Because the respirations of each infant are different, an apnea monitor can be set for a specific time period, based on the individual child (Nadkarni, Shah, & Deshmukh, 2000).

Another commonly used monitoring device is a pulse oximeter. A *pulse oximeter* measures oxygen saturation (the amount of oxygen that red blood cells carry) using a probe attached to the child's finger or toe with special tape. It is crucial to monitor blood saturation levels because this provides an indication of the amount of oxygen that is traveling to vital organs. Similar to the apnea monitor, this device can be set to alarm when the blood saturation level falls below a certain preset limit, which alerts care providers that oxygen supplementation is needed (Nadkarni et al., 2000). Both apnea monitors and pulse oximeters are portable devices that can accompany the child at all times and during most activities to provide almost constant respiratory monitoring. Both monitors are unfortunately susceptible to false alarms from probe displacement and/or excess movement of extremities, so they should be checked periodically.

## Mobility and Positioning Support

Infants and toddlers with delays related to neuromotor, orthopedic, or musculoskeletal disorders often require mobility and/or positioning support. *Mobility devices* can assist a very young child with moving or being moved around safely. *Positioning* support promotes proper body alignment to compensate for abnormal muscle tone and atypical postures. Providing proper positioning is one of the key interventions for addressing motor and muscle impairments associated with CP. In addition, positioning support can be used to prepare a child for independent mobility (Batshaw et al., 2013).

One of the first mobility devices to consider is an adapted car seat. Children with disorders such as CP and spina bifida require the use of a car seat that provides not only safety but postural and structural support to the head and trunk. Adaptive car seats use additional padding and strapping, and they offer a variety of tilting options to ensure an upright posture is maintained and respirations are not compromised. In addition to adaptive car seats, some children will need an adaptive stroller. *Adaptive strollers* provide support to the back while keeping the hips and head properly aligned through the use of headrests, trunk padding, and chest harnesses. Because such equipment may be expensive, some physical or occupational therapists will help families use rolled baby blankets and other materials to modify existing strollers before ordering special equipment. Adaptive strollers are intended to be used from infancy through toddlerhood until the potential ability of a child to ambulate has been determined by the medical team.

Determination of the ambulation ability of an infant or toddler is critical in determining the proper mobility support a family should use. As a child ages, if it appears that he or she will not be able to walk independently, medical and therapy providers will recommend options that provide for assisted ambulation or alternate modes of mobility. For a child who requires an alternative to walking, a wheelchair will be recommended. Wheelchairs come in a variety of designs with several options for propulsion. Manual wheelchairs are those that are propelled by the seated occupant through movement of the rear wheels by hand. A manual wheelchair can be fitted with a two-hand drive, which requires the occupant to have functional use of both hands, or a one-arm drive, which allows for operation by those who have functional use of only one hand. Power wheelchairs are propelled by motors that are controlled through a variety of methods, including a joystick, head switch, or foot pedal. In the event that a child is unable to operate a manual or power wheelchair due to significant cognitive and/or motor delays, the wheelchair can be pushed by a caregiver.

If it is determined that a child has the ability to learn to walk, either independently or with assistance, a gait trainer may be used to develop the strength, balance, and coordination needed to walk properly. A *gait trainer* offers the highest level of support for children learning how to walk because it provides both weight-bearing support and postural alignment. Gait trainers are customizable depending on the level of support necessary and are intended to be used to help a child progress from being able to partially bear weight to take reciprocal steps, to independent walking and weight-bearing with the support of the device. As a child becomes more independent in a gait trainer, he or she will likely progress to the use of a pediatric walker. Because a *pediatric walker* is used by a child who is already able to bear weight and take steps independently, the walker is merely used for balance support. Although a pediatric walker may be recommended for some children as a mobility support, it is not the same as the baby walker that is commonly sold in stores. Baby walkers are not recommended by physical therapists or the American Academy of Pediatrics (2001), who issued a statement recommending against their use due to the potential for injuries and associated motor delays.

Finally, for children who are beginning to walk, additional support to the lower extremities may be their only requirement. Orthopedic devices are frequently used to maintain range of motion, provide stability, and control involuntary movements that could interfere with walking. *Ankle-foot orthotics* (AFOs), like those that Jennifer's physical therapist used with her, are the most common orthotic for the leg. For children such as Jennifer, AFOs offer support by stabilizing the position of the foot and ankle while providing a constant stretch to the tendons of the lower leg in an effort to strengthen and lengthen them. With assistance from these mobility supports, children with cognitive and/or motor delays have the opportunity to be active participants in as many family and community activities as their parents choose.

## CHILDREN WITH SIGNIFICANT DISABILITIES

Children with significant disabilities, including those with deafblindness, traumatic brain injury, or multiple disabilities, often receive early intervention services for the longest duration because they are typically referred during early infancy (Hebbeler et al., 2007). Careful coordination of intervention supports is especially important due to the complex nature of their needs. Significant disabilities are discussed in the following sections.

### Deafblindness

Children who have dual impairments in vision and hearing that cause severe developmental delays may be described as having *deafblindness*. To fall into this category, a child must be either blind with an accompanying hearing impairment or deaf with an accompanying visual impairment. A child with these dual sensory impairments will likely have significant delays in most or all areas of development. Because of the significance of these delays, intervention often focuses on helping the child use the remaining senses to explore and learn. In many instances, strategies used to accommodate children with severe disabilities, such as tactile-based learning, will be employed as well (Batshaw et al., 2013). Often, a hearing or vision specialist will serve as a consultant to the primary service provider and the family to offer additional coaching in how to individualize learning and supports.

## Traumatic Brain Injury

Infants and toddlers who have physical damage to the brain or to the functioning of the brain due to a closed brain injury are considered to have *traumatic brain injury* (TBI). A closed brain injury results from an injury during which the skull remains intact, but there is significant damage to the brain itself. Severe injury may be caused by car accidents, falls, or physical abuse, such as shaken baby syndrome, which can result in moderate to severe lifelong disability (Accardo & Whitman, 2011).

## Multiple Disabilities

Infants and toddlers, such as Jennifer, who exhibit significant impairments in both cognitive and motor skills are often described as having multiple disabilities. Children with multiple disabilities typically have a combination of significant developmental concerns, such as having global delays and orthopedic impairment, as well as a sensory disability, such as hearing or vision loss.

## IMPLICATIONS FOR FAMILIES

When an infant or toddler has significant cognitive and/or motor delays or disabilities, the family is considered to be the one constant in the child's world of doctors, therapists, and other professionals (Bruder, 2010); therefore, it is critical to consider the impact to the family functioning when a child has a disability. Research clearly indicates that parents of children with disabilities and delays experience higher levels of stress and depression than parents of a child without disabilities (Brobst, Clopton, & Hendrick, 2009; Bruder, 2010; Dempsey, Keen, Pennell, O'Reilly, & Neilands, 2009; Lessenberry & Rehfeldt, 2004; Singer, 2006; Welch et al., 2012). When a child has cognitive, motor and/or other health-related conditions, parents are required to find more time, energy, and resources for their child for an extended period of time. For example, taking a child with spina bifida out to the grocery store may involve gathering the adapted car seat and stroller, packing a tank for supplemental oxygen, securing an apnea monitor to the stroller, and packing a bag with medical and self-care essentials for the child, as well as the usual toys. This stress can also affect the relationship between parents because it can be difficult to find adequate time for both the spouse and the child. As a consequence, the divorce rate of couples raising a child with a disability is 3%–6% higher than couples with typically developing children (Brobst et al., 2009; Risdal & Singer, 2004).

Due to the increased time required for caring for an infant or toddler with cognitive, motor, and/or health issues, parents may need to take a break from the daily responsibilities of caregiving. Because finding qualified, reliable home health staff is difficult, many parents seek out *respite services*. Respite is a service that provides families with the opportunity to take a short break from caring for a child while providing the child with enjoyable opportunities and trustworthy care based on the child's unique needs (Langer et al., 2010; Welch et al., 2012). Breaks offered through respite services vary in duration and frequency from 1–2 hours a day, to several days a week, to periods of a week or longer if necessary. Parents may need to be encouraged to use long-term respite services following surgical procedures that require the child to have constant supervision and assistance. Service providers can be a resource to families in identifying how to access respite services in the community.

## ROLES OF MEDICAL AND EARLY INTERVENTION PROFESSIONALS

Given the range of needs displayed by infants or toddlers with cognitive and/or motor disabilities, there will be a diverse group of professionals with medical, health care, and early intervention training to guide the family through the early intervention process. Collaboration among these professionals is essential to promote the health and well-being of the child with disabilities and the family.

### Medical Professionals

One of the first groups of professionals that families will have contact with after the birth of their infant with cognitive and/or motor disabilities are those from the medical field. Medical professionals include primary care physicians, such as pediatricians, other medical specialists, and surgeons. A primary care physician's role is to provide preventative and acute care for the child. In addition, the primary care physician may provide chronic care if the condition is within his or her scope of knowledge.

Because of the complexities of the medical conditions experienced by these infants, many will require referrals to specialists for diagnosis and treatment of chronic conditions, such as seizure disorders; heart, respiratory, and gastrointestinal conditions; and neuromuscular disorders. Table 10.2 provides a brief description of common medical specialists.

**Table 10.2.**    Descriptions of medical specialists

| | |
|---|---|
| Neurologist | A specialized physician who treats children with conditions related to the human nervous system, including the brain, spinal cord, and peripheral nerves. |
| Gastroenterologist | A physician with specialized training in diagnosing and treating conditions related to the digestive system, including the esophagus, intestines, liver, and pancreas. |
| Pulmonologist | A physician who has specialized knowledge and skill in the diagnosis and treatment of pulmonary (lung) conditions and diseases. |
| Cardiologist | A specialized physician who diagnoses and treats children with heart and blood vessel conditions. |
| Physiatrist | A specialist in physical medicine and rehabilitation who focuses on the management of chronic diseases, especially those that are neuromuscular. |
| Orthopedist | A surgeon who specializes in the treatment of muscles, joints, and bones. |

## Early Intervention Professionals

When a child has multiple and/or complex needs, the primary care physician is often the source of the child's referral to an early intervention program. These children typically qualify for services due to a combination of developmental delays and their diagnosed condition. Children with multiple disabilities often, but not always, receive more than one early intervention service, but, as with any child, which service(s) the child receives is dependent on the family's priorities for the child's development and the outcomes on the IFSP.

*Occupational Therapists*    When supporting a child with cognitive and/or motor delays or disabilities, an OT may work closely with the child and care provider (e.g., parent, other family member, child care provider) to provide intervention that focuses on independent functioning, adaptive skills, and play. Occupational therapy may be provided through direct services, with the OT interacting directly with the child, and indirect services, with the OT coaching the care provider in strategies that promote the child's development and participation in daily activities. In addition, an OT may provide intervention to assist in the modulation or balancing of sensory input (Accardo & Whitman, 2011; Coleman, 2006). In some instances, the OT will use assistive technology devices, such as built-up spoons or crayons or electronic toys modified to be activated using switches, to help the child learn.

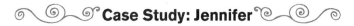

## Case Study: Jennifer

Jennifer's OT provided indirect services, in that she trained the PT in the strategies that she would have used with Jennifer had she been the primary service provider. The PT then in turn used coaching to guide Jennifer's parents, the playgroup leader, and Jennifer's brother in ways to encourage more independent play and improved eating skills within their daily interactions with Jennifer. In addition, the OT was an essential member of the early intervention team because she gave the team suggestions for promoting better oral-motor control with Jennifer's swallowing, which her mother reported was a "lifesaver" in getting the family through meals.

*Physical Therapists*    When working with an infant or toddler with cognitive and/or motor disabilities, a PT may address muscle strengthening, improving or maintaining range of motion and coordination, alleviating pain from contractures, and building up physical endurance. The PT uses a variety of therapeutic exercises for stretching and strengthening, as well as a range of positioning techniques to help the child learn the typical motor patterns for activities reflected in the child's IFSP, such as for learning to roll, sit, crawl, walk, or use whatever form of ambulation is most appropriate for the child (Accardo & Whitman, 2011). In addition, a PT may recommend the use of splinting or orthotic devices to assist a child in engaging in independent mobility.

## Case Study: Jennifer

Jennifer's PT employed the interventions and strategies offered by the OT. The PT also used positioning, play-based movement activities, and massage to reduce the muscle tightness that Jennifer experienced in her lower extremities. Shortly before Jennifer's first birthday, the PT fitted her with ankle-foot orthotics to keep her feet in proper alignment.

***Speech-Language Pathologists***   The SLP works closely with the child's family to find ways to promote the child's ability to communicate his or her wants and needs as clearly as possible. Many SLPs also have additional training in addressing oral-motor issues and feeding as well. For many children with cognitive and/or motor disabilities, speech therapy includes intervention strategies that encourage the child's use of sounds (and words as appropriate), eye gaze, body movements, sign language, and other means of augmentative and alternative communication.

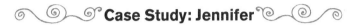 **Case Study: Jennifer**

Jennifer's SLP used a range of methods to support Jennifer's communication development. Like other children with cognitive and motor impairments, Jennifer was not able to communicate clearly via verbal speech. Her CP made swallowing, controlling airflow for speech, and tongue and lip coordination difficult for her. Because understanding Jennifer's communication was difficult for people outside the family, the SLP supplemented Jennifer's communication with a suitable alternative communication system, using a tablet with an application allowing Jennifer to touch pictures with her hand to request and label things she wanted or needed. When Jennifer went to her morning playgroup, she brought her communication tablet with her.

Although these three types of professionals have specialized training in their respective areas of expertise, when they work in early intervention they are expected to address the child's whole development, as opposed to focusing on one or two areas. Because early development is so interrelated, meaning that each area of development affects the others, all early intervention providers must be knowledgeable about all of child development and be willing to collaborate with other team members. This is especially important when supporting families of children with multiple disabilities or multiple areas of need.

***Service Coordinators***   The service coordinator has the important responsibility of coordinating with all individuals who are participating in the child's care during the creation of the IFSP and the delivery of services. Although most medical professionals are not directly involved in providing early intervention services, the service coordinator should obtain the family's permission to communicate with the child's medical providers. The service coordinator should maintain regular communication with medical providers to both obtain relevant medical information and provide information regarding significant changes to the child's development, as well as direct concerns regarding the child's medical status. Service coordinators may also assist parents in organizing a binder or folder in which to keep all of the child's medical information for quick reference. Relevant medical information is also incorporated into the IFSP. The service coordinator monitors the family's comfort with early intervention services to ensure that services are manageable within what may be a busy schedule, which also includes numerous medical appointments.

***Early Childhood Special Educators***   Another professional who might be part of a child's early intervention team is the early childhood special educator. When working with a child with cognitive and/or motor delays or disabilities, educators integrate information from other professionals to help the child's family learn ways to enhance the child's learning, problem solving, and engagement with others and the environment. For example, an educator may consult with the PT to learn the most appropriate positioning techniques to ensure that the child maintains head and trunk control; in this way, the child has the stability needed to use eye–hand coordination to play and learn. The educator may also consult with the OT on ways to use adapted materials or manage sensory differences. The educator and SLP may collaborate on functional communication techniques as well.

As stated before, any of these early intervention service providers, with the exception of the service coordinator, may serve as the primary service provider, depending on the IFSP outcomes and which provider has the expertise to best address the child's needs. With children with multiple delays or disabilities, having a single service provider may not be sufficient when expertise is needed from multiple providers. In this case, using a primary provider approach can be very helpful. The primary provider would receive support from other disciplines and help the family integrate strategies from the consultants into intervention activities and daily routines.

When the primary provider approach works well, the burden for families of having many professionals coming to the home and receiving different advice from different people can be reduced. The best way to ensure that a child's changing needs are being met is to regularly discuss with the team who the primary service provider is and if this professional is still the right individual to meet the child's and the family's present needs.

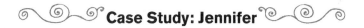

## Case Study: Jennifer

After Jennifer attended the playgroup for 2 months, her mother began to discuss the pros and cons of changing Jennifer's primary service provider with the service coordinator. Because of the family's priority to develop Jennifer's social and play development, Jennifer's mother was interested in working with an early childhood special educator. An IFSP meeting was scheduled, and Jennifer's IFSP outcomes were reviewed. Special instruction, the service provided by the educator, was added to the plan. Jennifer continued to receive physical therapy at a reduced frequency because her family felt confident with supporting Jennifer's motor development based on what they had learned so far. The educator consulted with the SLP and OT as needed as well.

## ASSESSMENT TOOLS AND STRATEGIES

To create an appropriate intervention plan, families must be involved in all aspects of the early intervention process, including evaluation and assessment, IFSP decision making and planning, and the delivery of the intervention (Ziviani, Feeney, & Khan, 2011). This becomes even more critical when children have significant and multiple challenges because a child's parents are often the best ones to interpret his or her behavior or intent, thereby assisting the professional team members with gathering accurate information and planning for intervention.

### Assessment

In preparation for the assessment of the child's strengths and needs, the service coordinator should communicate with the child's medical professionals (with parental permission) to obtain a well-rounded view of the child's unique biomedical differences. Next, the early intervention team of professionals will meet with the family in the home or other preferred setting to conduct observations of the child and complete the developmental assessment. Children with cognitive and/or motor involvement may require multiple opportunities to complete a comprehensive assessment due to the child's endurance and related health concerns. Adaptations of test items are also common, such as allowing a child with limited motor abilities to look at the correct hole in the shape puzzle to match the piece if he or she is unable to place the piece there.

Assessment team members, regardless of their discipline, use a combination of information gathered from formal assessment tools in their areas of expertise, information from tools assessing other domains, and informed clinical opinion to try to understand the child's overall functional strengths and needs. Professionals may have to rely more on clinical observations and judgment than with other children to establish an understanding of the child's abilities. Appropriate assessment tools for use with children with multiple delays and disabilities will present developmental skills broken down into their smallest components; this is important because identifying a child's abilities and tracking progress is more challenging when a child's skills are significantly limited and slower to develop. Some of the most commonly used assessment tools for children with disabilities, ages 0–3, are discussed here.

**Assessment Tools**    Although there are a variety of assessment tools for infants and toddlers, three of the most commonly used tools to measure skills across all domain areas are the Carolina Curriculum for Infants and Toddlers with Special Needs (Johnson-Martin, Attermeier, & Hacker, 2004), the Hawaii Early Learning Profile (HELP; Parks, 2006), and the Assessment, Evaluation, and Programming System for Infants and Children (AEPS®; Bricker et al., 2002). The diversity built into each of these tools provides for the collaboration needed to complete a thorough assessment, although it is common for PTs, OTs, and SLPs to use additional discipline-specific tools to gain a picture of a child's functioning level.

The Carolina Curriculum for Infants and Toddlers with Special Needs is intended to be used on infants and toddlers, ages 0–3, with mild to severe disabilities (Johnson-Martin et al., 2004). It assesses 26 total skill areas, which are organized into five domains of child development: cognition, communication, personal-social, fine motor skills, and gross motor skills. This tool includes developmental tasks broken down into components, as well as suggestions for how to adapt tasks for children with motor and sensory differences.

HELP is a criterion-referenced assessment used for identifying needs, tracking growth and development, and developing the next steps for instruction of infants and toddlers ages birth to 3 (Parks, 2006). Like the Carolina Curriculum, HELP focuses on the whole child and assesses 685 skills in the cognitive, language, gross motor, fine motor, social, and adaptive domains. This tool is commonly used because it promotes a cross-disciplinary approach and offers play-based activities and interventions for each skill assessed (Parks, 2006).

Finally, the AEPS tool (Bricker et al., 2002) helps one to identify developmental targets tailored for a child's specific needs. The AEPS is completed through parent report and direct observation of infants and toddlers in the domain areas of social-communication, fine motor, gross motor, adaptive, and cognitive skills. This tool also has a before and after evaluation component to measure the effectiveness of interventions.

Other tests used by assessment team members might include the Early Learning Accomplishment Profile (E-LAP; Glover, Preminger, & Sanford, 1988), the Peabody Developmental Motor Scales (Folio & Fewell, 2000), and the Infant/Toddler Sensory Profile (Dunn, 2002). The E-LAP is a comprehensive developmental assessment, whereas the Peabody focuses on motor development. The Infant/Toddler Sensory Profile is a parent-completed checklist that examines a child's sensory processing.

Which assessment tool is used depends on factors such as availability because programs may only have purchased particular tests, and appropriateness for assessing a particular child's development. Whenever possible, the decision about which tool will be used should be based on what is already known about a child's abilities and what information needs to be gathered to craft an individualized and accurate intervention plan.

## Strategies for Assessment

How a test is administered is equally as important as the choice about which test to use because accurately assessing the abilities of children with significant delays can be challenging. Some general strategies for assessing children with cognitive and/or motor delays and disabilities are provided here:

- *Coordinate the assessment to occur during the best part of the day for the child.* The service coordinator should ask the parent when the child is awake, alert, and the most comfortable during the day. This is a good strategy for any child, but it is especially important for children with significant disabilities because they may have limited endurance or be less alert following medication administration.

- *Ensure that the child is in a stable, supported position for assessment activities.* This is particularly important for activities that require attention, concentration, and the use of eye–hand coordination. If a child is unstable, he or she will likely be distracted and less successful completing activities.

- *Review the assessment tool for guidance in how to adapt test items.* Some assessments do not permit adaptations to how test items are administered or scored; these tests are typically not appropriate for use with children with significant delays or disabilities. Flexibility in how test items are administered is essential with children with motor limitations or visual or hearing loss. Using tests that provide suggestions for how to adapt and score test items is always a good idea.

- *Be careful to avoid overwhelming the child.* Many children with multiple delays or disabilities shut down or become easily frustrated with too many expectations. Moving slowly through test items at a pace that allows the child to be successful is the responsibility of the assessment team leader.

- *Begin the assessment with items that the child will be able to complete successfully.* This may require the assessor to begin with skills at an age much younger than the chronological age of the child. If the child was born prematurely, it is generally expected that the child will demonstrate skills closer to his or her *adjusted age,* or the age adjusted for the number of weeks of prematurity. A premature child's age is typically adjusted for assessment purposes until the child is either 18 or 24 months of age, depending on requirements in the state where the child lives. For example, a 6-month-old child who was born 8 weeks (or 2 months) early would be assessed as if he or she was 4 months old.

- *Interpret assessment results in terms of functional skill development.* It can be difficult for parents to hear how significantly their infant or toddler is delayed. Discussing assessment results in terms of a child's functional abilities and needs, rather than focusing on the age level of the child's skills, can help families put assessment results into perspective.

For example, at Jennifer's annual IFSP reevaluation, her development was assessed and found to be significantly delayed in all areas. Even after 2 years of receiving early intervention services, she was not yet using words to communicate due to the difficulties she continued to have with oral-motor coordination. As a result, her communication development appeared to be significantly delayed on the assessment tool. However, when the SLP used clinical judgment and included Jennifer's ability to communicate using her tablet and her use of body language to indicate her receptive understanding, her functional communication skills were much higher.

Most important, when assessing infants and toddlers with cognitive and/or motor impairments, strategies used must be individualized. Special attention must be paid to the child's health, body language, positioning needs, and how much physical and verbal support is needed to help the child complete assessment activities. These same considerations are also important when choosing intervention strategies that will be useful in promoting the child's development.

## INTERVENTION STRATEGIES

When selecting intervention strategies for infants and toddlers with multiple disabilities, it is important to remember that appropriate strategies are selected because they can be modeled by the early intervention service provider during intervention visits and used by parents during daily routines. The following nine general suggestions can help to maximize a child's participation in routine activities in the home or community:

1. *Do a quick inventory of the child's readiness to engage and keep interactions rewarding and brief.* It is imperative to understand that the child's health and abilities may vary from day to day, as well as across times of the day. Therefore, service providers must determine when the child's best time of day is and schedule intervention during that time. During intervention, the child should be observed carefully for fatigue. It is essential that professionals allow for frequent breaks during intervention activities based on how the child is interacting. Intervention activities should last as long as the child can tolerate without becoming exhausted or losing interest. Furthermore, intervention should not be attempted when the child is not feeling well. Finally, be sure to check in with medical professionals and regularly order medical records to keep up to date with the child's health status, limitations on activities, or medical signs to look for during intervention. Jennifer's intervention visits were typically scheduled in the mornings because this was when she was most alert and when she attended the church playgroup. Anytime she was not feeling well, her mother would call her service providers to reschedule the visit. Jennifer's service providers and her mother would monitor Jennifer closely for fatigue, which Jennifer indicated by keeping her eyes closed. When this occurred, they knew that they needed to give Jennifer a break.

2. *Acknowledge all attempts to communicate.* Jennifer tended to communicate using eye gaze and body language. For someone who was unfamiliar with her communication, it was not always easy to determine her intent. When they first began working with Jennifer and her family, the PT and SLP carefully observed Jennifer for consistent signs of communication. They also learned from her parents about how she indicated preferences and responded to communication from others. Jennifer was able to shift her eye gaze between two objects to make a choice, turn her head to indicate no or that she did not want to do something, cry or close her eyes when upset or tired, and vocalize when happy or excited. When she began using her communication tablet, her family was excited to see that she was able to touch pictures with her hand to communicate as well.

To make certain an infant or toddler is prepared to learn, caregivers and service providers must ensure that the child attends to their efforts to communicate and that they are in turn responding to any communication attempts that the child may make. It is important to talk to the child throughout the visit and encourage parents to narrate the child's activities throughout the week. Parents and service providers should assume that the child understands and is responding, even if it appears doubtful, because treating the child as if he or she understands and is communicating will help the child learn what his or her movements and sounds mean. Observe the child closely to determine how the child communicates and responds; watch for shifts in eye gaze, body movements, sounds/vocalizations, and/or changes in facial expressions. Assume any response is purposeful and develop this purposeful communication by responding to these communication attempts and labeling them for the child. For example, the SLP noticed that Jennifer tended to move her tongue out of her mouth whenever her brother mentioned food. When her family consistently labeled this behavior by asking, "Jennifer, are you hungry?" and offering her a snack, Jennifer soon learned that she could use this gesture to ask for something to eat.

3. *Allow extra wait time when prompting the child for a communication or motor response.* It is important to remember that a child with a disability may have slow or variable processing and response time, so service providers must be patient when waiting for a response. Once a child is prompted for a communication or motor response, such as if the child is asked to make a choice or activate a toy, it may be necessary to give the child as much as 45 seconds to process the instruction and coordinate a response. The service provider or parent should monitor this wait time to ensure that the child is given enough time to respond but not so much time that the child loses interest. After the prompt, the service provider should wait in silence and observe the child for a response. If the provider continues to immediately prompt the child, it could interrupt the child's processing and interfere with his or her ability to reply.

Because of Jennifer's motor limitations, it was challenging for her to coordinate the muscle movements needed to play with her toys and use her body to communicate. Based on a suggestion from the occupational therapist, the educator and Jennifer's parents made toys available to the left side of Jennifer's highchair tray to help her be more successful with activating them. This was due to the fact that Jennifer could coordinate movements with her left arm better than her right; therefore, with the toy placed to this side, she was less likely to exhaust herself with the movements required. Her family also noted that when they asked Jennifer a question, she would take about 20–30 seconds to indicate a response. After they noticed this need for wait time, communication became much easier and Jennifer cried less often because she was being understood.

4. *Create an environment that is accessible for the child.* Materials or toys should be placed within the child's visual field and reach, as Jennifer's parents and service providers did with her. If necessary, use physical supports, such as pillows under the elbows, to help the child interact with toys and materials independently. Be sure to adapt activities and materials so that the child can participate as independently as possible and teach turn-taking to help the child learn purposeful interaction. In Jennifer's case, she enjoyed taking turns with her brother activating her favorite switch toy, which was an electronic music box that had been adapted to be activated by a large flat switch. She also enjoyed popping bubbles in a game on her tablet and eventually learned to entertain herself with this game. To reduce the likelihood of fatigue, materials and toys should also be offered to the child in a variety of

positions. Toys and materials should be available wherever a child spends time. Positions that can support an infant's or toddler's independent movement while playing might include sidelying (lying on the child's side on the floor or in bed) and supported sitting, where the child's trunk is fully supported to maximize head control and stability.

5. *Offer toys and materials that are easily activated and provide input to multiple senses.* Independent play can be very challenging for children with significant needs. When developing a child's ability to play, finding toys and materials that interest the child is important so that the child does not have to rely on others for entertainment or for exploring the environment. Toys and materials that stimulate multiple senses, such as those with lights, sounds, and/or different textures for the child to feel, can be motivating and fun. However, service providers and parents need to be cautious that a toy does not overwhelm the child. Choosing the right toy is a decision based on the preferences of the child and the skills being addressed in the IFSP outcomes. Children with cognitive and/or motor limitations want to be able to interact with their toys successfully and have fun; this is an important consideration for any child.

6. *Remember to fade out any prompting or learning supports as the child is able to perform tasks more independently.* As with any child, two of the purposes of intervention are to encourage the child's participation and independence. For children with multiple needs, it can be easy to provide too much support. Service providers and parents should provide as much support as needed to help a child learn and practice new skills and abilities, but they should be ready to fade those supports as the child gains independence. For example, when Jennifer was learning to pop bubbles on her tablet, her mother became used to providing hand-over-hand assistance to help Jennifer accurately hit the bubbles. During one visit, the SLP suggested that they figure out how Jennifer might be able to touch the screen to pop the bubbles alone. After experimenting with ways to position Jennifer and the tablet, they determined that Jennifer could pop the bubbles while in her highchair with her mother only providing support under Jennifer's elbow. Jennifer eventually learned to play with her tablet independently, as long as she had elbow support from two towels rolled up and tucked beside her. She needed the elbow support to stabilize her arms, which helped her to control her wrist movements so that she could aim for the bubbles. This was a good lesson for her family in what Jennifer was capable of doing on her own. It also gave Jennifer a way to entertain herself without help.

7. *Provide verbal and physical cues before moving the child and before providing any physical assistance.* Infants and toddlers with motor limitations must rely on others to move them, and in many cases, to help them play and explore. Because these children often have very little control over their environment, parents and service providers should be encouraged to give physical and verbal cues before moving or manipulating the child so that the child will not be startled. Children should be moved frequently throughout the day so that they can be active participants in their environment. Providing verbal cues, such as "Time to get your diaper changed," can help the child prepare for the activity. It is helpful to use consistent phrases for frequently occurring events, such as diaper changes or feedings, to help the child associate the words with the activity. These cues can also be used to encourage the child's active participation by asking the child a question, such as "Are you ready to be picked up?" and then waiting for the child's response. For children with hearing loss or auditory processing difficulties, pairing a verbal cue with a physical prompt, such as gently tapping the child's sides before picking him or her up, is also a good idea.

8. *Individualize the number and frequency of services based on the IFSP outcomes, not on the child's diagnosis.* When children have complex medical or developmental needs, it can be easy to assume that they need multiple services from multiple service providers. Some children and families benefit from the support of several providers, but it should not be assumed that children who have these needs automatically require a high-intensity level of services. When a primary service provider is coaching parents in ways to enhance the child's development, the frequency and length of service provider visits can possibly be less intensive for the family. Reducing the number of people coming in and out of the home also reduces the child's exposure to germs, which can be important for children with health challenges. The decision about which service(s) a child needs is an IFSP team decision that is based on the child's and family's outcomes, and it often changes over time as the child's strengths and needs change. This decision should not be based on the child's diagnosis alone.

9. *Encourage caregivers.* Professionals are always willing to praise and encourage children as they attempt difficult tasks. Professionals need to remember to encourage caregivers as well. Because infants and toddlers with cognitive and/or motor disabilities may display a slow rate of learning, it can appear that the child has plateaued and progress is stalled. Sometimes, someone from outside the home can help the family notice tiny changes that show that progress is occurring. For example, Jennifer's father talked to the SLP because he felt that his daughter was not making progress with her swallowing and feeding. They decided to revisit Jennifer's IFSP outcomes and realized that Jennifer had progressed from gagging whenever any food was placed in her mouth to tasting soft foods, such as yogurt and mashed potatoes, without gagging. She was also using her tongue gesture to request food. Although she was not yet swallowing foods, she was tolerating different textures in her mouth without gagging, which was a significant step in the right direction.

Determining which intervention strategies will be most helpful to children and families takes time and careful attention to the child's cues. As with any child, early intervention service providers partner with family members and other important people in the child's life to ensure that the child is able to participate as fully as possible. Children with cognitive and/or motor delays and disabilities, like Jennifer, often require additional supports, such as specialized equipment, materials, and strategies, to promote their development and participation. These supports should be made available for the family to use with the child during and between intervention visits because, as with all children, these children benefit most when their parents are confident engaging them in ways that support development during daily activities. These infants and toddlers also benefit from well-coordinated care with involvement from medical and early intervention professionals who have knowledge of the causes of delays and disabilities and effective intervention strategies. This knowledge allows service providers to assist families in making informed decisions throughout the early intervention process and beyond. Many children who experience the delays and disabilities discussed in this chapter will continue to receive special education services after exiting the IDEA Part C system. The encouragement parents receive and the knowledge and skills they learn while participating in early intervention can last for many years to come.

## BEST PRACTICE HIGHLIGHTS

As service providers support very young children with significant needs and their families, it is important to remember these best practices:

- It is necessary to become familiar with the most common disorders associated with cognitive and/or motor delays, including neuromotor, chromosomal, genetic, metabolic, and endrocrine disorders; infectious diseases; and orthopedic and musculoskeletal disorders. In this way, service providers have an understanding of some of the developmental and health challenges that a child and the child's family may have to negotiate as they move toward realizing the child's potential.

- Children with significant delays and disabilities and their families benefit from well-coordinated services between medical and early intervention professionals to ensure that services are manageable and meet their needs.

- Infants and toddlers with cognitive, motor, and health issues require service providers who can support and encourage parents as they learn to use and provide nutritional, respiratory, mobility, and positioning supports for their child.

- To teach and reward purposeful communication, observe the child's behavior and respond to all communication attempts.

- Ensure that the child is properly positioned for play and interaction, and present toys or materials within the child's view and grasp.

- Make decisions about assessment tools, outcomes, services, and intervention strategies based on the child's abilities and needs and the priorities and interests of the family, not on the child's diagnosis or level of delay.

- Collaborate with families to learn about how they include their child in daily activities. Use this information to develop individualized intervention strategies that families can use every day to encourage their children's development. Provide support and encouragement, especially when development appears to be progressing slowly.

## CONCLUSION

As the case study with Jennifer demonstrated, infants and toddlers with cognitive and/or motor disabilities will experience a variety of strengths and needs. The precise needs will depend on the cause of the disabilities, as well as the child's accompanying chronic and complex medical conditions. A child's strengths and needs are also affected by the environment, so providing experiences and adaptations that allow the child to learn from and participate in family and community activities is an important goal of early intervention. It is also important to remember that these children will likely interact with many medical professionals, so collaboration and coordination between the child's medical specialists and the early intervention team is essential. Individualizing assessment and service delivery so that a child can be as successful as possible in communicating and demonstrating his or her abilities is necessary so that the team can provide the best support to the child. Partnering with the family throughout the early intervention process and providing emotional support and encouragement also helps ensure that the child and family have the knowledge and skills needed to meet their own needs while in early intervention and as the child continues to grow.

## DISCUSSION QUESTIONS AND APPLIED ACTIVITIES

1. Describe the four types of cerebral palsy (CP) and how they can affect an infant's or toddler's development in each developmental domain.

2. Explain how outcomes, services, and intervention strategies are determined when working with children with multiple disabilities and their families.

3. Interview an early intervention service provider in a local program about his or her experience working with very young children with cognitive and/or motor disabilities. Ask the provider to share how he or she coaches families to address the child's special communication needs during everyday activities.

## REFERENCES

Accardo, J.A., & Whitman, B.W. (2011). *Dictionary of developmental disabilities terminology* (3rd ed.). Baltimore, MD: Paul H. Brookes Publishing Co.

American Academy of Pediatrics. (2001). Policy statement: Injuries associated with infant walkers. *Pediatrics, 108*(3), 790–792.

Batshaw, M.L., Roizen, N.J., & Lotrecchiano, G.R. (2013). *Children with disabilities* (7th ed.). Baltimore, MD: Paul H. Brookes Publishing Co.

Brent, R.L. (2004). Environmental causes of human congenital malformations: The pediatrician's role in dealing with these complex clinical problems caused by a multiplicity of environmental and genetic factors. *Pediatrics, 113*(4), 957–968.

Bricker, D., Betty, C., Johnson, J.J., Pretti-Frontczak, K., Straka, E., Waddell, M., & Slentz, K. (2002). *Assessment, Evaluation, and Programming System for Infants and Children (AEPS®): Birth to three set* (2nd ed.). Baltimore, MD: Paul H. Brookes Publishing Co.

Brobst, J.B., Clopton, J.R., & Hendrick, S.S. (2009). Parenting children with autism spectrum disorder. *Focus on Autism and Other Developmental Disabilities, 24*(1), 38–49. doi:10.1177/1088357608323699

Bruder, M.B. (2010). Early childhood intervention: A promise to children and families for their future. *Exceptional Children, 76*(3), 339–355.

Centers for Disease Control and Prevention. (2013). *Facts about cerebral palsy.* Retrieved from http://www.cdc.gov/ncbddd/cp/facts.html

Cheng, J.C.Y., Wong, M.N., Ting, S.P., Chen, T.M.K., Phil, M., Shum, S.L.F., & Wong, E.M.C. (2001). Clinical determinants of the outcome of manual stretching in the treatment of congenital muscular torticollis in infants. *Journal of Bone and Joint Surgery, 83*(5), 679–687.

Cole, C., Binney, G., Casey, P., Fiascone, J., Hagadorn, J., & Kim, C. (2002). *Criteria for determining disability in infants and children: Low birth weight.* Rockville, MD: Agency for Healthcare Research and Quality.

Coleman, J.G. (2006). *The early intervention dictionary: A multidisciplinary guide to terminology* (3rd ed.). Bethesda, MD: Woodbine House.

Dempsey, I., Keen, D., Pennell, D., O'Reilly, J., & Neilands, J. (2009). Parent stress, parenting competence and family-centered support to young children with an intellectual or developmental disability. *Research in Developmental Disabilities, 30,* 558–566. doi:10.1016/j.ridd.2008.08.005

Dollard, S.C., Grosse, S.D., & Ross, D.S. (2007). New estimates of the prevalence of neurological and sensory sequelae and mortality associated with congenital cytomegalovirus infection. *Reviews in Medical Virology, 17,* 355–363. doi:10.1022/rmv.544

Dunn, W. (2002). *Infant/Toddler Sensory Profile.* San Antonio, TX: Pearson.

Fernandes, P., & Weinstein, S.L. (2007). Natural history of early onset scoliosis. *Journal of Bone & Joint Surgery, 89*(1), 21–33. doi:10.2106/JBJS.F.00754

Fingerhut, R., & Olgemöller, B. (2009). Newborn screening for inborn errors of metabolism and endocrinopathies: An update. *Analytical and Bioanalytical Chemistry, 393*(5), 1481–1497. doi:10.1007/s00216-008-2505-y

Flynn, J.M., Herrera-Soto, J.A., Ramirez, N.F., Fernandez-Feliberti, R., Vilella, F., & Guzman, J. (2004). Clubfoot release in myelodysplasia. *Journal of Pediatric Orthopedics, 13*(4), 259–262. doi:10.1097/01.bpb.0000124491.13918.b7

Folio, M.R., & Fewell, R.R. (2000). *Peabody Developmental Motor Scales* (2nd ed.). San Antonio, TX: Pearson.

Fowler, K.B., & Boppana, S.B. (2006). Congenital cytomegalovirus (CMV) infection and hearing deficit. *Journal of Clinical Virology, 35*(2), 226–231.

Giannoni, P.P., & Kass, P.H. (2012). Predictors of developmental outcomes of high-risk and developmentally delayed infants and children enrolled in a state early childhood intervention program. *Infants and Young Children, 25*(3), 244–264. doi:10.1097/IYC.0b013e318257ff83

Gilbert-Barness, E. (2010). Review: Teratogenic causes of malformations. *Annals of Clinical and Laboratory Science, 40*(2), 99–114.

Glover, M.E., Preminger, J.L., & Sanford A.R. (1988). *Early Learning Accomplishment Profile manual.* Lewisville, NC: Kaplan.

Hebbeler, K., Spiker, D., Bailey, D., Scarborough, A., Mallik, S., Simeonsson, R., ...Nelson, L. (2007). *Early intervention for infants and toddlers with disabilities and their families: Participants, services, and outcomes. Final report of the national early intervention longitudinal study (NEILS) (Project 11247).* Washington, DC: U.S. Office of Special Education Programs.

Horn, E., Chambers, C.R., & Saito, Y. (2009). Techniques for teaching young children with moderate/severe or multiple disabilities. In S. Raver (Ed.), *Early childhood special education 0–8 years: Strategies for positive outcomes* (pp. 255–278). Upper Saddle River, NJ: Pearson.

Individuals with Disabilities Education Improvement Act (IDEA) of 2004, PL 108-446, 20 U.S.C. §§ 1400 *et seq.*

Johnson-Martin, N., Attermeier, S.M., & Hacker, B.J. (2004). *The Carolina Curriculum for Infants and Toddlers* (3rd ed.). Baltimore, MD: Paul H. Brookes Publishing Co.

Kirby, R.S., Wingate, M.S., Van Naardn Braun, K., Doemberg, C.L., Arneson, R.E., Benedict, B.M., ... Yeargin-Allsoop, M. (2011). Prevalence and functioning of children with cerebral palsy in four areas of the United States in 2006: A report from the Autism and Developmental Disabilities Monitoring Network. *Research in Developmental Disabilities, 32*(2), 462–469. doi:10.1016/j.ridd.2010.12.042

Krägeloh-Mann, I., & Cans, C. (2009). Cerebral palsy update. *Brain & Development, 31*(7), 537–544. doi:10.1016/j.braindev.2009.03.009

Langer, S., Collins, M., Welch, V., Wells, E., Hatton, C., Robertson, J., & Emerson, E. (2010). *A report on themes emerging from qualitative research into the impact* of short break provision on families with disabled children. Retrieved from https://www.education.gov.uk/publications/standard/publicationdetail/page1/DCSF-RR221

Lessenberry, B.M., & Rehfeldt, R.A. (2004). Evaluating stress levels of parents of children with disabilities. *Exceptional Children, 70*(2), 231–244.

Long, S.H., Eldridge, B.J., Galea, M.P., & Harris, S.R. (2011). Risk factors for gross motor dysfunction in infants with congenital heart disease. *Infants and Young Children, 24*(3), 246–258. doi:10.1097/IYC.0b013e3182176274

Montagnino, B.A., & Mauricio, R.V. (2004). The child with a tracheostomy and gastrostomy: Parental stress and coping in the home—A pilot study. *Pediatric Nursing, 30*(5), 373–380, 401.

Nadkarni, U.B., Shah, A.M., & Deshmukh, C.T. (2000). Non-invasive respiratory monitoring in paediatric intensive care. *Journal of Postgraduate Medicine, 46,* 149–152.

National Institute of Neurological Disorders and Stroke. (2013). *Cerebral palsy: Hope through research.* Retrieved from http://www.ninds.nih.gov/disorders/cerebral_palsy/detail_cerebral_palsy.htm

National Scoliosis Foundation. (2013). *Information and support.* Retrieved from http://www.scoliosis.org/info.php

Nelson, K.B. (2008). Causative factors in cerebral palsy. *Clinical Obstetrics and Gynecology, 51*(4), 749–762. doi:10.1097/GRF.0b013e318187087c

Orton, J., Spittle, A., Doyle, L., Anderson, P., & Boyd, R. (2009). Do early intervention programmes improve cognitive and motor outcomes for preterm infants after discharge? A systematic review. *Developmental Medicine & Child Neurology, 51,* 851–859. doi:10.1111/j.1469-8749.2009.03414.x

Parker, S.E., Mai, C.T., Canfield, M.A., Rickard, R., Wang, Y., Meyer, R.E., … Correa, A. (2010). *National birth defects prevention network.* Atlanta, GA: Centers for Disease Control and Prevention, National Center on Birth Defects and Developmental Disabilities.

Parks, S. (2006). *Inside HELP: Administration and reference manual.* Palo Alto, CA: VORT Corporation.

Pass, K.A., & Neto, E.C. (2009). Update: Newborn screening for endocrinopathies. *Endocrinology Metabolism Clinics of North America, 38*(4), 827–837.

Reller, M.D., Strickland, M.J., Riehle-Colarusso, T., Mahle, W.T., & Correa, A. (2008). Prevalence of congenital heart defects in metropolitan Atlanta, 1998–2005. *Journal of Pediatrics, 153*(6), 807–813.

Risdal, D., & Singer, G.H.S. (2004). Marital adjustment in parents of children with disabilities: A historical review and meta-analysis. *Research & Practice for Persons with Severe Disabilities, 29,* 95–103.

Roizen, N.J., & Patterson, D. (2003). Down syndrome. *The Lancet, 361,* 1281–1289.

Rosenberg, S.A., Zhang, D., & Robinson, C.C. (2008). Prevalence of developmental delays and participation in early intervention services for young children. *Pediatrics, 121*(6), 1503–1509. doi:10.1542/peds.2007-1680

Sandberg, D.I. (2008). Endoscopic management of hydrocephalus in pediatric patients: A review of indications, techniques, and outcomes. *Journal of Child Neurology, 23*(5), 550–560. doi:10.1177/0883073807309787

Singer, G.H.S. (2006). Meta-analysis of comparative studies of depression in mothers of children with and without developmental disabilities. *American Journal on Mental Retardation, 111*(3), 155–169.

Ujházy, E., Mach, M., Navarová, J., Brucknerová, I., & Dubovický, M. (2012). Teratology—Past, present and future. *Interdisciplinary Toxicology, 5*(4), 163–168. doi:10.2478/v10102-012-0027-0

van Trotsenburg, A.S., Heymans, H.S., Tijssen, J.G., de Vijlder, J.J.M., & Vulsma, T. (2006). Comorbidity, hospitalization, and medication use and their influence on mental and motor development of young infants with Down syndrome. *Pediatrics, 118,* 1633–1639. doi:10.1542/peds.2006-1135

Welch, V., Hatton, C., Emerson, E., Robertson, J., Collins, M., Langer, S., & Wells, E. (2012). Do short break and respite services for families with a disabled child in England make a difference? A qualitative analysis of sibling and parent responses. *Children and Youth Services Review, 34,* 451–459. doi:10.1016/j.childyouth.2011.12.002

Westling, D.L., & Fox, L. (2009). *Teaching students with severe disabilities* (4th ed.). Upper Saddle River, NJ: Pearson.

Wirbelauer, J., & Speer, C.P. (2009). The role of surfactant treatment in preterm infants and term newborns with acute respiratory distress syndrome. *Journal of Perinatology, 29,* 18–22. doi:10.1038/jp.2009.30

Woolfolk, A., & Perry, N. (2012). *Child and adolescent development.* Boston, MA: Pearson.

Wren, C., Irving, C.A., Griffiths, J.A., O'Sullivan, J.J., Chaudhari, M.P., Hayes, S.R., …Hasan, A. (2012). Mortality in infants with cardiovascular malformations. *European Journal of Pediatrics, 171,* 281. doi:10.1007/s00431-011-1525-3

Young, N.K., Gardner, S., Otero, C., Dennis, K., Chang, R., Earle, K., & Amatetti, S. (2009). *Substance-exposed infants: State responses to the problem.* HHS Pub. No. (SMA) 09-4369. Rockville, MD: Substance Abuse and Mental Health Services Administration.

Ziviani, J., Feeney, R., & Khan, A. (2011). Early intervention services for children with physical disability: Parents' perceptions of family-centeredness and service satisfaction. *Infants & Young Children, 24*(4), 364–382. doi:10.1097/IYC.0b013e31822a6b77

# Index

Page numbers followed by *b*, *f*, and *t* indicate boxes, figures, and tables, respectively.

Open-ended questions
adult learning and, 88
to child, 130
coaching and, 93
collaboration of families/professionals and, 48t, 49, 96
individualized family service plan (IFSP) and, 64
during intake, 57, 57t
on routines/activities, 83
Optic nerve hypoplasia (ONH), 220
Orthopedic devices, 269
Orthopedic/musculoskeletal disorders, 263–265, 265f
Orthopedists, 271t
Orthotics, 173, 264
OSEP, see Office of Special Education Programs
Otoacoustic emission testing (OAE), 236, 238f–239f
Outcomes on individualized family service plan (IFSP), 280
adaptations to, 162
adult learning and, 88
assessment/evaluation and, 83–85, 84b
collaboration of families/professionals and, 41, 42
development of, 64–67, 66b, 171–172
family-centered, 11t, 34, 77–78
federal indicators versus, 6, 59
frequency/length of intervention and, 94, 212, 280
functional, see Functional outcomes
inclusion and, 71–72
legislation on, 22, 59
principles of intervention on, 11t–13t, 14–15
related goals as, 162
reviewing, 69–71, 70b, 240, 277
Outcomes/federal indicators
appropriate behavior to meet needs, 168
knowledge and skill acquisition/use, 136–138
multiple domain focus, 109, 136
overview of, 6–7, 7b
team goals versus, 6, 59
Overloading child (visually), 230b, 232, 233
Oximeter, pulse, 268

Parallel play, 150
Parallel talk, 42–43, 127–129
Parent professionals, 242
Participation, 19, 72, 132
see also Engagement; Inclusion
Participation-based intervention, 19
Peabody Developmental Motor Scales 2 (PDMS-2), 170, 275
Pediatricians, 62
Peekaboo game, 80, 179–180
Peer acceptance, 161
see also Inclusion
Perinatal causes of delay/disabilities, 257t
Permanence of objects, see Object permanence
Personal hygiene, 182–183
Phenylketonuria (PKU), 261–262
Physiatrists, 271t
Physical assistance
for appropriate motor/adaptive skills, 173
autism spectrum disorder (ASD) and, 204, 205, 205t

fading, 279
for objects in play, 155
visual impairments and, 228
Physical development
legislation and, 5
strength, 178, 179, 180
see also Motor development
Physical environment, see Environmental conditions; Natural learning environment intervention
Physical therapists
collaboration of families/professionals and, 44
motor development and, 40
motor/adaptive intervention by, 172–174
orthopedic/musculoskeletal disorders and, 264
role of, 174–175, 185, 272–273
Physical/verbal cues
attentiveness to, 129, 130, 161, 163, 192, 224–225, 277
of caregivers, 279
Piagetian theory
assessment and, 152
on cognitive development, 140–148, 144t–145t, 164
natural learning opportunities and, 154
on play, 149–151
Pilot caps/hats, 244
Pivotal response training (PRT), 208–209
PKU, see Phenylketonuria
PL 93-380, see Family Educational Rights and Privacy Act (FERPA) of 1974
PL 94-142, see Education for All Handicapped Children Act (EHA) of 1975
PL 101-476, see Individuals with Disabilities Education Act (IDEA) of 1990
PL 104-191, see Health Insurance Portability and Accountability Act (HIPAA) of 1996
PL 108-446, see Individuals with Disabilities Education Improvement Act (IDEA) of 2004
Planning
collaboration and, 93–94
everyday activities/experiences, 92
for generalization/maintenance, 211–212
motor, 198
program, 91
transitions, 21, 22, 25, 60, 68–69
for between visits, 98, 99t
see also Individualized family service plan (IFSP)
Play
autism spectrum disorder (ASD) and, 196–198, 199b, 210, 211
cognitive development and, 142, 148–151
motor development and, 178
object, 144t–145t, 147, 149, 155, 210
physical assistance for, 155
visual impairments and, 223–224
Positioning
for assessments, 276
feeding and, 181
hearing loss and, 249
for orthopedic/musculoskeletal disorders, 265, 268–269
overview of, 176–177, 176f, 177f
toys and, 177, 278–279
visual impairments and, 230b